THE ESSENTIAL

OF THE TEACHING OF

NICHIREN DAISHŌNIN

Translated and explained by

Martin Bradley

~

Dharmagate Press

THE ESSENTIAL OF THE TEACHING OF NICHIREN DAISHŌNIN

Translated and explained by
Martin Bradley

Edited and compiled by
Harley White

Book formatted by
Kirk W. Wangensteen

Communications Facilitator:
Michael Okoniewski

Cover fractal image courtesy of the late **Gerhard Lenz**

This work is licensed under the Creative Commons Attribution 4.0 International License. To view a copy of this license, visit http://creativecommons.org/licenses/by/4.0/ or send a letter to Creative Commons, PO Box 1866, Mountain View, CA 94042, USA.

Creative Commons Copyright © 2015 Martin Bradley
Dharmagate Press
Lulu Printing

ISBN 978-1-326-37190-6

MARTIN BRADLEY
Biography

Martin & Tatsu Bradley (at the end of the 1980s)

Martin Bradley was born in Richmond (Surrey, England) in 1931. From a very young age he discovered Far Eastern Culture (*Encyclopaedia Britannica*, Lafcadio Hearn, etc.). In 1947, he started learning Classical Chinese from Arthur Waley, who taught him how to teach himself. In 1951, he met William Willetts, the author of Foundations of Chinese Art from Neolithic Pottery to Modern Architecture, who guided him in his understanding of Sino-Japanese calligraphy. In 1954, he received lessons in Literary Tibetan from David Snellgrove. During this period he supported himself by means of his painting.

In 1960, Bradley obtained a travelling scholarship from the Brazilian Government, and he stayed in Brazil for two years, painting various pictures for the decoration of the new presidential palace in Brasília (o Palácio da Alvorada). Supported by a contract from his Parisian art dealer (R. A. Augustinci of the Galerie Rive Gauche), he was able to travel to Nepal where he studied the Buddha teaching and at the same time taught French at Kathmandu University. In 1970, he settled in Hong Kong, where he gave lectures on Western art history and also studied Buddhism under Hsin Kuang, who was then the Abbot of Tung Lin Temple. In 1972, he travelled on to Japan, where he studied the language and other aspects of Japanese culture.

In 1974, Martin returned to Italy and in 1975 met his wife, Tatsu, who was then a student at the Accademia di Belle Arti di Roma. He has been using Japanese as a daily language ever since. After living in Paris for ten years, he and his wife moved to Bruges. Due to his deep interest in the Buddha teaching over the last few decades, they moved to Japan in 2008, where Bradley now lives quietly and spends his time translating the various writings of Nichiren Daishōnin.

"From the onset, his biography is fascinating, almost what we could label as 'fictional', and even if we do not wish to delight in the anecdotal, it always helps us understand—albeit superficially—the circumstances that formed and shaped the author's personality in order to understand his accomplishments, especially in the case of Bradley, whose work displays a huge grasp of knowledge and life experience, which permeated his existential philosophy, and are transmitted and molded into his work."

Raquel Medina
Vargas, Art History
Director, AICA

The Essential of the Teaching of Nichiren Daishōnin

The Essential of the Teaching of Nichiren Daishōnin

Table of Contents

Preface

An Introduction

by Martin Bradley

Part 1: The Life of Nichiren	7
~	
Part 2: Utterness	15
~	
Part 3: *Myōhō*	33
~	
Part 4: *Renge*	55
~	
Part 5: *Kyō*	67
~	
Part 6: *Nam(u)*	69
~	
Part 7: A Chain of Twelve Causes	73
~	
Part 8: The Fundamental Object of Veneration	79
The Threefold Transmission on the Fundamental Object of Veneration	85

Buddha Writings of Nichiren Daishōnin

Treatise on Becoming a Buddha in a Single Lifetime   107

~

An Essay on the Chain of the Twelve Causes and Karmic Circumstances that Run through the Whole of Sentient Existence   113

~

Treatise on the Whole being Contained in the One Instant of Mind   127

~

Concerning the Ten Ways in which dharmas Make Themselves Present to our Six Sense Organs   141

~

Securing the Peace of the Realm through the Establishment of the Correct Dharma   147

~

A Reply to Shijō Kingo, Troublesome Worries are Not Separate from Enlightenment   195

~

The Esoteric Oral Transmission Concerning Plants, Trees and the Environment having their Inherent Buddha Nature made Manifest   201

~

A Letter to the Lay Practitioner Abutsu   207

~

Treatise on the Real Aspect of All Dharmas   211

~

Treatise on the Fundamental Object of Veneration
For Contemplating the Mind
Instigated by the Bodhisattva Superior Practice
(*Jōgyō, Vishishtachāritra*)
For the Fifth Five Hundred Year Period
After the Tathāgata's Passing over to Nirvana   223

~

Treatise on the Significance of the Actual
Fundamental Substance   273

~

The Oral Transmission on the Significance
of the Dharma Flower Sutra   305

~

Treatise on Questions and Answers
Concerning the Fundamental Object of Veneration
Addressed to the Lay Practitioner Jōken   311

~

A Collation of the Layers of the Various Teachings
of all the Buddhas of the Past, Present and Future
as to Which Specific Doctrines are to be
Discarded or Established   335

~ Translator's Note ~   401

~

The Matter of Accepting and Undertaking
to Serve the Three Esoteric Dharmas   409

~

**Explanations of Buddhist Terms and Concepts
as Applied to the Teaching of Nichiren Daishōnin**   419

The Essential of the Teaching of Nichiren Daishōnin

Preface

by Martin Bradley

It is now something like seventy years ago since I discovered the entry in the *Encyclopaedia Britannica* on the Chinese language, when I was little more than ten years old. I was immediately convinced that all those fascinating ideograms would one day reveal to me what life is all about and how we might alleviate the bundle of troublesome worries that tarnish all our existences.

Pictures may suggest, point to or even illustrate our intentions. They can even alter the atmosphere of a room. But they can never explain how we might liberate ourselves from our inherent schizophrenia.

Having no wisdom myself, I decided that I would translate a tiny portion of the writings of a person whom I perceive as being fundamentally enlightened.

Also, I would like to point out to various monks and scholars that any word to translate *Myō* has to include the simultaneity of all time and space. Otherwise such a complete teaching is reduced to a nonsensical caricature.

This book is an effort to repay the debt of being born in the world of humankind and to thank those who helped me turn away from the demonic insanity of a mad dog who snarls at his own bewilderment.

If it hadn't been for the encouragement of my friends, Harley White, Kirk W. Wangensteen, Michael Okoniewski, and the late Gerhard Lenz, this book could never have been called back into existence. For a number of years, I had the attitude that these translations would die their own death. However, here I am continuing to write the Preface for a new edition of *The Essential of the Teaching of Nichiren Daishōnin*, which is being typed out and rewritten into Standard English by Harley, who has not only served as editor, but has also made contributions to the writing of the text as well. As a faithful follower of the teaching of Nichiren Daishōnin, Harley has shown a purposefulness and perseverance in seeing this book restored to life, for which I am extremely grateful.

The essential of Nichiren's teaching is Nam Myōhō Renge Kyō, which means to devote our lives to and found them on (*Nam*[*u*]) the Utterness of the Dharma (*Myōhō*) [entirety of existence, enlightenment and unenlightenment] permeated by the underlying white lotus flower-like mechanism of the interdependence of cause, concomitancy and effect (*Renge*) in its whereabouts of the ten [psychological] realms of dharmas (*Kyō*).

Next, the question should be answered: What is a dharma?

A dharma is anything that exists, whether it be in the phenomenal world or anything that goes on in our heads. The word "dharma" stands in contraposition to the word "Dharma" with a capital D, which is a Sanskrit term for the whole of existence or the whole of the teaching of the various Buddhas. All Buddha Dharmas are the same in essence.

In the *Treatise on the Real Aspect of All Dharmas*, Nichiren says the following: "Even though the two Buddhas Shākyamuni and Tahō are carrying out their roles of Buddhas who are suspended in time and place, still it is the *Nam Myōhō Renge Kyō* – which means to devote our lives to and found them on (*Nam*[*u*]) the Utterness of the Dharma (*Myōhō*) [entirety of existence, enlightenment and unenlightenment] permeated by the underlying white lotus flower-like mechanism of the interdependence of cause, concomitancy and effect (*Renge*) in its whereabouts of the ten [psychological] realms of dharmas (*Kyō*) – that is really the original Buddha and the workings of existence."

There are numerous passages in the writings of Nichiren Daishōnin that urge his followers to 'embrace' Nam Myōhō Renge Kyō in every thought, word, and action. This is to say that because enlightenment is already inherent within us, the more we recite that single phrase, the more fully we experience the enlightened aspect of each facet of our lives – even more so as our understanding deepens – since Nam Myōhō Renge Kyō encompasses the entirety of existence.

The idea is that reciting the theme and title should become as natural as breathing. And Nichiren often equates faith in Nam Myōhō Renge Kyō with letting our wishes and desires flow forth as instinctively as we hunger for food, thirst for water, long for love, seek a cure for illness, and the like, even admonishing us that if we do not, we will regret it later. When we practise reciting Nam Myōhō Renge Kyō in such a manner, always maintaining a pure seeking spirit for the truth and the clear light of enlightenment, we are protected even from the delusions of our own minds, which might be considered the greatest protection of all.

Nam Myōhō Renge Kyō implies the whole of the Dharma and all dharmas. That single phrase is complete in itself and all-encompassing. Nothing else is needed. All imaginable meritorious virtues stem from its recitation alone – a practice sublime in its simplicity. And yet the profundity of Nam Myōhō Renge Kyō is fathomless.

This is the true practice as taught by Nichiren Daishōnin, and he encourages all of his followers to rely on him as they would depend on a wooden staff on treacherous paths. Furthermore, he assures us that he Nichiren is the guide on the difficult road to the attainment of enlightenment. Thus the aim of this book is to make these writings of Nichiren Daishōnin and the essential of his teaching, which is Nam Myōhō Renge Kyō, more accessible and understandable to worldwide readers of modern English.

Martin Bradley
Kagoshima, Japan

The Essential of the Teaching of Nichiren Daishōnin

THE ESSENTIAL OF THE TEACHING OF NICHIREN DAISHŌNIN

AN INTRODUCTION

by Martin Bradley

It seems that every time we come to die, we are, at some time or another, confronted with the clear light of the Dharma. It is the clear light of the original state which is, as the *Collation of the Layers of the Various Teachings of all the Buddhas* (*Sō Kan Mon Shō*) states, "mind just as it is, is light", our fundamental condition, the simultaneity of all time past, present, and future, as well as every imaginable space.

But, every time we die, there is always something inherent in us that makes us turn away from this fact, so that we find ourselves again in the entanglement of thoughts, which bring back old attachments that haul us all the way back to the cycle of living and dying, like roach and dace on the hook of a fishing line.

However hallucinating and disorientating our experiences in the intermediate state between dying and being reborn made us feel, we come back into the world of humankind all fresh, innocent, and clean, as though we had come out of a good bath. We are hardly aware that deep down in our psyches lurk many of the older reactions to the pitfalls of life that make us unhappy. As we grow up, we usually become less carefree and progressively burdened by our respective karma. We look in all directions for paradisiacal relief, either in the flesh or in the mind. There are all manners of heavens, all sorts of hells, and all kinds of spaces in between.

Nichiren Daishōnin's aim was to make us understand that the clear light of the Dharma realm is in no way apart from whatever situation we are living at this very moment. This essay and these translations are about the quest for an inner realisation and becoming an undivided self. And they are done in this spirit of bearing the intention of the Daishōnin in mind, which was to make all people aware of the fact that our real identity is life itself, and at the same time we can get on with being the persons we think we are in the business of living out our lives.

Probably the best way to introduce a collection of translations of the writings of Nichiren Daishōnin would be to first give the reader a resumé of the main events in his life. However, before I go a step further, I would like to explain the title Daishōnin.

In most Chinese and Japanese dictionaries, the ideogram *shō* is defined as a sage, wise and good, upright and correct in all his character. In Harajima's *Nichiren Daishōnin Goshō Jiten*, the standard dictionary of Nichiren Shōshū terminology, it says, "a person whose knowledge and insight is decidedly superior, and thoroughly versed in all principles. Therefore, such a person is able to discern the correct view of the Buddha wisdom." This word or ideogram could be translated as "sage-like", if we were to think of this word in its philological context as having an underlying meaning of "whole", "healthy" or "hail" or in Latin languages "saint", "*sain*", etc.

Placed in front of this word *shō*, we have the ideogram *dai*, a pictogram of a man with his arms and legs stretched out. This ideogram is defined in one of oldest glossaries of the Chinese language, *Discerning the Signs and Explaining the Ideograms* (*Shuowen jiezi, Setsubun kaiji*), as the following: "as enormous as the sky, as huge as the earth, and also, as vast as humankind. Therefore, this ideogram is in the shape of a human being. That is why it means universal or great."

So here, in contrast to the Buddha whose title might be translated as "the enlightener", we have the Daishōnin, who is the person who is universally sage-like.

It is in this light that I have translated a few of his writings, in order to break out of the sectarian limitations of the various schools that propagate something of his teachings. The aim of this book is to make the all-pervading enlightened wisdom of Nichiren Daishōnin available to a wider reading public.

Part 1: The Life of Nichiren

Nichiren Daishōnin was born on the 16th of the second month of the first year of Jō.ō (1222 CE) and died on the 13th of the tenth month in the fifth year of Kō.an (1282 CE). He is the founder of the Nichiren Shōshū School and is understood by Nichiren Shōshū believers to be the original Buddha of the final phase of the Dharma of Shākyamuni (*mappō*).

He was born in the fishing village of Kominato in the Tōjō district of the Awa province – the present-day village of Kominato in the Chiba Prefecture. His father was Mikuni no Taifu; his mother was called Umegikunyo, and they were said to have led a humble existence along the seashore. As a child he was called Zennichi Maro. At the age of twelve, he entered Seichōji Temple under the instruction of the Venerable Dōzen, who gave him the name of Yaku' ō Maro.

At about the same time, Nichiren made a vow to the Bodhisattva Kokūzō that he would become the wisest man in Japan. He took holy orders as a monk when he was sixteen and was renamed Zeshōbō Renchō. He then left for Kamakura for further studies. Three years later he came back to the Seichōji Temple and left again almost immediately for Kyōto, in order to study and practise the Dharma gateways of the Tendai School on Mount Hiei. More precisely, it was at the Onjōji Temple, the Tennōji Temple, and on Mount Kōya where he studied the doctrinal significance of each and every school, as well as reading through all the sutras and other Buddhist writings.

When he was thirty-one, he left Mount Hiei and returned to Seichōji Temple. On the morning of April 28th 1253, in the Hall of Holding to the Buddha (*Jibutsutō*) in the All Buddhas Monastic Residence (*Shobutsubō*) of the Seichōji Temple, in front of the whole assembly Nichiren announced his fourfold criterion: "Those who bear in mind the formula of Amida Buddha (*Amitābha*) (*Nembutsu*) bring about the hell of incessant suffering. The school of watchful attention (*Zen*) is the work of the Universal Demon of the Sixth Heaven. The Tantric (*Shingon*) school entails the ruin of the state, and the *Ritsu* School are the robbers of the land." He also announced that all sentient beings could be saved by the recitation of *Nam Myōhō Renge Kyō*, which means to devote our lives to and found them on (*Nam[u]*) the Utterness of the Dharma (*Myōhō*) [entirety of existence, enlightenment and unenlightenment] permeated by the underlying white lotus flower-like mechanism of the interdependence of cause, concomitancy and effect (*Renge*) in its whereabouts of the ten [psychological] realms of dharmas (*Kyō*).

When Tōjō Kagenobu the local ruler, who was a follower of the Nembutsu – i.e., the people who bear in mind the formula of Buddha Amida (*Amitābha*) – heard this, he flew into a rage and tried to have Nichiren arrested. However, the Venerables Jōken and Gijō, acting as guides, were able to organise his escape, and he made his way back to Kominato.

After taking leave of his parents, Nichiren embarked upon his life's destiny of propagating his teaching. He began his mission in Nagoe no Matsubatani outside Kamakura, where he had built a hermit's cottage. During that period, he converted numerous people who became his disciples and supporters. In the eleventh month of the fifth year of Kenchō (1253), he was visited by a monk from Mount Hiei called Jōben, who was later to become Nisshō, one of the six elder monks. In 1258, on a visit to the Iwamoto Jissōji Temple, the then thirteen-year-old Nikkō Shōnin became his disciple and was to remain so, until he became the second patriarch after the Daishōnin's demise in 1282. Among the other disciples, there was Toki Jōnin who was a samurai attached to the Shogunate, as well as other samurai, such as Shijō Kingo, Soya Kyōshin, Kudō Yoshitaka, and the two Ikegami brothers Munenaka and Munenaga.

On the 16th day of the seventh month of the first year of Bun.ō (1260), the Daishōnin, as a result of the good offices of Yadoya Nyūdō, was able to have his well-known *Treatise on Securing the Peace of the Realm through the Establishment of the Correct Dharma* (*Risshō Ankoku ron*) handed over to the regent Hōjō Tokiyori. The argument of this treatise is that if the correct Buddha teaching were established instead of the incomplete doctrines of the time, then the whole country would find peace and stability.

That same year, on the night of the 27th of the eighth month, the followers of Nembutsu and the Shogunate organised an attack on the Daishōnin's hermitage at Matsubatani. Fortunately, he was able to escape harm and moved to the estate of Toki Jōnin. On the 12th day of the fifth month of the first year of Kōchō (1261), under the orders of the Shogunate, the Daishōnin was exiled to the Izu Peninsula. His disciple Nikkō Shōnin, and Funamori Yasaburō and his wife accompanied him and were constantly in attendance. One year and nine months later, the Daishōnin was pardoned, and he returned to Kamakura.

In the first year of Bun.ei (1264), the Daishōnin returned to his birthplace in Awa, in order to take care of his mother during her illness. At the same time, he propagated his teaching throughout the whole of the Awa region. In the same year, on the eleventh day of the eleventh month, while Kudō Yoshitaka of Amatsu was returning towards his estate, his military escort was attacked by Tōjō Kagenobu, the local ruler, in Komatsubara. Both Kudō Yoshitaka and the Venerable Kyōnin were killed in the struggle. Nichiren was wounded on the forehead.

In 1268, the Mongolian court sent a delegation with a letter from Kublai Khan, demanding that the Shogunate become his vassal. This particular incident was evident proof of the prediction in the *Treatise on Securing the Peace of the Realm through the Establishment of the Correct Dharma* (*Risshō Ankoku ron*), which again urged the nation to take refuge in the correct Dharma. At the same time, Nichiren called for a public debate with the monks of all the other schools and sent letters to eleven various religious leaders. But he received no reply whatsoever.

During the eighth year of Bun.ei (1271), there was a terrible drought, from one end of the Japanese archipelago to the other. The then renowned monk Ryōkan performed the prayer ritual for rain but was unable to bring it about, whereas Nichiren Daishōnin's success is well established in the annals of Japanese history. The defeated Ryōkan left Kamakura for the north. This became an opportunity for the monks of the other schools to provoke the Shogunate with slanderous reports concerning the Daishōnin.

On the tenth day of the ninth month of that same year, the Daishōnin received a summons from Heinosaemon no Jō Yoritsuna to be interrogated by the Court of Enquiry. At the interrogation, Nichiren Daishōnin severely reprimanded the hypocritical stance of the Shogunate. The outraged Heinosaemon no Jō immediately had the Daishōnin arrested and taken in the middle of the night to Tatsu no Kuchi to face execution.

Just as the executioner's sword was about to strike, an enormous crystalline pure white light surged up and covered half the sky. In panic, the officials of the Shogunate and the samurai in attendance ran in all directions and hid. No one dared try to execute the Daishōnin. This was the moment when Nichiren Daishōnin reveals the original terrain of the self-received reward body that is used by the Tathāgata of the primordial infinity of the original beginning. It is also referred to as "eradicating the temporary gateway, in order to reveal the original".

[Tathāgata (*Nyorai*) signifies the following: one who has gone; one who has followed the Path and arrived at the real suchness; one of the ten titles of a Buddha. Tathāgata can be explained as a person who comes from the real suchness of existence, which is Nam Myōhō Renge Kyō – which means to devote our lives to and found them on (*Nam*[*u*]) the Utterness of the Dharma (*Myōhō*) (entirety of existence, enlightenment and unenlightenment) permeated by the underlying white lotus flower-like mechanism of the interdependence of cause, concomitancy and effect (*Renge*) in its whereabouts of the ten (psychological) realms of dharmas (*Kyō*) – and that person will return to it.]

On the tenth day of the eleventh month, he was exiled to the island of Sado. There he began to compose the *Treatise on Clearing the Eyes*, the *Treatise on the Fundamental Object of Veneration for Contemplating the Mind Instigated by the Bodhisattva Superior Practice (Jōgyō, Vishishtachāritra) For the Fifth Five-hundred-year Period After* the Tathāgata's Passing over to Nirvana (Kanjin no Honzon shō), and also completed a number of important treatises such as the *Treatise on the Unbroken Transmission of the Single Universal Concern of Life and Death*, the *Treatise on the Significance of the Actual Fundamental Substance (Tōtai Gi Shō)*, *An Account of the Buddha's Revelations for the Future*, and the *Treatise on Cultivating Oneself in the Practice as it is Expounded*. During Nichiren's exile, several of his admirers, such as the Lay Practitioner Abutsu and his wife, took refuge in his teaching.

At Tsukahara, where the Daishōnin was forced to spend his exile in the broken-down Sanmaidō Temple, the Nembutsu School challenged him to an open debate, in which each and every argument was completely refuted. At this point, the Venerable Sairen and the Honma family were converted to the Teachings of Nichiren. After two years or so, in 1274, on the 27th day of the third month of the eleventh year of Bun.ei, Nichiren was granted a pardon, and he returned to Kamakura.

On the eighth day of the fourth month of the same year, he was summoned a second time by Heinosaemon no Jō to appear before the Shogunate. This time, they calmly admonished the Daishōnin and told him to treat and see the monks from the other schools as equals. Naturally the reply was that, if the correct Dharma was not held to, then it could not be possible to assure the security of the land. The outcome of this interview was that the Daishōnin retired to the backwoods to a more hermit-like existence, as had other wise men of the past in China and Japan, when their efforts to save their country went unheeded.

In this case, Nichiren Daishōnin retired to the Hagiri district on Mount Minobu in the province of Kai, which is the present-day Yamanashi prefecture. There he gave lectures on the *Dharma Flower Sutra (Hokke-kyō)*. And, for the preparation and education of his disciples, he went into the subtlest details, so that the Dharma would be protracted into eternity. During this same period, he also wrote the *Treatise on Selecting the Time* and the *Treatise on the Requital of Grace*.

The Senior Monk Nikkō promoted propagation in the direction of Mount Fuji. His first major conversion was Nanjō Tokimitsu, then the Matsuno and Kawai no Yui families, and others from among the monks of Ryūsenji Temple in Atsuhara. Nisshū, Nichiben, and Nichizen also took refuge in the teachings of Nichiren Daishōnin. During the same period, a number of the local peasants and farmers did the same.

On the 21st day of the ninth month of the second year of Kō.an (1279), all the followers of Nichiren, both monks and laymen, were harassed and pestered as a single sect. Finally, twenty people, beginning with Jinshirō, were arrested. Heinosaemon no Jō interrogated the prisoners at his private residence and pressured them to change their religion. With profound faith, all of them persisted in reciting the title and theme Nam Myōhō Renge Kyō, which means to devote our lives to and found them on (*Nam[u]*) the Utterness of the Dharma (*Myōhō*) [entirety of existence, enlightenment and unenlightenment] permeated by the underlying white lotus flower-like mechanism of the interdependence of cause, concomitancy and effect (*Renge*) in its whereabouts of the ten [psychological] realms of dharmas (*Kyō*).

Jinshirō, Yagorō, and Yarokurō were beheaded, and the remaining seventeen were banished from Atsuhara. These events are often referred to as the adversity of the Dharma at Atsuhara.

Nevertheless, it was on account of this particular adversity of the Dharma that Nichiren Daishōnin felt that the time had come for him to fulfil his real purpose of coming into the world. On the 12th day of the tenth month of the second year of Kō.an (1279), he inscribed the Fundamental Object of Veneration (*gohonzon*) of the Altar of the Precept of the original gateway.

In order to perpetuate his teaching, the Daishōnin appointed six elder monks to help him in this task but decided to entrust the succession of the patriarchate to Nikkō. In 1282, while undertaking a journey to the hot springs in Hitachi for rest and recuperation, in the mansion of Ikegami Munenaka, he entered peacefully and auspiciously into nirvana, at the age of 61 years.

Some years ago I wrote in the introduction of one of my catalogues, "Is it the dream that dreams the dreamer, or are we just caught in rather a sticky trap?" The answer, I am afraid to say, is yes, we are. But, however sticky it is or to what extent we feel free depends entirely upon our own efforts.

The idea of presenting these translations of the writings of Nichiren Daishōnin is to show people a teaching that might open the way to their finding some kind of individuation. By individuation, I mean, as C. G. Jung does, a personality that is not divided, that can live in his or her own skin and is reasonably happy. The writings of Nichiren Daishōnin and the practice that accompanies his teaching could well be for many people a way to clean up and put back into their right place some of the elements that constitute our inherent schizophrenia or unenlightenment. What I am referring to is that unhappy voice inside us that says, "There is me, the other people, the other things and places that have nothing to do with how rotten and empty I feel."

This is not some hard and righteous evangelistic doctrine, although some practitioners may try to affirm that it is. All Buddha teachings and practice are based on universal compassion and a profound respect for all existence. Nevertheless, a sincere study and practice may help some people rediscover that the moon has a face, to become aware of the voices of the children playing at the end of the street, or how caterpillars have transformed the nasturtium leaves into organic pieces of lace. Also, there are not a few people who rediscover the entirety of existence in a single grain of sand.

The object of these translations is to help clear the way for that part of our mind that makes us smile when we read a haiku or look at a painting by Miró or Paul Klee. It is also that part of us that makes us struggle for human rights and dignity.

My intention is not to promote any particular one of the thirty-eight or so number of sects that base their doctrines on the teaching of Nichiren Daishōnin, but to try to make it known that such a Buddha teaching exists.

Part 2: Utterness

In order to have a clear idea of what the Daishōnin intended in his writings, it is essential to have a reasonable understanding of the word *Myō*, which I translate as Utterness. Unfortunately, until very recently, many of the translations of these writings have twisted the meaning originally intended, due to a misunderstanding of the significance of this ideogram. However, throughout these treatises and other writings, there are numerous instances in which the Daishōnin himself defines the word *Myō*, which is the essential point on which his doctrine rests.

At this juncture, I would like to quote two phrases from *The Oral Transmission on the Meaning of the Dharma Flower Sutra* (*Ongi Kuden*), to use as a cornerstone upon which the reader can build a deeper insight into this imponderably profound perception. "All-inclusiveness is the one instant of mind containing three thousand existential spaces (*ichinen sanzen*). But should we exchange the expressions 'the ever-present now' (*soku*) and 'all-inclusiveness' (*en*), they could be used as replacements for the word 'Utterness' (*Myō*)."

En means something that is round, circular, or encompassing, hence the use of the word "all-inclusiveness". *Ichinen sanzen* literally means "one mind at present – three thousand". The Chinese ideogram for "mind at present" (*nen*) is the ideogram for "now" placed above the ideogram for "heart".

Not so long ago, even in the west, people used to talk about the heart as an organ of thought ("my heart's desire", "my broken heart" or "completely heartless", etc.). It is only since the nineteenth century that people have really assimilated the notion that we think with our brains. It might be worth mentioning that one of the Sanskrit equivalents to the Chinese ideogram (*shin*) for mind or heart is *hrdaya* or *hrd*, which is obviously the same philological root as "heart" in English or "*coeur*" in French.

Within the domain of the Buddha teaching, the implication of the word (*Myō*) is closer to the idea of existence or being, rather than anything to do with the simple process of thinking. In the *Treatise on the Whole being contained in the One Instant of Mind*, Nichiren Daishōnin endorses a quotation from Myōraku (*Miao-lo*), by reiterating that the whole (of existence) is contained in the one instant of mind, which, in further detail, is divided into materiality and mind. Again in the *Treatise on the Fundamental Object of Veneration for Contemplating the Mind*, the Daishōnin writes, "These three thousand [existential spaces] are contained in a single instant of mental activity. If there is no mind, then that is the end of it." In other words, if there is no mind to perceive its own existence, then nothing can exist.

In the *Flower Garland Sutra* (*Kegon, Avatāmsaka-sūtra*), there are two lines that have the same inference: "All dharmas are only mind, and the three realms, *i*) where sentient beings have organs of sense as well as desires, *ii*) where there is a physical dimension, and *iii*) where there is only mental activity, i.e., thoughts, fantasies, dreams, and hallucinations – these three realms are merely ways of knowing."

At first glance, existence from the Buddhist point of view seems to be subjective. This may be so, since the only way we can be aware of the reality of existence is through the means of perception of a mind that has individualised itself. Even so, one instant or the ever-present now of the individualised mind is its own Utterness, which, at the same time, has been tarnished by our fundamental unenlightenment. This immediately becomes the materiality and mind within the oneness of mind. This fundamental unenlightenment is the karmic cause for both our bodies and their physical surroundings. Hence, the quality of how we perceive through our organs of sense and all our mental capabilities and defects has its origin in this extremely archaic way of understanding.

Nevertheless, this one flash of mind, which is a continuity of flashes that constitute the ever-present now, makes itself known to us by what is occupying our immediate consciousness. Then, behind the here and now, we have somewhat closer thoughts that may be even related to what is going on in the present. Further away, there are other thoughts, memories, knowledge, stored away experiences, with their corresponding traumas and epiphanies. At greater depth, there are darker urges. And, way below our most archaic mental forces, we come to that part of us that is the very thing of life, which is what really makes us function as sentient beings. This is the glint of gold at the bottom of the abyss that C. G. Jung so often alludes to in his writings.

It is this part of us that brings our inherent archetypes to life and is also the dimension within us that occupies all space, all time, simultaneously and effortlessly. It is the very thing of life itself. In the language of the Buddha teaching, it is the citadel of the ninth cognition (*kyūshiki no miyako*). For those people who are in some way familiar with the teachings of Nichiren Daishōnin, this is the Fundamental Object of Veneration (*gohonzon*) within us, which we project onto the same Object of Veneration (*gohonzon*) that is hanging in the altar (*butsudan*). Every nanosecond is the whole of existence, even though it may be only from a subjective, worm's-eye view.

Another way of looking at this one instant of mind containing the whole universe would be to say: I am here in Japan where I live, which is a part of Asia, on the continent that is on the planet Earth, which is a part of the solar system, which again is a part of the Milky Way, and so on and so forth. It can also be said that what is happening now, at this very instant, cannot be separate from what is going on, at this same moment, in New Delhi, or on the surface of the sun.

Returning to the subject of the Buddhist technical expression "three thousand existential spaces", even today in the Indian countryside there are not a few people who would find counting up to a thousand as an almost impossible undertaking, which would make such an amount practically innumerable. To treble such a sum would amount to incalculability. One can easily imagine that three thousand years ago such a numerical concept could easily imply totality.

The existential spaces are just as it says. They are the spaces where existence takes place. The "all-roundness", which is in the first quotation we are talking about, has the implication of the all-inclusiveness of the entirety of sentient existence.

Coming to the second sentence which I quoted a little earlier, it says, "But should we exchange the expressions 'the ever-present now' (*soku*) and 'all-inclusiveness' (*en*), they could be used as replacements for the word 'Utterness' (*Myō*)."

It is only in the writings of Nichiren Daishōnin that I have ever seen the ideogram *soku* used as a noun. In most dictionaries it is translated as "namely", "then", "forthwith", "immediately". Also, there are further interpretations which stem from the Tendai School in China, such as "not separate", "not two", and "inseparable from". It is also a participle that has something akin to the idea of implication – A implies B; B is implicit in A; B does not exist without A. In Harajima's *Nichiren Daishōnin Goshō Jiten*, we find, among various other definitions, "the inseparability of the sequence of time". Obviously, if we try to make a noun out of all these adverbs, adjectives, prepositions, and conjunctions, we get something like "the interdependence of time", "interdependence, i.e., all space, all time, simultaneously and effortlessly", or the paraphrase "the ever-present now".

The second sentence reads, "But should we exchange the expressions 'the ever-present now' for 'all-inclusiveness', they would become alternative words for 'Utterness' (*Myō*)." Now that we have the added ingredient of time, it would suggest that the real identity of life is that we live all space all time – which includes the past, present, and future – simultaneously, but always suspended in the ever-present now. We will go into the Buddhist concept of the interdependence of cause and effect further on in this essay.

Although it may be possible to dig out the secrets of the universe by thought, reason, logic, and mathematics, it is also possible to examine what life is, by means of our feelings, sensations, or intuition. And it also can be a combination of all of these.

All the schools that propagate the teachings of Nichiren Daishōnin emphasise that the only way to open up our inherent Buddha nature is to develop a solid faith in the idea that all beings and all things are fully endowed with the essence of enlightenment. Faith is very like our intuition, which is a preparation by the mind without reasoning. Faith is also a kind of trust that can lead to understanding. It is also a part of the process of our personal development. Any flat belief in a dogma without enquiry can only lead to mental stagnation and bigotry. With an open mind, we can explore a teaching, look into it, think about it, and maybe such a teaching could well be able to impart to us profound psychological truths upon which we can build our lives.

None of the Buddha teachings are philosophies simply based on empirical concepts. Instead, they are a real exploration into ourselves and our environment, which can never be separated from what we are. However, there is not only one Buddha teaching. Also, the profundity, the extent as to how much these teachings involve is entirely dependent on what Shākyamuni's intention was at the time when these doctrines were taught.

In order to clarify the role of Nichiren Daishōnin's Buddha teaching in the evolution of Buddhist doctrine, I will have to first introduce the word Dharma and then proceed into an oversimplified summary of how the Buddha teaching evolved.

First, we have this word Dharma. According to Sanskritologists, this word means something that maintains its own character, which in itself becomes a standard. Essentially, the word signifies the whole universe and everything it contains, as an object of thought. Since no single item can be divorced from the rest of existence, from the standpoint of the Buddha teaching of Nichiren Daishōnin as well as various other schools of Buddhist thought, even the tiniest grains of dust are fully endowed with the one instant of mind containing three thousand existential spaces (see *Treatise on the Real Aspect of All Dharmas*).

As far as we are concerned at the moment, the second meaning of the term "Dharma" is the Buddha teaching. It is here that the Dharma has various implications, which are unequal in their profundity or extent. During the first forty-eight years of Shākyamuni's teaching, with the scope of setting all sentient beings onto the path of enlightenment, he graded his teaching according to the needs and capacities of his hearers.

The first discourse of Shākyamuni was the *Flower Garland Sutra* (*Kegon, Avatāmsaka-sūtra*), which is a voluminous text that establishes the practices of a bodhisattva. However, this sutra, by being the first, is a revelation that describes the Buddha's own enlightenment, as well as emphasising that all sentient beings have a Buddha nature. Also, this sutra teaches that each and every other phenomenon, noumenon, or event, as well as each experience, although apparently independent, contains all things, experiences, and events, in an interdependent and mutually complementary relationship. It is recounted that Shākyamuni expounded this sutra to five of his co-practitioners, over a period of either three or six days.

Because the content of the *Flower Garland Sutra* (*Kegon, Avatāmsaka-sūtra*) was not readily accessible to people with little or no instruction, Shākyamuni then embarked upon the general teachings of the individual vehicle (*shōjō, hīnayāna*), which was the basic form of the Buddha doctrine based upon the Pāli Canon, whose main concern was the individual substantiation of Nirvana in the sense of it being the complete annihilation of any state of existence whatsoever.

In the Nichiren schools that use English, often this period is called the "Agon Period" (*Agonji*), which refers to the āgama sutras. But, since I try to avoid too many foreign words in writing English, or any other language for that matter, I refer to this period as "the general teachings of the individual vehicle", an expression which seems to cover this concept satisfactorily. Albeit these doctrines of the individual vehicle (*shōjō, hīnayāna*) were never intended to be ultimate teachings in themselves, even though Shākyamuni may have said so at the time, the real intention of these teachings as an expedient means was to lead people further into the Buddha Dharma, so that they could become fully enlightened.

The third of the five doctrinal periods of Shākyamuni is the period of the equally broad (*hōdō, vaipulya*) teachings. These teachings are said to have been expounded for the benefit of sentient beings within the three psychological and material realms (*sangai*), where 1) sentient beings have appetites and desires, 2) that are incarnated in a subjective reality with physical surroundings, 3) who, at the same time, are endowed with the immateriality of the world of thoughts, desires, and fantasies. This period of teachings lasted for sixteen years. Among the important sutras that were expounded were the *Sutra on the Golden Illuminating Light*, which is often mentioned in the *Treatise on Securing the Peace of the Realm through the Establishment of the Correct Dharma* (*Risshō Ankoku ron*), as well as the *Sutra on the Layman Yuimakitsu* (*Vimalakîrti*), who refuted the teachings of the followers of the individual vehicle (*shōjō, hīnayāna*) by showing that his own existence was based on relativity or the void – which is Nam Myōhō Renge Kyō and means to devote of our lives to and found them on (*Nam[u]*) the Utterness of the Dharma (*Myōhō*) [entirety of existence, enlightenment and unenlightenment] permeated by the underlying white lotus flower-like mechanism of the interdependence of cause, concomitancy and effect (*Renge*) in its whereabouts of the ten [psychological] realms of dharmas (*Kyō*).

The wisdom (*Hannya*) period is the fourth of these five periods of teachings. Most of the sutras expounded at this time usually have the expression "the wisdom that ferries sentient beings over the sea of living and dying to the shores of Nirvana" as a part of their titles. In these teachings, this particular wisdom is described as being the supreme, highest, or paramount, on account of its enlightenment and also due to its thorough understanding of the illusion of all existence. This doctrine was expounded as the principal means of attaining Nirvana.

The final and fifth doctrinal period of Shākyamuni is called the Dharma Flower and Nirvana period (*Hokke Nehanji*), which lasted eight years, in which most of the time was taken up with expounding the *Sutra on the White Lotus Flower-like Mechanism of the Utterness of the Dharma* (*Myōhō Renge Kyō*). This sutra comprises twenty-eight chapters, and the version that was translated by

Kumārajîva (344-409 CE) is the basic teaching of all the schools of Tendai (*T'ien T'ai*) and Nichiren.

The first fourteen chapters deal with events that occur in time and place and are called the "temporary gateway" (*shakumon*) to the Dharma. The following chapters refer to the timeless and fundamentally archetypal aspect of existence that is referred to as the "original gateway" (*honmon*) to the Dharma. This original gateway is the real revelation of the enlightenment of all the Buddhas of the past, present, and future.

The whole content of this sutra, with all its adjoining implications, was written out in the form of a mandala by Nichiren Daishōnin himself, as the Fundamental Object of Veneration (*gohonzon*). The *Nirvana Sutra* was taught by Shākyamuni, just before his death. Nirvana is understood as the cessation of all desires, delusions, mortality, and of all activity, thus passing over to a state of nonbeing that is beyond all concept.

Each one of these five periods has its own Dharma; each Dharma has its own "extent of the reaches of the mind of the Tathāgata". Incidentally, Tathāgata is a title that means "arrived at suchness", which obviously has extremely profound implications. But, since it is a title, I leave it untranslated.

[Tathāgata (*Nyorai*) signifies the following: one who has gone; one who has followed the Path and arrived at the real suchness; one of the ten titles of a Buddha. Tathāgata can be explained as a person who comes from the real suchness of existence, which is Nam Myōhō Renge Kyō – which means to devote our lives to and found them on (*Nam[u]*) the Utterness of the Dharma (*Myōhō*) (entirety of existence, enlightenment and unenlightenment) permeated by the underlying white lotus flower-like mechanism of the interdependence of cause, concomitancy and effect (*Renge*) in its whereabouts of the ten (psychological) realms of dharmas (*Kyō*) – and that person will return to it.]

However, out of all the different Dharmas, there is only one Utterness of the Dharma (*Myōhō*, *Saddharma*), which we will make an effort to explore in greater depth as we proceed.

In thirteenth century Japan during Nichiren's lifetime, there was no empirical science, nor any scientific progress. There was an arithmetic mainly based on the abacus. Physics existed in relation to practical needs. A kind of chemistry did exist, especially in relation to metallurgy, paint-making, and materials for dyeing. It was a chemistry that was beginning to crawl out of its alchemical phase as in China. On the whole, most of Japanese learning at that time came from China. Nearly all learning was Chinese, except for some poetry and traditional sagas (*monogatari*).

Outside of Buddhist doctrinal debate, which was always based on the fact that the Buddha always spoke the truth, there was no other discipline that really asked the whys and wherefores of existence. The Japan of Nichiren was an age of deep research into and a faithful reliance on the Buddha teachings, combined with an unshakable adherence to the mythology, folklore, and traditional values of the time.

We must not forget that Nichiren transmitted many of his teachings in writing to many of his followers. With this I would like to point out that all that we know about the doctrines of the Buddha Shākyamuni, Jesus Christ, and maybe many other religious founders, is what has been noted down by their followers. In the case of Nichiren, there still remain, here and there throughout Japan, many of his original writings, not to mention copies of these texts made by his closer disciples of the same period.

Coming back to our central discourse which is *Myō* and *Myōhō Renge Kyō*, I would like to give some other definitions of this pivotal word, before we explore the "theme and title" *Nam*[*u*] *Myōhō Renge Kyō* (*daimoku*) that is recited by all schools that claim to be a following of Nichiren Daishōnin:

– ***Kai*** means to open up, clear away, or make accessible. In this sense, those who do not do any of the practices of any of the schools of Nichiren are usually totally unaware that, at the bottom of their psyches, there is a force that is totally unsullied by any deed or action, yet at the same time it permeates the whole of existence, and yet it remains itself. In the technical language of the teaching of the Daishōnin, this is referred to as the triple body, independent of all karma (*musa sanjin*). People who follow other faiths may have deep intuitions about its existence or even visions of it, such as in near-death states or trances. What is more important is to know what this archetype consists of and to know that its contents are what make us what we are.

The whole of the constituents of what make up the forces of life were written out by the Daishōnin, who was completely enlightened to them, on the Fundamental Object of Veneration (*gohonzon*). In order to have a real access to this Object of Veneration (*gohonzon*), the followers of the various Nichiren schools recite the theme and title. This is Nam[u] Myōhō Renge Kyō, which means to devote of our lives to and found them on (*Nam[u]*) the Utterness of the Dharma (*Myōhō*) [entirety of existence, enlightenment and unenlightenment] permeated by the underlying white lotus flower-like mechanism of the interdependence of cause, concomitancy and effect (*Renge*) in its whereabouts of the ten [psychological] realms of dharmas (*Kyō*).

It is also possible to enrich our understanding of life through reading the Daishōnin's writings. And, for those people who can read the Chinese ideograms, they can study and ponder over these archetypal forces written out on the Object of Veneration (*gohonzon*). This again is a subject that will be studied in further depth, as we go forward.

- ***Gusoku*** means completely fulfilled. This expression is found here and there throughout the *Dharma Flower Sutra* (*Hokke-kyō*) and the writings of Nichiren Daishōnin. The implication of this term is "there is nothing lacking". This concept of completeness stands in contrast to other mandalas that usually have some defect or other, usually because they do not include our less noble urges or our darkest, hellish thoughts. If they do, then they are only conventionalised painted shapes. From the Buddhist point of view, these artisanally painted images only correspond to the axiom of phenomenon (*ke*), which is simply the outward form.

On the other hand, concerning written ideograms seen through the vision of the Daishōnin, his *Writing on Questions and Answers with regard to All the Schools* states the following: "Because written ideograms reveal the conditions of all the sentient beings who write them, people's handwriting lets us know what their mental capacities are. In the light of the equation of mind and materiality not being two separate dharmas, then what people write is a manifestation of those persons' poorness or fulfilment. It is only natural that written ideograms are the expression of the non-duality of materiality and mind of all sentient beings."

This statement tallies completely with the philosophy of the painters of the post-informal school in the 1950s, as well as the opinion of many graphologists. What we write or what we paint, or even whatever we sing or say at any given moment, is what we really are, along with the whole of existence. The non-duality of mind or materiality, colour or form, sound or odour, by being the "middle way of reality" (*chūdō jissō*) opens up the speculative thought that what artists, musicians, composers, poets, and calligraphers have given to humankind are perceptions that give us a greater understanding as to what life is all about.

In order that humankind could open up and substantiate the wisdom of the Buddha in each one of us, Nichiren inscribed the Fundamental Object of Veneration (*gohonzon*), which contains the ultimate equation of what constitutes life and inanimate existence, which he expresses in what might seem an oversensitive, and yet frighteningly dynamic, calligraphy. Since the Dharma of Nichiren Daishōnin is inseparable from the word "Utterness" (*Myō*), it can only have the implication of "being completely fulfilled".

– The next definition of Utterness is **enman**, which is the all-inclusive, replenished whole of the one instant of mind containing three thousand existential spaces. This replenishment refers to our living all space, all time, simultaneously and without effort. In the *Treatise on the Real Aspect of All Dharmas*, the Daishōnin makes the following remark: "The subjectivity and its dependent environment of the 'hell of incessant suffering' (*mukan jigoku*) are completely present in the minds of the supremely sage-like. So the person and the environmental terrain of persons such as the guardian Deva King of the North Bishamon (*Vaishramana*) do not go beyond the bounds of the universe contained in the instant of mind of ordinary people."

– Another important definition of Utterness is *sosei*, renewal, renovation, or rebirth. All of us are living in our own respective, ever-volatilising corridor of events, which at one end consists of the receding memories of a past which will eventually become the vagaries of history or personal myth. At the other end of this rapidly evaporating corridor, which is in fact the ever-present now, we also have the wildest dreams of a future that does not yet exist.

In a teaching that perceives existence as a oneness of space and time suspended in an interdependence of cause and effect, it is difficult to have a concept of a future in which we can lighten our karmic loads and look towards something brighter. It would seem that our ways of understanding our surroundings and ourselves are akin to the volatile corridor of time, which I mentioned before. This volatile corridor is essentially made up of a sequence of karmic relationships and requitals for what we have done in the past, as well as all our karmic potentials.

This sequence also gives rise to the chain of illusions that we call our lives. The end of this volatile corridor becomes more indistinct, as the immediate past dissolves into the memories, reminiscences that precondition us to our respective present attitudes. The past consists of these residues of impressions that are recalled to the mind's perceptions, to which we add our acquired knowledge of history, palaeontology, as well as other sciences. The front end of this volatile corridor is also blurred by our hopes, fantasies, wishes, and intentions, as it rushes along its karmic orbit. Our hopes for the future are affected by the circumstances of the past. But it is due to our various wants and intentions of what we should do about them that may change the course of our lives. Tomorrow I will shave. I will do my work and even do my practice.

Even though our subjective existences may have an apparently defined karmic tendency, it is through our intentions or determination or our neglectfulness and don't-care philosophies that the actual direction of what will happen in due time is shaped. So if we are to hold a determined faith in a teaching whose values are applicable to those of the 21st century and whose practice can be feasible in the societies that we live in, then without a doubt we can become wealthy, healthy, happy, and wise. Although our individual existences are not separate from time, space, and every possible psychological dimension, it is our individual intentions and efforts that can alter our karmic orbits.

In this sense, existence is continually renewing itself and changing. I cannot give a reason why, but it seems that life really started on earth when monocellular organisms found a way of dying, instead of multiplying and clustering together with each other ad infinitum. When we die, we enter the dimension that is called the *"antarābhava"* (*chūyū*), which is the intermediate state between dying and rebirth. Those people who are familiar with the text that is popularly known as the *Tibetan Book of the Dead* will recognise this period as the *bardo*.

Incidentally, we must not forget that Nichiren was most certainly familiar with the esoteric doctrines of the Shingon School and that the Fundamental Object of Veneration (*gohonzon*) itself contains Tantric elements. However, according to many other yogic and Tantric writings, people who are unused to mind-revealing experiences, or are unschooled in esoteric teachings, and who are also so attached to themselves that their only thought is "what is going to happen to me?", very often have very traumatic experiences in this intermediate state before being reborn again. It is my personal opinion that whatever happens to us during this state highly influences and moulds the archetypes of our minds, which in turn have a lot to do with our future bodies and their surroundings, since through such experiences, our fears, longings, tendencies to love or to hate, etc., are already firmly planted.

According to these Tantric texts, all our positive and negative reactions to the visions in the intermediate state before rebirth are our own choices, and our reaction to them stems from previous existences. Since we can never be separated from Nam Myōhō Renge Kyō itself – which means to devote our lives to and found them on (*Nam*[*u*]) the Utterness of the Dharma [entirety of existence, enlightenment and unenlightenment] (*Myōhō*) permeated by the underlying white lotus flower-like mechanism of the interdependence of cause, concomitancy and effect (*Renge*) in its whereabouts of the ten [psychological] realms of dharmas (*Kyō*) – then this idea might lead to a vague idea as to how karma works. This idea is fully implied in the following concept of Nichiren, in his *Collation of the Layers of the Various Teachings of all the Buddhas of the Past, Present and Future as to which Specific Doctrines are to be Discarded or Established*, where he states, "In as much as the mind and the Dharma of the Buddha are Utterness, and the mind and dharmas of sentient beings are also Utterness, and both of these two Utternesses are what make our minds work, therefore, outside of mind, dharmas do not exist at all."

Notwithstanding, the possibility of being reborn again opens up opportunities to seek an inner understanding of what our identity really is and all that it signifies. This also applies to our everyday reality, since all of us want to be happy. This realisation of happiness then comes about through a search for the right teaching and a sincere desire to understand what our lives are about. Because life is in no way separate from Utterness, since this is what sets everything in motion, then it is in this sense that this word means renewal.

– Utterness also has the **meaning of the Dharma nature**. This particular nuance is probably the hardest to explain, since it is beyond the bounds of ordinary experience. The Dharma nature is the "real suchness" (*shinnyō*) that underlies all existence. It is also understood as being indescribable, and sometimes it is referred to as the "Buddha nature" (*busshō*).

Within the limits of human experience and from reading Tantric texts, the Dharma nature might be described as the clear light that is often seen in near-death experiences, or in hallucinogenic and other visionary states. Some people who have had this kind of experience say that they become the clear light and that, by becoming so, they are completely free from any subjectivity or objectivity.

Nevertheless, this Dharma nature or Buddha nature not only exists for humankind, one might suppose that it exists also for other living creatures, and also that the insentient and the inanimate have a Dharma nature as well. This point is clearly revealed in the *Esoteric Oral Transmission Concerning Plants, Trees and the Environment having their Inherent Buddha Nature made Manifest*, in the following passages:

"The question is asked: In the *Dharma Flower Sutra* (*Hokke-kyō*), are both sentient beings and that which is insentient capable of revealing their inherent Buddha nature?

"The answer is given: The *Sutra on the White Lotus Flower-like Mechanism of the Utterness of the Dharma* (*Myōhō Renge Kyō*) is in itself the entirety or Utterness (*Myō*) of existence, which is also the Dharma (*hō*)."

This overwhelming title of this particular sutra would suggest that the absolute essence of reality and its substantiation entail the concurrence of all space and all the tenses of past, present, or future, suspended in an ever immediate present. Be that as it may, most of us are still stuck in the sticky trap with its karmically delineated boundaries.

What these boundaries really consist of are the five aggregates (*go.on*) that darken the awareness of our original enlightenment – *i*) a material form with its equally physical environment, *ii*) reception, sensation, feeling, and the functioning of the mind in connection with affairs and things, *iii*) conception, thought, discerning, and the functioning of the mind in distinguishing what is going on in both its psychological and material surroundings, *iv*) the functioning of the mind in its processes with regard to likes, dislikes, good and evil, etc., *v*) the mental faculty that makes us think we are who we are, on account of what we know.

Hence, due to such impediments, we are unable to see readily into the future or further back into the past beyond our own lived experiences, but we can have intuition and knowledge. In this light, C. G. Jung suggests that paranormal gifts and psychic phenomenon are something to do with a kind of "short circuit" between the realms of dharmas, which are really various states of consciousness, or even the whole.

It is here that I would like to make another digression. The Daishōnin, for the various reasons that are only sketchily described in the abbreviated biography at the beginning of this essay, received a summons to be interrogated by the Court of Enquiry. At this interrogation, Nichiren Daishōnin reprimanded the hypocritical attitude of the Shogunate. The outraged Minister Heinosaemon no Jō immediately had the Daishōnin arrested. In the middle of the night, he was taken to Tatsu no Kuchi, to face being put to death by beheading.

Just as the executioner's blade was about to swish down onto the Daishōnin's neck, a brilliant orb, brighter than the full moon, shot across the sky, from the southeast to northwest. It was shortly before dawn, yet still too dark to see anyone's face, but the radiant object lit up the whole surroundings, like a powerful magnesium flare. The executioner fell on his face, with his eyes so dazzled that he could not see. The soldiers were terrified and panic-stricken...

In spite of various astronomical explanations for this event, has anybody thought that this orb of clear diamond light, that could illuminate all its surroundings, was anything other than a projection, or some kind of spilling over of the utterly enlightened mind of the Daishōnin himself, as he was about to be decapitated?

It would be difficult to imagine a person who had a handwriting with such wise hypersensitivity and strength not being associated with some kind of paranormal event or other. The tears that the Daishōnin mentions in his *Treatise on the Real Aspect of All Dharmas* almost allude to the tears that were not uncommonly shed during the mind-revealing experiences of many people, during the latter half of the twentieth century. However, such events that occurred at Tatsu no Kuchi, where the Daishōnin was nearly executed, remain imponderably inexplicable.

This last term, "imponderably inexplicable", is also one of the many definitions of Utterness. Then, there is the concept of "Utterness in comparison with other teachings" (*sōtaimyō*).

Essentially, this particular view means that when the *Dharma Flower Sutra* (*Hokke-kyō*) is compared with all the other sutras, it is only this sutra that entails the interdependence of all space and all time, etc. On the other hand, with regard to existence, all the other Buddha teachings see time as a long piece of string which is really only a figment of our individual minds. Hence, all other sutras cannot measure up to the profundity of the Dharma Flower. This opens up the way for the idea of "Utterness as an absolute quality separate from all else" (*zettaimyō*). In any event, Utterness cannot exist without the comparability of the Dharma or dharmas.

Before leaving these definitions of Utterness and moving on to the word "Dharma", I would first like to explain that, in terms of the Buddha teaching, the ten [psychological] realms of dharmas, in everyday language, correspond to ten different states of mind. To give an example, when we are angry or rapturously in love, these particular states may be the dominant mood when they are happening, but, at the same time, even though we may be in the blindest of rages or at the height of orgasmic ecstasy, something of the rest of our lives remains somewhere in our heads.

What I am trying to say is that each one of the ten dharma realms is mutually endowed with the same ten realms, or, as some schools put it, the mutual possession of the ten [psychological] realms of dharmas. However, in order to understand this as a living experience, our heads know no simple joy or a sheet of pain that is not psychologically tinged by everything that happened prior to or after what is happening at any given moment. Our minds are as vast as the whole of existence.

Since Utterness sublimely includes everything that was, everything that is, and everything that will happen, as well as every imaginable space, we are confronted with the question about free will. Apart from the Dharma realm of the Buddha, the other nine realms of dharmas are seen as a network of interacting, volatile corridors of dream time and dream space, wherein people are only fully conscious of the actual instant they are living, so that they react according to their karmically construed personalities to situations that are also as illusory as the rest of their unenlightenment.

In *The Oral Transmission on the Meaning of the Dharma Flower Sutra* (*Ongi Kuden*), Nichiren states that "Utterness is the Dharma nature, and dharmas are its unenlightenment. The single entity of unenlightenment and the Dharma nature or enlightenment is called the Utterness of the Dharma (*Myōhō, Saddharma*)."

I have no doubt that the reader is fully aware that the word Dharma is a semantic minefield. However, whatever other meanings, nuances, and implications can be given to this word, within the boundaries of the Buddha teaching of Nichiren Daishōnin, dharmas are everything that we think, see, hear, smell, taste, touch, or no matter what comes onto the horizons of our consciousness, as well as all that lies submerged below any level of awareness. Whatever it is, it is existence and therefore a dharma. In a more verbose way, we could define dharma as the momentary configuration of events. There can be no dharma that stands alone.

As I have said earlier on, both the Buddha teachings of Shākyamuni and Nichiren tend to be expounded from a subjective angle. Hence, we have the Dharma that is the teaching of the enlightened, who perceive their existence in terms of the wholeness of the one instant of mind containing three thousand existential spaces (*ichinen sanzen*).

Dharmas are not separate from Utterness. But it is through studying the writings of Nichiren that one can have an idea of what the real implication is of becoming aware of our inherent Buddha nature not being separate from our respective personalities. To really substantiate this notion, then it becomes a question of doing the whole practice. At this point, it might be worth mentioning that there is no Buddha teaching without a practice that corresponds to it.

Part 3: *Myōhō*

Even though the concept of the one instant of mind containing three thousand existential spaces is included in the glossary at the end of this book, I am going to explain it so that the reader can grasp this concept in further detail. For the sake of putting our various mental states and moods that are often indefinable at the edges, such as our complexes, joys, angers, and sufferings, into a schema where they can be grasped more clearly, the Buddha teaching evolved the doctrine of the ten [psychological] realms of dharmas.

The unhappiest realm of dharmas is hell (*jigokukai*) and the suffering of its denizens. This would include all suffering, either physical or mental. Suffering begins at the stage of a thorn in your little finger, feeling the lash of pain caused by words that hurt, humiliations, the pain of broken relationships, illnesses and injuries. This also must include the horrors of war and the almost unimaginable mental dimension of the perpetrators and the victims of things that happened in the Second World War, as well as what has been going on in the Middle East, Africa, and other places in recent years. Hell is also hate.

Each and every one of us has suffered in some way or another. From a more conventional and stereotyped Buddhist point of view, there are, according to various teachings of the individual vehicle (*shōjō, hīnayāna*), eight hot hells, eight cold hells which are situated under the world of humankind. Usually the descriptions of these hells are mediaeval and sadistic and, in their iconographic way, far removed from the real pain, suffering, and mental anguish that many people experience. The object of the teaching of Nichiren Daishōnin is to lead people away from such torments.

Hungry demons (*gaki*), in the Buddhist teaching of Shākyamuni, are seen as ghosts who live in a purgatorial state, some say under the ground. It is their sad destination that they are condemned to continually hanker after food, sex, drink, and other such things that they covet. It is reported that there are 39 classes of these unfortunate creatures. This is the second of the three lower karmic destinations.

In traditional Buddhist iconography, these beings are depicted as having long, thin necks with swollen bellies that force them to crawl on the ground. There are also a number of Japanese paintings of the Edo period depicting hungry ghosts hanging around the more sordid and seedy establishments of the red-light districts. The present-day visualisation would be closer to heroin addicts in need of a fix, or alcoholic derelicts haunted by their thirst, or the need for a cigarette. This is the part of us that craves, wants, and must have in order to continue. From a positive angle, the perpetual desire for food, nourishment, money, etc., is the mechanism to defend the life within us, in order to do the things that make life positive. Again, like all the other realms of dharmas, the mental state of the hungry demon is also endowed with all the other ten.

In the teachings prior to those of Nichiren Daishōnin, the realms of dharmas of animality (*chikushōkai*) meant to be born as an animal, even though there must be psychic entities that can only be incarnated in the animal world. One of the definitions of animality is a sentient being who is essentially motivated by animal instincts and territorialities. Since we also have been described as hairless apes, then maybe we can recognise that our animal qualities are not only limited to eating, defecation, and sex, but are also partly responsible for our class systems, hierarchies and feudalism in the office or in the workplace. However, to be born with a human body also gives us the opportunity to open up our minds to comprehend what life is all about.

The *shura* (*ashura*), originally, in the Brahmanic and Vedic mythology, were titanesque beings who were always vying with the *deva* (*ten*) for superiority. Traditionally they are defined as being "ugly", "not *deva*" and "without wings". There are four categories of these beings that depend on the manner of their birth, which means they are born from eggs, or from a womb, or born by transformation, or as spawn in the water. Their habitat is the ocean which only comes up to their knees, but other less powerful *shura* (*ashura*) live in mountain caves in the West. In popular iconography, the kings of the shura are represented with three faces, and they have either four or six arms. They also have realms and palaces like the *deva* (*ten*).

In the teaching of Nichiren Daishōnin, this realm of dharmas corresponds to the psychological mechanism of wanting to be centre of attention, to be noticed by others, and the desire to control. Often when these tendencies are frustrated, they then turn into anger, rage, and jealousy. In simpler terms it has a lot to do with the show-off within us. In the *Treatise on the Fundamental Object of Veneration for Contemplating the Mind*, the Daishōnin refers to cajolery, wheedling, and "buttering up" as a part of this dimension. In a more positive sense, this is the part of us that says we need our own space, which enables us to mentally and physically carry on living – in other words, all that our egos need.

The realm of dharmas of humanity (*jinkai*) is the sense of equanimity and rationality. In spite of all our troublesome worries (*bonnō, klesha*), there is a part of us that reassures us that things are not as bad as they appear and that everything is all right. It is the part of us that gets on with our daily living without too many upsets – in other words, a satisfactory life. In the Buddha teaching of Shākyamuni, the realm of dharmas of humanity meant being born as a human being.

As far as the teaching of Shākyamuni is concerned, the realms of dharmas of the *deva* (*tenkai*) refer mainly to the merits of the divinities of Brahmanism and other Vedic teachings. The *deva* (*ten*) are said to have golden bodies, superhuman powers, and to have extremely long lives filled with joy and ecstasy. But, like all other lifespans, at some time or other, they have to come to an end.

Many *deva* are protectors of the Buddha teaching. According to the Daishōnin's writing on *Securing the Peace of the Realm through the Establishment of the Correct Dharma*, one gets the impression that the *deva* (*ten*) protect human interests and that they are also nourished by religious rites and especially by the recitation of the title and theme *Nam Myōhō Renge Kyō*, which means to devote our lives to and found them on (*Nam[u]*) the Utterness of the Dharma (*Myōhō*) [entirety of existence, enlightenment and unenlightenment] permeated by the underlying white lotus flower-like mechanism of the interdependence of cause, concomitancy and effect (*Renge*) in its whereabouts of the ten [psychological] realms of dharmas (*Kyō*). This is something we will explore further as this essay proceeds.

There are many cultures that have legends and mythologies concerning sentient beings who would come into the category of *deva* (*ten*), such as the elves, guardian spirits, local gods, saints, angels, and ancestral divinities. Since there are a number of names of *deva* who are important to the Buddha teaching of Nichiren Daishōnin inscribed on the Fundamental Object of Veneration (*gohonzon*), would not these tutelary essences be archaic archetypal elements in the depth of our psyches that have some influence over our lives in one way or another? Or when we create so much bad karma by doing things that are unwholesome that these archetypes can no longer take part in what we do, then these *deva* (*ten*) or whatever they may be no longer make their presences felt, which allows more destructive energies to take their place.

Anyone who has practised the teachings of the Daishōnin cannot help but be aware of forces that in some way guide our lives, often in the most unexpected way. What I have just said about the *deva* (*ten*) is obviously a personal intuition. However, somebody is likely to ask the question, "What are the *deva* (*ten*)?" Therefore, I thought an allusion to their existence might be food for speculation.

Because the *deva* (*ten*) have extremely happy and ecstatic long lives that unavoidably must come to an end in a protractedly distant future, the concept of the realms of dharmas of the *deva* (*ten*) in the teaching of Nichiren Daishōnin refers to our joys and epiphanies. Whatever our raptures and delights may be – like falling in love, getting the right job, a great night out, or the enjoyment of doing something useful or creative – however exhilarating or joyful our experiences may be, we are always sooner or later compelled to return to the more severe dimension of our normal realities of living. The realms of dharmas of the *deva* (*ten*) refer to the impermanence of all our joys, raptures, and delights.

The realm of dharmas of the hearers of the voice (*shōmonkai*) is a literal translation of the Sino-Japanese Buddhist term, which means "those who listen to or have heard the Buddha's voice". In the teaching of Nichiren Daishōnin, this term has the undertone of those who seek a meaning in their lives. Seen as a state of mind, it is the dimension of learning and wanting to find out. This process starts in our early childhood with continual questions in the form of "What is...?" and "Why?" This is the part of us that is the researcher and inquirer and the part of us where learning is still going on.

The realm of dharmas of the partially enlightened due to karmic circumstances (*engakukai*) is different from the search for understanding and wanting to know why. This psychological dimension is based on something comparable to the sensitivity of the mature painter and sculptor who perceive the phenomenal world around and within them as an aesthetic oneness, even though artists may pick and choose varying and contrasting colours and shapes in order to communicate their respective pictorial or sculptural messages. This is also true for composers who understand sound as a oneness that can be broken up, discriminated, and made use of. Again, it is the same with people who work with words, and no doubt there must be equivalents in the worlds of mathematics, science, and biology, etc., etc.

This realm of dharmas involves those people who have a deep understanding about what life itself entails, but not all its secrets. In the teachings that the Buddha Shākyamuni taught before the universal vehicle (*daijō, mahāyāna*), people who were partially enlightened due to karmic circumstances tended to be more involved in their own substantiation of nirvana, rather than taking into consideration all the people suffering in the bewilderment of the delusions of life around them. It is this point that evokes the essential difference between the individual vehicle (*shōjō, hīnayāna*) and the universal vehicle (*daijō, mahāyāna*) that strives for the Buddha enlightenment of all sentient beings.

The realms of dharmas of the bodhisattvas (*bosatsukai*), in the teachings of Shākyamuni up to the time of the original gateway (*honmon*) of the *Dharma Flower Sutra* (*Hokke-kyō*), indicated persons who seek enlightenment not only for themselves but also strive for the Buddha enlightenment of all sentient beings. However, the enlightenment of the Buddha teachings prior to the *Dharma Flower Sutra* (*Hokke-kyō*) is fundamentally flawed with the concept of a Buddhahood in the sense of attaining nirvana after arduous practices over a period of many kalpas. What this really entails is that, after becoming a Buddha with the body of a Buddha such as seen in Buddha images, one would then be extinguished into the void of relativity (*kū, shūnyatā*) and would no longer exist at all.

In contrast to such an attainment being hardly feasible, especially the continuous practices spread over many aeons, the possibility of the real happiness and inner realisation of the Buddha teaching of Nichiren Daishōnin, whose object is to open up our inherent nature with our persons just as they are, remains within the bounds of possibility. Bodhisattvas, especially with the connotation of bodhisattvas who spring from the earth, are understood as not only people who practise for themselves, but who also seek to set others onto this particular path, which is the practice and doctrine of all the Buddhas of the past, present, and future. At another level, the bodhisattva realm is that part of us which wants to do something for the benefit of others. Essentially, it is our altruistic nature.

To be more precise about the bodhisattvas who spring from the earth, I will have to digress from what I was saying about the altruistic qualities of those persons who belong to the dharma realm of the bodhisattvas, in order to deal with one of the most difficult doctrines of the Schools of Nichiren.

The bodhisattvas who spring from the earth are first mentioned in the *Fifteenth Chapter of the Dharma Flower Sutra on the Bodhisattvas who Swarm up out of the Earth*, which is the chapter that marks the beginning of the teaching of the original gateway. This gateway to the Dharma might well be thought of as a psychological description of the archetypal and fundamental state of all sentient existence.

In previous chapters, myriads and myriads of bodhisattvas who had come from realms such as ours asked the Buddha Shākyamuni for permission to propagate the *Dharma Flower Sutra* (*Myōhō Renge Kyō*) among the world of humankind after his demise into nirvana. Nevertheless, the Buddha refused, by stating that there were already bodhisattvas capable of carrying out this task. At the beginning of the *Fifteenth Chapter*, the ground shook and an astronomical number of bodhisattvas sprang from the earth, each one accompanied by his own coherent following of devotees. These bodhisattvas were led by four bodhisattvas – Superior Practice (*Jōgyō, Vishishtachāritra*), Infinite Practice (*Muhengyō, Anantachārita*), Pure Practice (*Jyōgyō, Vishuddhachārita*), and Firmly Established Practice (*Anryūgyō, Supratishthichārita*).

Since this gateway to the Dharma is so delicate and profound, I would rather quote the Daishōnin from his *Single All-embracing Item on the Bodhisattvas who Swarm up out of the Earth*, which is a part of *The Oral Transmission on the Meaning of the Dharma Flower Sutra* (*Ongi Kuden*) (*Goshō Shimpen*, p.1764):

"Number One, Concerning the Teachers who are Leaders of the Chant: *The Oral Transmission on the Meaning of the Dharma Flower Sutra* (*Ongi Kuden*) says, 'The whole of this particular *Chapter on the Bodhisattvas who Swarm up out of the Earth* deals with those bodhisattvas who were converted in the inherent infinity of existence.' The behavioural norm of the bodhisattvas who were converted in the inherent infinity of existence is *Nam Myōhō Renge Kyō*; this means that they recite it. 'To lead' means to induce and guide all sentient beings of the world of humankind to enlightenment. The leaders and tutors of the Final Period of the Dharma of Shākyamuni (*mappō*) who confine themselves to the original doctrine of the conversion within the inherent infinity of existence are referred to as teachers.

"Now, in order to make it clear what the Four Universal Bodhisattvas imply, it says, in the ninth fascicle of the *Supplementary Adjustments and Annotations to Myōraku's Textual Explanation of the Dharma Flower Sutra*: 'The four guides and teachers who are in the sutra actually depict four specific virtues. Jōgyō [lit., The Practice that is Supreme] represents me, Nichiren.

Muhengyō [lit., Practice without Bounds] stands for timelessness. Jyōgyō [lit., the Practice of Purity] represents purity itself. Anryūgyō, which literally means "the Practice that Establishes Tranquillity", portrays happiness. At one moment in time, there is one single person who is to be endowed with these four significant qualities.'

"The practice that dwells on the terrain that is completely free and unrestricted, as well as being exempt from the two kinds of death, one of which is the living and dying of ordinary sentient beings, whereas the other is seen by persons that are sage-like or bodhisattvas as nothing more than a transition – such an observance is called the Practice that is Supreme (*Jōgyō*). By going beyond the confinement of impermanency, this practice is thought of as the Practice without Bounds (*Muhengyō*). On account of the potential of this practice to rid ourselves of the polluting involvements of the five fundamental conditions that bring about troublesome worries (*bonnō, klesha*) in our physical surroundings along with their corresponding needs and desires, as well as the obstacles and attachments that lurk in the domain of our thoughts and ideas (*sangai, triloka*), this practice is spoken of as the Practice of Purity (*Jyōgyō*). Because the bodhi tree is a sphere of virtues, this adherence is said to be the Practice that Establishes Tranquillity (*Anryūgyō*)."

Now all those who follow Nichiren and reverently recite *Nam Myōhō Renge Kyō* – which means to devote our lives to and found them on (*Nam[u]*) the Utterness of the Dharma (*Myōhō*) [entirety of existence, enlightenment and unenlightenment] permeated by the underlying white lotus flower-like mechanism of the interdependence of cause, concomitancy and effect (*Renge*) in its whereabouts of the ten [psychological] realms of dharmas (*Kyō*)– follow the same course as the bodhisattvas who spring from the earth.

The Oral Transmission on the Meaning of the Dharma Flower Sutra (*Ongi Kuden*) also states that fire has the function of burning things; water is used for making things clean; wind has the role of blowing dust and dirt away; and the earth has the purpose of making plants and trees grow. These are the effective benefits of the four bodhisattvas. Even though the functions of these four bodhisattvas differ, all of them carry out the practice of the *Sutra on the White Lotus Flower-like Mechanism of the Utterness of the Dharma* (*Myōhō Renge Kyō*).

The explanation for the reason why these four bodhisattvas inhabit the nether region is said to be "that the Buddha nature is a bottomless abyss and the profundity of its essential point is unfathomable". "By being the nether region, it is where they abide. By being the nether region, it is where the actual intrinsicality of existence lies." In the *Supplementary Adjustments and Annotations*, it says, "With regard to the nether region, the Chinese monk Jiku Dō Shō (?-434) declared that by living in the nether region the four bodhisattvas themselves are the actual intrinsicality of existence."

But the actual intrinsicality of existence is said to come out of its abode and make itself apparent. Nevertheless, *The Oral Transmission on the Meaning of the Dharma Flower Sutra* (*Ongi Kuden*) does not say that the thousands of plants and myriads of trees are not the bodhisattvas who spring from the earth. Therefore, the bodhisattvas themselves who spring from the earth are said to be the original terrain, which is the inherent infinity of each and every instant. The origin is the effective benefit of a past, which would figuratively be described as a time that existed prior to a period which would amount to all particles of dust that go into the making of five hundred *kalpas*. This in fact refers to the effective benefit that has neither beginning nor end.

The bodhisattvas that spring from the earth are those that hold to the original Dharma, which is inherently infinite. The Dharma which is inherently infinite is *Nam Myōhō Renge Kyō*. Since this title and theme is decidedly what the bodhisattvas who spring from the earth hold to, then it is not in the possession of those bodhisattvas who were converted through the temporary gateway to the Dharma, which is made up of doctrines suspended in time and space. From the fundamental substance of this inherently infinite Dharma emerges its function, which expands into the one instant of thought containing three thousand existential spaces (*ichinen sanzen*).

This is made clear in Tendai's (*T'ien T'ai*) *Desistance from Troublesome Worries in order to See Clearly* (*Maka Shikan*). At a more general level, the explanations of the Universal Teacher Tendai (*T'ien T'ai*) the Teacher of Humankind consist of the propagation and the application of the Utterness of the Dharma (*Myōhō, Saddharma*), "This inherently infinite original Dharma is accepted and held to through the single word faith. The sharp sword that can confront and cure our primordial unenlightenment is the single word faith. You must realise that faith is defined as being free of doubt."

To finish this digression which nevertheless is very important for the understanding of the concept of a bodhisattva from the standpoint of the Nichiren Schools, I would like to add that Nichiren, in his *Treatise on the Fundamental Object of Veneration for Contemplating the Mind*, refers to a phrase in the *Sutra on the Buddha's Passing over to Nirvana*, where it says that "Even an unrepenting, wicked man can still have love and affection for his wife and children. This is the part of us that is the bodhisattva."

With regard to the Dharma realm of the Buddha (*bukkai*), here the word Dharma is in the singular because the Buddhas see the whole of existence as a oneness that is not separate from its synchronistic dynamo, Utterness. Since this is beyond the experience of anyone I know of, I shall simply quote from the second part of the *Collation of the Layers of the Various Teachings of all the Buddhas of the Past, Present and Future as to Which Specific Doctrines are to be Discarded or Established*:

"You must make the effort to substantiate the intrinsicality of the esoteric treasure [the Fundamental Object of Veneration (*gohonzon*)] through your practice, since this is what all the Buddhas of the past, present, and future originally had in mind. The two sage-like persons the Bodhisattva Sovereign Remedy (*Yaku' ō, Bhaishajya-rāja*) and the Bodhisattva Giver of Courage (*Yuze, Pradhānashura*), along with the two Deva Sovereign Guardians, Deva Sovereign Guardian who Maintains the Terrains upon which we Depend for an Existence (*Daijikoku Tennō, Dhritarashtra Mahādeva-rāja*), and Deva Sovereign Guardian Vaishravana (*Bishamon Tennō, Vaishravana Mahādeva-rāja*), as well as the Mother Numen of the Demonic Children (*Kishimojin, Hārītī*), will watch over you and protect you. When you die, you will be immediately reborn in the ultimate supreme terrain of silence and illumination.

"But should you for the shortest while return to the dream of living and dying, your person will completely fill all the realms of dharmas of the ten psychological dharmas, and your mind will be in the physical incarnations of all sentient beings. You will urge them on towards enlightenment from within, and on the outside you will show these sentient beings which path to take. Since there is a mutual correspondence between what is on the inside and what is on the outside, as well as there being a harmony between causes and karmic circumstances, you will busy yourself with the immense compassion that lies in the fullness of the reaches of your mind that is independently free to effectively benefit all sentient beings simultaneously."

Only the Buddha has a Dharma realm, because he and his environment, his teaching, are all the one enlightenment. But people like us live out our lives surrounded by all kinds of dharmas, which are either in our heads or are a part of the makeup of our external realities.

In the light of what I just quoted, I can only suppose that, for a person who has opened up his inherent Buddha nature with his personality just as it stands, there is somewhere in the depths of that person a consciousness of that person's identity being the Utterness of the Dharma (*Myōhō, Saddharma*) itself, as well as the wisdom to discern its subtlest workings.

Here I have to reiterate that each one of these realms of dharmas is furnished with the other ten, not as a sequel, nor in any order, but rather as an amorphous blob of ten potentialities of personality change. As I said a little earlier on, even when I am famished which is a condition that belongs to the realms of dharmas of the hungry demons, the affection I have for my friends does not diminish [the bodhisattva realm]. Yet my anger with that nasty civil servant is still lingering [the realm of the *shura*]. I am still enjoying the surroundings of my home [the realm of humanity];

and my ability to read the *Dharma Flower Sutra* in the original has not been overshadowed in any way [the realm of the hearers of the Buddha's voice]. And now I have made a fart which is something to do with the realm of dharmas of animality, and so on and so forth.

These ten [psychological] realms of dharmas that have now become a hundred, because each one of these ten [psychological] realms of dharmas is mutually endowed with the other ten – they become the basic fundamental of understanding this Buddhist view of life. Now we must look into the ten such qualities that define and describe in further clarity how we live out the first hundred psychological impulses.

In the *Treatise on the Whole being Contained in the One Instant of Mind*, the first sentence begins with, "The whole is contained in the one instant of mind. In further detail, this one instant is divided into a combination of materiality and mind."

The concept and the ideogram for "materiality" is just a little more complex than what it seems. Perhaps I should start by saying that colour, form, solidity, and their attractiveness or ugliness are not separate from each other. Originally, the ideogram for materiality was a pictogram of a human face. At first, it must have had the intended meaning of how someone appears to the outside world. Later, like all words, the significances and nuances attached to this ideogram multiplied as the centuries went by. Apart from the idea of colour not being separate from its form, in the grey rustic world of ancient China, complexions and pinkness became sexual fetishes. We have a famous sentence from the Analects of Confucius that says, "I have not yet seen anyone loving virtues as much as they like pink faces (i.e., sex)."

Be that as it may, here in my translations, materiality implies colour, its form, and in this context we should also include density, hence the translation of *shiki* as materiality. The opposite of this concept is mind. The original Chinese ideogram was a simplified picture of a human heart, which, as we have said before, was for the ancients the organ with which they thought. In the Buddha teaching we have the equation "mind and materiality are not two separate entities" (*shiki shin funi*).

It is virtually impossible to close one's eyes and not see at least an indigo backcloth on which to project our waking minds. Usually the backcloth moves and things like clouds, marshmallows, streaks of light, patterns, changing landscapes, strange architecture, and even nonexistent toys, faces, and strange animals appear in an endless procession, as our minds tick over at their own pace. But if we open our eyes and look at the space around us, whether it is outside with trees and houses or what have you, or an interior of a room with its furnishings, none of this could possibly exist, if we did not have a mind to perceive them.

Although materiality and mind may not be separate from each other, there is a difference between what goes on in our heads and what we see when we open our eyes. In addition to the images that float in our heads, there are also more abstract notions, such as words, figures, and imagined sounds and touch.

The second sentence of the passage quoted earlier on, says, "In further detail, this one instant [of mind] is divided into materiality and mind." Most people seem to see their lives in these terms. This leads us to the ten such qualities (*jūnyoze*), which in the *Dharma Flower Sutra* are ten modalities that are ingrained in every aspect and instant of life.

The first mention of these ten such qualities appears in the *Second Chapter on Expedient Means of the Dharma Flower Sutra* (*Hokke-kyō*), where the Buddha Shākyamuni states, "This real aspect of all dharmas is said to be (*Sho'i shohō*) in any way they make themselves present to any of our six sense organs – eyes, ears, nose, tongue, body, and mind [e.g., a carrot is orange; it tastes sweetish and may have a smell] (*Nyoze sō*), their various inner qualities which in any event must lead up to all the implications of Nam Myōhō Renge Kyō [e.g., which include all the words associated with carrots, i.e., zanahoria, carotte, carota, ninjin, and all our memories of carrots and all the way up to their essence which is Nam Myōhō Renge Kyō; when we see this carrot, we unconsciously see a carrot, and both what we see and the

45

associations in our heads automatically come together] (*Nyoze shō*), their substance or what they really are (*Nyoze tai*), their potential strength and energy (*Nyoze riki*), the manifestation of that energy and strength, which is their influence (*Nyoze sa*), their fundamental causes (*Nyoze in*), along with their karmic circumstances (*Nyoze en*), the effects they produce (*Nyoze ka*), and their apparent and karmic consequences (*Nyoze hō*); also in any way dharmas make themselves perceptible to any of our six sense organs – eyes, ears, nose, tongue, body, and mind – has a coherence with their 'apparent karmic consequences', which are present in every instant of life (*Nyoze hon makku kyō tō*)."

What this means is that 1) such an appearance is the way such a dharma presents itself and also the way it behaves. The Universal Teacher Tendai (*T'ien T'ai*) explains in the second fascicle of his *Recondite Significance of the Dharma Flower*, "An appearance is according to its manifest features, which have their own peculiarity. Hence it is referred to as an aspect." The Universal Teacher Myōraku (*Miao-lo*) mentions in the fourteenth fascicle of his Explanatory Notes on the *Recondite Significance of the Dharma Flower*, "An appearance is only a dharma's manifestation."

2) Such a nature is also its disposition, temperament qualities, and properties, etc. *The Recondite Significance of the Dharma Flower* defines "nature" as "the intrinsic, inborn disposition which one cannot change. This is why it is referred to as such a nature." What is ultimately intended in the fundamental nature of all dharmas is their various inner qualities which in any event must lead up to all the implications of Nam Myōhō Renge Kyō (*Nyoze shō*), that is to say, the whole of existence – i.e., *the Dharma body*, the wisdom to understand it, i.e., *Nam Myohō Renge Kyō, and* the way existence manifests itself. In Myōraku's (*Miao-lo*) *Explanatory Notes on the Recondite Significance of the Dharma Flower*, he says, "Nature or dispositions are only mind."

3) Such a substance, entity, or reality is what something or someone really is, their inner and outward realities combined. In the teaching of Nichiren, substance (*tai*) is the true form, which involves both "such an appearance" as well as "such a nature". In the second fascicle of the *Recondite Significance of the Dharma Flower*,

this is defined as, "The whole content of someone or something is referred to as its entity."

4) Such a strength refers to the strength that is on the inside and also what it can do. It also indicates hidden capacities. In the second fascicle of the *Recondite Significance of the Dharma Flower*, it says, "Merits and abilities become strength." *The Universal Desistance from Troublesome Worries in order to see Clearly* puts it this way: "The capabilities to achieve lie in the strength and the use of it."

5) Such an action is said to be an operation, a function, or its effect. It also means the manifestation of "such a strength", in terms of actions and behaviour. In the *Recondite Significance of the Dharma Flower*, "such an action" is explained as, "Constructing something indicates such an action."

6) Such a cause is understood as, that which directly brings about an effect or fruition is a cause. *The Recondite Significance of the Dharma Flower* defines causes as, "That which brings about a continuity of causes is seen as having one cause." In the *Universal Desistance from Troublesome Worries in order to see Clearly*, "A cause is something that invites an effect. This also could be thought of as karma."

7) Such a karmic relationship is a complementary cause that aids and abets the original one. In the second fascicle of the *Recondite Significance of the Dharma Flower*, it says, "A complementary cause becomes a karmic relationship." In the fifth fascicle of the *Universal Desistance from Troublesome Worries in order to see Clearly*, it mentions that "The reasons which bring about karma are called karmic relationships."

8) Such a fruition or effect is the result of cause. The explanation in the *Recondite Significance of the Dharma Flower* is "Whatever comes out as a result of a chain of causes is called a fruition." The fifth fascicle of the *Universal Desistance from Troublesome Worries in order to see Clearly* also mentions that "Such a fruition is a fruition as seen as the victorious attainment."

9) Such a requital is how "such a fruition" appears in reality. *The Recondite Significance of the Dharma Flower* says that "such a requital" is "The recompense that accompanies fruition is called a requital." *The Universal Desistance from Troublesome Worries in order to see Clearly* says that "such a requital" is a recompense for "such a cause".

10) Then from such an appearance to such a requital, all these nine such qualities are equally the ultimate dimension of the real aspect of all dharmas. The words "such a" refer to the nine particular qualities that are applicable to everything in existence, irrespective of existing in reality or whether they are things that only exist in our heads.

However, when Shakyamui first pronounced these ten such qualities, in the second chapter of the *Dharma Flower Sutra* (*Hokke-kyō*), he said, "The real aspect of all dharmas [that is to say anything we are capable of feeling, perceiving, knowing, dreaming about, or fantasising] can only be exhaustively fathomed between one Buddha and another." This statement opened the way for the replacement of the existing three vehicles of practice – that is, 1) the intellectuals who had heard the Buddha teach, 2) those who had been partially awakened through karmic relationships such as art, science, mathematics, music, etc., and a profound search for the meaning of existence, as well as 3) the bodhisattvas who are altruists. These three categories of people who were following the teachings of Shākyamuni were all to be put under the single label of those whose object is the path of Enlightenment.

This stage in the teaching of the *Dharma Flower Sutra* (*Hokke-kyō*) is referred to as clearing away the three vehicles in order to reveal the one that leads to opening the awareness of Buddhahood (*kaisan kenichi*). The phase of teaching of Shākyamuni that includes the ten such qualities was defined by the Universal Teacher Tendai (*T'ien T'ai*) as the "general clearing away of the three vehicles in order to reveal the one" (*ryakkaisan kenichi*).

For those who follow the Nichiren teachings of the Kōmon Schools and who, for the most part, in their daily practice (*gongyo*) recite the beginning of the *Second Chapter on Expedient Means, Hōben pon dai ni*, they may have asked why *Nyo ze sō, Nyo ze shō* . . . etc. are repeated three times over. We recite these ten such qualities in the way they are written in the Chinese text for ceremonial euphony. But the intention goes a long way deeper.

Nyo ze sō refers to the axiom of phenomena or the accepted principle of outward experience or *ke*. In literal English, *nyo ze sō* would be "such as this is present" or "such is its appearance". As I have already said, this "*sō*" applies to all colours, shapes, and behaviours of each and every dharma. When we recite *Nyo ze sō* . . . .etc. for the second time, what really is implied is *ze sō nyo, ze shō nyo* and so forth, which literally translated means, "This appearance is such, This nature is such . . . .".

When the ten such qualities are recited in this way, what is intended is that all dharmas are a suchness and that all dharmas are nothing but relativities in the void of existence *kū*. When we recite the ten such qualities for the third time, *Nyo ze sō*, it is to be understood as *sō nyo ze* which literally interpreted means "an existence such as this". This is also how the middle way of reality *chūdō jissō* is expressed in terms of the such qualities *nyoze*. All dharmas are such as they are according to the subjective circumstances and the location *seken* of the persons who are experiencing them. They are also the motivation for many people to start practising.

This brings us to the three existential spaces where the differentiation of individual qualities and environments occur. However, with regard to the first three of the ten such qualities as seen in the light of the original Buddha, such a presence would be what Nichiren looked like as a human being. In terms of the triple axiom of phenomenon (*ke*), the void of relativity (*kū*), and the middle way of reality (*chū*), then this phrase "such a presence" applies to the axiom of phenomenon. Such an inner nature is the mind and the Utterness of the wisdom of the Daishōnin, which by being the nature of mind is the axiom of relativity (*kū, shūnyatā*) or the void.

As for the axiom of the middle way of reality, we have not yet come to it. When the Buddha Shākyamuni expounded these ten such qualities in the *Chapter on Expedient Means* in the *Dharma Flower Sutra* (*Hokke-kyō*), the ten [psychological] realms of dharmas, which I have just explained, as well as the three existential spaces, which I will explain shortly, were merely an assumption. I presume that the inclusion of the ten [psychological] realms of dharmas was understood by the people who were listening at the time, and maybe the existential spaces could have been taken for granted also. But, at all events, they are not mentioned in the sutric text.

Scholars like Tendai (*T'ien T'ai*) took the view that Shākyamuni was only referring to the one thousand such qualities. That is to say, a hundred realms of dharmas possessed by the ten such qualities become a thousand such qualities. Since this concept of life only takes place in a subjective vision of it, it is seen as a temporary gateway to the Dharma and as a teaching that belongs to events suspended in time and place.

Whereas one might think of the one instant of mind containing one thousand such qualities as a somewhat indefinable mass of psychological complexes and confusions, the three existential spaces are the boundaries that separate us from one another and also delineate the boundaries in which that existence occurs. Here, even though the illusion of materiality is built into the structure of our unenlightenment, the fundamental nature of all the manifestations of existing is only mind, and what we perceive in it is only knowing.

In Shākyamuni's teaching there is no concept of an ego as in western psychology. Instead, there are the five aggregates (*go.on*), which overshadow any notion of awareness of our original state which is the Utterness and simultaneousness of all space and all time. This synchronistic Utterness is specified as our fundamental Dharma nature or as our basic enlightenment. Also, this can be described as the primordial Dharma nature that is the actual and unchangeable true suchness that is the basis of all existence.

In contrast, we are also endowed with a fundamental bewilderment, by which, due to our distraction from the fundamental Dharma nature, we find ourselves trundled away

The Essential of the Teaching of Nichiren Daishōnin

into the dreamlike delusions of unenlightenment. Since this unenlightenment is as fundamentally primordial as the Dharma nature, here, I use the word primordial in the sense that these two qualities of enlightenment and unenlightenment have always been, always are, and always will be in an ever-present now.

Here we can quote a passage from *The Oral Transmission on the Meaning of the Dharma Flower Sutra* (*Ongi Kuden*), to make this point clearer: "Utterness (*Myō*) is the Dharma nature, and dharmas (*hō*) are our respective unenlightenment. The single entity of unenlightenment and the Dharma nature is called the Utterness of the Dharma (*Myōhō, Saddharma*). The lotus flower (*renge*) is the two dharmas of cause and effect as a single interdependent event."

Judging by this statement, enlightenment and delusion exist side by side in an interdependence as part of the fundamental whole, if it were not for our basic bewilderment which brings about our various dispositions (*gyō*) that are inevitably choices inherited from former existences. This leads to an awareness that we have an existence that is our own, which entices us to invent *i*) the materiality (*shiki*) of a body and its necessary physical surroundings. This is the first of the five aggregates that darken our original enlightenment. Our bodies also involve the five organs of sense. This makes us *ii*) receptive (*ju*) to sensations and feelings, along with the functioning of the mind and senses in connection with affairs and things, then through *iii*) conception (*sō*), thought, discerning and the functioning of the mind in distinguishing. *iv*) The mind's volition (*gyō*) in it – processes with regard to likes and dislikes, good and evil, etc. – brings about the mental faculty that makes us know *v*) *shiki* who we are, on account of our acquired knowledge and experiences.

Because the combination of these five aggregates is an existential space in itself, it is said that this is what makes us separate individuals. It is also said, with the disappearance of the aggregate of materiality (*shiki.on*) after death which implies the loss of a body and its surroundings, this contributes enormously to our forgetting who we were in our previous lives.

Nevertheless, even though materiality can also exist within its own physical surroundings, we must now go further into the question of where existence takes place. The next existential space is called the existential space of sentient beings. The one thousand such qualities combined with the existential space of the five aggregates may well define what sort of individuals we are, but it is this existential space of sentient beings that is always the result of karma and is responsible for what our environments are to be.

According to Tendai's (*T'ien T'ai*) *Desistance from Troublesome Worries in order to See Clearly*, the existential spaces of sentient beings are circumscribed according to the ten [psychological] realms of dharmas. Even though these explanations have a highly mediaeval flavour, it is easy to speculate as to how things would be in the twenty-first century. "It is the red hot irons that are the makeup of the dwelling place of the realms of the dharmas of the denizens of hell. The abodes of the realms of dharmas of animality are to be found on the earth, in water, and in the air. The realms of dharmas of the *shura* abide along the seashores or at the bottom of the ocean. The realms of dharmas of humankind dwell upon the earth. The realms of dharmas of the *deva* (*ten*) who represent the transient quality of ecstasies and joys live in palaces. The bodhisattvas who carry out the six practices that ferry sentient beings over the sea of mortality to the shores of nirvana (*roku haramitsu*) live in the same places as humankind. The bodhisattvas of the interconnecting teachings (*tsukyō*) who have not yet overcome their delusions depend on the same living spaces as humankind and the *deva*. But those who have been able to sever their delusions about living and dying live on terrains that are an expedient means. The bodhisattvas of the particular (*bekkyō*) and all-inclusive (*enkyō*) teachings who have not yet exhausted their delusions about living and dying live in the terrains of expedient means among humankind and the *deva*. But those bodhisattvas of the particular and the all-inclusive doctrines inhabit the terrains of real reward (*jippōdo*), and the Tathāgatas dwell on the terrain of eternal silence and illumination (*jōjakkōdo*)."

[Tathāgata (*Nyorai*) signifies the following: one who has gone; one who has followed the Path and arrived at the real suchness; one of the ten titles of a Buddha. Tathāgata can be explained as a person who comes from the real suchness of existence, which is Nam Myōhō Renge Kyō – which means to devote our lives to and found them on (Nam[u]) the Utterness of the Dharma (Myōhō) (entirety of existence, enlightenment and unenlightenment) permeated by the underlying white lotus flower-like mechanism of the interdependence of cause, concomitancy and effect (Renge) in its whereabouts of the ten (psychological) realms of dharmas (Kyō) – and that person will return to it.]

Albeit it may be worthwhile to mention that the Buddha of the *Sixteenth Chapter on the Lifespan of the Tathāgata* in the *Dharma Flower Sutra* is always present in this actual world of ours that we have to put up with (*shaba sekai*), which for the enlightened is in no way different from the terrain of eternal silence and illumination, obviously all these different terrains are subjective. Hell can be in Buckingham Palace. And terrains of expedient means can be an artist's studio. Or the ecstasy and joy of the *deva* (*ten*) can be at the Christmas party.

The Buddha teaching of Nichiren Daishōnin does not flatly state that dharmas do not exist, but that their reality is flexible. Nevertheless, this teaching does emphasise that materiality and mind are not separate from each other, and also it teaches that subjectivity has to have a dependent environment. In addition to that, the quality of our materiality or environment is entirely in accordance with the state of our minds which can be modified from moment to moment.

Now we come to the last of the existential spaces, that of abode and terrain. In reality, this is the psychological and, to a certain extent, the physical barrier that lies between the denizens of hell, the hearers of the Buddha's voice, or the people who spend their time in the realms of the dharmas of animality. Certain people are not really welcome into our lives or living spaces. This has more to do with a sense of preservation than any moral judgement. This one instant of mind containing three thousand existential spaces (*ichinen sanzen*) is always on the move, according to the karmic circumstances that influence our lives from instant to instant.

Every single nanosecond that is lived by each and every manifestation of life however small – the substance of each of their lives is mind that can only be the totality of mind. In some way or another, it is the materiality of our brains and other simpler centres of psychic coordination that function as filters that only allow enough mind to seep through for biological or economic survival. Albeit even the tiniest scrap of mind contains the whole of mind, still, due to each one of these existential spaces, each individual mind has its unique window that looks out on to life as a whole.

A dirty, bad-tempered stray cat can become a much endeared house pet, due to karmic circumstances. Human beings, whoever we may be, can find fulfilment and happiness through our karmic relationship to faith and practice.

Probably the next question is – faith in what?

The answer is – faith in the existence of one's own Buddha nature, which is also present in every single event and object in our lives. The one instant of mind containing three thousand existential spaces (*ichinen sanzen*) is the *Myōhō*, the Utterness of the Dharma (*Myōhō, Saddharma*).

Part 4: *Renge*

Before going into the question of the lotus flower being the interdependence of cause and effect, I would like you to read an oral transmission from the Buddha Writings of Nichiren Shōshū (*Nichiren Shōshū Seiten*). Not only is this writing a little-known poetic vision of the lotus flower, but it also makes references to the eight-petalled lotus flower as being our own inherent Buddha nature. This text will also give the reader an idea as to how this lotus plant was seen in thirteenth century Japan. Nichiren says the following:

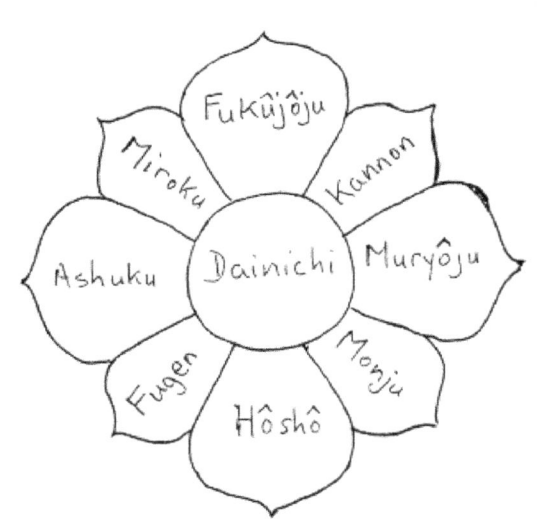

"To begin with, if we are to think of inquiring as to where the Lotus Flower grows, and as to what sort of pond, or in what sort of water, or in what kind of locality, or in what kind of environment this flower belongs, then are we to suppose that it grows among snowy mountains of the North? Or is it in tepid pools among the fragrant hills of the South that we find this unimaginable and ineffably wonderful flower, the all-embracing white lotus? Is this why we call it the Lotus Flower of the Utterness of the Dharma (*Myōhō, Saddharma*)?

"However that may be, the ponds of King Hokabara have lotus flowers that bloom with a thousand petals, but those that flower among humankind have only about ten petals each. Above us in the heavens, there are lotus flowers with a hundred petals, and those of the Buddhas and bodhisattvas have a thousand. Should we, for this reason, call them the lotus flowers of the Utterness of

55

the Dharma (*Myōhō, Saddharma*)? Or again should we not try to find out if there are lotuses growing up from the Pool of the White Heron or the waters of Kunming?

"You should carefully turn this matter over in your mind, without further inquiring into the distance or searching in places that are far away. These lotus flowers grow in the breasts of sentient beings such as us. In the midst of its foul slush of evil karma and troublesome worries, the mind is endowed with the cause proper of the Buddha nature that is designated by the name of the Lotus Flower of the Utterness of the Dharma (*Myōhō, Saddharma*).

"The lotus flowers of the ordinary world only bloom in summertime, but not the whole year round. They grow in muddy ooze and not on dry land. In the wind, they sink beneath the passing waves. They close up when it is icy and wilt in the blazing sun.

"Nevertheless, this is not the way of the lotus flower of the Buddha nature. By being the flower that is not limited by the past, present, or future, it keeps its petals throughout the four seasons of the year. And by being the flower whose bounds are unlimited, it flourishes in the six lower destinations of rebirth and the three realms of desire, materiality, and immaterial space. Since this is the flower of the non-duality of good and bad, it neither chooses the depth nor the shallowness of evil karma. Because it is the flower of the single suchness of right and wrong, it germinates in the foul slush of troublesome worries (*bonnō, klesha*). And, when it is grown, it is neither buffeted by the ten evil winds, nor is it submerged by the waves of the five deadly sins. The red lotus neither shrinks back from the icy cold, nor does it fade in the scorching heat.

"Even though we are in possession of the lotus flower of our Buddha nature just as it has been described, we are intoxicated by the liquor of unenlightenment, so that we are ignorant of its very presence within our bodies. By being beguiled by the murkiness of troublesome worries (*bonnō, klesha*), we are unawakened as to the real suchness of our own nature. This is like the poor woman who is oblivious of the treasure store in her own house and the *kirin* or dragon who is irritated by the jewel in his own body, without knowing that it is of worth. At all events, there are hidden things that we do not see, like the Buddha nature in sentient beings or the moon behind the clouds, the gold in the earth, or the flowers inside a tree. But there really is the Buddha nature stored within the hearts of sentient beings."

Previously, we had the explanation of the meaning of the two ideograms for the Utterness of the Dharma (*Myōhō, Saddharma*). Now, it must be made clear what the lotus flower means. The words imply both the dharmic and metaphoric lotus flower [just as earlier there was both the dharmic and metaphoric Utterness of the Dharma (*Myōhō, Saddharma*)].

Now the lotus flower of the actual fundamental substance has to be explained. Just as the metaphoric lotus grows out of the mire and remains unsullied, the lotus flower of the immaculate purity of our fundamental nature is not only unsoiled by muddy waters but is shown to be fully endowed with the fundamental substance and the functions of all the World Honoured Ones.

The lotus flower of the actual fundamental substance abides in the breasts of all sentient beings, in the form of a fleshy disc divided into eight parts. All of those who have received life everywhere – irrespective as to whether they are big, small, rough, or delicate, or as ungainly as crickets, ants, mosquitoes, and horseflies – all of them have within their bosom this immaculately white eight-petalled lotus flower.

In the eastern petal dwells the Buddha Ashuku (*Akshobhya*); in the southern petal dwells the Buddha Hōshō (*Ratnasambhava*). In the western petal, there is the Buddha Muryōju (*Amitāyus*); and the northern petal is the abode of the Buddha Fukūjōju (*Amoghasiddhi*). In the petal between the two astrological houses of the dragon and the snake, which is the southeast, resides the Bodhisattva Fugen; the petal in the southwestern direction of the sheep and the monkey is the seat of Bodhisattva Mañjushrī (*Monjushiri*). In the northwestern direction of the dog and the pig resides the Bodhisattva Kannon; and, in the northeastern petal, there is the abode of Bodhisattva Maitreya (*Miroku*). All eight petals entail four

Buddhas and eight Bodhisattvas. Enthroned in the centre is the Tathāgata Dainichi, who is the Buddha of the nine World Honoured Ones of the eight-petalled lotus. In actual fact, this is what is known as the Buddha nature, which can be none other than the Utterness of the Dharma (*Myōhō, Saddharma*).

In the western region, all the Buddhas are comprised in the one Buddha Ashuku (*Akshobhya*); in the eastern region, all Buddhas are comprised in the one Buddha Muryōju (*Amitāyus*); and, in the northern region, all the Buddhas are embodied in the Buddha Fukūjōju. So, all the Buddhas of the ten directions and of the past, present, and future are all included among the nine World Honoured Ones in the eight-petalled lotus. In this manner, sentient beings are exquisite *stupas* that comprise the innumerability of all the Buddhas.

When it comes to ordinary mundane *stupas*, sentient beings are ignorant of this essential element. They have to be taught that our own bodies are indeed *stupas* that embody all the Buddhas and what this implies. People with sharper propensities would know that our bodies are analogous to the *stupa* of the realm of the Dharma. This is called the beginning of enlightenment. The eight-petalled lotus that lies within our breasts is called the lotus flower of the nine World Honoured Ones, and Bodhisattvas upon it are called the Utterness of the Dharma (*Myōhō, Saddharma*).

This pragmatic aspect of the teaching of Tendai (*T'ien T'ai*) should be studied in these terms. This is by far the most esoteric gateway to the Dharma. When we do talk of the minds of sentient beings in this manner, it is then said to be the *Dharma Flower Sutra* (*Myōhō Renge Kyō*). Therefore, whenever we talk about the existence of the Precious Stupa in the *Dharma Flower Sutra* (*Myōhō Renge Kyō*) as not being real, then it has to be taught that the actual fundamental substance of sentient beings is just like the *stupa* of Tahō.

Accordingly, since all sentient beings are *stupas*, then the killing of people is a fearful wrongdoing. There is not even a tiny insect that settles in the palm of your hand that is not fully endowed with the eight-petalled lotus of the nine World Honoured Ones. If you begin to grasp the significance of this, then you will understand that should we fall into the flames of hell, then the eight-petalled Lotus Flower would also have to fall.

If you, in the tiniest way, consider that our minds are endowed with the fundamental substance and the function of the World Honoured Ones, then you are all but on the threshold of enlightenment. Even if you were to fall into the path of the hungry demons and deeply suffer the pangs of starvation, yet were in some small way to seize upon the idea that in our hearts there is a *stupa* of the Buddha who is totally awakened to *Myōhō Renge Kyō*, the *Sutra on the White Lotus Flower-like Mechanism of the Utterness of the Dharma* (*Myōhō Renge Kyō*), then this must be one's person not being separate from becoming a Buddha.

Since time immemorial, the omnipresent ten realms of the dharmas have been the shape of *Myōhō Renge Kyō*. This is how the eight-year-old Dragon King's Daughter in this manner fully realised what the Utterness of the Dharma (*Myōhō, Saddharma*) was. And, without altering the actual fundamental substance of her female body, she became a Buddha with her person intact. Therefore, "Of all the persons who hear the Dharma, there is not one who will not become a Buddha". This is the disclosure of the principle that of all the people everywhere that hear the *Dharma Flower Sutra* (*Myōhō Renge Kyō*), there is not a single one who will not be enlightened.

In spite of there being the *stupa* of the eight-petalled lotus of the nine World Honoured Ones, through the one instant of thought being dirtied by the bewilderment of an unenlightened attachment to fancies that cannot be cleared away, we become temporarily unknowing. So this lotus is hidden by life and death and its troublesome worries (*bonnō, klesha*). When you hear it expounded in the *Dharma Flower Sutra* (*Myōhō Renge Kyō*) that your own mind is the actual fundamental substance of the *Sutra on the White Lotus Flower-like Mechanism of the Utterness of the Dharma* (*Myōhō Renge Kyō*), with the fundamental substance and the function of the World Honoured One, and that the citadel of your mind is the abode of the *stupa* of Tahō, then the least understanding of this means that your person is not separate from becoming a Buddha.

What this teaching implies is in fact what can be made known, and knowing it is what we understand. What we comprehend is again according to our knowledge. Therefore, even if you do not read the *Dharma Flower Sutra* (*Myōhō Renge Kyō*), yet never give up meditating upon it, then seeing it in this way, you are someone who practises the Dharma Flower (*Myōhō Renge Kyō*). Albeit you do not understand this argument, it is still a meritorious virtue. Furthermore, when you know that the minds of all sentient beings are furnished with Buddhas of the eight-petalled lotus of the nine World Honoured Ones, you will, henceforth, always have the outlook of a person who practises the *Dharma Flower Sutra* (*Myōhō Renge Kyō*). Whether you are asleep or awake, you will be accompanied by the Buddha both day and night.

When you hear this gateway to the Dharma without letting it slip from your memory, and if you can hold faith in it and understand it, then your person is not separate from becoming a Buddha. We have inherited a personality which is in accordance to how we reacted to things in former lives. Again, according to the karma which our personalities bring about in this life, this will then be the fruition of how we become and react to things in lives to come. But by even having a tiny speck of understanding and faith in the *Sutra on the White Lotus Flower-like Mechanism of the Utterness of the Dharma* (*Myōhō Renge Kyō*), the Buddhas of the eight-petalled lotus of the nine World Honoured Ones will reveal themselves and make an impression on future lives. You will acquire a *Vajra* body and dwell in the lotus flower of the citadel of your own heart.

A *vajra* is the thunderbolt of Indra (Taishaku), often called the diamond club. Recent anthropological research sees the *vajra* as a sun symbol. Here the word diamond is a synonym of hardness, indestructibility, power, and being the least frangible of all minerals. At the time prior to Shākyamuni, the *vajra* is also seen to have been a weapon of Indian soldiers. It is viewed by the Esoteric and Tantric Schools as a symbol of power and wisdom to overcome delusions and evil spirits.

Then there is a text that says, "On the contrary, I do prostrate myself at the feet of all the Buddhas within my heart." The Dragon King's Daughter, whose person was not separate from becoming a

Buddha, became universally and correctly awakened and was enthroned on the Unsullied Precious Lotus Flower of the southern regions. This means that she dwelt in the awareness of the revelation that the nature of her own mind was *Myōhō Renge Kyō*, the *Sutra on the White Lotus Flower-like Mechanism of the Utterness of the Dharma* (*Myōhō Renge Kyō*).

This would indicate that when faith and understanding become just a little stronger and flourish a little more, then even now, at this very moment, the Buddhas of the eight-petalled lotus of the nine World Honoured Ones, as a matter of course, reveal the light they emit and beam it onto our respective realms of dharmas. This is why it says, in the *Collection of Given Decisions*, "Do not lose sight of the teaching, on account of my personal indolence. The Dragon King's Daughter became endowed with the thirty-two physical marks of a Buddha and bore witness to the silence and illumination of perfect enlightenment, on hearing the Sutra with undivided attention. What refers to all can be singled out with one example, since perceptive beings do think things out for themselves."

It is on this account that if your understanding and your clear insight into the sutra is lacking, then you will not be capable of becoming a Buddha with your person just as it is. So there would be no reason for the Buddhas of the essence of your mind to reveal themselves in the lives to come. Therefore, you must forge and hammer yourself into the shape of becoming a Buddha. In this context, it is taught that you do not have to look for the peerless cluster of jewels, since we ourselves already possess it.

When you do come to fully understand this eight-petalled lotus of the nine World Honoured Ones, you do not become a Buddha, even though you may be seated with the Buddha who has always been since the beginning. Nonetheless, it only takes a tiny shred of unenlightenment to obscure this understanding, so that we may never perceive it again.

Now we have come to the knowledge of the understanding which reveals that "You do not have to look for the peerless cluster of jewels, since we ourselves already possess it". So we have

Nangaku (*Nan-yüeh*), who says, "The *Sutra on the White Lotus Flower-like Mechanism of the Utterness of the Dharma* (*Myōhō Renge Kyō*) is the Universal Vehicle (*daijō, mahāyāna*), which, if sentient beings practise just as it teaches, then they will, as a matter of course, attain to the Buddha path. For instance, sentient beings who have rebuffed goodness, who are everywhere throughout the realms of dharmas, will decidedly, on a single hearing of the *Dharma Flower Sutra* (*Myōhō Renge Kyō*), attain to a mind of enlightenment."

The eight-petalled lotus of the nine World Honoured Ones is also the essence of the mind of the slanderous person of incorrigible unbelief, as well as the evil person who commits the five deadly sins or the ten acts that lead to evil karma. Should these people exercise a minimum of faith and understanding, there is no doubt that they will become Buddhas and naturally attain to the Buddha path. While hell is just being hell, it is endowed with the World Honoured One, with both his fundamental substance and function.

The universal and impartial wisdom, by being the actual fundamental substance throughout the ten [psychological] realms of dharmas of the *Sutra on the White Lotus Flower-like Mechanism of the Utterness of the Dharma* (*Myōhō Renge Kyō*), perpendicularly reaches through the past, present, and future. Horizontally, it embraces the whole of the ten directions and is totally unbiased towards the differences of things being high or low, great or small, coarse or delicate, because it is the universally impartial wisdom of the *Dharma Flower Sutra* (*Myōhō Renge Kyō*). As the sole vehicle has been expounded in this manner, then there can be no other path to attain; neither two nor three, since it is called the sole Dharma vehicle.

Indeed, what an outstandingly superlative Dharma gateway this is!

It does not teach that the eight-petalled lotus of the nine World Honoured Ones only dwells within the breast of the masculine. It extols with a sigh that women also receive it in their feminine frames. If it expounded that only high-ranking people were endowed with *stupas*, then those of inferior rank would bear a grudge. Because this is the *stupa* of universally impartial wisdom, there could be no circumstance for a deviation from the truth.

If the Dharma becomes a single vehicle, then there are no doubts concerning it. Although this is an easier Dharma for becoming a Buddha, it was as long as forty years before Shākyamuni exposed this treasury of esoteric wisdom, for fear that a simple explanation of universal significance of the Dharma would reduce it to insignificance.

The meritorious virtue of building and setting up a hundred thousand *stupas* made of precious metals does not amount to the meritorious virtue of holding faith in, and understanding that our minds are *stupas* of the Buddhas. So, when sentient beings do evil things, they are acts of perversity, because sentient beings are the fundamental substance of the Lotus Flower of the Utterness of the Dharma (*Myōhō, Saddharma*). Therefore, the enlightenment to this concept naturally consists in universal compassion. There is even great merit in giving up the seat of one's position, so that others may be placed upon it. But how much more is the boundless meritorious virtue of rolling back one's own unenlightenment, so as to reveal and know that the dwelling place of the five Buddhas and four Bodhisattvas is in the citadel of one's mind?

The Buddha, on giving an illustration, said that the ox-headed sandalwood tree is among all the kinds of wood the most renowned, so that one ounce of this wood is said to cost four *mon*. It is a treasure that has the value of a world where the sun shines from dawn to dusk under the four heavens. The capacity of this wood is like a wand with the wish-fulfilling jewel (*mani*) that can make all the treasures that one desires come raining down or bubble up like a spring. If you lay out this wood when it gets cold, it becomes warmer; and, if it is hot, it becomes cool. People who are sick are cured at once. Those who are impoverished become independently wealthy and honourable. So what would the meritorious virtue be, if one were to construct, from this precious wood, thirty-two halls, whose height is that of eight fan palms with a width of thirty-nine *jō* and two *shaku*, and then fill them with a hundred thousand fully ordained monks and members of the Order? Such a meritorious virtue would then be surpassed by myriads of billions of times, in a single instant of understanding and faith in the *Dharma Flower Sutra* (*Myōhō Renge Kyō*). All of this has been recounted in the sixth fascicle of this canon.

"Naturally, it must be the same as that which has just been said – that a hundred thousand myriad times that number of merits does not amount to the virtuous merit of one, which indeed is to be relied upon. What this Dharma amounts to is the reason for the Buddha coming into the world and is the direct path for all sentient beings, as well as the treasury of esoteric wisdom of all the Buddhas past, present, and future. Since this is the justification and the circumstances for the sole purpose of the Buddha appearing in the world, the Dharma that he expounded is of the ultimate significance.

"Nevertheless, the Buddha expounded the *Dharma Flower Sutra* (*Myōhō Renge Kyō*) from the podium of possessing eternal nirvana. Then what is the reason for sentient beings not understanding or having faith in it? Even Shākyamuni held it back for as many as forty years and taught the *Flower Garland Sutra* (*Kegon, Avatāmsaka-sūtra*), the sutras of the teachings of the individual vehicle (*shōjō, hīnayāna*), and the interrelated sutras instead, so as to entice the various propensities of his hearers towards the exposition of the *Dharma Flower Sutra* (*Myōhō Renge Kyō*). And this is its meritorious virtue."

Above all poetic and metaphorical considerations, the lotus flower is the interdependence of cause and effect. Nichiren, in his *The Oral Transmission on the Meaning of the Dharma Flower Sutra* (*Ongi Kuden*), makes this clear, when he says, "... The lotus flower is the two dharmas of cause and effect, as well as being the oneness of cause and effect... The lotus flower is the Buddha entity of the nine World Honoured Ones of the eight-petalled lotus."

Would this not be the part of us that lives all space, all time, which must include the past, present, and future – the part of us that cannot be destroyed? Is it the very essence of life itself?

However many lives or deaths we have had and will have to go through, or however much pain and suffering we may have had and may have to suffer in the future, it is on account of this interdependence of cause and effect that the substantiation of our own inherent Buddha nature comes about and, at the same moment, makes the Buddha nature manifest in all the plants, trees, and all the things and people that surround us.

The Essential of the Teaching of Nichiren Daishōnin

Part 5: Kyō

Now we come to the word "sutra". One of its most common interpretations is "the thread of the discourse". However, the Daishōnin in his explanation of *Nam Myōhō Renge Kyō* – which means to devote our lives to and found them on (*Nam[u]*) the Utterness of the Dharma (*Myōhō*) [entirety of existence, enlightenment and unenlightenment] permeated by the underlying white lotus flower-like mechanism of the interdependence of cause, concomitancy and effect (*Renge*) in its whereabouts of the ten [psychological] realms of dharmas (*Kyō*) – at the very beginning of his *The Oral Transmission on the Meaning of the Dharma Flower Sutra* (*Ongi Kuden*), defines it as, "... the realms of dharmas are the sutra".

Among the many meanings attached to the Chinese ideogram *kyō* that is equated with the word "sutra", as well as its Tibetan counterpart "*mdo*", this concept includes the warp of a fabric and things running lengthwise such as meridians, etc. It is probably due to the never-ending vertical threads of the warp in weaving that this ideogram acquired a secondary nuance of something that lasts forever, such as a scriptural canon or a philosophical classic.

Be that as it may, if we use this ideogram for sutra in the light of the doctrines of Shākyamuni, then it was at the first council on Spirit Vulture Peak (*Ryōjusen, Gridhrakūta*) in northern India, not long after the Buddha's demise into nirvana, that the Venerable Anan (*Ānanda*) was asked to repeat from memory all the teachings that the Buddha had expounded during his fifty years of teaching. It was because of Anan's (*Ānanda*) outstanding memory that he was able to reconstitute these orally transmitted discourses and have people write them down. Each one of these Buddha teachings begins, "As I heard upon a time". And, since then, this phrase has been used as a token to validate a discourse and call it a sutra.

It is within the Buddha teachings of Nichiren Daishōnin, whose education was almost entirely in classical Chinese – rather in the same way Latin was used in thirteenth century Europe – that we see the profundity of the word sutra extended to a far greater significance than a mere discourse. The way people used to read at the time of the Daishōnin was not like the way we read an Agatha Christie novel in the train. Because the content of the larger part of mediaeval writings had something to do with the meaning of life, readers projected the whole of their psyches into whatever was written, as a part of their search for an inner realisation.

I am firmly convinced that the way the Daishōnin read all his books was by thoroughly pondering over the significance of each and every ideogram, in whatever text he was examining, as though he was determined to find evidence to confirm his own enlightenment. For Nichiren, *Myōhō Renge Kyō* were not only five ideograms that made up the title of the sutra of the same name, each ideogram was a word.

A convenient translation would be *"The Sutra on the White Lotus Flower-like Mechanism of the Utterness of the Dharma (Myōhō Renge Kyō)"*. But a far profounder interpretation of this title would be to devote our lives to and found them on (*Nam[u]*) the Utterness of the Dharma (*Myōhō*) [entirety of existence, enlightenment and unenlightenment] permeated by the underlying white lotus flower-like mechanism of the interdependence of cause, concomitancy and effect (*Renge*) in its whereabouts of the ten [psychological] realms of dharmas (*Kyō*). In this way, the title becomes the "title and theme" (*daimoku*).

Part 6: *Nam(u)*

The word *Namu* is the Chinese version of the Sanskrit word *Namas*. The apt translation of this word is based on the Universal Teacher Tendai's (*T'ien T'ai*) definition of it, which is "to consecrate and found one's life on". In Japan, this expression of devotion or dedication is to be found inscribed on the images of every kind of bodhisattva, *deva* (*ten*), or Shinto divinity.

But nothing could be more deeply meaningful than consecrating and founding our individual lives on the very essence of life itself. This is the particular significance of the recitation of Nam Myōhō Renge Kyō. This is the lion's roar, as Nichiren expresses it in his *The Oral Transmission on the Meaning of the Dharma Flower Sutra* (*Ongi Kuden*): "The lion's roar is the Buddha's exposition of the Dharma. The exposition of the Dharma is the *Dharma Flower Sutra*, and in particular it is Nam Myōhō Renge Kyō."

According to the teachings of the Nichiren Schools, sentient beings possess nine modes of cognition (*kyūshiki*). The first five correspond to our faculties of seeing, hearing, smelling, tasting, and touch. *i*) The cognition of sight (*kenshiki*) depends on the organ of the eye, and its function is to discern shape, colour, and form. *ii*) The cognition of hearing (*nishiki*) depends on the organ of the ear, and its function is to discern and pick out sounds. *iii*) The cognition of smell (*bishiki*) has the function of discriminating odours, fragrances, and stenches. *iv*) The cognition of taste (*zesshiki*) depends on the tongue, whose function is to discern various tastes and flavours. *v*) The cognition of touching (*shinshiki*) and feeling depends on the body, whose role is to discern every variety of physical contact. *vi*) The cognition of conscious mental activity (*ishiki*) is the consciousness and the awareness of what we are feeling and perceiving, with regard to what is going on around us and within us.

The first five cognitions have their own organs to detect whatever they are supposed to sense, whereas the cognition of mental activity (*ishiki, manashiki*) is dependent on the mind as a faculty of thought. Perhaps one could say I know I am seeing, but that, in fact depends on the mind.

vii) The cognition of the mind as a faculty of thought (*i, manas*) – this cognition is in fact a little more complicated, since it has a strong power of attaching itself to the result of its own thinking. This cognition constantly perceives images, sounds, tastes, etc., even if they are only imagined, all of which induce this cognition to presume that it is the controller of the body and the part of us that makes decisions. It also sees itself as being independent by nature. The cognition of mind as an organ of thought first wills; then it discriminates (*funbetsu*), in order to judge. The process of judging entails an awareness of the individual particularities in concepts, ideas, and in matters and things – hence this cognition's habit of firmly attaching itself to a subjective and objective view of existence.

The cognition of mind as an organ of thought is always functioning, even during our sleep, unconsciousness, and comas, etc. As a result, unenlightened people such as us are always prey to illusions and ideas about our own existence, which to all intents and purposes belong to the nine realms of dharmas (*kyūkai*) that constitute our unenlightenment in the world of the dream.

viii) The storehouse cognition (*arayashiki*) strictly speaking is not a cognitive faculty and has no discerning powers of its own; rather, its role is accumulative. This storehouse cognition is the source of the previous seven cognitions, which are produced from "messages" (*shūji*) that are implanted in it. This storehouse is a sort of universal unconscious that stockpiles every conceivable dharma that is available to us, whether it be physical or mental, including the concept of our own bodies. When this storehouse cognition receives the outcome of the messages from the other seven cognitions, it passes these messages on to the cognition of conscious mental activity (*ishiki*), which in turn holds on to these impressions and discerns them as being real.

In this sense, the storehouse cognition is the basic element of the individual who mistakenly interprets the cognition of conscious mental activity as the sum total of the self. On this account, we have the tendency to think that we are what we know. The storehouse cognition is also the part of us that stores up the whole of our past and present karma. This deepest basement of our personalities also accompanies us through all our cycles of living and dying. It is through the distorted notion of being what we know that we become susceptible to deep traumas in the intermediate existence between death and rebirth, which tend to create distorted archetypes in our psyches. The scars of these deepest traumas from previous deaths may even assist in obscuring any intuition we may have, with regard to our original enlightenment. At any event, the storehouse cognition hoards up the whole of our existence, whose real identity is *ix*. the immaculate cognition (*amarashiki*), which is the fundamental of life itself.

This ninth cognition (*daikushiki, amarashiki, amala-vijñāna*) is not really a way of perceiving, since this particular cognition is the origin of all dharmas and mind. At the same time, it is the track upon which our lives roll. The object of most Buddha teachings suggests, through one practice or another, that the people who carry out these practices should shake themselves free of the storehouse cognition that is tainted with illusions and return to the original state of the superlative and absolutely pure, real suchness, which is the immaculacy of pure mind as the self nature of existence. In other words, it is the cognition of the Buddha, which is the original enlightenment.

This immaculate cognition is also seen as the sovereign of the mind and the foundation of all its workings. By being the real suchness, it is what life really is and completely inalterable. All things, both sentient and insentient, are endowed with this quality. In the teachings of Nichiren, this ninth and immaculate cognition is the *Sutra on the White Lotus Flower-like Mechanism of the Utterness of the Dharma* (*Myōhō Renge Kyō*). To be a little more explicit but perhaps not simpler, this sutra consists in devoting our lives to and founding them on (*Nam[u]*) the Utterness of the Dharma (*Myōhō*) [entirety of existence, enlightenment and unenlightenment] permeated by the underlying white lotus flower-like mechanism of the interdependence of cause, concomitancy and effect (*Renge*) in its whereabouts of the ten [psychological] realms of dharmas (*Kyō*).

Nichiren defines this dimension of us as the ninth cognition that is the capital of the real suchness and the sovereign of the mind. This aspect of ourselves is not merely an emptiness filled with light, but is also replenished with all the archetypal urges that pulsate throughout existence. Thus, it was Nichiren's all-embracing compassion for all sentient beings that made him draw up a mandala which includes all our primordial forces set in perfect proportion and in perfect relation to each other, just as they are in the *Dharma Flower Sutra* (*Myōhō Renge Kyō*). In this way, ordinary people who are burdened with karma, as we all are, can discover that this ninth cognition (*daikushiki, amarashiki, amala-vijñāna*) is our real identity.

Nichiren's intention was to show us a pathway that would lead to a real individuation, which is referred to in Buddhist technical language as the opening up of our inherent Buddha nature, with our persons just as they are. This psychologically alchemical process can be set about through reciting Nam Myōhō Renge Kyō in front of this mandala, which for those people who follow these teachings is the Fundamental Object of Veneration (*gohonzon*).

Part 7: A Chain of Twelve Causes

The next question is – how are we to understand this practice in terms of the twenty-first century?

Traditionally, the answer is through faith. But here we must make a distinction between faith and belief.

Here in the Western world, we are faced with the problem of not knowing the Japanese language. It is only in this essay, or in the translations that follow, that I know of any reasonable translation of *Nam(u) Myōhō Renge Kyō*, which is "the consecration and founding of our lives on the vertical threads of the sutra where existence takes place, into which is woven the filament of the interdependence of cause and effect of the entirety of existence that are the utter limits of the one instant of mind containing three thousand existential spaces". Then of course we can translate Nam Myōhō Renge Kyō literally, which is, "to consecrate and found our lives upon the *Sutra on the White Lotus Flower-like Mechanism of the Utterness of the Dharma (Myōhō Renge Kyō)*", the meaning of which Nichiren has explained with precise clarity in his *The Oral Transmission on the Meaning of the Dharma Flower Sutra* (*Ongi Kuden*).

From here on, we can say that the only place upon which we can found our lives and consecrate them to is the whole of life itself. I can also take on trust that all the Buddhas of the past, present, and future based their practice on reciting at least something that had the same meaning as the "theme and title" (*daimoku*) of the Dharma Flower, even if they were not the precise words.

What we are really talking about is the recitation of a paramount psychological truth. Where there is no subjective mind, such places cannot be explored. The boundaries of perception are always limited by the mandala-like circles that are created in the depths of the unconscious, and in most cases not even that.

I would say that nowadays in educated Western societies there are very few thinking and enquiring people who do not accept the subconscious of Freud and the collective unconscious of Jung as a part of our normal cultural heritage. Then would not Jung's archetype of the 'crock of gold at the bottom of the ocean' not be the immaculate cognition I mentioned a few passages ago? Is this not the source from which all culture, mythology, and faith come? Is this not the immaculate cognition squeezing and squirming through the various deep down archetypes of our minds, in order to impart to us that our respective identities are not who we think we are, but in fact we are none other than life itself?

No doubt this is what the Bodhisattva Not Holding Anyone or Anything in Contempt Ever (*Jōfukyō, Sadapāribbhūta*), in the *Twentieth Chapter on the Bodhisattva Not Holding Anyone or Anything in Contempt Ever (Jōfukyō, Sadapāribbhūta)*, saw in anybody who was a monk or a nun, or either a layman or female lay follower. He said, "I really admire you. How could I be arrogant and look down on you? Since you are all practising the path of the bodhisattva, you will certainly attain to the Buddha harvest."

It is not beyond the bounds of the imagination that there is an immaculate essence that is all space, all time, which includes the past, present, and future that is the real embodiment of what life really is, yet at the same time is not separate from people like ourselves who, due to our fundamental unenlightenment, find ourselves living lives that are not without problems. This is what makes us ask the question, "How and why did I get here, and what can I do about it?"

The simple answer would be to have enough trust in the Buddha teaching to accept the fact that we have a Buddha nature, just in the same way that we have an unconscious, along with our usual complexes and quirks. This would be a basis for faith. But it is not faith if we blindly listen to or take to heart inanities, such as we find in some silly books that say, "The *gohonzon* (i.e., the Fundamental Object of Veneration) is the body and mind of Nichiren himself. It is not different from a living human being..." Then this is the way to piousness, bigotry, blind belief, and a life that is cold, narrow, and nasty. Often, it is in the circles that pretend to have faith in the teaching of Nichiren Daishōnin where there is far too much sanctimoniousness and not enough faith.

In order to understand why we are the way we find ourselves in the world of humankind, the Buddha teaching describes this situation in a chain of twelve causes and karmic circumstances that run through the whole of sentient existence.

i) The first is *mumyō*. This is the part of us that does not want to know, that does not want to change our ways. It is our fundamental unenlightenment that leads to *ii*) *gyō*, the dispositions and volitions inherited from former lives, which are carried over to *iii*) *shiki*, which are the first signs of consciousness that takes place in the womb after conception. This then leads to *iv*) *Myō, shiki*, the body and mind evolving in the womb. The body then develops *v*) *rokunyū*, the five organs and cognitions of sense, as well as the cognition of conscious mental activity. After birth, this leads to *vi*) *shoku*, which is contact with the outside world. This opens the way for *vii*) *ju*, receptivity and budding intelligence and discernment from six to seven years onwards. At the age of puberty, we then develop *viii*) *ai*, the thirst and yearning for love and amorous relationships. All of this leads to *ix*) *shu*, the urge for an existence in which desires, hopes, and ambitions are fulfilled. But, even if these desires are not accomplished, we come to *x*) *yū*, which is the substance of karma to come in the future. Then we come to *xi*) *shō*, the completed karma ready to be born again. Naturally, this life is now irrevocably facing in the direction of *xii*) *rō, shi*, old age, and death. Nichiren explains this karmic process in his *Essay on the Chain of the Twelve Causes and Karmic Circumstances that Run through the Whole of Sentient Existence*.

Since people who live in the Western Hemisphere are endowed with a healthy dose of doubt, as well as a tendency to ask how or why the Fundamental Object of Veneration (*gohonzon*) is seen to have the properties it does, the answer has to be, "It is the people who do the practices of the Nichiren teachings who invest the Fundamental Object of Veneration (*gohonzon*) with the qualities it has." What this basically amounts to is the faith of the practitioners in the existence of their own Buddha nature.

This of course is also true for all the crosses, images of saints, Buddha images, and any other object that is thought of as being sage-like. But in the same way as beauty lies in the eyes of the beholder, the numinous quality of an object of worship resides in the faith of those people who hold it sacred. Faith can bring about an intuitive understanding. Deeper insight can lead to greater faith. And, as a follower of the teachings of Nichiren, a deep faith can make us aware of our inherent Buddha nature, without becoming something different from what we are, even if this may only happen at the time of our deaths.

However that may be, the Fundamental Object of Veneration (*gohonzon*) is as it is defined in the Second Consideration of the religious ceremony of the Nichiren Shōshū School, which is as follows: "I consecrate my life to the essence of the *Chapter on the Lifespan of the Tathāgata* of the original gateway – the universal Dharma that lies esoterically submerged within the text – the subtle integration of the objective realm and the subjective insight of the original terrain that is so hard to understand – the primordial infinity of the original beginning – the actual fundamental substance of the self-received reward body that is used by the Tathāgata – the inherently infinite existence of the ten [psychological] realms of dharmas, the pragmatic one instant of mind containing three thousand existential spaces – the oneness of the person and his Dharma – the one and only Universal Fundamental Object of Veneration (*gohonzon*) of the altar of the precept of the original gateway."

[Tathāgata (*Nyorai*) signifies the following: one who has gone; one who has followed the Path and arrived at the real suchness; one of the ten titles of a Buddha. Tathāgata can be explained as a person who comes from the real suchness of existence, which is Nam Myōhō Renge Kyō – which means to devote our lives to and found them on (*Nam[u]*) the Utterness of the Dharma (*Myōhō*) (entirety of existence, enlightenment and unenlightenment) permeated by the underlying white lotus flower-like mechanism of the interdependence of cause, concomitancy and effect (*Renge*) in its whereabouts of the ten (psychological) realms of dharmas (*Kyō*) – and that person will return to it.]

Now having quoted all of this, obviously I must now give the reader some explanations, starting with the essence of the *Chapter on the Lifespan of the Tathāgata*. This is the *Sixteenth Chapter of the Sutra on the White Lotus Flower-like Mechanism of the Utterness of the Dharma* (*Myōhō Renge Kyō*), in which Shākyamuni refuted the concept that he had attained enlightenment for the first time in Bodhgaya under the bodhi tree in northern India. Instead, he announced that he already had become enlightened in the dimension of the original source of existence in the primordial infinity in time, which is the interdependence of cause and effect that perpetuates throughout the whole of existence.

This chapter begins with three exhortations, where the Buddha says, "Indeed, you must sincerely give your attention to having faith and accepting what the Tathāgata says." The Buddha was about to repeat this phrase a fourth time when the Bodhisattva Maitreya (*Miroku*) said three times over, "World Honoured One, we only wish to hear your teaching. We do indeed accept with faith what the Buddha says."

After this ritual of the Buddha announcing that he would teach without being asked to, a situation which throughout all the Buddha teachings is extremely rare, the Tathāgata said, "You must listen attentively to what I have to say about the extent of the esoteric and almost inaccessible reaches of the mind of the Tathāgata." The Buddha then goes on to say that his enlightenment existed prior to a period of time that would amount to all the grains of dust that would go into the making of five hundred *kalpas*.

[Tathāgata (*Nyorai*) signifies the following: one who has gone; one who has followed the Path and arrived at the real suchness; one of the ten titles of a Buddha. Tathāgata can be explained as a person who comes from the real suchness of existence, which is Nam Myōhō Renge Kyō – which means to devote our lives to and found them on (*Nam*[*u*]) the Utterness of the Dharma (*Myōhō*) (entirety of existence, enlightenment and unenlightenment) permeated by the underlying white lotus flower-like mechanism of the interdependence of cause, concomitancy and effect (*Renge*) in its whereabouts of the ten (psychological) realms of dharmas (*Kyō*) – and that person will return to it.]

Rather than being an immense distance in time, I would suggest that we really are talking about a very great psychological depth. This statement is referred to as, "the clearing away of what is close at hand, in order to reveal the distance". The Lifespan in the title of this chapter alludes to the longevity of the Buddha as being all time, which is an inherently infinite existence that includes all the past, present, and future, even though this infinity is expressed in terms of a time that is like a long piece of string, or perhaps as a circle instead of a synchronicity. This is the meaning of the *Chapter on the Lifespan of the Tathāgata* that is esoterically submerged within the text.

The original gateway to the Dharma is the second half of the *Dharma Flower Sutra* (*Myōhō Renge Kyō*). The first half of this sutra concerns itself with teachings and events that are suspended in space and time, and therefore only temporary. In contrast, the original gateway to the Dharma points to things that exist in the original state that is more like a profound dream that unfolds to us psychological truths as to the nature of our real existence.

Another important point is that, apart from the Buddha stating that his life is inherently eternal, he also said that he is always present in "this world that has to be put up with" (*shaba sekai*), which means that there is no other Buddha terrain apart from the world we are living in now. The *Chapter on Expedient Means* of the *Dharma Flower Sutra* (*Myōhō Renge Kyō*) emphasises that the dharma realm of the Buddha is present in all the other nine realms of dharmas of ordinary people. But in the *Chapter on the Lifespan of the Tathāgata*, it is pointed out that these realms of dharmas are also endowed with that of the Buddha.

Part 8: The Fundamental Object of Veneration

Since most of our societies are based on human rights and we are not into submissive knuckling under, we have a problem as to how we shall comprehend the Fundamental Object of Veneration of the Nichiren Schools (*Gohonzon*).

To begin with, I refer to the *gohonzon* as the "Fundamental Object of Veneration", instead of as the "Fundamental Object of Worship". The reason for this is that the words 'to venerate' have the undertone of looking upon something with deep respect and awe, or to revere it on account of its enlightenment, etc. The word 'revere', means to hold in deep affection or religious respect, whereas the word 'worship', according to the Oxford Dictionary, has been defined as homage or reverence paid to a deity, etc. The word worship of course implies the pitfall of grovelling or snivelling towards some object of a cult or 'juju stick'.

The Fundamental Object of Veneration is a diagrammatic representation that indicates the cosmic nature of Nichiren Daishōnin, as well as being a symbol of the workings of the universe in terms of the culmination of Shākyamuni's teachings, as revealed in the *Dharma Flower Sutra* (*Myōhō Renge Kyō*). This Object of Veneration has been referred to as the "Self-received Wisdom Entity of the Tathāgata which he uses to save humankind". This expression has been misinterpreted as the "Buddha of Absolute Freedom".

In spite of this misnomer, this Fundamental Object of Veneration contains every conceivable psychological ramification of existence. Hell, which is represented by Daibadatta, is the dimension that includes every possible manifestation of suffering, from a thorn in our little toe to a normal headache, and even the pains of being mutilated in one of the many war zones that infest our planet. Next we come to the 'hungry ghosts'. These are those unfortunate people who resort to bars and are addicted to alcohol, or the junkies in need of a fix. This dimension also represents poor and starving people of the less developed countries, or even children who beg their parents to give them more pocket money. Overall, this realm of dharmas is the world of wanting, needing, or feeling the lack of something.

The dharma realm that follows is animality and can often be connected to the realm of hungry ghosts. These people are motivated by animal desires, such as for sex, food, or love. At the lowest level, this realm of dharmas is represented by a child wanting to pee. This can even be extended to the sadist who hurts other sentient beings on account of deep-rooted instincts, which no doubt modern psychology can explain. Animality is the realm of dharmas of the psychological world of brutish behaviour. Now we come to the realm of the *ashuras* or *shura* in Japanese. This is the realm of the show-off or even the salesman who wheedles, cajoles, and pushes in order to sell something. However, this psychological wavelength of wanting to impose oneself on other people could readily be extended to being bad-tempered or even in a blind rage.

This realm of dharmas is followed by that of human equanimity which implies that, in spite of the four former, rather tempestuous psychological dimensions, things are not as bad as they seem and everything is all right. This realm of dharmas is represented by a polite, "Good morning. How are you?" The realm of dharmas that follows human equanimity is that of ecstasy, characterised by getting the right part in a play or falling in love, from a great night out, or from having a book published. As with all our joys and epiphanies, we go up into the air, only to come down again to our respective, mundane realities.

The following realm of dharmas is a high-class avidity. It starts with when we are children and we ask, "Why?" or "What is…?" And it finally goes on to deep study of some abstruse subject or other. The realm of dharmas that comes next is that of when we have assimilated our learning and have a deeper knowledge of our chosen subjects. We then become the people who are partially enlightened. In my translations, I tend to render the Buddhist technical words *engakukai, pratyekabuddha* as the term "people who have made a profound search for the meaning of life".

Now comes the dharma realm of bodhisattva. Bodhisattvas, according to the teachings of the Tendai and Nichiren Schools, are persons who not only seek enlightenment for themselves, but also for others as well. However, this starts at giving some food to a stray cat or dog and can be extended to being rich enough to donate scholarships. The highest altruistic gesture is to teach people as to what the meaning of life is, and this means to rectify all that is not right in their lives. This would imply teaching the Buddha Dharma.

The realm of dharmas or the Dharma realm of the Buddha is the hardest for me to define, because it is beyond my experience. A Buddha is said to be wise, good and upright, and correct in all his character. This word is related to *Budh*, which means to "be aware of", "conceive", "observe", or "to be awakened to the significance of existence as well as to fully understand how it works". There is an eternal Buddha that is cited in the "Sixteenth Chapter of the Dharma Flower (Lotus) Sutra" and is said to have three facets to his person.

1) *Hosshin, Dharma-kāya* is the entity of the highest aspect of the threefold body of the Buddha. It is the absolute nature of the Buddha mind. It is ineffable, unmanifested, and without substance.

2) The second entity of the Buddha is his reward entity (*hōshin, sambhoga-kāya*) and is his wisdom and perception. For those that do the practices of the Nichiren Schools, it contains every possible manifestation of human existence.

3) *Ojin, nirmāna-kāya* is either the manifestation of Nichiren or Shākyamuni as persons, or anything that can awaken our perceptions to the truth of what existence really is. For the practitioners of the Nichiren Schools, Nichiren is the Buddha of the beginningless and endless original state. This is Nam Myōhō Renge Kyō, which entails devoting our lives to and founding them on the Utterness of the Dharma [entirety of existence, enlightenment and unenlightenment] permeated by the underlying white lotus flower-like mechanism of the

interdependence of cause, concomitancy and effect in its whereabouts of the ten [psychological] realms of dharmas. If one were to think about it, existence can only take place within the ten psychological realms of dharmas. As to the 'where' – where existence takes place, nobody can know. However, every facet of our lives is inscribed on the Fundamental Object of Veneration (*gohonzon*).

All mandalas are used for aiding and abetting meditational practices and for reciting formulas for enlightenment to, i.e., *dhāranīs* or mantras – in other words, to help the practitioner concentrate. The problem that lies within the Fundamental Object of Veneration is that this mandala is written out in Chinese, with two rather distorted letters from the Sanskritic Siddham alphabet. This makes this mandala unreadable for people who are neither Chinese nor Japanese.

Here is a case for the Fundamental Object of Veneration to be inscribed in the Roman and other alphabets or *Gongyō* to be recited in English and other languages. How this is to be done is not my responsibility. But I have it made it my obligation to render these teachings accessible to humankind, since they are so easily misunderstood.

The Object of Veneration is something to focus our faith on. In itself it has no intrinsic power, except for what is written on it. But that strength depends on who drew up this Fundamental Object of Veneration. The Fundamental Object of Veneration that was inscribed by Nichiren, and which is even available on the internet, is the calligraphy of a person who was completely enlightened and whom many people consider the Original Buddha.

With Sino-Japanese calligraphy, it is not necessarily what is written, but, like all in visual arts, what is important is how it has been put down to be made perceptible. This is not a question of skill, although ability does come into it. But ultimately it is what the calligrapher is, as a manifestation of his entire personality.

If the reader is curious enough, then there is the treatise of *The Threefold Transmission on the Fundamental Object of Veneration*

(*Honzon San Sōden*) by Nichiren, written out by one of his close disciples Nichigen, which is included below. Other than this, I have no wisdom of my own.

The Essential of the Teaching of Nichiren Daishōnin

The Threefold Transmission on the Fundamental Object of Veneration

These three all-embracing matters were transmitted to Nikkō [and Nichigen] and signed and sealed by Nichiren.

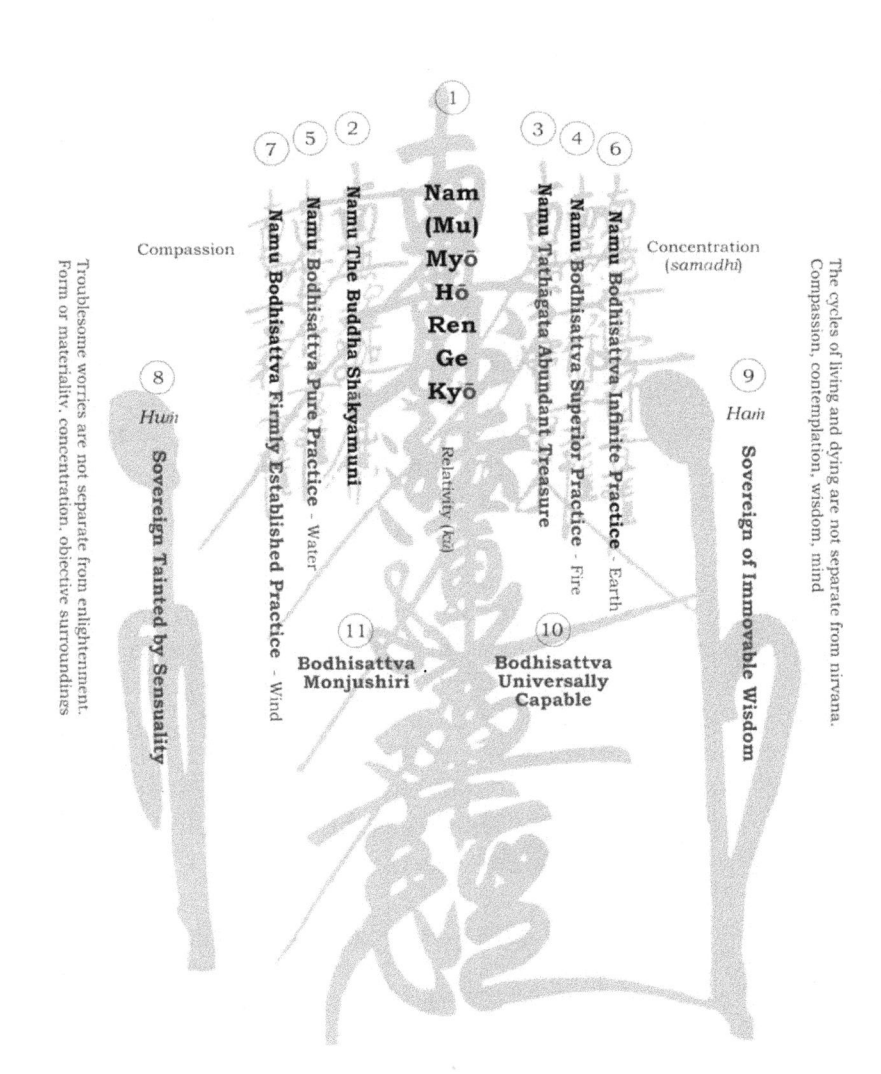

1. Nam (Mu) Myō Hō Ren Ge Kyō — Relativity (ku)
2. Namu The Buddha Shākyamuni
3. Namu Tathāgata Abundant Treasure
4. Namu Bodhisattva Superior Practice – Fire
5. Namu Bodhisattva Pure Practice – Water
6. Namu Bodhisattva Infinite Practice – Earth
7. Namu Bodhisattva Firmly Established Practice – Wind
8. Hūm — Sovereign Tainted by Sensuality
9. Ham — Sovereign of Immovable Wisdom
10. Bodhisattva Universally Capable
11. Bodhisattva Monjushiri

Compassion

Concentration (samadhi)

The cycles of living and dying are not separate from nirvana. Compassion, contemplation, wisdom, mind

Troublesome worries are not separate from enlightenment. Form or materiality, concentration, objective surroundings

85

Part 1: An explanation of the archetypes inscribed on the Fundamental Object of Veneration (*gohonzon*)

(1) *Nam Myōhō Renge Kyō* – which means to devote our lives to and found them on (*Nam*[*u*]) the Utterness of the Dharma [entirety of existence, enlightenment and unenlightenment] (*Myōhō*) permeated by the underlying white lotus flower-like mechanism of the interdependence of cause, concomitancy and effect (*Renge*) in its whereabouts of the ten [psychological] realms of dharmas (*Kyō*).

(2) The Buddha Shākyamuni – the historical founder of the Buddha teaching. According to Chinese Buddhist tradition, he was born on April 8th, 1029 BCE and died on February 15th, 949 BCE. However, there are a number of uncertainties regarding these dates. Western Buddhist scholarship puts these dates at above five hundred years later.

(3) The Tathāgata Abundant Treasure (*Tahō Nyorai, Prabhūtaratna*) – This is the Buddha who appeared, seated in the *stupa* made of precious materials, during the ceremony in empty space, and verified the teachings of Buddha Shākyamuni in the *Dharma Flower Sutra* (*Myōhō Renge Kyō*). [See the *Eleventh Chapter on Seeing the Vision of the Stupa made of Precious Materials.*]

(4) The Bodhisattva Superior Practice (*Jōgyō, Vishishtachāritra*) was one of the four leaders of the bodhisattvas who swarmed up out of the earth. He appears in the *Fifteenth Chapter on the Bodhisattvas who Swarm up out of the Earth* of the *Dharma Flower Sutra* (*Myōhō Renge Kyō*). Nichiren suggests in various writings that he himself is the incarnate manifestation of the Bodhisattva Superior Practice (*Jōgyō, Vishishtachāritra*), whose real identity is the original Buddha of the ever-present infinite in time (*kuon ganjo*).

(5) The Bodhisattva Pure Practice (*Jyōgyō, Vishuddhachārita*) was one of the four leaders of the bodhisattvas who swarmed up out of the earth. He appears in the *Fifteenth Chapter on the Bodhisattvas who Swarm up out of the Earth* of the *Dharma Flower Sutra* (*Myōhō Renge Kyō*).

(6) The Bodhisattva Infinite Practice (*Muhengyō, Anantachārita*) was one of the four leaders of the bodhisattvas who swarmed up out of the earth. He appears in the *Fifteenth Chapter on the Bodhisattvas who Swarm up out of the Earth* of the *Dharma Flower Sutra* (*Myōhō Renge Kyō*).

(7) The Bodhisattva Firmly Established Practice (*Anryūgyō, Supratishthichārita*) was also one of the four leaders of the bodhisattvas who swarmed up out of the earth. He appears in the *Fifteenth Chapter on the Bodhisattvas who Swarm up out of the Earth* of the *Dharma Flower Sutra* (*Myōhō Renge Kyō*).

(8) The Sovereign Tainted by Sensuality (*Aizen Myō' ō, Raga-rāja Vidyā-rāja*) is also one of the forces of the Buddha teaching that is able to release people from their troublesome worries (*bonnō, klesha*) and the suffering that comes from sensual desires in particular. In the Esoteric School (*Shingon*), he is represented on the mandala of the Existential Dimension of the Diamond Thunderbolt (*Kongōkai, Vajra-dhātu*) as being coloured red, with three eyes and an angry expression. He holds a bow with arrows in his hand. The Sovereign Tainted by Sensuality (*Aizen Myō' ō, Raga-rāja Vidyā-rāja*) is on the left-hand side of the Fundamental Object of Veneration (*gohonzon*) [as one faces it]. The germ syllable of his name "*Hum*" is written in the Siddham letters from a medieval Sanskrit alphabet and represents that "troublesome worries are not separate from and can lead to enlightenment".

(9) The Sovereign of Immovable Wisdom (*Fudō Myō' ō, Achala Vidyā-rāja*) is one of the psychological forces that help practitioners overcome obstacles and negative energies that hinder Buddhist practice. The images of the Sovereign of Immovable Wisdom (*Fudō Myō' ō, Achala Vidyā-rāja*) are represented by this personage as being the colour indigo and being immersed in a meditation that produces flames (*kashō zammai*), which destroy all karmic impediments. Like the Sovereign Tainted by Sensuality (*Aizen Myō' ō, Raga-rāja Vidyā-rāja*), the images of the Sovereign of Immovable Wisdom (*Fudō Myō' ō, Achala Vidyā-rāja*) are wrathful and holding a rope and sword. The germ syllable (*Ham*) that is used to evoke this entity is on the right side of the Fundamental Object of Veneration (*gohonzon*) [as one faces it] and implies that

"the cycles of living and dying are not separate from nirvana" (*shōji soku nehan*).

(10) The Bodhisattva Monjushiri (*Mañjushrī*), whose name is often shortened to Monju, is a bodhisattva who appears in a number of sutras as a symbol of the perfection of wisdom. He is also described with the Bodhisattva Universally Worthy (*Fugen, Samantabhadra*) as one of the bodhisattvas who are assistants to the Buddha Shākyamuni. The Bodhisattva Monjushiri (*Mañjushrī*) is usually depicted on the left of the Buddha and the right-hand side on the Fundamental Object of Veneration (*gohonzon*) [as one faces it]. He is seated on a lotus flower on the back of a lion and symbolises the truth and practice of the Buddha teaching.

(11) The Bodhisattva Universally Worthy (*Fugen, Samantabhadra*), along with the Bodhisattva Monjushiri (*Mañjushrī*), is one of the bodhisattvas who assists the Buddha Shākyamuni in giving directions and advice to the other bodhisattvas. He is usually represented on the right side of the Buddha, which is the left-hand side on the Fundamental Object of Veneration (*gohonzon*) [as one faces it], the Buddha being Nam Myōhō Renge Kyō. The Bodhisattva Universally Worthy (*Fugen, Samantabhadra*) is normally depicted as seated on a lotus flower and riding a white elephant with six tusks. In the *Flower Garland Sutra* (*Kegon, Avatāmsaka*), he made ten vows with regard to Buddhist practice. In the *Twenty-eighth Chapter on the Persuasiveness of the Bodhisattva Universally Worthy* (*Fugen, Samantabhadra*) of the *Dharma Flower Sutra* (*Myōhō Renge Kyō*), he made a vow to protect this sutra along with those that do its practices. Both the Bodhisattva Monjushiri (*Mañjushrī*) and the Bodhisattva Universally Worthy (*Fugen, Samantabhadra*) symbolise the truth of the Buddha teaching and its practices.

Facsimile of a diagram from *A Collection of the Essential Studies of the Fuji School, Volume 1*, originally published by Soka Gakkai, Shōwa, p. 35, Japan, 1974

A Transmission on the Fundamental Object of Veneration (*gohonzon*)

It is pointed out that these five mental images (*gokei*) for Myōhō Renge Kyō are what really constitute our own bodies and persons. In the teachings derived from the external events of the Buddha Shākyamuni's life and work, these five images were either indicated as separate entities, or they were generally lumped together and included in the explanations of our objective surroundings. In this sense, these five mental images as separate entities are applicable to the wisdom of the Buddha Shākyamuni's initial enlightenment in Buddhagāya [which originated from and became the Buddha enlightenment of the original archetypal state]. Here we have, in the *Second Chapter on Expedient Means* of the *Dharma Flower Sutra* (*Myōhō Renge Kyō*), the phrase, "the wisdom and discernment of all the Buddhas is exceedingly deep and immeasurably profound", and then the sutric text continues right on to the real aspect of all dharmas.

This passage in the sutra is explained by saying that the objective environment of the Buddha is like a yawning abyss, without any boundaries to it. Therefore, it is exceedingly deep, and the water of the Buddha wisdom can only be fathomed with difficulty, which to quote the sutric text, is immeasurably profound. Again, it can be said that all dharmas are his objective surroundings and that their real aspect is represented by the wisdom of the Buddha.

At the time of the *Eleventh Chapter on Seeing the Vision of the Stupa made of Precious Materials*, the Tathāgata Abundant Treasure (*Tahō Nyorai, Prabhūtaratna*) represents the objective surroundings of the Buddha, and the Buddha Shākyamuni stands for the wisdom to be able to understand them. Both of these Buddhas are seated in the same *stupa*, so as to indicate that our objective surroundings and the wisdom to perceive them are not separate entities.

What then is the concept of our objective surroundings and the wisdom to perceive them not being separate entities?

They are and have been, from beginningless time to the present, the lives and deaths that we sentient beings have received that consist of the inseparability of mind and materiality, as well as our subjective and objective existences and the movement and stillness of a thousand blades of grass and ten thousand trees.

Because the Tathāgata Abundant Treasure (*Tahō Nyorai, Prabhūtaratna*) has already passed over to the extinction of nirvana, he symbolises death. And, because the Buddha Shākyamuni had not yet entered into the extinction of nirvana at that time, he represents life. When the two concepts of mind and materiality are placed in front of each other, then it is the mind that is always on the move and represents mobility, whereas materiality being inanimate stands for stillness. As a result, the Tathāgata Abundant Treasure (*Tahō Nyorai, Prabhūtaratna*), as the aspect of death, symbolises our dying one death after the next, and the Buddha Shākyamuni, as the aspect of life, represents the continuity of living and dying being the characteristics of our total existence.

This is said to be the workings of the all-embracing nirvana (*hosshin, Dharma-kāya*), that neither comes into being, nor does it ever cease to exist. If we are to apply the fundamental principle of this phenomenon and the wisdom to perceive it (*richi*), the Buddha

Shākyamuni represents four of the five aggregates of our minds and bodies, which are [1) physical form (*shiki*), 2) the receptivity of our sense organs (*ju*), 3) that provokes our thinking (*sō*) and 4) influences our behaviour (*gyō*), 5) thereby resulting in our individual understandings of existence (*shiki*)]. This is because the mind has the function of going round and round in our heads.

In Buddha Shākyamuni's explanation of the Dharma, the Tathāgata Abundant Treasure (*Tahō Nyorai, Prabhūtaratna*) stands for the first of the five aggregates which is our physical (*shiki*) aspect. And, since materiality as such is silent, the Tathāgata Abundant Treasure (*Tahō Nyorai, Prabhūtaratna*) does not expound the Dharma. If we really can absorb this concept, neither our minds nor our bodies are ever really set in motion; they are entirely the working of the Buddha Shākyamuni or the Tathāgata Abundant Treasure (*Tahō Nyorai, Prabhūtaratna*).

This notion, however, was expounded as the opening up of our inherent Buddha nature with our persons just as they are, according to the teachings derived from the external events of the Buddha Shākyamuni's life and work (*shakumon*). [In many of the teachings prior to the *Chapter on the Lifespan of the Tathāgata*, such as those of the Tantric (*Shingon*) and Zen Schools, all dharmas were expounded as relativity (*kū, shūnyatā*).]

In the teachings of the original archetypal state, the Buddha Shākyamuni declares, in the *Sixteenth Chapter on the Lifespan of the Tathāgata*, "(Since) I really became a Buddha . . . ." [including the whole of the passage from *The Oral Transmission on the Meaning of the Dharma Flower Sutra* (*Ongi Kuden*)]. The explanation for this is that materiality (*shiki*) and mind (*shin*) have existed since beginningless time and are the immutable reality of the Utterness (*Myō*) of the objective environment [of the Fundamental Buddha (*honbutsu*)] and the Utterness of his wisdom that can perceive it.

The Universal Teacher Dengyō (*Dengyō Daishi*) says, "The whole of the underlying significance of the whole teaching consists of this particular wisdom and objective environment." The words "the whole of the teaching" refer to all the contents of the *Dharma Flower Sutra* (*Myōhō Renge Kyō*), and the "underlying significance" is the five ideograms for Myōhō Renge Kyō [which means the Utterness of the Dharma (*Myōhō, Saddharma*) (entirety of existence, enlightenment and unenlightenment) permeated by the underlying white lotus flower-like mechanism of the interdependence of cause, concomitancy and effect (*Renge*) in its whereabouts of the ten (psychological) realms of dharmas (*Kyō*)], and is fundamentally subtle. What we understand by the word "fundamental (*fukai*)" is that it comes from the profoundest of causes and is therefore significant.

On the whole, all that the twenty-eight chapters of the *Dharma Flower Sutra* (*Myōhō Renge Kyō*) imply are simply the wisdom and objective environment of the five ideograms of the Utterness of the Dharma (*Myōhō, Saddharma*) [entirety of existence, enlightenment and unenlightenment], even though the significance of the objective environment and perceptive wisdom of the teachings of the original archetypal state (*honmon*) and those derived from the external events of the Buddha Shākyamuni's life and work are discussed, to the bewilderment and misunderstanding of his listeners, caused by his initial enlightenment in Buddhagāya [which originated from and became the Buddha enlightenment of the original archetypal state]. Therefore, any ineptitude in his ability to be compassionate never really came about. This is placed on the side of wisdom on the left side as you face the Fundamental Object of Veneration (*gohonzon*) where Buddha Shākyamuni is also placed.

On coming to the teachings of the original archetypal state, that were discussed according to the virtue of his awareness of the original enlightenment and consequently on account of this essential truth, he was unable to break the bonds of having all the qualities of a sentient being. So, on the surface of the Fundamental Object of Veneration (*gohonzon*), Buddha Shākyamuni established it as a gateway to the unimpeded interaction of noumena and phenomena. The Tathāgata Abundant Treasure (*Tahō Nyorai, Prabhūtaratna*) is on the right-hand side as you face the Fundamental Object of Veneration (*gohonzon*). The right-hand side represents the ruling principle.

Nevertheless, both the left and the right elements of this Fundamental Object of Veneration (*gohonzon*) are fully endowed with the qualities of subjective and objective existence, mind and materiality, intent, contemplation (*samādhi*), and compassion, as well as living and dying. All these aspects of existence are referred to as the fusion of the objective environment and the wisdom to experience it (*kyōchi myōgo*) of the completely enlightened.

The rest you ought to know.

Here, for instance, the all-embracing, wise Bodhisattva Monjushiri (*Mañjushrī*) is present in the *First and Introductory Chapter* and, therefore, represents the whole subject matter of the sutra; the Bodhisattva Universally Worthy (*Fugen, Samantabhadra*) appears at the end of this sutra and represents the propagation of this canonical text. After the testimony of the Tathāgata Abundant Treasure (*Tahō Nyorai, Prabhūtaratna*), in the *Chapter on Seeing the Vision of the Stupa made of Precious Materials* is where the two Buddhas [Shākyamuni and Abundant Treasure] are seated in the one *stupa*. This expresses the significance of the Fundamental Object of Veneration (*gohonzon*).

Coming to the point, what do all these various deep meanings imply? – They are only the subjectivity and objective environment of the five ideograms for Myōhō Renge Kyō, whose meaning is the entirety of our existences permeated by the underlying white lotus flower-like mechanism of the interdependence of cause, concomitancy and effect in its whereabouts of the ten realms of dharmas.

Since our physical existence, in terms of the Tathāgata Abundant Treasure (*Tahō Nyorai, Prabhūtaratna*), and our mentally subjective existence, in terms of the Buddha Shākyamuni, have already been discussed, the part of us that is incapable of words is represented by the Tathāgata Abundant Treasure (*Tahō Nyorai, Prabhūtaratna*), who does not explain the Dharma. And the part of us that expresses opinions is represented by the Buddha Shākyamuni, who does expound the Buddha teaching. The explanation for this is as easy to see as a mango in the palm of the hand; it is obviously the essence of the *Dharma Flower Sutra* (*Myōhō Renge Kyō*).

This essence is the five ideograms for Myōhō Renge Kyō that is the fundamental source of our existence. This gateway to the Dharma is esoteric and should never be divulged to anybody.

Next, there are the two wrathful emanations of enlightenment (*myō' ō, vidyārāja*). The Sovereign Tainted by Sensuality (*Aizen Myō' ō, Raga-rāja Vidyā-rāja*) is the entity that represents that our troublesome worries are not separate from and can lead to enlightenment. His red colouring stands for our love of beauty and our sexual desires. That is to say that this wrathful emanation of enlightenment is the way we look upon beauty and carnal desires. The Sovereign of Immovable Wisdom (*Fudō Myō' ō, Achala Vidyā-rāja*) is the entity that represents that our cycles of living and dying are not separate from and can lead to nirvana. The blackness of his colouring represents the eternally inaccessibly black karma within the realms of dharmas, which is impossible to renew and is, therefore, the Sovereign of Immutable Wisdom (*Fudō Myō' ō, Achala Vidyā-rāja*).

Nevertheless, the Wrathful Sovereign Tainted by Sensuality (*Aizen Myō' ō, Raga-rāja Vidyā-rāja*) bestows loving-kindness, whereas the Sovereign of Immovable Wisdom (*Fudō Myō' ō, Achala Vidyā-rāja*) represents the psychological immobility of one's perfect absorption into the one object of meditation (*samādhi*).

What then do these two dharmas of our loving-kindness and mental immobility represent? They are the two dharmas of our subjective perception and our respective objective environments.

So what then are the two dharmas of our subjective perception and our respective objective environments? They are simply where we stand in terms of the Utterness of the Dharma (*Myōhō, Saddharma*).

By this we mean that, by enjoying and taking pleasure in the sutra, as well as appreciating it, we then become capable of discriminating with discernment a thousand myriads of different ways of speaking and skilfully putting concepts into words, so that we can explain it in a way to induce people to hold to it.

It is said that, when the Buddha entered into the absorption of the *Sutra on Implications Without Bounds* (*Muryōgisho zammai, ananta nirdesha pratishthāna samādhi*) [the meditation on the infinite meaning of existence (*Nam Myōhō Renge Kyō*), which is the *samādhi* into which the Buddha entered before expounding the *Dharma Flower Sutra* (*Myōhō Renge Kyō*)], neither his body nor his mind stirred.

When the Sovereign Tainted by Sensuality (*Aizen Myō' ō, Raga-rāja Vidyā-rāja*) and our troublesome worries (*bonnō, klesha*) disturb us, we should then recite the title and theme (*daimoku*), in order for this Wrathful Sovereign (*Myō' ō Vidyā-rāja*), who is an emanation of enlightenment, to lead us towards a deeper understanding. When we are taken aback by the rotations of living and dying, then we should contemplate and mentally take in the implications of the Fundamental Object of Veneration (*gohonzon*), so that the Sovereign of Immovable Wisdom (*Fudō Myō' ō, Achala Vidyā-rāja*), who is a wrathful sovereign that is an emanation of enlightenment, can teach us that nirvana implies the way existence works.

Apart from the Sovereign Tainted by Sensuality (*Aizen Myō' ō, Raga-rāja Vidyā-rāja*) and the Sovereign of Immovable Wisdom (*Fudō Myō' ō, Achala Vidyā-rāja*), there is no other meaning of existence – only our physical and mental bodies, their subjective perception and objective environment, along with our wisdom and the directions where our minds lead us, as well as all that takes our fancies. All this is the Utterness of the Dharma (*Myōhō, Saddharma*). The rest you already know.

These orally transmitted instructions, concerning the Fundamental Object of Veneration (*gohonzon*), contain esoteric material, and you should not make the least attempt to transmit them.

Here is a transmission on placing the palms of our hands together in reverence.

There exist three references with regard to putting the palms of our hands together with a mind of complete veneration, because we wish to listen to the path of enlightenment. Tendai (*T'ien T'ai*) said, "Even though we do not open our mouths to speak, the tips of our tongues are empowered with a myriad of virtues." Myōraku said that if you have understood these concepts, then you should know that the essence of the *Dharma Flower Sutra* (*Myōhō Renge Kyō*) is like looking at a mango in your hand.

These three all-embracing matters were transmitted to Nikkō and signed and sealed by Nichiren.

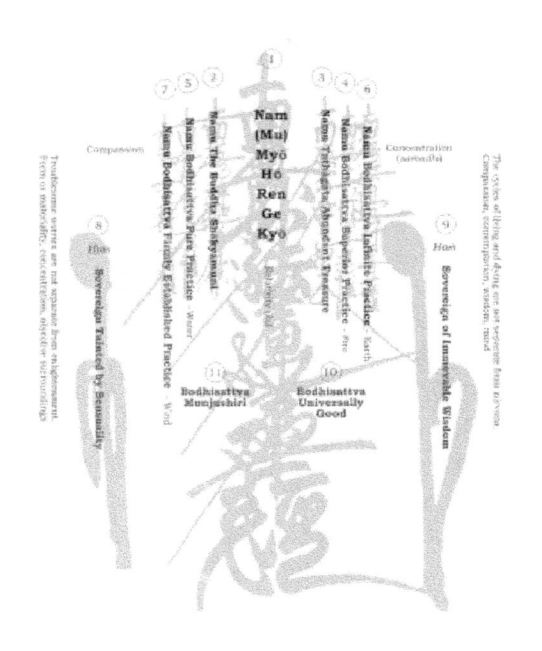

There is also a transmission that this mandala, as the Fundamental Object of Veneration (*gohonzon*), is inscribed in a way so as to express the assembly of the ceremony on Vulture Peak (*Ryōjusen, Gridhrakūta*). This was in order that, during the final period of the Dharma of Buddha Shākyamuni (*mappō*), which is a time for the broad propagation of this teaching, the people who are capable of accepting and holding to the *Sutra on the White Lotus Flower-like Mechanism of the Utterness of the Dharma* (*Myōhō Renge Kyō*), which is the fundamental truth of the original archetypal state that is to be widely published, will be able to directly see this assembly on Vulture Peak (*Ryōjusen, Gridhrakūta*).

In the *Dharma Flower Sutra* (*Myōhō Renge Kyō*), it says, "Even if it is in a garden or if it is in the middle of the woods, or even if it is at the base of a tree, or even if it is in the living quarters of the monks or the residence of an ordinary person, all such locations are unquestionably the raising of a *stupa* made of seven precious substances (gold, silver, lapis lazuli, crystal, agate, ruby, cornelian). After the Buddha's extinction into nirvana, people must certainly accept and hold to this sutra. Without a doubt, such persons are definitely set upon the path to enlightenment."

Part 2: What I have heard and written down, concerning the Fundamental Object of Veneration (*gohonzon*)

(1) The Buddha Shākyamuni and the archetypal numen Amaterasu both appear in the western sky, so as to express the fundamental pledge of all the Buddhas to explain that existence is Myōhō Renge Kyō, which means the Utterness of the Dharma [entirety of existence, enlightenment and unenlightenment] (*Myōhō*) permeated by the underlying white lotus flower-like mechanism of the interdependence of cause, concomitancy and effect (*Renge*) in its whereabouts of the ten [psychological] realms of dharmas (*Kyō*), and to assert that all sentient beings everywhere are the Buddha's children [endowed with the Buddha nature]. Again, on account of the appearance of these archetypes, one should directly throw away all teachings that are an expedient means, so as to requite this essential desire and the pledge that people should keep it in their heads.

Now in this muddled age of the end of the Dharma of the Buddha Shākyamuni, Nichiren reveals the original thinking of all the Buddhas. Nevertheless, the Buddha Shākyamuni, the Bodhisattva Superior Practice (*Jōgyō*, *Vishishtachāritra*), the archetypal numen Amaterasu, and Nichiren Daishōnin are being referred to as a single entity. [Nichiren writes his name underneath the Nam Myōhō Renge Kyō in the centre of the Fundamental Object of Veneration (*gohonzon*).]

The enclosure of the hundred sixty-second radical in Chinese ideograms ⌐ is written with three dots ⌐ instead of two, so as to express 1) Nichishin [sun numen] as the archetypal numen of the sun Amaterasu, 2) the Buddha Shākyamuni, by using his childhood name Nichishu (*Sūryavamsha*) [sun seed], and 3) Nichiren himself [sun lotus]. [All these names refer to the clear light often seen in near-death states.]

Regarding Amaterasu, the Buddha Shākyamuni, and Nichiren Shōnin as being a single entity, Nichiren uses the childhood name of the Buddha Shākyamuni, Nichishu (*Sūryavamsha*), as well as the childhood name of Amaterasu, who was called Numen of the Sun (*Nichishin*). When Nichiren was Amaterasu, his entity was present in the assembly of the *Dharma Flower Sutra* (*Myōhō Renge Kyō*), during the time of the teachings derived from the external events of the Buddha Shākyamuni's life and work (*shakumon*) as well as those of the original archetypal state (*honmon*).

Superficially, Amaterasu appears with a body of a woman, but, in fact, she sat at the assembly as a spirit that harmonises both the qualities of yin and yang. The ideogram for heaven (*ama*) is written as a combination of two ideograms 二 and 人. In this way, once put together, they both imply yin and yang. The word "bright" in the other appellation of Amaterasu, Brightness of the Heavens, is written with the ideogram for the "sun" next to the ideogram for the "moon". Both these ideograms together have the undertone of yin and yang, as well as the gateway to the teachings derived from the external events of the Buddha Shākyamuni's life and work (*shakumon*), along with those that belong to the original archetypal state (*honmon*).

(2) Nichiren is seated as the Bodhisattva Superior Practice (*Jōgyō, Vishishtachāritra*) and the four bodhisattvas who surged up from the earth. The wrapping that makes half of the ideogram for lotus 辶 and is read "gyō", in the sense of practice and people, should be at one with the concept of practice. With regard to the ideogram that is half the wrapping of the ideogram for lotus, another dot has been added onto the two dots, both intentionally and unintentionally. However, the extra dot has to be shown 辶.

(3) When inscribing the name of the four *Deva* Guardians of existence, Bishamon Tennō (*Deva* Sovereign Guardian, *Vaishravana, Mahādeva-rāja*) should guard the northeast corner of the Fundamental Object of Veneration (*gohonzon*) [the demon gateway through which spirits can come and go], albeit it is not quite the same with the Fundamental Object of Veneration (*gohonzon*) in the Honmonji Temple.

The altar (*kaidan*) of the Honmonji Temple faces west. The reason for this is that, during the period when the Buddha teaching was more like a superficial show than a teaching that could instigate the deepest of contemplation (*zōbō*), the Buddha teaching in the East was on the decline and gradually passed over towards the west. During the final period of the Dharma of the Buddha Shākyamuni (*mappō*), the Buddha teaching will cross over towards the countries in the West, so the western direction had to be protected. In this instance, the western direction was made the demon gateway through which the spirits could come and go.

(4) The entity of Hachiman Daibosatsu (Universal bodhisattva) is the same as the *Dharma Flower Sutra* (*Myōhō Renge Kyō*). The word "*hachi*" means eight and refers to the eight scrolls of the *Dharma Flower Sutra* (*Myōhō Renge Kyō*). [Hachiman Daibosatsu is probably a deification of the Emperor Ojin. The title Daibosatsu (Universal bodhisattva) was conferred on him, circa 765 and 781 C.E. by the Imperial Court. Often referred to as the god of war, he is also sometimes said to be a deification of the Empress Jingu, who invaded Korea in the third century.]

At the side of the "man" part of Hachiman's name, this ideogram is put into the category (radical 50) of articles of clothing. [The meaning of this ideogram in Buddhist texts is a tubular banner.] At the top of the phonetic part of this ideogram is the character for "wild rice"; underneath it is the ideogram for "field". Therefore, this ideogram has the latent meaning of "rice". But since this ideogram is put into the category (radical) of articles of clothing, the name Hachiman is endowed with the benevolence and virtue of both food and clothing. One should think in the terms of the seeds of Buddhahood being sown in the field of the mind. Since Hachiman is on a par with the Bright Universal Numen (*Amaterasu*), the ideogram for Brightness ought to be placed before Hachiman's name.

(5) The reason for placing the Bodhisattva Superior Practice (*Jōgyō, Vishishtachāritra*) at the side of the Tathāgata Abundant Treasure (*Tahō Nyorai, Prabhūtaratna*) is in conformity with Indian etiquette, where the guest is placed next to the host. Since the Tathāgata

Abundant Treasure (*Tahō Nyorai, Prabhūtaratna*) is the Buddha who is the guest, Bodhisattva Superior Practice (*Jōgyō, Vishishtachāritra*), as the leader of the bodhisattvas who swarmed up out of the earth, is placed by the side of the Tathāgata Abundant Treasure (*Tahō Nyorai, Prabhūtaratna*).

(6) Since the Fundamental Object of Veneration (*gohonzon*) is inscribed almost entirely in Chinese, then why are the Sovereign of Immovable Wisdom (*Fudō Myō' ō, Achala Vidyā-rāja*) and the Sovereign Tainted by Sensuality (*Aizen Myō' ō, Raga-rāja Vidyā-rāja*) written in Sanskrit? The reason is that Nichiren knew the Siddham alphabet [a medieval Sanskrit alphabet used in Tibet, China, Korea, and Japan, for ritual purposes] and that he knew both Sanskrit and Classical Chinese as well.

Although Amaterasu is worshipped as a venerable numen of good, there are also numina of negative qualities. Amaterasu is the expression of our original Buddha nature. The Demon Sovereign of the Sixth Heaven above Mount Sumeru (*Dai Roku Ten no Ma' ō*) represents our fundamental unenlightenment. Both Amaterasu and The Demon Sovereign of the Sixth Heaven above Mount Sumeru are inscribed on the Fundamental Object of Veneration (*gohonzon*), in a way similar to husband and wife, thereby being an expression of the concept that our troublesome worries (*bonnō, klesha*) are not separate from and can lead to enlightenment.

Furthermore, this venerable numen of the sun (*Amaterasu*) is placed on the Fundamental Object of Veneration (*gohonzon*), in a dimension beyond the clouds in her palace. The sun, figuratively speaking, is the Dharma nature, whereas the clouds are a representation of our inherent unenlightenment. Nevertheless, when Amaterasu finally comes out of her rocky cave, this venerable numen shines forth as a single individuated entity. For instance, when the morning sun comes up in the east, it is first covered up by clouds stretching horizontally across the sky. But, when the sun rises, the clouds disappear. In this way, we get an insight of the truth that our unenlightenment sinks downwards, so that the Dharma nature increases in brightness.

Part 3: The Buddha Transmission on the Fundamental Object of Veneration (*gohonzon*)

Nichiren states that, apart from the enlightenment of the Buddha mind, the essence of reality which can be perceived is Myōhō Renge Kyō [which means the entirety of existence (enlightenment and unenlightenment) permeated by the interdependence of cause, concomitancy and effect in its whereabouts of the ten realms of dharmas]. He also says that, after the two thousand two hundred thirty or so years after the Buddha's extinction into nirvana, this is the all-embracing mandala that has never been seen before in the world of humankind (*Ichienbudai, Jambudvīpa*). In the morning, we should bow our heads towards it, as well as putting the palms of our hands together. And, in the evening, we should reverently sit upright with admiration and praise for our teacher and guide.

The Fundamental Object of Veneration (*gohonzon*) shows the ten [psychological] realms vertically in front of you, whereas the contiguous quality of materiality (*ke*), relativity (*kū*), and the middle way of reality as we perceive it (*chū*), are clearly apparent when you look at the Fundamental Object of Veneration (*gohonzon*) horizontally.

Why should this be so?

This is solemnly suggested by the title of the sutra running down the centre [Nam Myōhō Renge Kyō], which is the all-inclusive reality and the inclusion of all dharmas of existence that are the five [or seven] ideograms for the Utterness of the Dharma (*Myōhō, Saddharma*), without leaving a single item out. Nevertheless, there is not a single entity that is not swallowed up by it. The reason for this is that it is only a proof for the time being of the relativity (*kū*) that engulfs the whole of existence.

Each entity of the ten [psychological] realms of dharmas shown on the Fundamental Object of Veneration (*gohonzon*) implies that each of these ten [psychological] realms of dharmas is to be found in one another, or each of these ten [psychological] realms of dharmas contains the other nine realms within itself. But in this case, they are named according to their physical (*ke*) appellations.

The Buddha Shākyamuni and the Tathāgata Abundant Treasure (*Tahō Nyorai, Prabhūtaratna*), along with the Buddha emanations of the ten directions, represent the Dharma realm of the Buddha. The Bodhisattva Superior Practice (*Jōgyō, Vishishtachāritra*), the Bodhisattva Infinite Practice (*Muhengyō, Anantachārita*), the Bodhisattva Pure Practice (*Jyōgyō, Vishuddhachārita*), and the Bodhisattva Firmly Established Practice (*Anryūgyō, Supratishthichārita*) are the four bodhisattvas who were converted in the original archetypal state of existence (*honmon*).

The Bodhisattva Universally Worthy (*Fugen, Samantabhadra*), the Bodhisattva Monjushiri (*Mañjushrī*), Maitreya (*Miroku*), and the Sovereign Remedy (*Yaku' ō, Bhaishajya-rāja*), and so forth, are all bodhisattvas who were converted during the time of the teachings derived from the external events of the Buddha Shākyamuni's life and work (*shakumon*). The revered sages Kashō (*Mahākāshyapa*), Anan (*Ānanda*), Sharihotsu (*Shariputra*), Mokuren (*Maudgalyāyana*), along with others, represent the two realms of dharmas of 1) the people who exerted themselves to attain the highest state of the individual vehicle (*shōjō, hīnayāna*) through listening to the Buddha [the intellectuals of today] (*shōmon, shrāvaka*) and 2) the realms of dharmas of people who have become partially enlightened, due to a profound search for the meaning of existence (*engaku, pratyekabuddha*). Bonten (*Brahmā*), Taishaku (*Indra*), the *deva* of the sun and the moon, along with the four major guardian *deva* who protect existence, represent the realms of dharmas of the *deva* (ecstasy).

The sage-like sovereigns, whose chariot wheels roll everywhere without hindrance (*tenrinnō, chakravartin*), King Ajase (*Ajāshatru*), as well as others, represent the realm of dharmas of human equanimity. The *shura* [titans or giants] and the sovereigns of the dragons (*ryū, nāga*) represent these two realms of dharmas of 1) the titan-like behaviour of the *shura*, as well as 2) the realm of dharmas of animal-like behaviour, when human beings act without conscious intention. The Demon Mother Numen (*Kishimojin, Hāritī*) and her ten cannibalistic demon daughters (*rasetsu, rākshasī*) are the two leaders of the hungry ghosts. The extremely evil Daibadatta (*Devadatta*) represents the innate idea of the realm of hellish suffering. However, it is undecided as to whether the two revered personages, the Sovereign of Immovable Wisdom (*Fudō Myō' ō, Achala Vidyā-rāja*) or the Sovereign Tainted by Sensuality (*Aizen Myō' ō, Raga-rāja Vidyā-rāja*), harvest the effects of the ten [psychological] realms of dharmas.

Amaterasu [the Sun goddess] and the Universal Bodhisattva Hachiman [the god of war], along with others, are appended to other numina and demons. Furthermore, Ryūjū (*Nāgārjuna*), Tenjin (*Vasubandhu*), Tendai (*T'ien T'ai*), Dengyō, and others, have been added as representatives of the Universal Teachers of the two periods of when 1) the Dharma was correct and could bring people to enlightenment, and 2) when it was an ostentatious and superficial show of piety (*zōbō*).

On the whole, all the personages have been recommended and invited – not even the most humble has been left out – because this is the supreme and universal mandala of the original archetypal state, in which the auspicious, iniquitous, ordinary, and sage-like qualities of the universal vehicle (*daijō, mahāyāna*) and the individual vehicle (*shōjō, hīnayāna*) have all been thoroughly pounded and sieved.

How sublime it is!

With the Buddha realm at the top, from where one goes down to the hellish regions at the bottom, each realm of dharmas is endowed with the other nine, so that they become a hundred realms of dharmas, which are multiplied by the ten ways in which dharmas make themselves present to our six senses (*nyo ze*). In this way, we have a thousand ways in which dharmas make themselves perceptible to our six senses.

Then, when this thousand is bundled together with the three existential spaces upon which sentient beings depend in order to exist (*san seken*), we then open up the gateway to the Dharma [of the one instant of thought containing three thousand existential spaces (*ichinen sanzen*)]. For the sake of argument, this is called, "each of the ten realms of dharmas contains the other nine in itself (*jikkai gogu*)".

For a more detailed explanation, you should look into Tendai's (*T'ien T'ai*) *Universal Desistance from Troublesome Worries in Order to See Clearly* (*Maka Shikan*). However, the *Desistance from Troublesome Worries in Order to See Clearly* (*Maka Shikan*) is for the subjective inspection of our own minds, since it is based on the teachings derived from the external events of Buddha Shākyamuni's life and work (*shakumon*).

When we look upon the Fundamental Object of Veneration (*gohonzon*) that is in front of us and written out on paper, it reveals the original archetypal state of existence (*honmon*). It is the all-inclusive, unobstructed accommodation of both the dharmas of relativity (*kū*) and materiality (*ke*), bound together just as they are, neither being two nor separate. This is the view that the name and words applied to phenomenal existence are only provisional and are not separate from the middle way of reality (*chū*), as we perceive it in our ordinary lives. This is explained as materiality (*ke*), relativity (*kū*), and the middle way of reality (*chū*) not being separate (*soku*) from each other. Or it could be said that, even if the axiom of the middle way of reality (*chū*) and relativity (*kū*) are two concepts, they are not really separate.

The question is asked that, when we look upon the Fundamental Object of Veneration (*gohonzon*) with all the depths of reverence and esteem in our minds, why is everything inscribed in Chinese, except for the names of the Sovereign of Immovable Wisdom (*Fudō Myō' ō, Achala Vidyā-rāja*) and the Sovereign Tainted by Sensuality (*Aizen Myō' ō, Raga-rāja Vidyā-rāja*), which are written out in Sanskrit? Although the answer to this question refers to another topic, I will say something about its meaning.

The favourable influences of both the Sovereign of Immovable Wisdom (*Fudō Myō' ō, Achala Vidyā-rāja*) and the Sovereign Tainted by Sensuality (*Aizen Myō' ō, Raga-rāja Vidyā-rāja*) are the Sanskrit germ syllables themselves. The Chinese ideograms for these names have been omitted and replaced with the Sanskrit germ syllable. In the same way as, if people hear the sound of the incantations in the

Chapter on Dhāranī, they can derive benefit from [hearing] them, the Sanskrit version of these two germ syllables is given, without translating them into Chinese.

All this is the deep purpose and the all-embracing esoteric, practical content of our school.

If the occasion and conditions are not right, then, even for a thousand pieces of gold, you must not transmit these teachings to anyone else. All I ask is that when disciples choose this receptacle of the Dharma, it should be transmitted to them face to face, and in secret.

This *Threefold Transmission on the Fundamental Object of Veneration* was written out by Nichigen.

FOOTNOTE:
Nichigen 1263 – 1315 C.E. was a disciple of Nichiren during his lifetime. Before he took up the holy orders, his name was Harima Hōin. He was schooled at Jissō Temple and became known as Chikai (Ocean of Wisdom). In 1278, he gave up all his lands and took refuge in the teaching of Nichiren, in Minobu. Later, he returned to Jissō Temple, where he converted and taught the clerical community (*sō, sangha*). He also founded temples in Marashi, which is now part of Tōkyō, and also in Suraga, which is now in the Shizuoka Prefecture.

The Essential of the Teaching of Nichiren Daishōnin

Treatise on Becoming a Buddha in a Single Lifetime

Isshō jōbutsu shō
Goshō Shimpen, pp. 45-47

The seventh year of Kenchō (1255), at 34 years of age

If those who are detained, in the beginningless chain of living and dying, should this time firmly decide to substantiate their supreme enlightenment, then they ought to contemplate the inherently infinite existence of the intrinsic Utterness in the lives of sentient beings. The intrinsic Utterness in the lives of sentient beings is *Nam Myōhō Renge Kyō*, the *Sutra on the White Lotus Flower-like Mechanism of the Utterness of the Dharma*. Therefore, reverently reciting *Nam Myōhō Renge Kyō* is to contemplate the inherently infinite existence of the intrinsic Utterness in the lives of sentient beings.

[Nam Myōhō Renge Kyō means to devote our lives to and found them on (*Nam[u]*) the Utterness of the Dharma (*Myōhō*) (entirety of existence, enlightenment and unenlightenment) permeated by the underlying white lotus flower-like mechanism of the interdependence of cause, concomitancy and effect (*Renge*) in its whereabouts of the ten (psychological) realms of dharmas (*Kyō*).]

Because this textual line of the *Dharma Flower Sutra* (*Myōhō Renge Kyō*) is entirely correct, it is the king of sutras, whose words and ideograms are not separate from the real aspect of all dharmas; and the real aspect is not separate from the Utterness of the Dharma (*Myōhō, Saddharma*). However, what this comes down to is that to expound and reveal the meaning of the Dharma realm, as the oneness of mind, is to say that it is the Utterness of the Dharma (*Myōhō, Saddharma*). Therefore, this sutra is said to be the wisdom and discernment of all the Buddhas.

The significance of the ten [psychological] realms of dharmas and their three thousand existential spaces of the Dharma realm is the oneness of mind, its subjectivity, its dependent environments, its materiality as well as mind, its insentient plants and trees, without ignoring its empty space, the flash of time in the terrain of where the one instant occurs, or even one particle of its dust – all of these are stored away in a single instant of mental activity. What this one instant of mind means is that it is the whole content of the Dharma realm. This is referred to as all of the dharmas. To be knowingly aware of this principle is to have to admit that the Dharma realm is the oneness of mind.

Nevertheless, even though you may hold to reciting Nam Myōhō Renge Kyō, if you think that the Dharma is somewhere outside your mind, then it is in no way the Utterness of the Dharma (*Myōhō, Saddharma*), but some inferior teaching. Such inferior teachings are not the present sutra.

If it were not for this sutra, then it would be an expedient means, or something from the provisional gateway to enlightenment, and it could not be the direct path for becoming a Buddha. By not being the direct path, then it will be an attempt to become a Buddha through practising for numerous lifetimes, over countless *kalpa*s, and it would be impossible to become a Buddha in a single lifetime.

You must give rise to a deep mind of faith to understand that when we recite and read Nam Myōhō Renge Kyō – which means to devote our lives to and found them on (*Nam*[*u*]) the Utterness of the Dharma (*Myōhō*) [entirety of existence, enlightenment and unenlightenment] permeated by the underlying white lotus flower-like mechanism of the interdependence of cause, concomitancy and effect (*Renge*) in its whereabouts of the ten [psychological] realms of dharmas (*Kyō*) – it refers to the one instant of thought containing three thousand existential spaces that make up our lives. They too are Nam Myōhō Renge Kyō, which means to devote our lives to and found them on (*Nam*[*u*]) the Utterness of the Dharma (*Myōhō*) [entirety of existence, enlightenment and unenlightenment] permeated by the underlying white lotus flower-like mechanism of the interdependence of cause, concomitancy and effect (*Renge*) in its whereabouts of the ten [psychological] realms of dharmas (*Kyō*).

You must under no circumstance ever imagine that the repository of the eighty-four thousand Dharmas of a lifetime of enlightened teaching, as well as all the Buddhas of the past, present, and future of the ten directions, exist anywhere else, other than in your own mind. Although you may well have studied the Buddha teaching, if you do not contemplate the nature of your own mind, you will never get entirely away from the cycles of living and dying.

If you do search for a path outside of your own mind and then do ten thousand austerities and ten thousand good deeds, they will all be as useless as a poor man who counts his neighbour's wealth day and night, without gleaning from it a share as small as half a brass coin. Hence, among the explanations with regard to this, in the writings of Tendai (*T'ien T'ai*), we have, "If you do not contemplate your own mind, you will never eradicate the layers of karmic entanglements in your life."

Through not contemplating our own minds, we condemn ourselves to a lifetime of countless, bitter austerities. Moreover, even though the people who behave in such a way have studied the Buddha Dharma, they bring shame upon it, by becoming just like those of other cults. With regard to this, there is a comment in the *Universal Desistance from Troublesome Worries in order to See Clearly (Maka Shikan)* that says, "Although they study the Buddha teaching, their views become the same as those of the heretics."

Withal, in the meantime you must build a mind of faith, by reciting the name of the original Buddha, reading the sutra, spreading flowers, and offering pinches of powdered sandalwood over burning incense, all of which in the oneness of our minds become the meritorious virtues of good roots. In the sutra concerning Yuimakitsu, it makes it very clear that, should one look for the freedom and release that is inherent in all the Buddhas and from the sufferings of living and dying, then it is to be found embedded in the minds and practices of sentient beings. This is because sentient beings are not separate from the enlightenment of which they are capable of attaining, as those who suffer in the cycles of living and dying are not separate from nirvana of which they are capable of reaching.

Again, if sentient beings befoul their minds, their dependent terrain is also befouled. Likewise, if they purify their minds, then also their dependent terrains become purified. Still, at the same time, the terrain that is befouled or the one that is purified are not two places. They are seen as such, due to the good and evil in our minds.

So it is the same with whom we refer to as sentient beings and those whom we refer to as Buddhas. When a person is bewildered, he is spoken of as being a sentient being. But, on his enlightenment (*satori*), he is then called a Buddha.

For instance, a tarnished metal mirror, when polished up, will shine like a jewel. When the mind is bewildered, even for one instant, by its fundamental unenlightenment, it immediately becomes like a mirror that has been neglected. But, once it is polished, it will attain the brilliance of the true suchness of the dharma nature. You must give rise to a deep mind of faith, in order to polish this mirror mornings and evenings. How should you polish it then? This is done just by reverently reciting Nam Myōhō Renge Kyō, which is what this polishing is called.

Now then, what does Utterness (*Myō*) really mean? Utterness is the part of our one instant of thought that can neither be thought out nor be expressed [since it is utterly all-embracing]. It is what the mind cannot ponder over nor put into words. However, as soon as you diligently look for it in your mind, you find that it has neither a colour nor a shape to show that it exists. Again, if you say it is not there, then all sorts of things come into your mind to show that it is. You cannot say that it does not exist; neither can you say that it does. The two words for existence or nonexistence do not cover it; nor can it be explained by the meanings of these two words either. It is neither existence nor nonexistence, yet it is omnipresent in both. By being the embodiment of Utterness of the sole reality of the middle way, it becomes imponderably inexpressible and goes by the name of Utterness (*Myō*).

By giving such implications to the word Utterness, it is then referred to as dharmas [as its manifestation] (*Myōhō*). [*Nam* means to devote our lives to and found them on.] This gateway to the Dharma, with its revelation of the imponderably inexpressible, alludes to the Dharma assuming the role of the lotus flower, which is the interdependence of cause and effect (*renge*). When you realise that your own mind is its entirety, both enlightened and unenlightened, then in turn you realise that other minds are the Utterness of the Dharma (*Myōhō*, *Saddharma*) also [*kyō* signifying the whereabouts of the ten (psychological) realms of dharmas]. This is called the sutra which is its own utter and intrinsically infinite path. It is the king of sutras, and the direct path to becoming a Buddha, since it explains that the actual fundamental substance, from which both good and evil arise, is the fundamental substance of the Utterness of the Dharma (*Myōhō*, *Saddharma*) [entirety of existence], both its enlightened and unenlightened aspects.

If you hold a deep faith in the significance of this and recite Nam Myōhō Renge Kyō, you will, without any doubt, become a Buddha in this lifetime. This is because in the text of the sutra it tells us that, "After my passing over to extinction, you must indeed hold to this sutra. Those people who do so shall decidedly, without any doubt whatsoever, be on the path of enlightenment." On no account, must you have any doubts.

With awe and respect.

You must have a mind of faith and become a Buddha in this lifetime. Nam Myōhō Renge Kyō, Nam Myōhō Renge Kyō.

Nichiren [formal signature]

An Essay on the Chain of the Twelve Causes and Karmic Circumstances that Run through the Whole of Sentient Existence

Jūni In.nen Goshō
Goshō Shimpen, pp. 53-56

The first year of Kōgen [1256], at 35 years of age

If we are to talk about becoming Buddhas in a general way, then it is through knowing what our persons consist of, and that we are able to become such. What is said to be knowing our own persons is to know that they are Buddhas from the very origin.

All sentient beings, including such creatures as crickets, ants, horseflies, and mosquitoes, are all endowed with bodies that are comprised of the eighteen ways of understanding through the six organs of sense – *i*) the eyes, *ii*) the ears, *iii*) the nose, *iv*) the tongue, *v*) the body, *vi*) the mind. The six objective realms of these senses are the fields of *vii*) sight, *viii*) sound, *ix*) odours, *x*) flavours, *xi*) touch, and *xii*) ideas, as well as the capabilities of *xiii*) seeing, *xiv*) hearing, *xv*) smelling, *xvi*) tasting, *xvii*) touching, and *xviii*) a consciousness of any one or all of these events that are taking place.

Hence, all sentient beings are incarnations of the five aggregates that darken the awareness of our original enlightenment, through having *i*) a physical form which *ii*) has ways of perceiving, which bring about ways of *iii*) thinking, which lead to ways of *iv*) behaviour, which results in *v*) all these aggregates amounting to how this sentient being sees himself in relation to his own existence.

Among the explanations, it says, "By giving a name to the combination of these five aggregates, we refer to a sentient being." The combination of these five aggregates that darken our original enlightenment is therefore the chain of the twelve causes and karmic circumstances that run through the whole of sentient existence.

This chain is made up of *i*) a fundamental unenlightenment, which leads to *ii*) dispositions that are inherited from former lives. Then, *iii*) the first consciousness after conception takes place in the womb, whilst *iv*) the body and mind are evolving, which leads to *v*) the five organs of sense and the functioning of the mind, as it makes *vi*) contact with the outside world. This becomes *vii*) the receptivity or budding intelligence and discrimination from six to seven years old onwards, which evolve into *viii*) the thirst, desire for love at the age of puberty, and *ix*) the urge of sensuous existence, which *x*) forms the substance of future karma. Then, *xi*) the completed karma is ready to be born again, as it takes its direction towards *xii*) old age and death.

This chain of the twelve causes and karmic circumstances is said to be spread over the two levels of cause and effect, which are understood as past cause and present effect and present cause and future effect. Also, this chain is carried over from the past to the present and on to the future.

The first link of this chain of causes and karmic circumstances is our fundamental unenlightenment. The eighth link is a thirst, desire, or love at the age of puberty; and the ninth link is the urge for sensuous existence. These three links are seen as troublesome worries (*bonnō, klesha*). The second link is made up of the various dispositions inherited from our former lives, and the tenth link is the substance of future karma. These are to be understood as being the workings of karma.

The first spark of consciousness that takes place in the womb after conception, the body and mind that evolve in the womb, the five organs of sense and the functioning of the mind, contact with the outside world, receptivity or budding intelligence and discrimination from six to seven years onwards, the karma that is

The Essential of the Teaching of Nichiren Daishōnin

completed and ready to be born again, as well as old age and death – all these seven links in the chain are seen as suffering. The chain of the twelve causes and karmic circumstances that run through the whole of sentient existence consists of the three paths of troublesome worries (*bonnō, klesha*), the workings of karma, and suffering.

The two links in the chain of fundamental unenlightenment and the various dispositions that are inherited from former lives have their causes in the past. The five links of the consciousness that originates in the womb, the body and mind that also evolved there, the five organs of sense and the functioning of the mind, contact with the outside world, and the receptivity and intelligence and discrimination that evolved from six years onwards, are five visible effects that are now in the present. The three links in the chain, which are *i)* the thirst, desire for love that starts at the age of puberty, *ii)* the urge for sensual existence that forms *iii)* the substance of karma, are the causes of the present state of affairs. On the other hand, the completed karma ready to be born again is already facing in the direction of old age and death, of which the outcome is to be seen in the future.

As far as our bodies are concerned, there are the three bitternesses of taking life, robbery, and sexual abuse. As far as our mouths are concerned, there are the four oral transgressions of being foul-mouthed, double-tongued, recounting wild fantasies, and the use of false flowery language, which bring about the workings of karma. Then, with regard to the mind, there are the three kinds of troublesome worries (*bonnō, klesha*) of indulgence, hatefulness, and unprofundity.

If you hold to and believe, as in the same way you would in the Dharma, in this particular chain of the twelve causes and karmic circumstances that run through the whole of sentient existence, then there is no doubt that you will become aware that your own inherent Buddha nature is not separate from what you are now. What this amounts to is that, if a person vilifies and destroys this sutra through his unbelief, then he will cut off all his Buddha seeds, throughout all the existential spaces. Outside of our own persons, there exists neither a separate Buddha nor a *Dharma Flower Sutra* (*Hokke-kyō*).

The cause of existence, brought about by karmic circumstances, or not coming into existence, as a result of karmic circumstances, is brought about by two of the twelve zodiac branches that refer to the past.

[The animals of the twelve zodiac branches are the rat, ox, tiger, hare, dragon, snake, horse, goat, monkey, rooster, dog, and boar.]

To come into existence, as a result of causes due to karmic circumstances, or not to come into existence, is brought about by karmic circumstances, which is brought about by two of the twelve zodiac branches that refer to the future. The other eight of the twelve zodiac branches that are suspended between the past and the future all have the cause of their existence brought about by karmic circumstances, as well as having come into existence as a result of causes due to karmic circumstances. Not coming into an existence caused by karmic circumstances and not having come into existence as a result of causes due to karmic circumstances are dharmas free from causation.

Now if we think of the chain of the twelve causes and karmic circumstances that run through the whole of sentient existence in terms of the past, present, and future, then our fundamental unenlightenment is when our pasts have become completely solidified. Dispositions inherited from the past refer to every single disposition we ever had.

When the first consciousness takes place in the womb is when we inherit a mind that is consistent with our surroundings. When the body and mind are evolving in the womb is the time when we receive the continuity of life, even though the capabilities of seeing, hearing, smelling, and tasting are not yet developed, nor are the five organs of sense and the functioning of the mind coherent as yet. The five stages within the womb are seen as the growth of the formation of a *stupa*.

[Originally this *stupa* was a tower-like reliquary which represents the Dharma body in three-dimensional form. Later, this representation of the Dharma body became the pagodas of China, Japan, and Korea.]

[In the esoteric symbolism which Nichiren refers to, proceeding from the base upwards is a square, a circle, a triangle, a moon-shaped semicircle, and a jewel in the shape of a flame, called a *mani*, which is a symbol for the wisdom of the Buddha. The square symbolises matter; the circle symbolises cognition; the triangle represents mind; the new moon shape stands for the Dharma; and the flame stands for the Buddha nature.]

The first stage in the womb is called *karara, kalala*, which represents the first sequence of seven days. This is defined as a union of the sperm and ovary and the subsequent development. The second stage is called *abudomu, arbuda*, which is translated as a bud and represents the second week after conception. The third stage, *heishi* [Skt.: *peshî*], is understood as an agglomeration of flesh and blood. The fourth stage is *kennan, ghana*, which denotes bodily growth from the fifth week onwards. The fifth stage, *barashakya, prāshakhā*, is when the foetus is fully formed to bide its term until birth.

This is followed by the foetus leaving the womb and becoming a human being. This means to be a sentient being.

In the *Broad Elucidation of the Universal Desistance from Troublesome Worries in order to See Clearly*, it says, "The head is round just like the heavens, and the feet are square just like the earth. Within the body, there are empty cavities which are like empty space. The warmth of the bowels is comparable to spring and summer. The hardness of the backbone is like that of winter. The four limbs of the body are like the four seasons, and the twelve major joints throughout the body are like the twelve months of the year. The three hundred sixty lesser joints throughout the whole body are comparable to the three hundred sixty days of the year. When we breathe in and out through our noses, it is like the wind that blows down from the mountains, over the marshes, and through the ravines and valleys. The breath that comes in and out through our mouths is like the wind that blows through empty space. The eyes are comparable to the sun and moon, and their opening and shutting are like day and night. Our hair is like the stars and other heavenly bodies. The eyebrows are like the seven stars of the Big Dipper. Our veins and arteries are like the rivers and streams. Our bones can be likened to gems and stones. Our flesh is like the soil and the earth. And the hairs on our bodies are like the thickets and woods. The five viscera are like the five planets – Venus, Jupiter, Mercury, Mars, and Saturn; or these five viscera are like the five sacred mountains on earth that mark the boundaries of China [Taisan (Taishan in Shandong), Kōsan (Hengshan in Hunan), Kasan (Huashan in Shanxi), Kōsan (Hengshan in Hebei), and Sūsan (Sungshan in Henan)]."

The flesh on our bodies is symbolised by the element earth. The runny marrow in our bones is seen as the element water. Blood is symbolised by the element fire. The skin is symbolised by the element wind. And the muscles are understood as being the element wood. Now when it comes to the five organs of sense and the functioning of the mind, the eyes are for seeing shapes and colours; the ears are for hearing sounds; the nose is for smelling odours; the tongue is for tasting flavours; and the body suffers pain and discomfort, when it is touched by heat, cold, coarseness, and things that irritate it. It is easy to see with our eyes how these five senses work. As for the sixth sense which is the workings of the mind, this is a propensity that is to be found within the bodies of all sentient beings. But they do not know its totality.

This is something I cannot see and know nothing about. How is it then, for those superior to humankind? At the present time, is there anybody capable of knowing the totality of mind?

It is said that the mind of the Buddha cannot be thought out, nor deliberated upon. Then why should it not be so for those with lesser propensities?

What people do not know is that this totality is separate from being long or measuring less, or being round or square in shape. It is not blue, yellow, vermilion, white, or black. It is a Dharma that is beyond any verbal expression or pondered thought. It cannot be compared to walking, standing, sitting, or lying down – which are understood as the four noble positions of the Buddha – or to any other state. It silences anything that is composed of words or any manifestation of cause and karmic circumstances. It is not something that could be depicted by painting a picture; nor is it anything that can be learned through study; nor is it something that comes from the Buddha's foretelling when a disciple will attain enlightenment, nor from any oracular message from the gods; nor is it anything that can be handed down from one's parents or teachers. It does not rain down from heaven; nor does it spring up from the earth. It is something so utterly all-embracing that it is impossible to ponder over or deliberate upon.

In response to such charlatans that claim to be enlightened, the two sage-like personages Tendai (*T'ien T'ai*) and Myōraku (*Miao-lo*), in the *Recondite Significance of the Dharma (Hokke Gengi)* and the *Explanatory Notes on the Recondite Significance of the Dharma Flower (Hokke Gengi Shakusen)*, say, "The mind is as elusive as the sparks of fireworks which, when burned out, only remain as remembered words. But on naming these illusions we call them mind. As you would expect, some people will insist that these sparks existed, and when they say so, they perceive neither their colour nor their inherent qualities. Naturally, there are other people who say that these sparks do not exist, and, when they say so, only their memory comes to mind. You should not even go as far as wondering whether something exists or not, because it is the imponderable quality of Utterness. That which acts in the same way as the Utterness of mind is referred to as the dharma(s). The dharmas of the mind are not the cause, nor are they the fruition. If you contemplate this matter in the light of it being a fundamental principle, you will come to understand that cause and effect are interdependent; this is what we call the lotus flower-like mechanism. Then, when you have contemplated this matter as being the oneness of mind and pass this concept on to other minds in order to teach them, then this is what we call a sutra."

In the *Explanatory Notes on the Recondite Significance of the Dharma Flower (Hokke Gengi Shakusen)*, it says, "The instant it is said that something exists, it does not mean to say that the totality of existence is not there. So why should it not be the quality and appearance of all the ten [psychological] realms of dharmas? When it is said that something does not exist, then again three thousand thoughts come to mind, which do not exclude the actual instant of reflexion on the realms of dharmas at hand. You should not bother yourselves as to whether anything exists or not, since one instant of mental activity is simply the way the middle way is. This is because, as you already know, mind is Utterness itself."

At this point it is well understood that our minds are the *Dharma Flower Sutra* (*Hokke-kyō*), and the *Dharma Flower Sutra* (*Myōhō Renge Kyō*) is what our minds really are. Through not knowing the *Dharma Flower Sutra* (*Hokke-kyō*), we cannot know what our persons really are.

The idea of moving house and forgetting about one's wife could be used as an analogy for the person who cannot become a Buddha, because he has forgotten about the need for the *Dharma Flower Sutra* (*Myōhō Renge Kyō*) for his existence to come. Therefore, anybody who goes against and vilifies the *Dharma Flower Sutra* (*Myōhō Renge Kyō*) goes against all the Buddhas, all the *deva* (*ten*), one's father and mother, lord and teacher, the mountains, the seas, the sun and the moon, and everything that exists.

The *Dharma Flower Sutra* (*Hokke-kyō*) has to be all the ten comparisons that the Bodhisattva Sovereign Remedy (*Yaku' ō, Bhaishajya-rāja*) used to show that this sutra is superior to all others, when he said to the Bodhisattva Shukuōke, ["Just as out of all watercourses, effluents, streams, rivulets, and great rivers, the sea is the greatest, so it is the same with this *Dharma Flower Sutra* (*Myōhō Renge Kyō*), which is the most all-embracing and profound out of all the sutras that the Tathāgata has expounded. Just as out of all the mountains, black mountains, the lesser ring of iron mountains that surround the world, the larger range of iron mountains that surround the world, Mount Sumeru is the greatest, so it is the same with this *Dharma Flower Sutra* (*Hokke-kyō*), which is the highest peak among all sutras. Just as, out of all the stars, the moon as a prince of the *deva* (*ten*) is the first among the heavenly bodies at night, again, it is the same with this *Dharma Flower Sutra*

(*Hokke-kyō*), which shines the brightest out of the thousands of myriads of millions of different kinds of sutric Dharmas that exist. Again, just as the sun as prince of the *deva* (*ten*) can take away all darkness, so it is the same with this *Dharma Flower Sutra* (*Hokke-kyō*) that is able to reverse the darkness of everything that is not good. Again, in the same way a sage-like sovereign whose chariot wheels roll everywhere without hindrance (*tenrinnō, chakravartin*) is monarch among all the lesser kings, it is the same with regard to this sutra, which is the most revered out of all the others. Again, just as the thirty-third heaven of Taishaku is the ultimate of all heavens, so it is the same with this sutra that is paramount among all the others. Just as the Universal King Bonten is the father of all sentient beings, it is the same with this sutra, which is the parent of all those who aspire to the mind of a bodhisattva, all those who are sage-like and wise, and all those who are still studying to get rid of their delusions and those who have begun to cast them off. Again, just as those whose practice is beyond the stream of transmigratory suffering, or those whose practice requires only one more lifetime before reaching nirvana, or those who have attained the supreme rewards of the individual vehicle, or those who realise nirvana for themselves and without a teacher, are foremost among ordinary people, so it is the same with this sutra, whether it be expounded by the Tathāgata, or by a bodhisattva, or even by a person who has heard the Buddha's voice. Among all the Dharmas, this sutra is superior to all. Also, the person who is able to receive and hold to this archetypal sutra takes first place among sentient beings. Just as the bodhisattvas are foremost among the hearers of the Buddha's voice and those who realise nirvana for themselves without a teacher, so it is the same with this sutra. Out of all the sutric Dharmas, this sutra is superior to all. Just as the Buddha is the sovereign of all Dharmas, so it is the same with this sutra that is the most important of all."].

It says in the *Recondite Significance of the Dharma Flower Sutra* (*Hokke Gengi*), "The eyes, ears, nose, and tongue are the gateway to being free from troublesome worries and distress." In the *Explanatory Notes on the Recondite Significance of the Dharma Flower Sutra* (*Hokke Gengi Shakusen*), it says, "The eternally abiding, real aspect of all dharmas is like the sweet dew from the *deva* (*ten*) that is the elixir of immortality. Now that the Utterness of the Dharma (*Myōhō*,

Saddharma) has been explained, the real aspect of all dharmas is opened up to us. This is why it is referred to as a gateway."

Being free from troublesome worries and distress is the *Dharma Flower Sutra* (*Hokke-kyō*). Also, the *Dharma Flower Sutra* (*Hokke-kyō*) is the sweet dew of the *deva* (*ten*) [that is the elixir of immortality]. It says in the third fascicle of the *Universal Desistance from Troublesome Worries in order to See Clearly* (*Maka Shikan*), "The bundles of sutric scrolls of the all-pervasive wisdom and discernment of the Tathāgata exist in every detail within the persons of sentient beings. But because they are beset by the absurd ideas of ordinary people, this wisdom is obscured, so that they neither perceive it, nor do they think it is true."

What I am saying you must attentively take into deep consideration. You must close your eyes, set your mind completely at rest, and fully take this in. All the six organs of sense – the eyes, ears, nose, tongue, body, and mind – are all the embodiment of the *Dharma Flower Sutra* (*Nam Myōhō Renge Kyō*) [where the interdependence of cause and effect of the Utterness of the Dharma (*Myōhō, Saddharma*) occurs]. Have no doubts about the mind being the fundamental substance of the *Dharma Flower Sutra* (*Nam Myōhō Renge Kyō*) and that the other five sensory organs are its embodiment.

The mind is king, and the five organs of sense are its retinue. Although there is sight in our eyes and our auditive sense is in our ears, it is the mind that really makes us see and hear. Nevertheless, the behaviour of the five organs of sense is in accordance with the workings of the mind. Because seeing things is something that is done by the mind, then the eyes are also the *Dharma Flower Sutra* (*Nam Myōhō Renge Kyō*). Also, hearing with our ears is brought about through our minds, hence the ears being the *Dharma Flower Sutra* (*Nam Myōhō Renge Kyō*). It is also the same with the other organs of sense.

When we die, five of our organs of sense – the eyes, ears, nose, tongue, and body – no longer function. Even though the actual substance of these five organs is dead, their outward shape still remains. However, because there is no mind, when has a person who is dead ever been able to see or hear? It does not follow common sense.

It is exactly the same with those who slander the *Dharma Flower Sutra* (*Hokke-kyō*). Since our minds are the *Dharma Flower Sutra* (*Nam Myōhō Renge Kyō*), to go and vilify it implies losing our minds, so that our six organs of sense are incomplete. Does that then mean that by losing one's mind, that is to say the *Dharma Flower Sutra* (*Nam Myōhō Renge Kyō*), we should establish the teachings that came before it?

By vilifying the *Dharma Flower Sutra* (*Hokke-kyō*), means that this person no longer has faith in it; and since his mind has gone in the direction of all the schools of all the provisional Dharmas of the individual vehicle that were taught prior to the Dharma Flower, this person's mind is indeed that of a dead body.

Now, the school of the Dharma Flower is said to be the *Dharma Flower Sutra* (*Myōhō Renge Kyō*) itself. Since we do not throw our minds away, we do not become like the corpses that have lost their six organs of sense. If the mind is not separate from the five sensory organs and the five sensory organs are not separate from mind, when the mind becomes a Buddha, our physical attributes will become Buddhas at the same time. Since outward appearances and the mind are not a duality, there is the mutual possession of an inner and an external existence.

In the *Explanatory Notes on the Recondite Significance of the Dharma Flower Sutra* (*Hokke Gengi Shakusen*), it says, "The eight petals of the Lotus Flower represent the eight classifications of the doctrines of Shākyamuni and the calyx of the lotus stands for the one and only doctrine to which all the others relate. In the one, there are eight, and in the eight, there is one. There is always one, and there are always eight. There is only one and only eight. If it becomes one, then it becomes eight. There is neither a first, nor a last."

[The eight classifications of the doctrines of Shākyamuni are *i*) the teachings of the three receptacles, *ii*) the interrelated teachings, *iii*) the particular teaching, *iv*) the all-inclusive teaching, *v*) the direct teachings that reveal the Buddha's enlightenment without any preamble, *vi*) the gradual teachings where the Buddha reveals his enlightenment in stages, *vii*) the esoteric and secret teachings, and *viii*) the indeterminate teachings.]

In the *Universal Desistance from Troublesome Worries in order to See Clearly*, it says, "In the single instant of mind, there are ten [psychological] realms of dharmas. Even if there is only the tiniest scrap of mind, then there are three thousand existential spaces." In the *Broad Elucidation to Support the Practice of the Universal Desistance from Troublesome Worries in order to See Clearly*, it says, "Indeed you should know that the one instant of thought of the self and its dependent terrain contain three thousand existential spaces. This is because, when we put this fundamental principle of the attainment to the path into words, then it becomes the one instant of our own minds being replenished with all the existing realms of dharmas."

In the *Recondite Significance of the Dharma Flower* (*Hokke Gengi*), we have, "Even if you say three thousand existential spaces, or even if you say the realms of dharmas, they are just alternative names for the *Dharma Flower Sutra* (*Myōhō Renge Kyō*)." In the *Chapter on the Bodhisattva Sovereign Medicine* (*Yaku' ō, Bhaishajya-rāja*), it states, "There will be a broad propagation throughout the world of humankind."

The world of humankind is the sky, the earth, and our fathers and mothers. Also, the same chapter goes on to say, "The good medicine is for the illnesses of the people of the world of mankind." The good medicine is the sky, the earth, and our father and mother. In this manner, we ourselves who are sentient beings are none other than the substance of the Dharma Flower. We like to think that the *Dharma Flower Sutra* (*Myōhō Renge Kyō*) is an entirely different country or another Japan, and we think of the sky, the earth, water, as other dimensions and other places. In this way, we regardlessly end up by throwing our noble selves away. Apart from berating ourselves, we tend to fall into evil places. How can we be such wretched and sorry beings?

Therefore, when we have faith, our persons become something unthinkably wonderful, just as it is recounted in the *Eighteenth*

Chapter on the Joy of the following Meritorious Virtues of Practice. But the adversities we may meet when we vilify our persons are recounted in the *Twenty-Eighth Chapter on the Persuasiveness and Quest* [for Buddhahood] *of the Bodhisattva Universally Worthy (Fugen, Samantabhadra)*. In this chapter, it says, "This enlightened text of the universal vehicle (*daijō, mahāyāna*) is the treasure store of all the Buddhas. It is the eyes of all the Buddhas of the ten directions of the past, present, and future. It is the seed from whence all the Tathāgatas of the past, present, and future come into being. The person who holds to this sutra takes care of the Buddha, as well as carrying out his tasks."

In the *Third Chapter on Similes and Parables*, it says, "If somebody vilifies this sutra through having no faith in it means that this person denies all his Buddha seeds throughout all the existential spaces." In the *Chapter on the Persuasiveness and Quest [for Buddhahood] of the Bodhisattva Universally Worthy (Fugen, Samantabhadra)*, it says, "All the Buddha Tathāgatas are the offspring of the actual reality of the Dharma. Through doing the practice of the universal vehicle (*daijō, mahāyāna*), you will not be denying the seeds of the Dharma."

Nichiren [formal signature]

Treatise on the Whole, being Contained in the One Instant of Mind

Sōzai ichinen shō
Goshō Shimpen, pp. 111-116

The second year of Shōka [1258], at 37 years of age

In the sixth fascicle of the *Explanatory Notes on the Recondite Significance of the Dharma Flower*, it says, "The whole is contained in the one instant of mind, which, in further detail, is divided into materiality and mind."

The question is asked: What are the implications of the whole, being contained in the one instant of mind?

The answer is given: It is not easy to give an even perfunctory answer. There is, however, one significant point that is decided. It must be what happens in the primal instant of life of sentient beings, when they are first conscious.

If one carefully investigates the *samādhi* of stopping all mental activity and allowing no distraction whatsoever, then one can say that nothing is repressed by it, nor is anything recorded by it. Nothing is taken for being good, and nothing is taken for being evil. It is a state of mind that is like the ocean depths overflowing with darkness.

This is said to be the eighth consciousness. This eighth consciousness, by being the embodiment of all existence, and because it contains all dharmas, is said to be the whole, contained in the one instant of mind. It is, however, the one instant of mind of the eighth consciousness, in a practical sense.

However, when this one instant of mind moves and fluctuates, looking out towards the environments that are determined by karma, it does not yet discern what those karmically determined realms, with which it associates, are. This is called the seventh consciousness. This seventh consciousness, by fluctuating and being agitated by confrontation with good and evil situations and its delight in joyfulness and grief through sadness, gets itself entangled with both good and bad karma. This is called the sixth consciousness (*dairokushiki*). When this sixth cognition is made aware of its karma, it then becomes aware of its physical form [*shiki*] and the karmically deserved situation, such as family, race, country and economic conditions, etc, for life in the future [*hō*].

It is as though the primal one instant of mind is cavernous, unfathomable water. By its undulation and swell, it faces all kinds of situations. But even if the wind blows and makes the water billow, it does not break into waves and bubbling foam.

Through the fluctuations of being agitated, through facing both good and evil environments that are conditioned by karma, the delight in joyfulness and the grief in sadness are like the appearance of the undulating waves of the water, rising to their height. Then, with the acquisition of the physical form and the requitals for life in the future, the waves break upon the rocks and turn into a mass of foaming bubbles, both large and small. The bursting of those bubbles is like a return to death. You should skilfully and thoroughly think this through.

Whether one refers to waves, or whether one refers to bubbles, both come from the one water we have been using as a metaphor. In terms of the Dharma, the progressive changes of the primal one instant of mind become our physical characteristics and what we karmically deserve. This is due to the fact that there is absolutely no exception to the totality of mind becoming our person and body.

You must take care that every single exception to this concept has to be discarded. For instance, when all this water becomes extremely cold, it turns into smaller or larger pieces of ice. Consequently, one might say that this is a person who falls into hell in the midst of a cavern of raging fire, and becomes completely consumed by the flames. We can continue until we come to the reality of the Buddha realm, which becomes its own sublime and solemn manifestation.

Nevertheless, this is all the working of the oneness of the mind. Similarly, when wickedness comes to the surface, we become sensitive to the embodiment of the three evil paths, and, when we resolve to attain to a mind of enlightenment, we feel the personification of the Buddha and the bodhisattvas. In this way, the awareness of the workings of karma solidify into pack ice in the ocean of the oneness of mind, with the ten realms of dharmas becoming separate entities, since the source of the ten [psychological] realms of dharmas is the singularity of the fundamental substance.

[This singularity of the fundamental substance is Nam Myōhō Renge Kyō, which means to devote our lives to and found them on (*Nam*[*u*]) the Utterness of the Dharma (*Myōhō*) (entirety of existence, enlightenment and unenlightenment) permeated by the underlying white lotus flower-like mechanism of the interdependence of cause, concomitancy and effect (*Renge*) in its whereabouts of the ten (psychological) realms of dharmas (*Kyō*).]

Although there may only be one realm of dharmas called hell, hell is also endowed with nine realms of dharmas. It is also the same with all the realms of dharmas, including that of the Buddha. In this way, the ten [psychological] realms of dharmas are mutually furnished with the same ten realms, so that the total of these dharma realms becomes one hundred. Then, as each single one of these hundred realms of dharmas is equipped with the ten ways in which dharmas make themselves present to any of our organs of sense, the hundred realms of dharmas become a thousand ways in which dharmas make themselves present to our six sense organs – eyes, ears, nose, tongue, body, and mind. These thousand qualities, by being furnished with the existential spaces of sentient beings, the existential space of the five aggregates, and the existential space of abode and terrain – the thousand such qualities become three thousand.

The Dharma gateway of these three thousand existential spaces is fully present in the primal instant of mind, without any omission whatsoever. It is due to the fact that the one instant of mind is not separate from the physical body, but is endowed with the three thousand existential spaces. This is the Dharma gateway of the one instant of mind containing three thousand existential spaces (*ichinen sanzen*).

In this way, the realm of hell is not to be feared, nor is the Buddha to be particularly venerated. They are the perfect combination of our physical aspect and what we are essentially. You should abide completely in the unshakeable silence of the oneness of mind, without any further thought.

The Dharma gateway, which I have just mentioned, is an insight that is referred to as the contemplation of the real aspect. Superfluous cogitation becomes the movement of thought. The movement of thought becomes a lack of clarity, and this unenlightenment becomes bewilderment. But if one abides in the contemplation of the real aspect, then what is projected from the inseparability of our person and the fundamentally existing three thousand existential spaces is called the Buddha.

In view of this, the Universal Teacher Myōraku (*Miao-lo*) says, "Indeed, you should know that, in the body and its terrain, there are three thousand existential spaces. Because when one attains to the path it is in accordance with this fundamental principle, the one instant of mind in the body includes all the realms of the dharmas." Those who cannot hold on to this insight pass on to other contemplations, but they should contemplate the state of mind that arises out of the primal instant of thought.

The condition of mind that arises and sets the stillness of this one instant of thought in motion becomes one of bewilderment. This movement of thought is entirely the triple axiom of existence – relativity (*kū, shūnyatā*), materiality (*ke*), and the middle way of reality as we perceive it (*chū*). The triple axiom is in the midst of the fundamental substance of our minds. The instant of thought that arises in it is phenomenon. And the non-existence of self-nature, in the one instant of mind, is relativity (*kū, shūnyatā*). When this threefold contemplation of the dharmas is realised, the instant of mind that moves becomes inseparable from the instant of mind that is immovable.

This insight into the inseparability of enlightenment and unenlightenment is referred to as the insight that existence is nothing other than consciousness. Nonetheless, even though it becomes the insight that existence is nothing other than consciousness, it is ultimately the insight into the real aspect of all dharmas. Myōraku (*Miao-lo*) says in his explanation, in *Illustrations of the Significance of Desistance from Troublesome Worries in order to See Clearly*, "The roots and the branches reflect each other. Phenomena and its intrinsicality are not two."

The roots are the insight of the real aspect of all dharmas. The branches are the insight that existence is nothing other than consciousness. Phenomena become the insight that existence is nothing other than consciousness. And the essential point of that insight is the insight into the real aspect of all dharmas.

When this imponderably unutterable insight is attained, then one ascends to the consequent fruition of temporarily cutting off and destroying the ever-revolving cycle of birth and death. This is called the single fundamental substance of phenomena, and its essential quality is that "the whole of existence is contained in the one instant of mind and noumena".

The manifestation of each and every thing being endowed with the one instant of thought containing three thousand existential spaces (*ichinen sanzen*) is the revelation of the thirty-two bodies of Kannon (*Avalokiteshvara*), and the luminosity of everything being endowed with this intrinsic fundamental of the one instant of thoght containing three thousand existential spaces (*ichinen sanzen*) is the manifestation of the thirty-four bodies of Myō.on. If it were not so, then the various emanations of the Buddha or the transformations of the bodhisattvas would have no reason to become apparent.

Again, when this principle of the one instant of thought containing three thousand existential spaces (*ichinen sanzen*) is not adhered to, then the one thousand two hundred Buddhas of the two mandalas of the Womb Store Realm (*Garbhadhātu*) and the Vajra Realm

(*Vajradhātu*), the homogeneous body of the Tathāgata Dainichi (*Mahāvairochana*) as well as his transformations, would be difficult to know. The essential to these gateways to the Dharma is each and every thing being endowed with the one instant of thought containing three thousand existential spaces (*ichinen sanzen*). You must retain this secret and keep it to yourself.

On explaining this one instant of thought containing three thousand existential spaces, Tendai (*T'ien T'ai*) said: "In the oneness of mind, there are ten [psychological] realms of dharmas [qualified by the ten ways in which dharmas make themselves present to any of our six sense organs – eyes, ears, nose, tongue, body, and mind]. And then, when each realm of dharmas is again furnished with the same ten realms, it comes to one hundred. Each realm of dharmas is then provided with the three sorts of existential space, so that the thousand existential spaces amount to three thousand. These three thousand are present in the one instant of thought in the mind. If there is no mind, we need go no further. But if there is even the tiniest scrap of mind, it is provided with the three thousand." Myōraku (*Miao-lo*) said, on explaining the words "tiniest scrap", "It alludes to the feeblest presence of mind. What is intended is hardly any."

Consequently, we must understand this as, whatever the occasion, the oneness of mind is the root, and the ten [psychological] realms of dharmas are the branches. This is a gateway to the Dharma that can be thought out and deliberated upon. But when it is taken as being imponderable, so that it cannot be deliberated upon, it is because the whole fundamental substance of the oneness of mind is the ten dharma realms of dharmas becoming the three thousand. There is no one thing that can be set apart from it. Neither has it an inside nor an outside. The oneness of mind is not separate from the three thousand, and neither are the three thousand separate from the oneness of mind.

One could make a comparison with the unknowing person who believes that ice exists apart from water. Therefore, one should realise that there is no disparity between the one instant of thought and the three thousand. They are both a single Dharma.

Accordingly, Tendai (*T'ien T'ai*) explains this, by saying, "At all events, mind is all dharmas, and all dharmas are mind. There is neither a vertical nor a horizontal, and there is neither oneness nor multiformity. It is abstruse, utter, profound, and superlatively all-embracing. There is no way of knowing that can know it, and there are no words that can formulate it. Therefore, we refer to it as the imponderable that cannot be deliberated upon. It is here where the meaning lies."

[That is to say, the meaning lies in Nam Myōhō Renge Kyō, which means to devote our lives to and found them on (*Nam[u]*) the Utterness of the Dharma (entirety of existence, enlightenment and unenlightenment) (*Myōhō*) permeated by the underlying white lotus flower-like mechanism of the interdependence of cause, concomitancy and effect (*Renge*) in its whereabouts of the ten (psychological) realms of dharmas (*Kyō*).]

The one instant of thought is not the one instant of thought, by being inseparable from the three thousand. The three thousand is not the three thousand, by being inseparable from the one instant of thought. Therefore, it is the Dharma gateway to the cultivation of the essential non-duality of the fundamental substance and its intrinsicality.

What is unthinkably unutterable about this one instant of thought containing three thousand existential spaces (*ichinen sanzen*) is that the existential space of abode and terrain is a part of the three thousand, so that plants, trees, tiles, and stones, by being also furnished with the three thousand, are completely filled with the fundamental substance of enlightenment.

However that may be, because we are provided with three thousand existential spaces, we, too, are the originally existent, fundamental substance of the Buddha. Therefore, it follows that the sentient beings in the hell of incessant suffering, by being endowed also with the three thousand existential spaces, are at one with the fundamental substance of the Tathāgata, who is enlightened to Utterness without any discrepancy whatsoever.

[Tathāgata (*Nyorai*) signifies the following: one who has gone; one who has followed the Path and arrived at the real suchness; one of the ten titles of a Buddha. Tathāgata can be explained as a person who comes from the real suchness of existence, which is Nam Myōhō Renge Kyō – which means to devote our lives to and found them on (*Nam[u]*) the Utterness of the Dharma (*Myōhō*) (entirety of existence, enlightenment and unenlightenment) permeated by the underlying white lotus flower-like mechanism of the interdependence of cause, concomitancy and effect (*Renge*) in its whereabouts of the ten (psychological) realms of dharmas (*Kyō*) – and that person will return to it.]

This is why, in the *Twelfth Chapter on Daibadatta*, Daibadatta (*Devadatta*) – who was in the flames of the hell of incessant suffering, due to his unpardonable sins of creating a schism in the clerical community (*sō, sangha*), stoning the Buddha to the shedding of his blood, and killing a nun – received, contrary to all expectation, the prophecy by the Buddha that he would become the Tathāgata Sovereign of the *Deva* (*Tennō*).

If this is the case of a person in hell, then why should it not be so with the other nine realms? When their discriminative thinking and intellectual knowledge is cleared away, and even people of the two vehicles can become Buddhas, then why should it not be so with people of the remaining eight realms?

As each and every blade of grass – trees, as well as all the rest of the environment – is the originally existent Buddha substance with its three thousand existential spaces, it is not a matter of casting aside evil thoughts and evil dharmas, nor adopting good thoughts and good dharmas.

Because this principle is being discussed and revealed in the present sutra, it is given the title *Myōhō renge kyō*, the *Sutra on the White Lotus Flower-like Mechanism of the Utterness of the Dharma*. The Utterness of the Dharma (*Myōhō, Saddharma*) is furnished with the ten [psychological] realms of dharmas and the three thousand existential spaces of plants and trees, without a single dharma being left out.

As for the Lotus Flower, the persons who have become enlightened to this principle must, as an equal to the Buddha, be placed upon the calyx of the Lotus Flower. The Lotus Flower solemnly ennobles that person, and it is said that the Lotus Flower is the adornment of abode and terrain. That is to say that their bodies are not separate from the fundamental substance of all the Buddhas of the past, present, and future.

Without a grasp of this principle, it cannot be referred to as the seeds of the Buddha. Myōraku (*Miao-lo*) explains this, when he says, "If it is not the objective realm of the Buddha wisdom, if it is not a random counterfeit, even then it cannot be the seeds of enlightenment."

You are already aware that, since all the sutras that were expounded prior to the Dharma Flower have provisional dharmas entwined into them, even if one were to accept and hold to them for a continuity of *kalpas*, as many as there are grains of dust, they can never become the seeds of enlightenment. This is due to the fact that the sutras do not reveal and account for the totality of the Buddha wisdom; nor do they expound the whole of the wisdom of the Buddha; nor do they state that women and people of evil disposition can become Buddhas.

Among the elucidations of Tendai (*T'ien T'ai*), it says: "In the other sutras, the Buddha prophesied that only his disciples who were bodhisattvas would become Buddhas, and that people of the two vehicles would not be able to do so, and that only good people could become Buddhas and wicked people could not. He prophesied that only men could become Buddhas and that women were excluded, that only male humans and *deva* (*ten*) could become Buddhas but not animals. But in the present sutra, all these categories are foretold as being able to become Buddhas."

Myōraku (*Miao-lo*) justifies this, by saying, "Even if there are sutras that are designated as the King of Sutras they are not said to be the foremost to have been expounded, are expounded or will be expounded in the future. You must be able to understand the significance of the doctrine that this particular teaching stands in addition to the others, that it is only the teachings of the three receptacles, that the equally broad teachings (*hōdō, vaipulya*) were in answer to people who had the propensities for the four teachings, and that the wisdom (*hannya, prajña*) teachings include both the interrelated and particular doctrines, in preparation for the all-inclusive teaching." Just as these explanations infer, all the sutras prior to the Dharma Flower are an expedient means and are not the direct cause for becoming a Buddha.

The question is asked: Among all the sutras that came before the Dharma Flower, are there any that illustrate the so-called all-inclusive teachings as being particularly superior, and how is it that you pick out all those sutras that came prior to the Dharma Flower as not being the seeds for Buddhahood?

The answer given is that, even though the all-inclusive teachings are dealt with, the teachings prior to the *Dharma Flower Sutra* (*Hokke-kyō*) let the Buddha seeds go astray since they do not discuss the hearers of the voice, those who are partially enlightened due to a profound search for the meaning of existence (*engaku, hyakushibutsu, pratyekabuddha*), people of evil disposition, and women becoming Buddhas. This sutra is the ultimate extremity of the all-inclusive teaching. Without this final superlative, they would not uphold the original intention of the Buddha. And also because they are devoid of the Buddha's wisdom, they could not be the seeds for becoming enlightened.

It is on this account that I have pointed to all the sutras in contrast to the Dharma Flower. Referring to this point, there is a Universal Teacher, who said, "Both people who are refined and those who are coarse have made this mistake [through not understanding the interdependence of cause and effect], which means that both those who are refined and those who are coarse can be referred to as being crude and oversimple." Consequently, none of the other sutras are called the *Sutra on the White Lotus Flower-like Mechanism of the Utterness of the Dharma* (*Myōhō Renge Kyō*).

The question is asked: What advantage would a dunce who cannot read have in reciting Nam Myōhō Renge Kyō?

Answer: Even though somebody who may be illiterate and who does not even know one ideogram were to exert his faith by reciting it, then, out of the three karmas of body, mouth, and mind, it would be his mouth that would be the first to realise its meritorious virtue. When this meritorious virtue is accomplished with the Buddha seeds being stowed within his breast, he evidently becomes a person who is coming out of the bewilderment of the realm of life and death.

The fact that this sutra surpasses all other sutras, it is taught that those who ridicule and disparage it reverse their karmic relationship for enlightenment and become people whose values are a mean disregard and vilification.

What would one then say about the people who exert a mind of faith and comply with the affinities to become a Buddha?

Accordingly, the Universal Teacher Dengyō (*Dengyō Daishi*) wrote, "It is decidedly preordained that both the persons who slander and the persons who have faith will become Buddhas."

The question is asked: On becoming a Buddha, what is the significance of the three bodies?

Answer: The three thousand existential spaces that are in our bodies, by being completely merged into each other, are the same as dharmas. The body whose wisdom exhaustively knows this principle is that which is called the reward body. As this principle is present in every instant of life, then, from the eighty-four thousand features and distinguishing marks on the body of the Buddha to the bodies of the tigers, wolves, and jackals, which are made apparent for the effective benefit of all beings, all are understood as being designated as the corresponding body.

The *Dharma Flower Sutra* (*Hokke-kyō*), in its exposition of these three bodies, says, "Such an appearance, such a nature, such a substance". The appearance is the corresponding body; the nature is the reward body; and the substance is the Dharma body. We have been endowed with these three bodies since the primordial infinity, with no exceptions whatsoever. However, the clouds of our bewilderment hide these three bodies, so that we are not aware of their existence. But he who is referred to as the enlightened Buddha knows this essential element and is also the practitioner of the *Dharma Flower Sutra* (*Hokke-kyō*).

Having been unaware and ignorant of these three bodies since time immemorial, we become closer to an enlightenment to them, by being induced by the instruction of a moderated Buddha discourse, which is called the temporary gateway. Without any sort of confusion with regard to the fundamental principle of our being endowed with these three bodies, it is also explained that they have their abode in the past, present, future, and throughout eternity. There is no dimension that is not pervaded by these three entities. This is referred to as the original gateway to the Dharma.

Even though it may be that the difference between the original and temporary gateways is merely a matter of the relatively recent past and primordiality, the fundamental substance of the Dharma remains the same. This is the reason why Tendai (*T'ien T'ai*) says in his explanations, "Even though the original and temporary teachings have their peculiarities, their oneness is their imponderable inexplicability."

When we say enlightenment, it simply means to be enlightened to and to know what the intrinsicality of the fundamental substance is. It could be compared to the opening of a door of a storehouse of wealth and taking away the treasure within.

Enlightenment does not come from the outside. When we clear away the clouds that bewilder the oneness of mind, it becomes the substance of dharmas, which is the axiom of relativity (*kū, shūnyatā*), materiality (*ke*), and the middle way of reality as we perceive it (*chū*) that always abides in the past, present, and future, and throughout eternity. It is like a mirror that no longer reflects, because it is covered with dust. But when it is cleaned, every kind of image glides across it. The dust is removed by people cleaning the mirror. But if it were not cleaned, the images would not appear.

It is supposed of course that the person who transforms bewilderment into an enlightened awakening is the one who practises. The intrinsicality of the substance that is the three thousand existential spaces, the three axioms of relativity (kū, shūnyatā), phenomena (ke), and the middle way (chū), as well as the three bodies, is inherently and infinitely existing, which has nothing to do with the makings of humankind.

Again, even though the cultivation of bewilderment is something that is done by human beings, one does not see this bewilderment going away of its own volition. It is like sitting in a dark room for a hundred years with a burning candle, wherein the lightlessness does not go away entirely. This transforming of bewilderment into an enlightened awakening is to turn back the flow and finish at the source.

The inseparability of enlightenment and unenlightenment, as only being bewilderment and enlightenment [satori], is none other than the single entity or the oneness of the substance of unenlightenment and the Dharma essence. I respectfully fear and beg of you to be prudent and discard all other ways of knowing. If you ever perceive bewilderment and enlightenment as two separate entities, you will be distancing yourself from becoming a Buddha. It will be like climbing one Mount Sumeru after another.

Those who, since the origins, have been bewildered about the non-dual nature of the intrinsicality of the fundamental substance are called sentient beings, and the person who is enlightened to this non-duality is called the Buddha. You must really get to understand the all-embracing significance of what I have written, without any omissions or misconceptions.

These writings involve the Buddha's one universal concern about living and dying. Also, these writings are the Buddha's fervent desire to come into the world, in order to save people from the bewilderment of living and dying.

How can you enter into a treasure mountain and come out with empty hands? It would bring about a thousand myriad regrets, and there would be no advantage to it whatsoever.

When Emma takes someone to task or the lictors of hell raise their staves, they do not choose people at random, but only those who have done wrong. If these wrongdoers can get away from this harsh situation by being born as human beings, they will live through hundreds of thousands of myriads of *kalpas*, without even hearing of the name or ideogram for the Buddha.

They will also become progressively immersed into the three realms where *i*) sentient beings have appetites and desires, which *ii*) are incarnated in a subjective materiality with its physical surroundings, who, *iii*) at the same time, are endowed with the immateriality of the realms of thoughts and ideas (*sangai, triloka*), as well as being persons who must drift about the six paths of unenlightenment.

To not be able to hear the essential Dharma, in order to escape from the bewilderment of the realm of life and death, is sad indeed. It is also as frightening to suffer the punishment of the ox-headed demon lictors of hell.

Concerning the Ten Ways in which dharmas Make Themselves Present to our Six Sense Organs

Jū.nyoze ji
Goshō Shimpen, pp. 104-106

The second year of Shōka [1258], at 37 years of age

With regard to our persons being the originally enlightened Tathāgata, whose three bodies [of the Dharma, wisdom, and corresponding bodies] are not separate from the one, it is expounded in the present sutra, where it says, "Such a way in which dharmas make themselves present to any of our six sense organs [eyes, ears, nose, tongue, body, and mind] [1] *Nyoze sō*], their various inner qualities [2] *Nyoze shō*], such a substance or what they really are [3] *Nyoze tai*], such a potential strength and energy [4] *Nyoze riki*], such a manifestation of that energy and strength which is their influence [5] *Nyoze sa*], their fundamental causes [6] *Nyoze in*], along with their karmic circumstances [7] *Nyoze en*], the effects they produce [8] *Nyoze ka*], their apparent and karmic consequences [9] *Nyoze hō*], and then in any way dharmas make themselves perceptible to any of our six sense organs [eyes, ears, nose, tongue, body, and mind] has a coherence with their 'apparent karmic consequences' [10] *Nyōze hon makku kyō tō*] – all these nine such qualities (*nyoze*) are equally the ultimate dimension of the real aspect of all dharmas which are present in every instant of life."

To begin with, "such way in which dharmas make themselves present to any of our six sense organs [eyes, ears, nose, tongue, body, and mind]," refers to how the colours and shape of our bodies look. This is said to be the corresponding body of the Tathāgata, as well as his freedom and release from transmigration, karma, and illusion and is also the axiom of phenomena. Next, we have "such an inner quality". This refers to the inner quality of mind. It is the wisdom body of the Tathāgata, which is his wisdom and discernment and is said to be the axiom of relativity (*kū*, *shūnyatā*). Thirdly, we have "such a substance", which is the fundamental reality of what we are. This is the Dharma body of the Tathāgata, the middle way of reality, and the fundamental nature of the Dharma (*hosshin, Dharma-kāya*), which is said to be silence and extinction.

Therefore, these three such qualities are the triple body of the Tathāgata. Since these three such qualities are the triple body of the Tathāgata, you must have thought that they were distantly set apart from the rest of us. Instead, this is something that concerns our very own persons. Those that know this to be so are said to be those who are enlightened by the *Dharma Flower Sutra*. These three such qualities are the basis out of which the other seven such qualities emerge, bringing the total up to ten such qualities.

These ten such qualities, combined with the hundred realms of dharmas [i.e., suffering, craving or wanting, animality, the angry show-off, human equanimity, ecstasy, intellectual seekers, the partially enlightened due to a profound search for the meaning of existence, altruists, and the fully enlightened] – each realm of dharmas being endowed with the other ten, hence a hundred realms of dharmas – become a thousand such qualities. And then, combining again with the three existential spaces, they become the three thousand existential spaces. Thus, by being such multifarious gateways to the Dharma, it could be thought of as the receptacle of the eighty-four thousand particles that make up the human body.

All of this is but the single Dharma of the triple axiom of existence – relativity (*kū, shūnyatā*), temporary phenomenal existence (*ke*), and the middle way of our perception of reality (*chū*). Outside of this triple axiom, there are no gateways to the Dharma. This is the reason why we refer to the ten [psychological] realms of dharmas as the axiom of phenomena (*ke*), the thousand ways in which dharmas make themselves present to our six sense organs – eyes, ears, nose, tongue, body, and mind – as the axiom of relativity (*kū, shūnyatā*), and the three thousand existential spaces as the middle way of reality (*chū*). On account of the triple axiom of phenomena, relativity, and middle way, the hundred realms of dharmas (things), the thousand such qualities, and the three thousand existential spaces become a multifarious gateway to the Dharma.

Consequently, the triple axiom of the three such qualities, at the beginning, and the seven such qualities that come afterwards, are but one triple axiom. Also, from the beginning to the end, they are the intrinsicality that runs through the whole of our being. Then, there is this one item that is imponderable and inexplicable. It is regarded as being the ultimate superlative that runs equally from the beginning to the end of these nine such qualities. This is the *Hon matsu kukyō tō* that we recite.

With the first three such qualities, being the beginning, and the seven last such qualities, being the end, together they make up the ten ways in which dharmas make themselves present to our six sense organs that are the triple axiom of existence within ourselves. This triple axiom refers to relativity (*kū, shūnyatā*), temporary phenomenal existence (*ke*), and the middle way of our perception of reality (*chū*). Since we are saying that this triple axiom is the triple body of the Tathāgata, then apart from the good and evil that sticks to our minds and bodies, there is not even the trace of a dharma to deny that our persons are not, in the long run, the inseparability of the three bodies from the one of the originally enlightened Tathāgata.

Thinking about this in another way, you could say that this is what sentient beings, people who are bewildered, and common mortals are. When we come to understand that this refers to our own persons, then you can say it is the Tathāgata, the enlightenment, the enlightened man (*shōnin*), or a person who knows. If we look upon it with clear understanding, we can say that our persons, in this present life, are finally none other than the manifestation of the originally enlightened Tathāgata. This means that becoming a Buddha is not separate from our persons just as we are.

For instance, because the fields are planted in spring and summer, we are able to collect the harvest in autumn and store it in winter. Likewise, the mind can be worked on in the same way. The time between spring and autumn seems to be drawn out, and we still have to wait most of the year. Similarly, it must seem that it takes an awfully long time, before we attain a stage where we can open our inherent Buddha nature and reveal our enlightenment. But, even so, within one lifetime, it can be shown that our persons are indeed the three bodies that are not separate from the one of the Buddha.

Accordingly, among the people who enter into the path, irrespective as to whether they have superior, middling, or lesser capabilities, all of them equally have the possibility to reveal their inherent Buddha nature in a single lifetime. People with greater propensities, on hearing this teaching, can decidedly unveil their enlightenment to their inherent Buddha nature. Those whose capacities are average may take a day, a month, or even a year before it emerges.

But those of lesser capacities do not need more time, however thoroughly deadlocked they may become. This deadlock is only limited to a lifetime, so that when they come to the point of dying, it is as though they are startled into wakefulness from all the dreams they have had. It is only at that particular moment that their wild ideas that came from the cycle of living and dying, their strangest thoughts, and the reason for their resentments disappear without a trace. Through being startled, returning to the original enlightenment, they experience the Dharma realm and the uttermost joy of everything being silence and illumination. Then they may think of their normal lives as being something rather squalid, now that their persons can be the three bodies that are inseparable from the one of the Tathāgata of the original enlightenment.

Just as there are three sorts of rice plants that ripen in autumn – those that are harvested early, those that are reaped a bit later, and those that are gathered last of all – they are all collected within the one year. In the same way, even though there is difference between those of superior, average, and lesser propensities among humankind, they can all figure out, within a single lifetime, that they are in fact without any duality, the oneness of the fundamental substance of the Buddha Tathāgata.

With regard to the exquisiteness of the fundamental substance of *Myōhō Renge Kyō*, the *Sutra on the White Lotus Flower-like Mechanism of the Utterness of the Dharma*, you may ask: What is its composition?

It is the part of us that is the eight-petalled white lotus flower of the self-existing original mind. This means that the nature of our fundamental substance is *Nam Myōhō Renge Kyō*. Even if there were no name for this sutra, yet at the same time if we had the knowledge of the fundamental substance of our persons, it would in due course turn out to be *Nam Myōhō Renge Kyō*, which is to devote our lives to and found them on (*Nam[u]*) the Utterness of the Dharma (*Myōhō*) [entirety of existence, enlightenment and unenlightenment] permeated by the underlying white lotus flower-like mechanism of the interdependence of cause, concomitancy and effect (*Renge*) in its whereabouts of the ten [psychological] realms of dharmas (*Kyō*).

Due to the Buddha's words, the *Dharma Flower Sutra* names and reveals what the fundamental substance of our persons really is, so that, in fact, at last we are able to become the three bodies that are not separate from the one of the originally enlightened Tathāgata. When we have deeply realised this, all the habitual worries we have had since the primordial infinity, as well as all our resentments and flights of the imagination, will become like the kinder reminiscences of those dreams gone by that have dissipated without a trace.

If you believe this and recite *Nam Myōhō Renge Kyō* just once, becoming aware of what the *Dharma Flower Sutra* entails, it will be as though you were to read through the whole of this sutra with reverence, just as the Buddha expounded it. So, if you were to recite *Nam Myōhō Renge Kyō* ten, a hundred, or a thousand times, it would be as though you had read and recited the whole sutra, the same number of times in the same way as the Dharma teaches. Therefore, you should hold faith in the person who practises in the same way as the Buddha taught. *Nam Myōhō Renge Kyō*.

Nichiren [formal signature]

The Essential of the Teaching of Nichiren Daishōnin

Securing the Peace of the Realm through the Establishment of the Correct Dharma

Risshō ankoku ron
Goshō Shimpen, pp. 234-250

The 16th day of the seventh month of the first year of Bun.nō [1260], at 39 years of age

Once a passing guest [who, in this discourse, represents the majority who have little notion of what the Buddha teachings really are and, at the same time, represents the supreme ruler of Japan at the time of Nichiren] came by, and said with indignant regret to his host: From the last few years up to the present day, the weather has swung from one thing to another, and just as nasty things are happening on the ground, such as hunger, starvation, and contagious diseases that affect everything under the sky and spread over the breadth of the land. Oxen and horses drop down dead in the alleyways, and their skulls and bones litter the roads. More than half of the fellows of humankind have been called away by death. I daresay there is not a single person from any family that is not in mourning.

In the meantime, some people concentrate their faith on the phrase in Zendō's work, *In Praise of the Ship that Carries All*, which says, "The sharp sword of reciting the name of the Buddha of Boundless Light (*Amida, Amitābha*) cuts off all troublesome worries (*bonnō, klesha*), karma, and bitterness." So they go chanting the name of this Lord of the Immaculate Terrain in the West, whereas others depend on the phrase from the vow of the Tathāgata *Master of Healing* (*Yakushi Nyorai, Bhaishajya Guru*) and recite the *Sutra on the Tathāgata of the Immaculate Lapis Lazuli Terrain* in the eastern direction.

Then there are other people who revere the words of the sentence that embraces Utterness, from the *Chapter on the Bodhisattva Sovereign Medicine* (*Yaku' ō, Bhaishajya-rāja*) in the *Dharma Flower*

Sutra (*Myōhō Renge Kyō*), which is a prayer of the Tendai School, and reads, "This sutra is the good medicine for all the illnesses of the world of humankind. Any who hear this sutra will have their ailments eradicated, and there will be neither old age nor death." Or instead they hold faith in the Tendai prayer from the *Sutra on the Wisdom that Ferries Sentient Beings to the Shores of Nirvana*, that deals with the benevolent king who protects his realm, which says, "If one is to read aloud and praise the texts of the wisdom that ferries sentient beings over the sea of living and dying to the shores of nirvana, then the seven hardships will be extinguished, and the seven happinesses will arise. The people will be happily at peace, and the imperial sovereign will be filled with joy." Then ceremonies are arranged, in which a hundred monks read out loud the *Sutra on the Benevolent King*.

There are also some who carry out the rite of exorcism of the esoteric and secret Shingon teaching, in which five vessels of water are in turn sprinkled onto the heads of the participants. Others, of the Zen School, sit in perfect absorption into the one object of meditation, which is to perceive all existence as the emptiness of relativity that in itself is only mind and as unblemished as the full moon.

Then there are people who write out and paste on their doorways the names of the seven kinds of evil spirit that are mentioned in the *Kyaku.onshin Jukyō*, which is a sutra on mantras to exorcise disease, so that these demons do not force their way into people's houses. Again, there are other people who paint images of the five all-powerful bodhisattvas from the *Sutra on the Benevolent King* and stick them on the doors of where they live.

On the other hand, there are people who worship the Shinto gods of the heavens and the deities of the earth. They also organise ceremonies at the four northeast, southeast, southwest, and northwest corners, and the four boundaries of the capital [Kamakura], where the deity who eliminates epidemics and the deity of medicine are enshrined. Also, the sovereign and all those who govern the realm take pity on the common people, and make sure that the existing government is benevolent and upright.

Nevertheless, no matter to whatever extreme we sincerely endeavour to put things right, plague and starvation still pursue their inflamed course forward. Homeless people on the street and vagrants overwhelm the eyes. The dead are such a common sight that those who are stretched out and piled on top of each other look like observation platforms, or when they are laid out side by side, they give the impression of being planks on a bridge.

On careful consideration, we see that the sun and moon follow their regular course and that the spacing between the lines, upon which the jewels of the five planets are placed, is quite normal. The three treasures of the Buddha, consisting of the Buddha, the Dharma, and the clerical community (sō, sangha), are still here in the world. Again, at the time of the fifty-first Emperor Heizei (r. 806-809 CE), there was the oracular vow from the Bodhisattva Hachiman, who swore to safeguard a hundred generations of sovereigns, but we have not yet come as far as the hundredth monarch!

Then why is it the world has fallen into decline so soon? For what reason have the laws of the world become obsolete? To what do we owe these calamities? What is the error that brought them about?

The host replied: On my own I have pondered over what is happening, and I am angry because of my ominous feelings, but I would like to talk about it. Now that you have come to visit me, let us gripe about these things together and see where this conversation leads us.

When people leave home in order to enter upon the path of the Buddha, they expect, by means of the correct Dharma, to open up their inherent Buddha nature. But now even resorting to the Shinto gods is useless. There is not a sign of the majestic virtues of the Buddhas, such as the Buddha of Boundless Light (Amida, Amitābha), the Tathāgata of Healing (Yakushi Nyorai), or the Tathāgata of Universal Sunlight (Dai Nichi Nyorai).

When I take in the reality of the present age in detail, many people, due to their unknowingness, have doubts about their existences to come in the hereafter. As a result, looking up to the sky all around and above them, they swallow their resentment. Then they look downwards to the ground on all four sides and sink into deep apprehension. With my modestly restrained vision, rather like trying to see things through a narrow tube, I have read a number of the sutric texts, in search of an answer.

The people of the world today have turned their backs on what is right and committed themselves to evil. On this account, the spirits of good have abandoned the nation. The persons who are whole and saintly have gone away and are not coming back. Instead, their places have been taken by demons and hateful spirits, who bring about disasters and calamities. I do have to say this, and I cannot help being afraid.

The guest said: I am not the only one who is distressed by the disasters that are happening everywhere under the sky and the calamities that occur throughout the realm. The whole populace deplores them. Now that I have entered the refined surroundings of your house, I hear, for the first time, such an illuminating discourse. From which sutra do you get the concept that when the spirits of good and the people who are sage-like and wise leave the realm, then disasters and calamities come about? I would like to hear your evidence for this.

The host replied: Since the number of these sutras is enormous, there is amply broad material for testimony. It says, in the *Sutra on the Golden Illuminating Light*: "At that time, the four *deva* kings who are the Guardians of the World put the palms of their hands together, and said to the Buddha, 'World Honoured One, if there is a sovereign who is humankind, who, though his kingdom and terrain are in possession of this sutra as yet has not had it propagated, then the sovereign, by putting it aside, separates himself from it and takes no pleasure in hearing its teaching. Neither does he make offerings to it, nor does he solemnly revere it, nor does he express his admiration for it. Even though he sees the monks, nuns, and both the lay men and women who follow the correct Dharma holding to this sutra, this sovereign is incapable of seriously venerating or making offerings to it.

"'As a result, we, Taishaku (*Indra*) and the four *deva* kings, with our respective retinues that are made up of countless *deva* (*ten*), will depart and, on account of this sovereign's refusal to listen to the Utterness of this profound Dharma as well as turning his back on this elixir of immortality, the flow of the correct Dharma in his realm will become lost, and his aura of majesty and authority will come to nothing. Therefore, among the people in his kingdom, denizens of hell, people who act like hungry demons, and others who are almost animals or domineering bullies, will be on the increase. Those persons with human values and those of the *deva* (*ten*) will dwindle away through falling into the troublesome worries (*bonnō, klesha*) of the cycles of living and dying, without having any interest in opening up their inherent Buddha nature.

"'World Honoured One, when we, the four *deva* kings, all our retinues, as well as the army of *yasha* (*yaksha*) who are the protective demons, see that the sovereign does not propagate this correct Dharma, we shall then abandon this realm and terrain, since we have no more mind to go on protecting it. It is not only we who will abandon this sovereign, but all the countless spirits of good, who have protected and kept this realm safe. All of them everywhere will abandon it and just go away.

"'When all the *deva* (*ten*) and spirits of good have departed, various kinds of disasters and calamities will indeed occur in this realm, and its prestige will be lost. Out of the whole of the population, there will be nobody whose mind is healthily directed towards good. There will be nothing but restraint and being hindered, hurting and killing, anger and quarrels. People will slander each other and twist their words to curry another's favour. Their crookedness will involve even those who have done nothing wrong. Plague and disease run through the realm and its terrains. Comets will often appear in the sky, and two suns will shine side by side. Also dust storms and eclipses will blot out the sun and moon, with unusual frequency. There will be black and white arcs across the sky, forewarning of some imminent evil. There will be falling stars, and the earth will tremble; voices will come from inside the wells. There will be cloudbursts of rain and destructive typhoons that come out of season. The people will come up against famine and starvation, because the seedlings do not grow, and other produce cannot mature or become ripe. Adding to the already bitter troubles that burden the populace, hard-faced robbers from other regions will attack and pillage the realm, so that there is nowhere where people can live in safety.'"

In the *Sutra on the Great Assembly of Bodhisattvas*, it says, "When the Dharma of the Buddha really becomes obscured and fades away, then ordinary people and even monks will let their beards, hair, and fingernails grow long. Also the laws of society will be forgotten and fall into disuse. At that time, extremely loud noises will be heard in the sky, making the earth shudder. Everything everywhere will go round and round, like the wheel of a watermill. The walls of cities will crumble and fall down and, at the same time, the houses and dwellings will split apart and collapse. The curative qualities that are inherent in the roots, branches, leaves, petals, or fruit from the plants and trees in the woods will come to an end. With the exception of the six *deva* realms, that are between the realms of the Bonten (*Brahma deva*) and the earth, the seven different kinds of taste [sweet, pungent, sour, bitter, salty, acrid, and insipid], as well as the three pure energies that give life [which are *i*) the life force of the earth to produce vegetation, *ii*) the life-giving force of the Buddha Dharma and the laws of humankind, and *iii*) the life-giving force of humanity and society] will all dwindle and decline, so much so that nothing will remain.

"When all these things happen, there will be no efficacy in all the sane discourses that lead to the understanding of and liberation from living and dying. The flowers and fruits that grow in the earth will become scarce, and their flavours will become unpleasant. All the wells, streams, and ponds will become parched and dried up. Everywhere all the ground will become salty, brackish, and furrowed, and cracks will open up between the hillocks. All the mountains will be scorched and set ablaze, and the dragons of the skies will not send down rain. The seedlings, crops, and trees will shrivel and die; everything that is alive will wither and die; no new vegetation will ever grow again. Due to whirlwinds caused by the heat, dust will rain down, and it will get so dark that the brightness of the sun and moon will be blotted out.

"In all the four directions, the water will evaporate, and there will be drought. Time and time again, evil omens will make their appearance. The ten paths of bad karma, as well as covetousness and indulging in it, and that inborn angry hatred and the stupidity of wanting to remain ignorant – all these defects will be on the increase."

[The ten paths are the three physical evils of *i*) taking life, *ii*) stealing, and *iii*) wrongful sexual relations, as well as the four evils of speech, which are *i*) telling lies that are really fantasies, *ii*) engaging in duplicity, *iii*) deceiving, and *iv*) defaming, and the three evils of mind – *i*) greed, *ii*) anger, and *iii*) stupidity.]

"Sentient beings, on looking at their fathers and mothers, will think no more of them than do the hornless river deer. The lifespan, the physical strength of sentient beings, as well as their feeling to be able to enjoy life with dignity, will become disconnected from the normal pleasures of humankind, and the *deva* (*ten*) and all sentient beings everywhere will lapse into the courses of wrongdoing.

"Consequently, the karma of wrongdoing of the bad sovereign and the dissolute monks will break down and destroy the correct Dharma of the Buddha, thus handicapping and diminishing the paths of people being reborn among humankind or in the realms of the *deva* (*ten*). Then all the *deva* (*ten*) and spirits of good, who would normally have compassion for and sympathise with the sentient beings who are subjects of this king, will abandon this filthily evil country and look towards other places to go."

In the *Sutra on the Benevolent King*, it says, "When the realm becomes disorganised, it is due to the demons and the archetypal spirits who are first in disorder. The reason for the demons and spirits being out of control is because the populace has become anarchical. Marauders come into the realm and lay it waste; the ordinary people are faced with the despair of annihilation. The ministers, the ruling class, the prince that is heir to the throne, and princes of royal blood all squabble with each other over what is right and wrong. There are dreadful abnormal things happening in the sky and on the ground. The twenty-eight constellations [of ancient Chinese astronomy], the paths of stars as well as those of the sun and the moon, are all out of time and have lost their proper order. Also, there are many people who have become rebels."

Then it goes on to say, "I am now, with the five kinds of vision [that of *i*) humankind, *ii*) the *deva* (*ten*), *iii*) wisdom of the individual vehicle, *iv*) vision of the bodhisattvas, and *v*) that of Buddhas], clearly able to see the past, present, and future. As for all the sovereigns of nations, they all became emperors, kings or rulers, because they attended on five hundred Buddhas in former existences. It is on account of this meritorious virtue that all the men who are sage-like and all those who have attained the supreme rewards of the individual vehicle (*arhat*) strive to do what is beneficial for the rulers of the countries where they were born. But if there is a time when the blessedness of the rulers comes to an end, all the sage-like men will abandon such a sovereign and depart. If the men that are sage-like do depart, then the seven calamities are certain to come about."

[These seven calamities are *i*) the sun and moon neither appearing at the right time nor being on course, *ii*) the constellations appearing in the wrong order; *iii*) everywhere there being conflagrations of different sorts, *iv*) heavy rainfall and floods, *v*) disasters caused by great winds, *vi*) heaven and earth rising and falling, *vii*) marauders attacking from all directions.]

It says, in the *Sutra on the Master of Healing*, "If the correct Dharma is slandered in the realms and domains of anointed kings and the ruling warrior caste (*kshatriya*), calamities will occur, such as contagious diseases among the populace, incursive aggressions from other countries, rebellion and treachery within their own domains, ominous changes in the stars and constellations, eclipses of the sun and moon or their radiance suddenly becoming less bright, winds and downpours out of the proper season, and also no rain during the period of the monsoon."

In the *Sutra on the Benevolent King*, the Buddha says to the Sovereign Hashinoku (*Prasenajit*): "Great King, the places where people have been converted to my teaching now amount to a hundred billion worlds of Mount Sumeru. Again, each Mount Sumeru has, under its skies, four continents. In the southern continent (*Ichi.enbudai, Jambudvîpa*), which is the world of humankind, there are sixteen great nations, five hundred medium-sized nations, and ten thousand smaller nations."

[These Mount Sumerus are the central mountains of each world system. At the top is the heaven of Taishaku (*Indra*) and below are the four *deva* kings. Around this central mountain are eight circles of mountains, and between them are eight seas. Each world system has its own sun and moon.]

"In these realms and domains, there are seven calamities to be feared. Therefore, all the sovereigns of these nations know that when these calamities occur, they are real dangers. In fact, what are these calamities?

"It is when the sun and the moon move off their regular paths, when the seasons come in the wrong order, when there appears a sun that is red throughout the whole day, or a sun that appears to be black, or when there are one, two, three, four, or five suns appearing at the same time, when there is an eclipse of the sun without a corona, or when the sun appears in either one, two, three, four, or five layers – all of these are counted as the first calamity.

"When the twenty-eight constellations are not on their regular courses, also when the Golden Stars, the Yard Broom-shaped Stars, the Wheel Stars, the Demon Star, the Fire Star, the Water Star, the Wind Stars, the Ladle-shaped Stars, both the Northern and Southern Dippers, all the stars that astrologically govern the Lord of the Realm, the three royal aides and the hundred civil and military officials, appear in a different way from what they usually do – then all of this constitutes the second calamity.

"Then we come to those huge conflagrations that rage throughout the realm and burn tens of thousands of people to death. Either these fires are caused by demons, or their origins are unknown, or they are caused by dragons or falling thunderbolts. There are fires caused by the *deva* (*ten*), or something from the sky. Other fires are caused by the mountain spirits who induce volcanoes to erupt. Then there are those fires that are caused by the wilfulness or the negligence of humankind. There are raging fires that spontaneously break out in the forests. Also there are fires that are set alight by marauders and arsonists. Such strange and uncanny events are taken to be the third calamity.

"When enormous floods wash away and drown the people, when the seasons come in the opposite order with monsoon rains in wintertime and snowfalls in the summer, when in winter there are lightning flashes and the deafening booms of noisy thunder, also when there are ice, frost, and hailstorms in June, or when it pours down red water, black water, or a rain that is bluish green, when mountains of earth and stone come precipitating down, or when it rains sand, pebbles and stones, when the course of the rivers flows backwards, when mountains are afloat and river boulders are swept away, when such peculiar seasons come about – then it is the fourth of the seven catastrophes.

"When huge winds blow many people to their deaths, and the realm, its domains, its mountains, its rivers, its trees and shrubs are also at the same time blown into annihilation, then when typhoons rage out of season and black winds, red winds, winds that blow bluish green, winds that whirl towards the sky, winds that rake the earth, fiery hot winds, and winds that are sopping wet – when such out of the ordinary winds occur, then it is the fifth calamity.

"When the heavens over the earth, on which the realm and its domains stand, become so overbearingly hot, so that air feels like rising flames, then all the vegetation shrivels up, and the five staple grains fail to grow, the soil on the ground is scorched red hot, and the people can no longer exist – when such monstrosities occur, it means that the sixth calamity has come.

"Finally, when enemies emerge from the four quarters to attack and invade the realm, there are also traitorous rebels causing troubles within it. There will then be criminals who will add to the wretchedness of the people, through causing disasters of fire, water, wind, as well as other demoniacal acts. The people are subjected to madness and confusion, and the clash of arms and plunder will break out everywhere. When tragedies of this kind occur, it is the seventh calamity."

It says in the *Sutra on the Great Assembly of Bodhisattvas*: "Suppose there were a sovereign of a realm, who through countless lifetimes had always given alms as unsullied charity, observed the precepts, and acted with the wisdom and discernment of the Buddha teaching. One day, this sovereign became aware that the correct Dharma was dwindling away, but he just stood by and did nothing to support or protect it. In this way, all the uncountable good seeds that he had planted during numerous lives would be completely destroyed and lost forever. His kingdom would become a place where the three unfortunate circumstances would come about. The first of these misfortunes is the rising prices of staple grains; the second is war; and the third is contagious disease.

"All the spirits of good everywhere in this realm will reject it and go somewhere else. Then, when this sovereign tries to instruct or give orders, no one will follow or obey him. There will be continual aggressions and other provocations from neighbouring states. Fierce fires are likely to break out for no apparent reason. There will be vicious winds, and enormous downpours of rain and floods will increase, so that the people are blown about by storms and washed away by floods. The paternal and maternal relatives of the monarch will plot together to bring about his downfall. After this, the sovereign will have a severe illness and, when his lifespan has come to its end, he will be reborn in one of the larger hells. Likewise, a similar destiny will await the consort of the sovereign, the princes, the ministers of state, the lords of the cities, the military leaders, the protectors of the regions, and the government officials."

The implications of these quotations from the *Sutra on the Golden Illuminating Light*, the *Sutra on the Great Assembly of Bodhisattvas*, the *Sutra on the Benevolent King*, and the *Sutra on the Tathāgata Master of Healing* are very clear indeed. Not one person in ten thousand could have doubts about them.

However, there are those monks who are incapable of discerning what the correct teaching really is, whose blindness and bewilderment have made them hold faith in distorting and incomplete doctrines such as the Nembutsu teaching. Because of the influence that their distorting doctrines have on people of all classes, the people then are inclined to turn away from and abandon all the sutras that are not of the Nembutsu School and have lost any resolve to protect the correct Dharma. Consequently, all the spirits of good and the people who are sage-like will abandon the realm and leave the places where they used to dwell. As a result, evil demons and people who follow distorting and incomplete teachings bring about disasters and calamities on the people.

The guest flushed angrily, and said: The Emperor Kō Mei (r. 57-75 CE) of the latter Kan (*Han*) Dynasty, who revealed the doctrine, saw a golden personage in a dream. When the emperor had realised that this person was the Buddha, he had the Buddha teaching brought to China on the backs of white horses. In Japan, after Prince Shōtoku had subjugated the anti-Buddhist rebellion of Mononobe no Moriya, he then set about building *stupas* and temples throughout the land for the prosperity of the Buddha teaching. From that time onwards, from the single person of the emperor down to the tens of thousands of ordinary people, Buddha images have been venerated and devotion has been paid to the sutric texts.

Starting with the Enryakuji Temple on Mount Hiei, the Onjōji, and Eastern Temples in Nara the southern capital, then all over the country surrounded by the four seas, including the five home provinces and the seven districts that are controlled directly by the emperor, the sutras and teachings of the Buddha are like the mesh of stars arrayed across the sky, and temples and monasteries are like the clouds draped over our heads. The wise monks who adhere to the tradition of Sharihotsu (*Shariputra*) continue their practice of contemplation, meditating on the Dharma, and those who hold to the direction of Kakuroku (*Haklenayashas*) devote themselves to the doctrinal teachings.

How can anyone say that the Buddha teaching of a lifetime has become petty and cramped, or that the three treasures of the Buddha, Dharma, and the clerical community (sō, sangha) have fallen into decline? If you have evidence to support what you say, I would like to hear your reasoning and all the details.

The host said reprovingly to his guest: The tiled roofs of temples stand in row upon row, and the eaves of the sutra storehouses are lined up one after another. Monks are as numerous as bamboo plants or reeds, and members of the clerical community (sō, sangha) are as common as rice or hemp seedlings. What is more, all these monks and temples have been highly regarded year after year since ancient times, and again each day they are venerated and honoured anew.

Nevertheless, teachers of the Dharma have become flatterers of power and wealth who deviously confuse the people about what ethics and human relationships ought to be. The sovereign and his ministers lack the depth of understanding to be able to distinguish between what is correct and what is distorting and incomplete.

In the *Sutra on the Benevolent King*, it says, "There are many bad monks, many of whom seek worldly fame for their own profit. Now and then, they appear before the sovereign, the heir apparent, and other princes. These monks teach their own variety of the Buddha Dharma that is contrary to the correct teaching. In turn, these sermons become the cause and complementary causes for the ruin of the state. The sovereign indiscriminately listens to these teachings, which are fabricated, nonsensical legislation that have nothing to do with the Buddha precepts. These are the causes and circumstances that destroy the Buddha teaching and bring about the collapse of the realm."

Again, we have, in the *Sutra on the Buddha's Passing over to Nirvana*, "Bodhisattvas, do not let mad elephants in your mind terrify you. What ought to scare your thoughts is an evil acquaintance. Even though you may be killed by a mad elephant, it will not be as bad as falling into one of these evil paths [of the hells, hungry demons, or the realm of animality]. If you are killed on account of an evil friend, then you are most likely to fall down into one of these unfortunate paths."

In the *Dharma Flower Sutra* (*Hokke-kyō*), we have the following: "The monks in that age when things are bad will, through their incomplete and distorted insight, become devious flatterers. They will say they have reached enlightenment when they have attained nothing of the sort, and their minds will be full of conceit and pride. There will also be people wearing the three regulation garments of monks, living like hermits who have forsaken the world. They will say that they are the ones who practise the correct path. Yet, at the same time, they will hold ordinary people in contempt. There will also be other monks who, with an eye for their own nourishment and personal gain, will expound the Dharma to the laity and be respected and venerated by society, as though they had attained the supreme reward of the individual vehicle (*arhat*), which includes the six reaches of the mind [i.e., *i*) the sight of a *deva* (*ten*), *ii*) the hearing of a *deva* (*ten*), *iii*) the ability to penetrate the minds of other people, *iv*) to be able to understand the inherent karma of sentient beings, *v*) to be able to manifest oneself according to the propensities of sentient beings as well as being able to mentally travel elsewhere, and *vi*) the ability to cut off all troublesome worries (*bonnō, klesha*)]."

This text then continues, until, "These evil monks will always, in some way or another, be present among the people, seeking to denigrate those who hold to the correct Dharma. They will also turn to the rulers of nations, great ministers, Brahmins, lay supporters of the Buddha teaching, and also other monks, in order to vilify and make evil remarks about those who follow the correct way, by saying that such persons who do follow the correct Buddha path have distorting and unwholesome views that are outside the Buddha Dharma.

"Throughout the long filthy lapse of time that is the degenerate age, there will be many different things to be afraid of. There will be evil demons who will take possession of other persons, in order to slander and besmirch and humiliate those who follow the correct Dharma. Bad monks of this turgid age, who do not understand the expedient means of the Buddha teaching or the

Buddha Dharma, will hurl foul language at those who are on the correct path, as well as having them marginalised or banished time and time again."

In the *Sutra on the Buddha's Passing over to Nirvana*, it says: "After my passing over into extinction, when uncountable hundreds of years have gone by, those who hold to the fourfold path of sage-like persons – who *i*) rely on the Dharma and not on the person who teaches it, *ii*) who rely on the significance and not on the wording, *iii*) who rely on wisdom and not on knowledge, and *iv*) who rely on the sutra of the ultimate implication and not on the sutras whose significance is incomplete – all those persons everywhere will have passed over into complete extinction. After the correct phase of the Dharma has ended and the formal phase of superficial appearances has already begun, there will be monks who give the impression that they are holding to the precepts, but they will be hardly reading or reciting the sutras at all. They will be greedy and epicurean about the food that nourishes and fattens their bodies.

"Although they may wear the robes of a monk, they will have the sharp eye of a huntsman in seeking out those who give alms, just as a cat stalks a mouse. These monks are forever dwelling upon the same litany, saying that they have attained the supreme reward of the individual vehicle (*arhat*). Outwardly they will appear to be wise and good but inwardly they will be consumed with greed and jealousy. When they are asked to say something about the Dharma, they will act dumb, like the Brahmins who have made the vow of silence. They may appear to be monks who have diligently brought their minds and passions to quietude, but these are only appearances. In actual fact, they are not monks at all. Also, by being completely gobbled up by their own incomplete and misguided ways of seeing things, they revile and slander the correct Dharma."

If we look at the world around us, as it is seen according to these sutric references, then indeed the situation is just as it has been described. If we do not admonish these counteractive and distorting monks, how can anything be done to correct things?

The guest, getting more outraged than ever, said: An enlightened sovereign models his government according to the principles of heaven and earth. The sage-like man (*shōnin*), through his capacity to see into what is right or wrong, is able to set the world in order. As for the monks in the world, people throughout the land take refuge in them and have faith in them. If they were such evil monks, an enlightened sovereign would not put his trust in them. Also, if these monks were not saintly, virtuous people with understanding, people would not look up to them. Now, since people of virtue and wisdom do profoundly revere these monks, they must be, as you already know, religious dignitaries of exceptional virtue and wisdom.

How can you severely slander them, by throwing up such silly nonsense? To whom are you referring, when you speak about monks being degenerate? I would like to hear what you really mean.

The host said: When the Emperor Go-Toba (r. 1184-1198 CE) was on the throne, there was a monk called Hōnen who compiled *The Only Choice is the Nembutsu School, which is the Original Vow of the Buddha of Boundless Light* (*Amida, Amitābha*), a work that brought so much bewilderment to sentient beings everywhere throughout the ten directions. The text of *The Only Choice* quotes the Teacher of Contemplation, Dōshaku (*Dao Chao*) of the Tō (*Tang*) Dynasty, as saying, "He makes a distinction between the two gateways to enlightenment, one being the path that is sage-like [individuating and non-schizophrenic], and the other being the immaculate terrain. People should abandon the path that is sage-like and take the correct step of putting their faith in the immaculate terrain. To begin with, the path that is sage-like is made up of two gateways to enlightenment, the individual vehicle (*shōjō, hīnayāna*) and the universal vehicle (*daijō, mahāyāna*)."

The text continues, until, "On careful consideration, the path that is sage-like also includes the esoteric teachings, both the provisional and the real universal vehicles, as well as the Dharma Flower. If that is so, then all the eight schools of the present day – Shingon, Zen, Tendai, Kegon, Sanron, Hossō, Jiron, and Sharon – are also the path that is sage-like and should be set aside.

"The Teacher of the Dharma, Donran (*Tan Luan*, 476-542 CE), in his *Annotations on Being Reborn in the Immaculate Terrain*, expressed these concepts in the following manner, 'On carefully reading *The Options to be made by Bodhisattvas at the Tenth Stage of Abiding in the Faith* by the Bodhisattva Nāgārjuna (*Ryūju*), it suggests that there are two sorts of practice for those bodhisattvas who aspire to the state where there is no retrogression. One is the difficult path; the second is the easier path.' Out of these two paths, the one that is difficult to practise is the one that is sage-like. The other that is the easier practice is the gateway to enlightenment through the immaculate terrain. First those that wish to study the practice of the immaculate terrain must understand this point. Even though they may have studied the gateway to enlightenment of the path that is sage-like, but if they are determined to practise this gateway to enlightenment through the immaculate terrain, they must necessarily renounce the path that is sage-like and give their complete trust to that of the immaculate terrain."

Again Hōnen says, "The Chinese monk Zendō (*Shan Dao*, 618-681 CE), in his *Devout Praise of being Reborn in the Immaculate Terrain*, establishes that there are two kinds of practice, the Nembutsu that is the correct one, and the other, a miscellany that is not right. This miscellany of practices should be discarded and one should devote oneself to the correct practice of the Nembutsu. Essentially, with regard to the miscellany of practices of reading and reciting sutras, apart from the *Sutra on Contemplating the Buddha of Infinite Life* (*Amida, Amitāyus*) and the other two sutras of the immaculate terrain, the *Sutra on the Buddha of Infinite Life* (*Amitāyus*), and *The Buddha Expounds the Sutra on the Buddha of Boundless Light* (*Amida, Amitābha*), all other reading, reciting, or holding to any universal vehicle (*daijō, mahāyāna*), individual vehicle (*shōjō, hīnayāna*), or exoteric or esoteric sutra anywhere, is to be defined as the practice of reading and reciting sutras wrongly. With regard to the third practice of wrongful worship, with the sole exception of devoutly worshipping the Buddha of Boundless Light (*Amida, Amitābha*), all the veneration and devout worship of all the Buddhas, bodhisattvas, and *deva* (*ten*) who are elsewhere or amongst humankind, are to be regarded as practices of devout worship that are wrong. With regard to this passage, I [Hōnen] tell myself that I must definitely renounce the medley of wrongful teachings and cultivate the practices of the Nembutsu, to the exclusion of all others. Therefore, should one not practise the Nembutsu teachings, which specify that, out of a hundred practitioners, a hundred will be reborn in the Heaven of Ultimate Bliss of the Buddha of Boundless Light (*Amida, Amitābha*), instead of hanging on to the miscellany of disciplines and practices that cannot enlighten one person in a thousand? Fellow practitioners, you should ponder this very carefully."

Hōnen goes on to say, "In the inventory of the sutras selected for the Jōgen Treasury, it starts with the six hundred fascicles of the *Universal Wisdom that Carries Beings over to the Shores of Nirvana* and ends with the *Sutra of the Eternal Existence of the Dharma*, including all the exoteric and esoteric sutras of the universal vehicle (*daijō, mahāyāna*), which together amount to six hundred thirty volumes that are made up of two thousand eight hundred eighty-three fascicles. All of these texts must be substituted by the recitation of the single phrase of the universal vehicle (*Namu Amida Butsu*)."

Furthermore, Hōnen says, "Indeed you should realise that, before the Buddha taught the Dharma in accordance with the propensities of his listeners, he propounded for the time being the two gateways to enlightenment of practices for minds that were ordered by contemplation and the minds of ordinary people, who had not the discipline of contemplation. Later, when the Buddha taught from the standpoint of his own enlightenment, he then stopped teaching these two gateways. But the Buddha teaching, having once been made known, can never be taken back. This is the single gateway to enlightenment of bearing in mind the doctrine of the Nembutsu."

Again Hōnen states, "The text that says practitioners of the Nembutsu School must be equipped with the three states of mind that are the assured ways of reaching the immaculate terrain [*i*) the perfect sincerity to do so, *ii*) the profound resolve to reach it, and *iii*) the decision to turn one's merit over to all sentient beings] is to be found in the *Sutra on Contemplating the Buddha of Infinite Life*. Zendō also says, in his commentary on the same sutra, 'The question is asked. If a person's understanding and practice are different from the Nembutsu teachings, would he not be a perverse follower of the miscellany of other teachings, and, how can we prevent him from creating difficulties through his erroneous, divergent views?' Evil people like this, who have divergent understanding and different practices, are similar to the gangs of thugs who call back travellers that have set out on one part or two parts of their journey to the immaculate terrain. What I mean to say is that all the divergent understandings, various studies, and distinct points of view, which are referred to in these passages, all point to the gateways of the path that is sage-like."

Finally, in the text where Hōnen sums up his point of view, he says, "For those who wish to be quickly released from the cycles of living and dying, there are the two prevailing dharmas of the correct Dharma of the immaculate terrain and the other path that is sage-like. They should put the gateway to the Dharma of the path that is sage-like aside and enter through the Dharma gateway of the immaculate terrain. For any who wish to pass through the gateway to the Dharma of the immaculate terrain, they should abandon all the miscellaneous practices, and take refuge in the immaculate terrain."

On looking at these passages more closely, we see that Hōnen, through making misrepresentations from Donran, Dōshaku, and Zendō, establishes classifications, such as the path that is enlightened, the immaculate terrain, a practice that is difficult, and a practice that is easier. He then bunches together all the six hundred thirty-seven volumes, which comprise two thousand eighty-three fascicles, which constitute a lifetime of Buddha teaching of the universal vehicle (*daijō, mahāyāna*).

This also includes the *Dharma Flower Sutra* (*Myōhō Renge Kyō*), the Tantric teachings of the Shingon School, which all go under the label of the miscellaneous teachings, the practices that are difficult to carry out, together with all the Buddhas, bodhisattvas, and *deva* (*ten*) of the heavenly and human realms – which Hōnen then incites people to either throw them all away, close them, put them aside, or abandon them entirely. Nearly everybody has been led into following what is not true, on account of these injunctions.

In addition to this, he points to the monks that are sage-like, from the three countries of India, China, and Japan, along with all the disciples of the Buddha teaching, and calls them a gang of thugs who are obstructing the practice and cultivation of the Nembutsu doctrine. Thus he makes people insult and speak ill of these sage-like personages.

To be a little more precise, the three sutras of the Nembutsu School [*i*) *The Sutra on the Adornments of the Immaculate Terrain*, *ii*) *The Sutra on the Buddha of Infinite Life*, and *iii*) *The Sutra on the Buddha of Boundless Light* (*Amida, Amitābha*)] contradict the original vow of the Buddha of Boundless Light (*Amida, Amitābha*) to save all beings, by saying that, "through taking refuge in and reciting the name of the Buddha of Boundless Light (*Amida, Amitābha*), everybody can be reborn in the immaculate terrain of ultimate bliss, except those who have committed the five deadly sins [of *i*) killing one's father, *ii*) killing one's mother, *iii*) killing an arhat, *iv*) shedding the blood of a Buddha, and *v*) destroying the harmony of the clerical community (*sō, sangha*)], or those who slander the correct Dharma."

From a more distant standpoint, the Nembutsu School seems to be misguided over the text of Shākyamuni's severe warning in the *Second Chapter of the Dharma Flower Sutra*, which is the very essence of the five periods [*i*) the Flower Garland, *ii*) the Doctrine of the Individual Vehicle, *iii*) the Equally Broad Doctrine, *iv*) the Wisdom Teachings, and *v*) the period of the Dharma Flower and Nirvana sutras] which constitute a lifetime of the Buddha's instruction. This passage says, "If a person does not hold faith in this Sutra and destructively reviles it", and the text then continues, until, "at the end of this person's life he will fall into the hell of incessant suffering".

Now that we have reached the present age that is the final era of the Dharma of Shākyamuni (*mappō*), there is nobody around who is supremely virtuous, wise, and is a person that is enlightened. Practically all the people have been led astray by the distorting and incomplete doctrine of Hōnen, so that each one has arrived at his own dark crossroad, because the direct path to become a Buddha has been forgotten.

It is so sad that nobody can shake the people out of their deluded religious fantasies, and how painful it is to see that more and more people attach themselves to distorting and incomplete faiths. From the sovereign down to the myriads of ordinary people, everybody thinks that there are no other sutras outside the three volumes that are used by the School of the Immaculate Terrain. As for the Buddha, everyone thinks there can be no other than the Buddha of Boundless Light (*Amida, Amitābha*), with his two attendant bodhisattvas, the Bodhisattva Perceiving the Sounds of the Existential Dimensions (*Kanzeon, Avalokiteshvara*), and the Bodhisattva He Who has Arrived at Enormous Strength (*Mahāsthāmaprāpta, Seishi*), which make up the trinity that is venerated by the School of the Immaculate Terrain.

Formerly, there were monks like Dengyō (*Dengyō Daishi*), Gishin, Jikaku, and Chishō, who either crossed over ten thousand leagues of ocean in order to find the teachings that are enlightened, or who travelled all around the mountains and rivers of Japan, searching for venerated Buddha images so that they might acquire them. In order that they might be enshrined, they built temples on the tops of high places, or else they established hermitages at the bottom of deep valleys, where these representations of holiness could be honoured with faith.

Both the Buddhas, Shākyamuni who is enshrined in the western pagoda of the Enryakuji Temple on Mount Hiei, along with the Tathāgata Master of Healing (*Yakushi*) who is placed in the Central Hall of the eastern pagoda of the same temple, radiated their majestic light from the living sum total of the whole of the past onwards into the ages to come. Also the Bodhisattva *Receptacle of the Relativity of Happiness and Wisdom* (*Kokūzō, Ākāsagarbha*), enshrined in the Hannyadani Temple, and the Bodhisattva Repository of the Earth (*Jizō, Ksitīgarbha*) [who was entrusted by Shākyamuni to save people], installed in the Kaishindani Temple, were both an enormous benefit that reached beyond our present existence to our lives in the hereafter. The reason for this was that the rulers of the nation made the contribution of either one village or one county, in order to keep the lamps before the Buddha images burning, whereas the lords of the manors made offerings of fields and rice paddies, so as to help the maintenance of temples and monasteries.

Because of this book, *The Only Choice*, by Hōnen, Shākyamuni, the Lord of the Teaching for the world we live in, has been forgotten by the people, and all honour has been attributed to the Buddha of Boundless Light (*Amida, Amitābha*), the Buddha of the western direction. All of those who had been entrusted with the assignment of the Buddha, for the formal period of the Dharma, have been cast aside, and all the significance of the Tathāgata Master of Healing (*Yakushi Nyorai, Bhaishajya Guru*)), has been neglected. All faith and devotion is particularly directed towards the four fascicles of the three volumes that make up the sutras of the School of the Immaculate Terrain, to the detriment of Shākyamuni's lifetime of teachings that are enlightened, which have ended up as though they were nothing at all.

Consequently, if the places of worship are not dedicated to the Buddha of Boundless Light (*Amida, Amitābha*), people will not make offerings to the Buddha images enshrined inside them. If there are no monks who recite the Nembutsu (*Namu Amida Butsu*), any thought of making donations to temples is soon forgotten. Hence the halls of the Buddha are in a tumble-down state, their roofs are covered with so much moss that they look like pine trees. Since hardly any monks live there, no smoke rises from between the tiles. The monks' living quarters are also in a state of dilapidation, with their courtyards thick with weeds that are sodden, soggy with the wettest of dews.

Even though things have come to this pass, there seems to be nobody who cares enough about the Dharma to try to protect it, or who would make an effort to restore these temples. Since the monks of the clerical community (*sō, sangha*) have left and are not coming back, the spirits of good who gave them protection have also departed and are unlikely to return. These unhappy events are entirely due to *The Only Choice* of Hōnen. What is so sad about all this is that, during the past ten years or so, hundreds, thousands, or even tens of thousands of people, due to their demonic association with Hōnen, have been completely led astray, with regard to the Buddha Dharma. Because the people take to a teaching that is no more than a doctrinal sideshow, they forget what the real teaching is.

How can the spirits of good not be enraged? Since the people have abandoned the all-inclusive teachings and favoured a doctrine that is less than complete, how can they not be spooked by evil presences? Instead of offering up myriads of prayers to remedy these calamities, the best thing to do would be to prohibit this Nembutsu teaching that is the sole source of our misfortunes.

This time, on hearing how the host had branded Hōnen as an evil monk and the cause of the present calamities, the expression on the guest's face became even more agitated, as he said: Because our Original Teacher Shākyamuni expounded the three volumes of the sutras on the immaculate terrain, we have the teacher of the Dharma, Donran, abandoning the three explanatory discourses of Nāgārjuna (*Ryūju*) and also the discourse of the Bodhisattvas Seshin (*Vasubhandu*) and Daiba (*Kanadeva*), so that he could dedicate his entire faith to the teaching of the immaculate terrain. The Master of Contemplation Dōshaku renounced his extensive study and practice of the *Sutra on the Buddha's Passing over to Nirvana* and then wholeheartedly set about propagating the doctrine of the Buddha of Boundless Light's (*Amida, Amitābha*) Heaven of Ultimate Bliss in the western region. The Venerable Abbot Zendō discarded the miscellaneous practices and concentrated on the cultivation of the practice of the immaculate terrain. The Director of Monks Eshin collated the doctrinal essence of all the sutras and proclaimed that they all imply the single practice of the Nembutsu. Indeed such was the manner that these monks fervently venerated the Buddha of Boundless Light (*Amida, Amitābha*) that they were able to bring about the rebirth of countless individuals in the immaculate terrain.

I should also like to point out that the wise Hōnen entered the Tendai Monastery on Mount Hiei, when he was a child. At the age of seventeen, he had read through all the literary works of Tendai (*T'ien T'ai*), the *Recondite Significance of the Dharma Flower*, the *Textual Explanation of the Dharma Flower* (*Hokke Mongu*), and the *Universal Desistance from Troublesome Worries in order to See Clearly* (*Maka Shikan*). In addition to this, he had also read all the explanatory works of Myōraku (Miao-lo), *Explanatory Notes of the Recondite Significance of the Dharma Flower, Notes on the Textual Explanation of the Dharma Flower,* and the *Broad Elucidation to Support the Practice of the Universal Desistance from Troublesome Worries in order to See Clearly.* All these works amount to sixty fascicles. At the same time, he had looked into the teachings of the eight schools and had grasped the essential meaning of all of them. Apart from this, he had read through all the sutras and discourses seven times and had made a study of all the general commentaries, critical explanations, and biographies related to the Buddha teaching. His wisdom was equal to the sun and moon, and his virtue surpassed the earlier teachers.

In spite of all this, he was confused over what direction should be taken, in order to be free of the troublesome worries (*bonnō, klesha*) of mundane existence; also he was unable to comprehend the implications of nirvana. Because of this, Hōnen read all the sutras and discourses he was able to. He deeply considered them in every detail, pondered over them in depth, and deliberated over them in the farthest reaches of his mind. In the end, he put all the sutras aside and exclusively dedicated his practice to the reciting of the Nembutsu.

Furthermore, Hōnen's decision was confirmed through his seeing Zendō in a dream, which he took to be an answer to a prayer. From then on, Hōnen propagated the teaching of the immaculate terrain throughout the length and breadth of Japan, to friends, relatives, and strangers. Later on, people looked up to Hōnen as the manifestation of the Bodhisattva Seishi [who, in the iconography of the Immaculate Terrain School, stands with the Bodhisattva Kannon on either side of the Buddha of Boundless Light (*Amida, Amitābha*)], or he was seen as the reincarnation of Zendō. Irrespective of whether people were of high or low birth, all of them everywhere inclined their heads towards Hōnen in respect; men and women throughout Japan fervently sought after him for his teaching.

Ever since that time, springs and autumns have followed one another; sparkling, hoary winters have accumulated one on top of another. Nevertheless, you say that the causes of our calamities are due to Hōnen, yet you sacrilegiously marginalise the teachings of Shākyamuni, who expounded the Nembutsu doctrine, and you deliberately berate the texts that concern the Buddha of Boundless Light (*Amida, Amitābha*). Why do you assign the origin of the calamities of recent years to the past age of the saintly Hōnen? You do all you can to vilify the former teachers Dōnran, Dōshaku and Dōzen of the School of the Immaculate Terrain, and, to make matters worse, you heap abuse on Hōnen the sage. From the way you talk and behave, it seems that you are blowing between the hairs on a fur, in order to reveal a cut or flaw in the leather, or knowingly snipping at the pelt with scissors, to see if any blood will come out. From ancient times up to the present, such evil speech has never been heard. It is really frightening and you should be more thoughtful. If you build up the karma of slander, how can you expect to avoid being punished? I am afraid even to sit in front of you. I think I must pick up my staff and take my leave!

The host smiled, so to restrain his guest from leaving, and then went on to say: You know the insects that cut the knotweed [Polygonum] are unaware of its salty, acrid taste; people who spend a long time in lavatories forget their stench. In the same way, after having lived for so many years with a distorting and incomplete Buddha teaching, when you hear the good words of the real truth, you think they are just evil talk. You refer to an individual like Hōnen as being saintly, who slanders the Dharma and turns his back on the real intention of the Buddha. By doubting a correct teacher, you brand him as an evil monk. Your bewilderment is indeed profound, and not knowing what you are about is no shallow matter at all. If you would like to hear how this confusion came about, then we can discuss the sequence of events in detail.

The course of Shākyamuni's lifetime of expounding the Dharma can be apportioned to the five doctrinal periods of *i*) the Flower Garland, *ii*) the Doctrinal Period of the Individual Vehicle (*Agon, Āgama*), *iii*) the Equally Broad, *iv*) the Wisdom, and *v*) the Dharma Flower Period. The order of these periods has already been justified by Tendai, and the distinction between the provisional and real teachings is quite clear. Nevertheless, since the founders of the School of the Immaculate Terrain, Donran, Dōshaku, and Zendō, were so attached to the provisional doctrines, they had entirely forgotten about the real teaching. The practice and teaching of these founders was according to those sutras that were expounded by Shākyamuni during a period of forty years, which represent the first half of his practice. The second half, which consisted of the eight years the Buddha expounded the *Dharma Flower Sutra* (*Myōhō Renge Kyō*), were just thrown away. Donran, Dōshaku, and Zendō were not yet aware of the utter depth of the Buddha teaching.

Hōnen was indeed the inheritor of the teaching of Donran, Dōshaku, and Zendō, but he was ignorant of the origins of what they taught. What he did not know was that his precursors were confused over the provisional and the real teachings, which was to add uncleanliness to filth and pile wrong on top of wrong. The reason for saying this is that, with regard to all the sutras of the universal vehicle (*daijō, mahāyāna*), which are two thousand eight hundred fascicles contained in six hundred thirty-seven volumes, along with all the Buddhas, bodhisattvas, and all the *deva* (*ten*) in their celestial and terrestrial dimensions of existence, Hōnen said, "Throw them away and close them, or put them aside and abandon them."

On this account, Hōnen had mishandled the minds of all sentient beings, particularly through his own personal viewpoint and wording that distorted what the Buddha had expounded, and his total disregard for the sutras. In fact, all that he said amounts to absurd verbiage. As for the distorting evil from his mouth, there are no words to describe it; nor is there a censure that is harsh enough.

But the whole populace of Hōnen's time put their faith in his absurd wordiness, and all held his work, *The Only Choice*, in high esteem. As a result, through the people's veneration for the three volumes of sutras on the immaculate terrain, all the other sutras were neglected. They only worshipped the one Buddha of Boundless Light (*Amida, Amitābha*) of the Heaven of Ultimate Bliss, whereas all the other Buddhas were forgotten. Indeed, this Hōnen was the bitter antagonist of all the Buddhas, all the sutras, and the archenemy of all the monks that are wise, and ordinary people as well. This incomplete and distorting doctrine has now spread to every nook and corner of Japan, pervading the ten directions throughout.

Now then, you were terribly upset when I pointed out that the cause of the calamities in recent years was due to the propagation of the incomplete and distorting qualities of Hōnen's doctrine. Maybe, by quoting examples from previous periods, I can persuade you to see things with more understanding.

In the second fascicle of the *Desistance from Troublesome Worries in order to See Clearly (Maka Shikan)*, there is a quotation from a passage of the [Chinese] Historical Records, where it says, "When the dynasty of the Kings of Shū (Zhou), (1122-255 BCE) was coming to an end, there were people who went around with dishevelled hair and naked to the waist, who ignored all etiquette and propriety." [Etiquette and propriety were the foundation of the Shū Dynasty social behaviour.] In the *Broad Elucidation to Support the Practice of the Universal Desistance from Troublesome Worries in order to See Clearly*, Myōraku (Miao-lo) gives a more precise explanation with regard to the end of the Shū dynasty, where he quotes, from *The Spring and Autumn Annals*, "During the reign of the thirteenth King of Shū, King Hei (770-719 BCE), when he had first moved his capital further towards the east to Rakuyō (Loyang) in order to evade the western barbarians, saw by the river Izen (I Ch'üan) people with their hair hanging long and untidy, performing their religious rites in the open wilds. A man with deep insight said, 'It will not be a hundred years before your dynasty comes to an end, because the devotional rites for the divinities are being desecrated.'" As you already know, the appearance of the omens comes first, then the calamities come later.

The *Universal Desistance from Troublesome Worries* goes on to say, "In China, during the Western Jin Dynasty (265-313 CE), there was a well-known poet of exceptional talent called Gen Seki (Juan Chi), whose hair was always messed up and his clothes untidy. Later, the sons and younger relatives of the nobles at court all imitated him, until those who acted like foul-mouthed hooligans were thought to be behaving normally, whereas those who valued politeness and were restrained in their conduct were referred to as unfashionable, rustic conformists. These were the signs that heralded the downfall of the Shi Ba family who were the kings of the Western Tsin Dynasty."

The Universal Teacher Jikaku mentions, in his *Pilgrimage Through China in Search of the Dharma*, that, in the first year of the reign entitled Kai Shō (*Hui Chang* 841 CE), the Emperor Bu Sō (*Wu Zong*) commanded the Teacher of the Dharma Kyōsō (*Jing Shuang*) of the Shōkyōji Temple (*Chang Jing Shi*) to transmit the teaching of the immaculate terrain of the Buddha of Boundless Light (*Amida, Amitābha*) to every temple. From then on, the Venerable Kyōsō went unceasingly from one temple to another lecturing and teaching.

In the following year [842 CE], armies of the Uighur people from Turkistan made inroads into the Chinese frontier. In the third year of the same reign, the military governor of the provinces that lie north of the Yellow River unexpectedly raised a revolt. Later, the Chinese tributary kingdom of Tibet again refused to obey orders, and the Uighurs repeatedly seized land from China. Generally speaking, the military engagements and other disturbances were similar to those during the reign of Shi Kō Tei (*Shih Huang Ti*, 221-209 BCE) or when Kō U (*Hsiang Yu*) of the State of So (*Chu*) was defeated, a time when towns and villages were put to the torch as well as other atrocities. But what was even worse was the Emperor Bu Sō's drive to annihilate the Buddha Dharma, during which many temples, monasteries, and *stupas* were destroyed. This emperor was never able to quell the revolts, nor his need for military interventions. Sick at heart, due to his negative karma, he finally died.

If we look at these events in the light of the fashionableness of the teaching of the immaculate terrain being the cause that brings about the destruction of the state, Hōnen was active during the reign called Kennin (1201-1204 CE), when the retired emperor Go-Toba tried to assert his authority and take back the reins of government in the Jōkyū Disturbance (1221 CE). Hōjō Yoshitoki, the second regent, put down the uprising within a month and sent Go-Toba and two other former emperors into exile.

The downfall of Go-Toba is right in front of our eyes. Hence we have a previous example of this kind of situation in China and also another testimony in our own country Japan. You must not doubt this or even have any misgivings. All you must do to abandon this affliction of the Nembutsu teaching that was diffused by Hōnen is to take refuge in the *Sutra on the White Lotus Flower-like Mechanism of the Utterness of the Dharma*. You must destroy and get rid of *The Only Choice*, so that we can block the advance of these disasters and calamities, by cutting them off at their source.

The guest, who had by now calmed down a little, said, in a reconciliatory way: Even though I have not yet understood this matter as profoundly as you do, I think I know what you are trying to say. Nevertheless, from Kyōto, where the emperor reigns, to Kamakura, the headquarters of the Shogunate, there are within the realm of the Buddha teaching numerous excellent monks who are pivotally essential to our society. But there is not yet a single person who has written a letter of complaint, pointing out Hōnen's errors, either to the Shogunate, or had it presented to the throne. You, however, as a person of lowly rank, throw up slanderous words without the slightest concern. What you say is not entirely right, so perhaps it would be better not to declaim your reasoning.

The host said: Although I am not particularly gifted, I have attentively made a study of the universal vehicle (*daijō, mahāyāna*). A bluebottle fly, which hangs on the tail of an excellent steed, can cross over ten thousand miles. The green creeper, that entwines itself up to the top of the pine tree, can grow to a thousand feet. I may not be quick-thinking, but I was born a disciple of the one Buddha Shākyamuni, and I dedicate myself to the sovereign of all sutras, the *Sutra on the White Lotus Flower-like Mechanism of the Utterness of the Dharma*. Therefore, how can I watch the deterioration of the Buddha teaching, without having pity for it and feeling sorrow?

Besides, it says in the *Sutra on the Buddha's Passing over to Nirvana*, "If there is a fully ordained monk who sees a person vilifying the

Dharma and wilfully neglects to scold him, or turn him out, or to forcibly show him where this person is at fault, then you must realise that this person is an enemy in the midst of the Buddha Dharma. But if this monk ousts or scolds or forcibly shows this person what his errors are, then this monk is my disciple and a real hearer of the Buddha's voice."

For my part, even though I may not be a good monk, in order to avoid a scolding for being an enemy within the Dharma, I have taken a general view and only vaguely pointed to a part of the matter in hand.

Furthermore, during the Gennin era (1224 CE), both the Enryakuji Temple of the Tendai School on Mount Hiei and Kōfukuji Temple of the Hossō School in Nara submitted petitions to the throne, on repeated occasions, with the scope of having the Nembutsu School banished. As a result, there was an imperial command and a letter of instruction from the Shogunate that the wood blocks for printing Hōnen's book, *The Only Choice*, should be confiscated and brought to the Great Lecture Hall of the Enryakuji Temple. There they were burned, in order to repay the benevolence and kindness of the Buddhas of the past, present, and future. In addition, the people in the service of the Gion Shinto Shrine, who are called "the dog spirit wardens", were given the order to dig up and destroy Hōnen's grave. At the same time, the disciples of Hōnen, Ryūkan, Shōkō, Jōkaku, and Sasshō were all exiled to faraway provinces and have never been pardoned. So how can you say that nobody sent a letter of complaint with regard to these matters?

The guest replied, in a tone of voice that was still calm: It would be difficult to say that denigrating sutras and vilifying monks is solely limited to Hōnen, since you also drag the three sutras of the immaculate terrain through the mud and vilify the monk Hōnen. However, it is quite true that Hōnen takes the six hundred thirty-seven volumes that comprise two thousand eight hundred eighty-three fascicles of sutras of the universal vehicle (*daijō, mahāyāna*), along with all the Buddhas, bodhisattvas, and *deva* (*ten*) of both the heavenly and human existential spaces, and then incites the people either to throw them all away, or close them, or put them aside, or abandon them. There is no doubt that these are Hōnen's words, and the meaning of this injunction is obvious. But because you keep on holding up this flaw in the precious stone and call Hōnen names for it, I cannot say whether he made the injunction out of his bewilderment or his awakening. What is more, it is difficult for me to work out who is the wise and who is the fool, or who is right or who is wrong.

You assert that the origin of the calamities and disasters that have happened on our abode and terrain is due to *The Only Choice* of Hōnen, and then you loquaciously build up your discourse, in order to emphasise its implications. But what this all comes down to is that the peace of the world and the tranquillity of the abode and terrain are what is asked and prayed for by the rulers, ministers, and the people of the land. The realm prospers and succeeds through the Buddha Dharma, because the Dharma is venerated by the people. If the realm were to be destroyed, and the people were to perish, who would be left to revere the Buddha or to hold faith in his Dharma? Therefore, first we must all pray for the peace and tranquillity of the nation, and then we must strive for the establishment of the correct Buddha Dharma. Now, if you have the means to ward off calamities and bring disasters to an end, I would like to hear what you have to say.

To this, the host replied: When you said it was difficult for you to work out who is the wise and who is the fool, then it is I who am the stubborn fool. I would never dare to say that I am wise. Nevertheless, I would like to quote some passages from the sutras that I have been thinking about. To begin with, both within and outside the Buddha teaching there are numerous texts that deal with various means to quell catastrophes and disasters. It would be difficult to mention them all. In my own modest way, I have been dwelling upon this problem ever since I entered upon the Buddha path. It would seem to me that, by curbing people who vilify the Dharma and respecting and taking seriously the monks who follow the correct path, this would be the best way of securing order and tranquillity in the realm and peace throughout the world.

In the seventh fascicle of the *Sutra on the Buddha's Passing over to Nirvana*, it says, "The Buddha said, 'Apart from the one particular kind of person, if you are to give alms, or the Dharma, as unsullied charity to all the others, those people, who do the practice of giving, will be praised and admired by all.'

"Junda asked, 'What do you call the one particular kind of person, who is apart from all the others?'

"The Buddha replied, '[I mean] the sort of person that is discussed in this sutra, as the one who breaks the precepts.'

"Junda then said, 'I still do not understand what you mean. Would you explain it further to me?'

"The Buddha addressed Junda, saying, 'A person who breaks the precepts is referred to as a person of incorrigible disbelief (*issendai*). With regard to all the other kinds of persons to whom you may bestow alms, all of them will praise you, because you will obtain universal fruition and reward.'

"Again Junda asked the Buddha, 'What are the implications of a person of incorrigible disbelief?'

"The Buddha said: 'Assume that there was either a monk or a nun, or a layman or a laywoman, who let out crude and injurious words that vilify and slander the correct Dharma, who continually built up this serious karma, without any sense of repentance in his or her heart, then this individual has taken the direction of a person of incorrigible disbelief.

"'Let us suppose that there is a person who commits the four grave sins of killing, stealing, wrongful sex, and lying, or a person who commits the five irreversible, noxious acts of killing one's father, killing one's mother, killing an *arhat*, shedding the blood of a Buddha, and destroying the harmony of the clerical community (*sō, sangha*), and is consciously aware of committing such wrongdoings, who from the outset remains fearlessly unrepentant. In addition to keeping back any admission to having committed these crimes, this person feels no inclination to help, establish, or to care about protecting the correct Dharma. Instead, such a person despises the Dharma and is foul-mouthed about it. Also, the speech of such an individual is satiated with hate and resentment. Again I would say that such a person has taken the direction of the path of one who is an incorrigible unbeliever. Accordingly, except for the people who are of incorrigible unbelief, if you give alms or the Dharma, as an unsullied charity to all the others, you will be praised and admired by everyone.'"

Again, in the *Sutra on the Buddha's Passing over to Nirvana*, in the *Seventh Chapter on Sage-like Practice*, it says, "When I think about the past, I was once the sovereign of a great country in the world of humankind. My name then was Senyo. As this king, I looked upon the sutras and teachings of the universal vehicle (*daijō, mahāyāna*) with love and deep reverence. My mind was pure, good, and without any malice, coarseness, jealousy, or small-mindedness.

"All you good people, at that time I took the teachings of the universal vehicle (*daijō, mahāyāna*) very seriously. When I caught the Brahmins slandering and vilifying the Equally Broad doctrine of the universal vehicle (*daijō, mahāyāna*), the moment I heard them, they were put to death on the spot. All you good people, from that time onwards, due to this cause and the karmic circumstances of undoubting faith, I never fell into hell."

Again, further on in the same sutra, it says, "In the past, the Tathāgata had the affinities to become the sovereign of a nation, a period in which he was doing the practices of a bodhisattva. He also put to death a number of Brahmins."

Then, in the same part of this sutra, we have, "There are three categories of killing, which are called the least heinous, the moderately heinous, and the most heinous degrees of taking life. The least heinous degree consists of killing the grubs of ants, on up to the slaughter of animals. This excludes the slaughter of a bodhisattva who has chosen to be born as an animal. The cause and the circumstances of the least heinous degree of taking life can lead to being reborn in the realms of the hells, animality, or those of the hungry demons. But, to be precise, they will only have to suffer in a way that corresponds to the least heinous degree of taking life. The reason for this is that, whatever scanty good roots an animal may have, the one who kills it must pay for the sin of taking its life.

"The moderately heinous degree of killing involves the murder of an ordinary common mortal, up to persons who have attained the stage of the individual vehicle of not having to be reborn in the world of humankind, but in one of the heavens where there is real physical contact, or where there is only mental activity. The karma that results from this offence is to fall into the realms of hell, animality, or that of the hungry demons, where the person who committed this crime will suffer torments that correspond to this moderately heinous category.

"The most heinous degree of taking life consists of parricide, along with the killing of a person who has attained the supreme rewards of the individual vehicle (*arhat*), or one who has been awakened by affinities [who has understood something of the meaning of life but not all its secrets (*Hyakushibutsu, Pratyekabuddha*)], or a bodhisattva who [through a practice perpetuating through countless *kalpas*] has reached the state where no regression is possible. The killer of such persons will fall into the great hells of incessant suffering. But should someone kill a person of incorrigible disbelief, they would not fall into the three degrees of taking life I have just mentioned. All you good people, all those Brahmins were people of incorrigible disbelief."

In the *Sutra on the Benevolent King*, it says, "The Buddha informed King Hashinoku (*Prasenajit*), 'I intend to entrust the protection of the Dharma to all the rulers of state, rather than the monks and nuns of the order. Why should this be so? Because the monks and nuns do not possess the majesty and power that is normal for a king.'"

Also it says, in the *Sutra on the Buddha's Passing over to Nirvana*, "I now entrust the safekeeping of the correct Dharma to all the Kings, great ministers, councillors of state, and also to the monks, nuns, laymen, and laywomen. If there is anybody who vilifies the correct Dharma, then the great ministers, monks, nuns, laymen, and laywomen must harshly scold this person and correct his faults."

Again it says, in the same sutra, "The Buddha said to the Child Bodhisattva Kashō (*Mahākashyapa*), 'Due to the cause and karmic circumstances of being capable of holding to and protecting the correct Dharma, I have been able to bring this indestructible *vajra* [diamond-like] body to fulfilment.' Good people, those who intend to guard and hold to the correct Dharma have no need to receive the five precepts against killing, stealing, wrongful sex, lying, and the consummation of intoxicating substances, or the need to practise dignified courtesies. Rather, they should carry knives, swords, bows, arrows, halberds, and spears."

Quoting the *Sutra on the Buddha's Passing over to Nirvana* once more: "There are some people who receive and hold to the five precepts against killing, stealing, wrongful sex, lying, and taking intoxicating substances, but they do not inevitably deserve to be called practitioners of the universal vehicle (*daijō, mahāyāna*). However, a person may not have received the five precepts against killing, stealing, wrongful sex, lying, and taking intoxicating substances, but, by defending the correct Dharma, then this person is a practitioner of the universal vehicle (*daijō, mahāyāna*). A person who defends the correct Dharma ought to be armed with swords, knives, and other weapons. Even though they may carry weapons and swords, I will refer to these people as those who keep the precepts."

In the *Chapter on the Vajra Body of the Sutra on the Buddha's Passing over to Nirvana*, it says: "All you good people, in past ages, in this city of Kushinajō (*Kushinagara*), a Buddha came into the world called the Tathāgata of the Increasing Benefit of Gladness and Joy (*Kangi Zōyaku Nyorai*). After this Buddha had passed over to nirvana, his correct Dharma era lived on for countless millions of years.

"Then when there were only forty years left before this Buddha's Dharma was to come to an end, there was a monk that held to the correct Dharma, whose name was Kakutoku. Also, during that period, there were numerous monks who were vilifying the Buddha teaching. When these decadent monks heard the Venerable Kakutoku finding fault with their amassing wealth, evil rose in their minds. They armed themselves with knives and staves and set out to attack this teacher of the Dharma.

"At this time, the sovereign of the realm, who was called Utoku, on hearing reports of what was happening, and in order to protect the Dharma, went straightaway to the place where the Venerable Kakutoku was expounding it. There and then, the sovereign fought with all his might against the evil monks who had broken the precepts. Thus the Venerable Kakutoku was able to avoid serious harm. On the other hand, the king's body was covered with so many wounds, from knives, swords, arrows, and halberds, that there was not even the space of a mustard seed that was left untouched.

"Immediately the Venerable Kakutoku praised the king, acclaiming him with words such as, 'Splendid, extraordinary!' The Venerable Kakutoku then said, 'You really are a protector of the correct Dharma. In ages to come, your person will become a vessel for uncountable Dharmas.'

"After the king had finished listening to the Dharma, his heart was overwhelmed with joy and gladness. Then the lifespan of the king came to its end. He was then reborn in the Eastern Realm of the Joy of Utterness of the Buddha Ashuku (*Akshobhya*). This king became the principal disciple of the Buddha Ashuku (*Akshobhya*). Then all those who were under King Utoku's command in the skirmish, irrespective as to whether they were ordinary people or from court circles, were all overjoyed. Nobody had any further doubts about having the notion of an enlightened mind that perceives the real behind the seeming – that believes in the consequences of karma, that everything has a Buddha nature – and aims at a Buddha awakening.

"When the life and destiny of the Venerable Kakutoku finally came to an end, he also was reborn in the realm of the Buddha Ashuku, where he became the second among the hearers of this Buddha's voice. When it is the time for the correct Dharma to come to its close, it should be held to and defended in this manner.

"Listen, Kashō (*Kashyapa*), my disciple. The sovereign at that time was I myself, and the monk who expounded the Dharma was the Buddha Kashō (*Kashyapa*) [who was the seventh in a line of Buddhas that ended with Shākyamuni]. Those people who protect the correct Dharma will receive countless benefits and rewards. It is due to such causes and karmic circumstances that today my person is adorned with all kinds of special characteristics, which make it the manifestation of the Dharma which is indestructible."

The Buddha pointed out to the Bodhisattva Kashō (*Kashyapa*): "It is for this reason that lay believers who wish to defend the Dharma should arm themselves with staves and swords, in order to protect it in this fashion.

"All you good people, after my passing over to nirvana, when the foul and evil age has come into being, the nation and its terrain will become wild and ungoverned, where people will plunder and steal from each other, and the populace will suffer from want and hunger. During this period, on account of hunger and want, many people will resolve to attain a mind of enlightenment and leave their families to become monks and nuns. If we are to give such persons a name, then they are shavepates. But should any of these shaven-headed bonzes see a person holding to and protecting the correct Dharma, then they would chase after him and drive him away. Either they would kill him or do him harm. It is for this reason that I allow those who hold to the precepts to associate with those laymen who carry swords and staves. Even though they carry swords and staves, these people, as I have already expounded, are referred to as those who keep the precepts. But even though they are armed with swords and staves, they do not use them to take life."

In the *Dharma Flower Sutra* (*Myōhō Renge Kyō*), we have, "If there is a person who refuses to have faith in this sutra, but instead berates and vilifies it, he will immediately deny all the Buddha seeds in his heart that would mature and bring about his enlightenment." The text continues, until, "At the end of his life, he will fall into the hell of incessant suffering."

The Essential of the Teaching of Nichiren Daishōnin

This extract from the sutra is perfectly clear, and there is no need for me to add any more words. Broadly speaking, if we are to comply with the *Dharma Flower Sutra* (*Myōhō Renge Kyō*), then we must accept that vilifying the sutras, and other writings of the universal vehicle (*daijō, mahāyāna*), is more serious than committing the five irreversible sins [of *i*) parricide, *ii*) matricide, *iii*) killing an *arhat*, *iv*) shedding the blood of a Buddha, or *v*) destroying the harmony of the clerical community (*sō, sangha*)]. Therefore, anyone who does so will fall into the iron-walled penitentiary of the hell of incessant suffering and need not expect to be set free for an unbearably long time.

According to the *Sutra on the Buddha's Passing over to Nirvana*, "One may give alms to a person who has committed the five irreversible sins, but one must never make donations to a person who has vilified the Dharma. A person who kills the grub of an ant will fall into the three evil paths, but a person who prevents others from vilifying the Dharma will ascend to the state of no-retrogression." These passages show that the monk Kakutoku later became the Buddha Kashō (*Kashyapa*) and that the King Utoku finally was incarnated as the Buddha Shākyamuni.

Both the *Dharma Flower Sutra* (*Myōhō Renge Kyō*) and the *Sutra on the Buddha's Passing over to Nirvana* represent the five periods of *i*) the Flower Garland, *ii*) the Doctrines of the Individual Vehicle, *iii*) the Equally Broad Doctrine, *iv*) the Wisdom Teachings, and *v*) the *Dharma Flower Sutra* (*Myōhō Renge Kyō*), which all together comprise everything that Shākyamuni taught during his lifetime. Therefore, the implications of these injunctions not to vilify the Dharma are very grave indeed. Who would not pay serious attention to them? Besides, all those people who belong to the schools that vilify the Dharma have forgotten all about the correct way, which is to hold to the *Dharma Flower Sutra* (*Myōhō Renge Kyō*). Instead, their stupidity sinks further downwards, through their attachment to Hōnen's *Only Choice*.

For the same reason, some people, who remember what Hōnen looked like when he was alive, paint pictures or sculpt images of him in wood, whereas others, who believe his humbug doctrine, engrave printing blocks of his wickedly distorting verbiage, in order to propagate them to every corner of the land. This is why, at present, all the people in the realm look up to the Nembutsu School of Hōnen and make donations to his disciples.

Also, this situation has come to such that we see artisans removing the hands from the images of Shākyamuni and replacing them with hands making the gestures (*mudrā*) that are characteristic of the Buddha of Boundless Light (*Amida, Amitābha*), or temples, formerly dedicated to the Buddha Master of Healing (*Yakushi*) of the Eastern Direction, are renovated with statues of the Tathāgata of Boundless Light (*Amida, Amitābha*) of the Western Direction. Also, the ceremony of copying out the *Dharma Flower Sutra* (*Hokke-kyō*), which has been perpetuated by the Tendai School for some four hundred years, has been replaced with the ritual of transcribing the three volumes of the sutras on the immaculate terrain in the west. In addition to this, we see that the traditional annual lectures of the Universal Teacher Tendai (*T'ien T'ai*), which are held on the twenty-fourth of November each year, have been stopped, and ceremonies of Zendō, etc., are carried out instead.

There is no end to counting the disciples of the Buddha who are led astray by Hōnen. They are the people who thwart the Buddha, the Dharma, and the clerical community (*sō, sangha*). And their distorting and incomplete doctrine is entirely due to Hōnen's *Only Choice*.

How awful and sad it is that people should turn their backs on the Buddha's forbidding admonitions about vilifying the Dharma! Also, it is such a tragedy that people are misguided by the vulgarly commonplace utterances of that stupid monk Hōnen. If we swiftly wish to bring about peace and serenity to humankind, then we must stop all those people throughout the realm who vilify the Dharma.

The guest said: If we are to get rid of those people who vilify the Dharma or those who go against the Buddha's severe admonitions about speaking ill of the Buddha or the Dharma, are they condemned to be beheaded, as it suggests in the sutric passages you have just quoted? If it is so, then have we also come to the stage of killing and harming others? What about the karma for having committed such sins?

Accordingly we have, in the *Sutra on the Great Assembly of Bodhisattvas*, "If a person shaves his head and puts on the robe of a monk, whether this person holds to the precepts or breaks his vows, both the *deva* (*ten*) and humankind should make offerings to him. As a result, these offerings become donations to the Buddha, because this person is the Buddha's son. But should anyone curse and abuse this person, then they are reviling and insulting the Buddha himself."

On giving this matter some thought, it is not a question of whether someone is good or bad, right or wrong, but, by the fact that this person is a member of the clerical community (*sō, sangha*), he ought to have offerings made to him. This is because, by hitting and insulting the son, how can you not bring grief and sadness to the [father] Buddha? Did not those Brahmins, who thrashed the Buddha's disciple, the Venerable Mokuren (*Maudgalyāyana*), with staves and bamboo sticks, sink down to the bottom of the hell of incessant suffering for an eternity? Or did not Daibadatta (*Devadatta*) spend a very long time choking in the flames of the same hell of incessant suffering, for killing the nun Renge?

The sutric evidence of the past is apparent, yet in ages to come the most foreboding of all is the fear of committing the offence of harming members of the clerical community (*sō, sangha*). What you intended to be a dissuasion, to prevent the vilification of the Dharma, would be to infringe the Buddha's admonition about speaking ill of it. I feel very uneasy about the whole matter. How am I supposed to understand it?

The host replied: You clearly saw the passages from the *Sutra on the Buddha's Passing over to Nirvana* that I have just shown you, and yet you say a thing like that! Can your mind not assimilate what these passages mean, or are you incapable of understanding the reasoning behind them?

This has nothing to do with scolding the disciples of the Buddha, but it has a lot to do with deeply loathing any vilification of the

Dharma whatsoever. According to the Buddha incarnations, prior to that of Shākyamuni, the monks who vilified the Dharma were sentenced to be beheaded. However, after the advent of Shākyamuni, whose compassion was so great that his patience could endure the slander and insults of all sentient beings, it was decided forthwith that members of the clerical community (*sō, sangha*), who vilified the Dharma, were to have the donations offered to them discontinued.

Now then, if the four kinds of people faithful to the Buddha teaching, who are the monks, nuns, male and female lay believers, that live within the four seas and the myriads countries, would no longer give alms to those monks whose concept of the Dharma is distorting and incomplete, and if everybody were to take refuge in the right and wholesome doctrine, then how could we be further plagued with troubles or forced to face disasters?

The guest, as a gesture of respect, moved off his floor cushion to sit on the tatami, and then adjusted the neck-band of his robe, and said: The Buddha teachings have many divergences; it is difficult to look into all of them and decide which is the kernel or the ultimate truth. I have doubts about many points, and I am not sure about what is right or where I go astray.

However, the errors of Hōnen's *Only Choice* are blatantly obvious, through his placing all the Buddhas, all the sutras, all the bodhisattvas, and all the *deva* (*ten*) together, and exhorting the people to "either throw or shut them away, or put them aside and abandon them". The meaning of this text is perfectly clear. Also, it is on account of this text that the people who are enlightened have left the realm, and the spirits of good have abandoned the areas they frequented. Hence, there is drought and famine throughout the land, with plague and disease everywhere.

Now that you have quoted a broad range of passages from the sutras, you have clearly pointed out what is right, and where one might easily go astray. I have already turned away from my former prejudices, which were my attachment to delusion, and my eyes and ears have been made more aware, each time you raised a point.

The gist of the matter is that everybody, from the single person of the Emperor down to the myriads of ordinary people, has the desire to enjoy serenity and tranquillity in the places where they live, and peace and security in every corner of the realm. If we could put an end to these persons who are incorrigibly misguided, and insure that people will always make offerings to sustain the monks and nuns who follow the correct Dharma, we should be able to calm down the white foam of misleading and bewildering doctrines that rages on the surface of the Ocean of the Buddha, along with cutting down the greenwood that overgrows the Mountain of the Dharma. Then the world will become as prosperous as it was during the Chinese reigns of Fu Ki (*Fu Hsi*, 2852-2737 BCE) and Shin Nō (*Shên Nung*, 2737-2697 BCE), and the nation will become ideally perfect, as it was in the age of the Emperors of China, Gyō (*Yao*, 2357-2255 BCE), and Shun (*Shun*, 2255-2205 BCE). Naturally, after that we will have time to think over and decide which the shallows are and which are the depths of the Buddha teaching, and to pay deep reverence to the pillars and rafters that hold up the house of the Buddha.

The host burst out, with an exclamation of joy: Just as it says in folk tales, the dove has turned into a hawk, and the sparrow into a clam. This is really something to be glad about. Through your friendly visits to my house, you have accepted to hold to the correct Dharma, and, unlike the tangled weeds in the hemp field, at last you stand up straight. You have let go of the teachings that are distorting and incomplete and have taken refuge in the Dharma that is whole. Indeed, if you are to look over your shoulder to the disasters of yesterday and today and devotedly believe the words of the Buddha, then, through the correct Dharma, the winds will blow softly, and before long there will be plentiful harvests.

However, a person's heart may change according to the times, and the nature of an object may change according to the conditions surrounding it, just as the reflection of the moon on water is distorted by the waves, or the vanguard of an army may be intimidated by the blades of the enemy. Even though at the present moment you say you hold faith in the correct Dharma, still I fear that later on you will forget all about it.

If we wish to pray for the peace and tranquillity of the abode and terrain, on which we depend for an existence, as well as our happiness and well-being for the present and the future, then we must concentrate our thoughts and hastily increase our efforts to resolve this question of these deluding and incomplete teachings that vilify the Dharma.

This is because, out of the seven calamities that I quoted to you earlier from the *Sutra on the Master of Healing*, five of them have already happened, only leaving the remaining two to appear. One is "the calamity of being invaded by another country", and the other is "the calamity of revolt and disorder in our own [country]". It also says, in the *Sutra on the Great Assembly of Bodhisattvas*, that when two of these disasters have already been seen, there is only one left to occur, which is the disaster of armed rebellion.

It seems that all the calamities mentioned in the *Sutra on the Golden Illuminating Light* have already happened, but the disaster of "heartless marauders invading our country for plunder" has not yet made an appearance or come about. Out of the seven disasters that are foretold in the *Sutra on the Benevolent King*, six of them are raging around us. The only disaster left to be seen is "aggressors will come on all four sides, in order to violate the country".

However, the same sutra takes care to mention that, "When the abode and terrain on which we depend for an existence falls into disorder, then the demons, and even the more enlightened spirits, start behaving wildly and violently. Then, when this happens, the whole populace goes on the rampage."

With regard to this sutric text, I would particularly like to insinuate that hundreds of demonic spirits have earlier shown violent and erratic behaviour, which has brought about death and ruin to much of the population. Since it is obvious that the first of those disasters, predicted in the sutras, has already come to pass, why should we have any doubts about those to come? When the remaining disasters, of rebellion within our own frontiers and invasion from abroad, which are caused by people's belief in evil dharmas, are all to come rushing down upon us, then what is that time going to be like?

The Emperor, as the foundation of the state, governs all that is under its sky; the ministers and the people have dominion over the fields and gardens of the realm and supply all its needs. However, should marauders from other regions force their way into it, or should rebels within our shores seize and take hold of the lands of the people, then why should there not be screams of people going out of their minds with terror? If the state is lost and families are wiped out, then where is the place where people could run to safety? If you are in any way thinking about your own protection and security, then first solemnly pray for the peace and tranquillity of all the four directions of our realm.

Also, you should devoutly pray that the people will abandon those teachings that are distorting and incomplete and take refuge in the correct Dharma. Among other things, I have the impression that all individuals, who are living in the world at present, have fears about their existence after death, hence the reason for their having faith in erroneous teachings and their veneration for things that vilify the Dharma.

For my part, I feel compassion for and yet am exasperated with people who are confused over which is the correct Dharma and which teachings are distorting and incomplete. But when you think that it is the various Buddhist sectarian dogmas that they have taken refuge in, then it makes me feel distressed. With the strength of faith that they hold to them, I wonder how it is that, without any second thought, they can revere such rambling, whose significance is so unfulfillingly untrue? If people continue in this manner to attach themselves regardlessly to these sectarian, distorting, and incomplete teachings, together with having a distorted view of the true significance of the correct Dharma, they will sooner or later be leaving the world of the living and no doubt fall into the hells of incessant suffering.

This is why, in the *Sutra on the Great Assembly of Bodhisattvas*, this point is expounded in the following manner: "Should there be a king of a nation, who, for countless existences, practised giving donations, keeping the precepts and acting with discernment, but when he sees the Buddha Dharma fading away, remains indifferent, doing nothing to sustain or protect it, then all the countless good roots that he had accumulated would all be entirely lost and eradicated forever." The text continues, until, "Before long this sovereign will fall seriously ill, and, after his lifespan has come to its end, he will fall into one of the great hells. Likewise, the same fate will befall the sovereign's consort, princes, ministers, the lords of the cities, and the rulers of the provinces as well."

Also we have, in the *Sutra on the Benevolent King*: "If somebody destroys the Buddha teaching, this person will have children who have no respect or affection. There will be disharmony between father, mother, elder and younger brothers, wife and offspring; also there will be no help from the *deva* (*ten*) or the spirits of good. Raging illnesses and evil demons will infest this person, in order to do harm. Misfortune and something eerie and nasty will pursue this person, bringing obstacles and bad luck. When death comes, this person will either fall into one of the hells, or the realms of dharmas of the hungry demons, or even that of animality. Should this person escape this torment and be born in the realm of dharmas of humankind, he will receive the fruition and reward of a subordinate in the army.

"Just as echoes reiterate the sound, or shadows extend from the original form, or, when, after writing at night-time, one puts out the light and, even if what is written cannot be seen, the writing is still on the paper, in the three realms of desire, form, and all that goes on in our heads, the fruitions and retributions of karma work in the same way."

[These three realms are *i*) where sentient beings have organs of sense, which have the capacity to desire or need, *ii*) where there is real physical contact, and, at the same time, where *iii*) there is mental activity, which can also act independently from the body.]

It says, in the second fascicle of the *Dharma Flower Sutra* (*Myōhō Renge Kyō*), in the *Chapter on Metaphors and Similes*, "If there is a person who will not hold faith in this sutra, but, instead, vilifies and disparages it. . .", the text continuing, until, ". . .when this person's lifetime has come to an end, he will fall into the hell of incessant suffering." Also, it says, in the seventh fascicle of the same sutra, in the *Chapter on the Bodhisattva Not Holding Anyone or Anything in Contempt Ever*, "For a thousand *kalpas*, they suffered agonies and torments, in the hell of incessant suffering."

In the *Sutra on the Buddha's Passing over to Nirvana*, we have, "By keeping away and separating oneself from a good friend who has accepted and holds to the correct Dharma, even though this person has no wish to hear about it, but instead abides by the teachings that are distorting and incomplete, this will be the cause and karmic circumstances of making such a person sink down to the depths of the hell of incessant suffering, where there will be torments and agonies that defy description."

When we broadly look through all the sutras, we see that they all explain that the offence of vilifying the Dharma is the most serious of all. It is the saddest thing that people should depart from the gateway of the correct and hence the Utterness of the Dharma (*Myōhō, Saddharma*) and get themselves caught up in doctrines that are distorting and incomplete. How stupid it is to be entwined in the coils of erroneous teachings, or to be ensnared forever in the net of doctrines that deviate from and vilify the reality of the Utterness of the Dharma (*Myōhō, Saddharma*)! Such people lose their way in the smog of these erroneous teachings, and, when they die, they sink down to the bottom of hell. How these people must grieve and suffer!

[The Utterness of the Dharma (*Myōhō, Saddharma*) signifies the entirety of existence, both the enlightened and unenlightened facets of it.]

Now, you must renew yourself and break away from your narrow-minded beliefs concerning the Dharma, and quickly direct your faith towards the real vehicle of the individuating goodness of the Utterness of the Dharma (*Myōhō, Saddharma*). By doing so, the three realms of desire, form, and all that goes on in our heads become the abode of the Buddha. How could it possibly be that a

Buddha abode should fall into decay? Throughout its ten directions, everywhere is a terrain that is supereminently sublime. How could such a supereminently sublime terrain be possibly harmed?

If the abode does not decline or diminish, and the terrain is neither broken nor dismantled, then our persons are able to have peace and fulfilment. What goes on in our minds will be stable and at rest, through our immovable faith. You must really take notice of and hold faith in these words that I am saying.

The guest said: When it comes to the life we are living now and also the lives to come after our deaths, who would not be concerned about such a grave matter? Now, when I read through the passages of the sutras you quoted earlier, I understand the purport of what the Buddha said. I realise that vilifying the Dharma is a very serious offence, and to destroy or ruin the Buddha teaching is a wrongdoing that penetrates deeply into our lives. Through a misguided single belief in the one Buddha Amida (*Amitābha*), I rejected all the other Buddhas. I worshipped the three sutras on the immaculate terrain, but I entirely disregarded all the other sutras. This was not some distorted way of thinking of my own. I was simply following the words of eminent forerunners, such as Donran, Dōshaku, Zendō, Eshin, and others. It must be the same for all the people of the ten directions, who have been following the doctrines and practices of the immaculate terrain.

The practices, which in this life impair the clarity of our original, unsullied mind, in the next life will drag us down to the hell of incessant suffering. The passages you have quoted are quite clear about this point. The reasoning is detailed, and there is no reason for doubt. The more I listen to your compassionate instruction, and also when you have upbraided me for my own benefit, I am able to clear away the blockages that have been keeping me back.

I must quickly set up a policy to rectify all this vilification of the Dharma, in order to re-establish peace and order throughout the land. First, peace must be brought to this present life, in order to be a help to what will happen after death. This is not a faith for myself alone, but I would like to see that others are forewarned about the hidden dangers of vilifying and distorting the Dharma.

A Reply to Shijō Kingo, Troublesome Worries are Not Separate from Enlightenment

Shijō Kingo Dono Go Henji (Bonnō Soku Bodai)
Goshō Shimpen, pp. 597-599

The second day of the fifth month of the ninth year of Bun.ei [1272], at 51 years of age

I must herewith express my heartfelt thanks for your visit, your offerings, and your enquiries about the hardships I have encountered. By being involved as a practitioner of the *Dharma Flower Sutra*, I do not consider these hardships to be something to be upset about. For however many times one receives a lifetime, one must also meet so many deaths. But it seems hardly believable that I have received a lifetime with so much reward and fruition as this. Also I wonder – were it not for all these trials, I would probably still be in the cycle of lives and deaths of the three or four evil tendencies of hell, hungry ghosts, animality, and *shura* (*ashura*). Now, to my deepest joy, I have cut away the rotation of living and dying and am sure to attain the fruition of a Buddha.

Even Tendai (*T'ien T'ai*) and Dengyō (*Dengyō Daishi*), who propagated the temporary gateway of the one instant of thought containing three thousand existential spaces in theory (*ichinen sanzen*), still had to face the problems brought about by other people's resentment and jealousy. In Japan, this teaching was transmitted from Dengyō (*Dengyō Daishi*) down to Gishin, Enchō, and Jikaku, as well as to others. The eighteenth enthroned lord of the world of mankind was the Universal Teacher Jie, who had a great number of disciples. Among them, the four most outstanding were Danna, Eshin, Soga, and Zen.yu.

At that time, this gateway to the Dharma was divided into two digressions. The Abbot Danna transmitted the doctrine of the

Tendai School, whereas the Senior Monk Eshin, its contemplation of the mind. The relationship between doctrine and contemplation was like the sun and the moon. The doctrine itself was not so deep, because it was not all-inclusive. The contemplation of the mind was deeper. The gateway to the Dharma that Danna taught was so spread out that it became shallow. The gateway that Eshin taught was narrow, but profound.

Now, although the gateway to the Dharma that is propagated by Nichiren seems to be constricted, it is utterly fathomless. The reason for this is that it penetrates that one layer deeper than the Dharma gateways that were spread abroad by Tendai (*T'ien T'ai*) and Dengyō (*Dengyō Daishi*), because it deals with the three esoteric dharmas of the *Chapter on the Lifespan of the Tathāgata* of the original gateway. Reciting the seven ideograms for *Nam Myōhō Renge Kyō* – which means to devote our lives to and found them on (*Nam[u]*) the Utterness of the Dharma (*Myōhō*) [entirety of existence, enlightenment and unenlightenment] permeated by the underlying white lotus flower-like mechanism of the interdependence of cause, concomitancy and effect (*Renge*) in its whereabouts of the ten [psychological] realms of dharmas (*Kyō*) – may seem to be constricted, but, because it is the teacher and example for all the Buddhas of the past, present, and future, the teacher and guide for all the bodhisattvas of the ten directions, and the compass for all sentient beings to attain to the path of becoming a Buddha, it is unfathomable.

In the sutra it says, "The wisdom and discernment of all the Buddhas is infinitely profound and incalculable." In this sutric text, the expression "all the Buddhas" means all the Buddhas of the ten directions and of the past, present, and future, which includes the Tathāgata of Universal Sunlight (*Dainichi Nyorai*) of the Shingon school, the Buddha Amida (*Amitābha*) of the Jōdo school, as well all the Buddhas and bodhisattvas of each and every school and their respective sutras – also all the Buddhas of the past, future, and present in general and even the Shākyamuni of our present time. Next, we come to "wisdom and discernment", and if we ask what indeed this wisdom and discernment is, then it is the fruition of substantiating the ten such qualities of the real aspect, as being the fundamental substance of the Dharma.

So what is this fundamental substance of the Dharma?

It is Nam Myōhō Renge Kyō, the consecration and foundation of one's life on the *Sutra on the White Lotus Flower-like Mechanism of the Utterness of the Dharma (Myōhō Renge Kyō)*. This is explained as the "*Sutra on the White Lotus Flower-like Mechanism of the Utterness of the Dharma (Myōhō Renge Kyō)*, which is the fundamentally existing and underlying intrinsicality of its real aspect".

Also, what we refer to as the real aspect of all dharmas is apprehended through the two Buddhas Shākyamuni and Tahō seated side by side in the *stupa* made of precious materials. Tahō summarises all dharmas, and their real aspect is represented by Shākyamuni. These are the two dharmas of the objective realm of the Buddha and his subjective insight that is able to understand it. Tahō stands for the realm of objectivity, and Shākyamuni is the wisdom that penetrates into it. Although objectivity and subjectivity are a duality, the non-duality of objectivity and subjectivity is the inner testimony of enlightenment.

These gateways to the dharmas are profoundly serious and all-embracing matters. They are referred to as our troublesome worries (*bonnō, klesha*) not being separate from our inherent enlightenment, or that the cycle of living and dying is not separate from the universality of the workings of existence. In fact, for those men and women who recite Nam Myōhō Renge Kyō, even when they are in sexual union, everything that goes on in their minds is in no way separate from their inherent enlightenment, and their cycles of life and death are not separate from the ultimate unchanging void or relativity of nirvana. Outside of becoming awakened to the fact that the actual fundamental substance of life and death does not come into being nor does it cease to exist, there can be no other cycles of living and dying that are separate from nirvana.

It says in the *Chapter on the Persuasiveness and Quest* [for Buddhahood] *of the Bodhisattva Universally Good (Fugen, Samantabhadra)*, "Without cutting off their troublesome worries or freeing themselves from the five desires [that are induced by form, sound, smell, taste, and touch], they were able to purify their senses and eradicate all their wrongdoings." It also says in the *Universal Desistance from Troublesome Worries in order to See Clearly (Maka Shikan)*, "All the toil and dust of our unenlightenment are, at the same instant, inseparable from our enlightenment. The cycles of living and dying are simultaneously inseparable from the ultimate unchanging relativity of nirvana."

Then, in the *Chapter on the Lifespan of the Tathāgata*, we have, "What is present in my thoughts is – how can I get sentient beings to enter onto the supreme path and speedily attain to becoming realised as a Buddha?" Again, we have the statement, "The essence of the appearance of the realms where existence takes place is fundamentally eternal." This must be the intended meaning of these quotations. Thus, there is no other existence apart from the substance of the Dharma, which can only be Nam Myōhō Renge Kyō.

In the past, I used to tuck this exquisitely perfect and all to be venerated *Dharma Flower Sutra* under my knee, or I looked down upon it with a scowl, having no faith in it whatsoever. Also, in some way or another, I maliciously ridiculed anybody who would edify another person by teaching them the *Dharma Flower Sutra* in order that the destiny of the Dharma should be passed on to the future. I tried to get people to leave this sutra alone in this life, since it was far too difficult, and made them embrace the Buddha Amida (*Amitābha*) teaching which would correspond more to their present need to be reborn in the immaculate terrain, where they would be more equipped to study the Dharma Flower.

It is through countless vilifications and disparagements that, in this life, I Nichiren am faced with all kinds of great hardships. Because of my having abased the supreme summit of all the sutras, now, in my present realm of existence, I am humiliated and not taken into consideration. It is taught in the *Chapter on Similes and Parables*, "Through having slandered the Dharma Flower in former lives, even though he would like to make friendly relationships with other people, they will not be sympathetic towards him and will keep him out of their way."

Nevertheless, you are also a practitioner of the *Dharma Flower Sutra*, and, as a result, you too have come up against great difficulties. But, even so, you came to the aid of Nichiren. In the text of the *Chapter on the Dharma as a Teacher*, it clearly states, "I will send Buddhas and *deva* (*ten*) in the guise of people and also the four assemblies of monks, nuns, with male and female lay believers, so that they can listen to his explanation of the Dharma." If this reference to lay believers does not apply to you, who could it point to? On hearing the Dharma, you accepted it without any recalcitrance whatsoever. How marvellous, how unthinkable and ineffable!!

Consequently, you have no doubts about Nichiren being the teacher of the Dharma of the *Dharma Flower Sutra*. Then, I would appear to be "the emissary of the Tathāgata" and also the person who, in his practice, "carries out the affairs of the Tathāgata".

Nichiren has roughly spread abroad the five ideograms of the theme and title, that was handed down to the Bodhisattva Superior Practice (*Jōgyō, Vishishtachāritra*), at the time when the two Buddhas Shākyamuni and Tathāgata Abundant Treasure (*Tahō Nyorai, Prabhūtaratna*) sat side by side in the *stupa* made of precious materials. Was this not then the assignment of the Bodhisattva Superior Practice (*Jōgyō, Vishishtachāritra*)? You too, as a follower of Nichiren and a practitioner of the Dharma Flower, talk about it to everybody. How can this not be circulating the transmission of the Dharma?

Hold fast to your mind of faith in the *Dharma Flower Sutra* (*Myōhō Renge Kyō*). If you give up striking the flint while trying to ignite the tinder, you will get no fire. Summon up a compelling and overflowing strength of faith. Shijō Kingo must become renowned throughout all the people, high and low, in Kamakura and also among all the sentient beings in Japan, as the Shijō Kingo of the Dharma Flower School. Even a bad reputation gets around, so why shouldn't it be the same for a good one? Then why would it not be so for the sake of the *Dharma Flower Sutra* (*Myōhō Renge Kyō*)?

You must carefully tell your wife about the purpose of all this. You must be as coordinated as the sun and moon or the eyes and wings of a bird. How can there be a path of bewilderment for the dead, if there is a sun and a moon? You must have no doubt that, with two eyes, you will be able to gaze upon the countenances of the three Buddhas, Shākyamuni, Tathāgata Abundant Treasure (*Tahō Nyorai, Prabhūtaratna*), and all the Buddha emanations of the ten directions. With a pair of wings you can fly in a timeless instant to the precious instant of silence and illumination.

I will talk about this more in detail another time.

With awe, reverence and respect,
Nichiren [formal signature]

The second day of the fifth month [1272]

A reply to Sir Shijō Kingo

The Esoteric Oral Transmission Concerning Plants, Trees and the Environment Having their Inherent Buddha Nature Made Manifest

Sōmoku Jō Butsu Kuketsu
Goshō Shimpen, pp. 522-523

The 20th day of the second month of the ninth year of Bun.ei [1272], at 51 years of age

The question is asked: With regard to plants and trees having their inherent Buddha natures made manifest, how does it apply to living beings and to that which is insentient?

The answer is given: Plants and trees having their inherent Buddha natures made manifest means that things that are insentient are also endowed with the Buddha nature and therefore are Buddhas in themselves.

The question is asked: In the *Dharma Flower Sutra* (*Hokke-kyō*), are both sentient beings and that which is insentient capable of revealing their inherent Buddha nature?

The answer is given: Yes, by all means.

Then it is asked: What textual proof do you have?

The answer is given: It is Myōhō Renge Kyō [which means the Utterness of the Dharma (*Myōhō*) (entirety of existence, enlightenment and unenlightenment) permeated by the underlying white lotus flower-like mechanism of the interdependence of cause, concomitancy and effect (*Renge*) in its whereabouts of the ten (psychological) realms of dharmas (*Kyō*)].

[Nam Myōhō Renge Kyō means to devote our lives to and found them on (*Nam*[*u*]) the Utterness of the Dharma (*Myōhō*) (entirety of existence, enlightenment and unenlightenment) permeated by the underlying white lotus flower-like mechanism of the interdependence of cause, concomitancy and effect (*Renge*) in its whereabouts of the ten (psychological) realms of dharmas (*Kyō*).]

The Utterness of the Dharma (*Myōhō, Saddharma*) means that sentient beings can open up their inherent Buddha nature, whereas the lotus flower which symbolises the interdependence of cause and effect means that vegetation, insentient objects, and the environment can have their inherent Buddha nature made manifest as well. Sentiency means that all that is alive can open up its inherent Buddha nature. Insentience implies that all that is inanimate can have its inherent Buddha nature made manifest.

What is referred to as life and death having their inherent Buddha nature made manifest is the opening up of the Buddha nature of the animate and inanimate. This is why when people die, a stupa is raised and then a ceremony of offerings that nourish are performed over it, as well as the ritual for opening the eyes of Buddha images. This means that if the dead have their Buddha nature made manifest, then it must be the same for plants, trees, and the environment.

In the first fascicle of the *Universal Desistance from Troublesome Worries in order to See Clearly* (*Maka Shikan*), it says, "Any materiality that is endowed with some kind of colour, so as to give it form or even any odour which can be perceived, is seen to belong to the middle way which spans both relativity and phenomenon." Myōraku (*Miao-lo*) said, "Even though people can admit that materiality, colours, and odours are the reality of the middle way, the idea that plants and things that are inanimate are also endowed with the Buddha nature perplexes their ears and puzzles their minds."

Out of which of the five colours is this single colour?

The five colours of blue, yellow, red, white, and black are each recognised as colours on their own. But the singleness is the

Dharma nature that is explained here by Myōraku (*Miao-lo*) as the middle way between relativity and phenomenon [or the bridge-like instant between the appearance of something and the recognition of what it is]. The Universal Teacher Tendai (*T'ien T'ai*) also said that there is nothing that is not the middle way. The singleness of the one colour or the single odour is not the singularity that stands in opposition to the numbers two or three, but points to the oneness of the middle way of the Dharma nature.

In the last analysis, there is nothing that is not endowed with the ten [psychological] realms of dharmas or the three thousand existential spaces. What this means is that all materiality, its colours and odours, etc., can have its Buddha nature made manifest. This is not different from the lotus flower with its interdependence of cause and effect making its inherent Buddha nature manifest. Should we then exchange the words "lotus flower" for colour and odour, it would still be plants, trees, and the environment making their inherent Buddha nature manifest.

According to Myōraku (*Miao-lo*), "Both plants and trees can become Buddhas, by making their inherent Buddha nature manifest." This means that by making their inherent Buddha nature manifest, they can become the Shākyamuni of the *Chapter on the Lifespan of the Tathāgata* [i.e., the Fundamental Object of Veneration (*gohonzon*)]. This is referred to in the *Dharma Flower Sutra* as the extent of the reaches of the mind of the Tathāgata. It is said that the Dharma realm can only be the embodiment of the Tathāgata Shākyamuni [of the primordial infinity].

The revelation of the principle of the original terrain as the ultimate superlative means that alongside this primordial infinity there are uncountable sentient beings who, due to their unenlightenment, are endlessly suffering in the dream of living and dying. This is called the principle of the real suchness that is immutable in essence that belongs to the temporary gateway. But a gateway to the Dharma that is suspended in time and place implies impermanency and therefore entails extinction.

The revelation of the original terrain in practical terms is its own original source in the ever-present infinity in time [as well as being the integrated treatise of the triple Utterness]

[The triple Utterness refers to *i*) the Utterness of the original cause. Myōraku (*Miao-lo*) bases his explanation of this Utterness of original cause on the following phrase from the *Chapter on the Lifespan of the Tathāgata*, "'Since I originally practised the path of a bodhisattva' is a reference to time without an intermediary space. This is the path before (Shākyamuni) became a Buddha. By giving a name to this path, it becomes the origin." The Utterness of the original cause is the recitation of the title and theme of the original gateway. *ii*) The Utterness of the original fruition is explained by Myōraku (*Miao-lo*) again from the *Chapter on the Lifespan of the Tathāgata*, as follows: "Since I became a Buddha at the other extremity of the enormous infinity of primordiality" is a proof of the Buddha being infinitely enlightened. In concrete terms, the Utterness of the original fruition is the Fundamental Object of Veneration (*gohonzon*) of the original gateway. *iii*) The Utterness of the original abode and terrain is also explained by Myōraku (*Miao-lo*) from the *Chapter on the Lifespan of the Tathāgata* as, "Ever since then, I have been in this existential realm that must be endured (*shaba sakai, sahāloka*), expounding the Dharma and converting others." This points to the concept that whatever existential realm there may be, the Buddha is always present. Again, in practical terms the "Utterness of abode and terrain" is the altar of the precept of the original gateway in the place where the Fundamental Object is enshrined.]

This revelation of the original terrain in practical terms is referred to as the fundamental of life, as well as the lotus flower which represents the interdependence of cause, concomitancy and effect. The revelation of the principle of the original terrain through its connection with temporality and death presides over that which is sentient, whereas the revelation of the original terrain in practical terms through its connection with the fundamental of life presides over insentience.

What sentient beings such as us have to depend on is the lotus flower that is inanimate, which is used to represent the interdependence of cause, concomitancy and effect. So the sound, voice, speech, and words of sentient beings such as us, in our capacity of being alive, make the Utterness of the Dharma (*Myōhō, Saddharma*) become animate. Our bodies too are endowed with animate and inanimate qualities. Our hair and nails have no feeling, and if they are cut, it does not hurt. However, the rest of our bodies do have feeling, and it causes pain and suffering if they are cut.

Our bodies that are both sentient and insentient are also endowed with the two dharmas of cause and fruition in the ten such qualities. The three existential spaces of *i*) the existential space of sentient beings, *ii*) the existential space of the five aggregates that darken our awareness of the original enlightenment, and *iii*) the existential space of abode and terrain – all three of these existential spaces are common to both the animate and inanimate. It is the mandala that is kneaded and soaked in the gateway to the Dharma of the one instant of thought containing three thousand existential spaces that is quite unknown, even in the dreams of the scholars of the present age, whose learning is incomplete.

Tendai (*T'ien T'ai*), Myōraku (*Miao-lo*), and Dengyō (*Dengyō Daishi*) understood this teaching, but they did not propagate it. They played down and de-emphasised the doctrine of the single colour and the single odour, whispering that it would confound the ears and shatter the minds of those who were attached to the provisional teachings. Instead, they advocated that people should adhere to the *Sutra on the White Lotus Flower-like Mechanism of the Utterness of the Dharma* (*Myōhō Renge Kyō*) with its all-inclusive and direct meditation of the desistance from troublesome worries (*bonnō, klesha*) in order to see clearly. Therefore, by making manifest the Buddha nature of plants and trees means that those who have died can have their Buddha natures made manifest also.

These gateways to the Dharma are known to a few people only. What this amounts to is that, through not knowing the implications of the *Dharma Flower Sutra* (*Hokke-kyō*), other gateways to the Dharma can become misleading. On all accounts, these teachings must not be forgotten or lost.

With awe and respect,
Nichiren [formal signature]

The 20th day of the second month [1272]

A reply to the Venerable Sairen

A Letter to the Lay Practitioner Abutsu

Abutsu-bo Goshō
Goshō Shimpen, p. 792

The 13th day of the third month of the 9th year of Bun.ei [1272], at 50 years of age

I have finished reading through your letter attentively. Well now, as offerings for the *stupa* made of precious materials, there was one string of a thousand coins, some white rice, and various other gifts, all of which I received intact. To this effect, I have respectfully made it known to the Fundamental Object of Veneration (*gohonzon*) and the *Dharma Flower Sutra* (*Myōhō Renge Kyō*). So please set your mind at rest.

In your letter you ask, "What is the significance of the *stupa* made of precious materials of the Tathāgata Abundant Treasure (*Tahō Nyorai, Prabhūtaratna*) springing up into view out of the earth?"

This gateway to the Dharma is a matter of grave importance. The Universal Teacher Tendai (*T'ien T'ai*), in the eighth fascicle of his *Textual Explanations of the Dharma Flower* (*Hokke Mongu*) said, in regard to this *stupa* made of precious materials, that there are two ways of seeing its significance. One is as a testimony to the truth of the theoretical doctrine, and the other, as a pointer to what was to come afterwards.

[A *stupa* is a building that is a representation of the Dharma realm, which in the *Dharma Flower Sutra* (*Hokke-kyō*) can only imply its Utterness.]

The testimony to the truth refers to the temporary gateway, and what was to come afterwards indicated the original gateway. Or, if you like, the closed *stupa* refers to the temporary gateway, and what was to come afterwards stands for the original gateway. These are in fact the two dharmas of the objective realm and the subjective insight of the original terrain. Since this is getting very involved, I shall put it aside for now.

What this really comes down to is that, when the hearers of the voice of the Buddha [who were enlightened by one of the three modes of the teaching in the Dharma Flower] were actually listening to the sutra, they saw it in their own minds in terms of the *stupa* made of precious materials.

[The three modes of the teaching in the Dharma Flower were *i*) through the Dharma itself, *ii*) through metaphors and parables, or *iii*) through references to the lives of Buddhas in the past.]

It is also just the same with the disciples and supporters of Nichiren at the present time. In the final period of the Dharma of Shākyamuni (*mappō*), there is no *stupa* made of precious materials other than the configurations of the men and women who hold to the *Dharma Flower Sutra* (*Myōhō Renge Kyō*). Without making any distinction between the honourable and the humble or the higher and the lowly, the people who recite Nam Myōhō Renge Kyō are those whose persons are that of the Tathāgata Abundant Treasure (*Tahō Nyorai, Prabhūtaratna*).

Outside of Myōhō Renge Kyō, the *Sutra on the White Lotus Flower-like Mechanism of the Utterness of the Dharma* (*Myōhō*), the *stupa* made of precious materials does not exist. The title and the theme of the *Dharma Flower Sutra* (*Myōhō Renge Kyō*) is the *stupa* made of precious materials. This *stupa* made of precious materials is also Nam Myōhō Renge Kyō [which means to devote our lives to and found them on (*Nam*[*u*]) the Utterness of the Dharma (*Myōhō*) (entirety of existence, enlightenment and unenlightenment) permeated by the underlying white lotus flower-like mechanism of the interdependence of cause, concomitancy and effect (*Renge*) in its whereabouts of the ten (psychological) realms of dharmas (*Kyō*)].

[This is the consecration and founding of our lives on the vertical threads of the sutra, into which is woven the simultaneousness of the Utterness of existence.]

Now, the whole person of the saintly Abutsu is composed of the five universal elements of earth, water, fire, wind, and relativity (*kū, shūnyatā*). These five universal elements are the five ideograms for the title and the theme. Hence, the Lay Practitioner Abutsu is just like the *stupa* made of precious materials, and the *stupa* made of precious materials is just like the Lay Practitioner Abutsu. Apart from this, no other discursive thinking is to any advantage.

This *stupa* is adorned with the precious materials of the seven treasures of *i*) listening to the dharmas, *ii*) receiving it with faith, *iii*) holding to the precept, *iv*) intense concentration on the object of meditation, *v*) diligent progression, *vi*) the ability to let go of attachments and troublesome worries (*bonnō, klesha*), and *vii*) a sense of modesty.

When you thought you were making offerings to the *stupa* made of precious materials of the Tathāgata Abundant Treasure (*Tahō Nyorai, Prabhūtaratna*), it was not so at all. You were offering them to your own person.

Moreover, your own person is made up of the three bodies that are inseparable from the one of the Tathāgata awakened to the inherent infinity of time. It is in the spirit of this kind of faith that you must recite *Nam Myōhō Renge Kyō*. The place where you dwell is just like the *stupa* made of precious materials. In the sutra, it says this: "At the place wherever the *Dharma Flower Sutra* (*Myōhō Renge Kyō*) is expounded, this *stupa* made of precious materials will spring up and appear before them."

Because I am so moved and grateful for your faith, I shall write out for you and reveal the *stupa* made of precious materials [in the form of mandala]. If you do not have a son, you must bequeath it to no one; nor should you let anybody see it if they do not have a mind of faith that is strong and diligent, because this concerns the ultimate aspiration of my whole being.

The Lay Practitioner Abutsu should be known as the guiding teacher of this northern region. Could you not be the reincarnation of the Bodhisattva Pure Practice (*Jyōgyō, Vishuddhachārita*) who came to pay Nichiren a visit? It is something so imponderable that

I do not know what to say. It is beyond the understanding of Nichiren why you have such determination and is something I will have to leave until the appearance of the Bodhisattva Pure Practice (*Jyōgyō, Vishuddhachārita*), who has the power to know these things. It is beyond all reasoning.

You and your wife should in private pay reverence to the *stupa* made of precious materials. I will eventually go over this again in detail.

With awe and respect,
Nichiren [formal signature]

Addressed to the abode of the Lay Practitioner Abutsu

Treatise on the Real Aspect of All Dharmas

Shōhō Jissō Shō
Goshō Shimpen, pp. 664-668

The 17th day of the fifth month of the tenth year of Bun.ei [1273], at 52 years of age

The question is asked: In the *Second Chapter on Expedient Means* in the first fascicle of the *Dharma Flower Sutra*, it says, "The real aspect of all dharmas can only be exhaustively scrutinised between one Buddha and another. This real aspect of all dharmas is said to be (*Sho'i shohō*) in any way they make themselves present to any of our six sense organs – eyes, ears, nose, tongue, body, and mind (*Nyoze sō* [*ke*]). [For instance, a carrot is orange; it tastes sweetish and may have a smell.] Next are their various inner qualities (*Nyoze shō* [*kū*]). [These include all the words associated with a carrot, i.e., zanahoria, carotte, carota, ninjin, and all our memories of a carrot; when we see this carrot, we unconsciously see a carrot, and both what we see and the associations in our heads automatically come together.] Then there is the substance or what they really are (*Nyoze tai* [*chūdō jissō*]), which includes Nam Myōhō Renge Kyō. Next come their potential strength and energy (*Nyoze riki*), the manifestation of that energy and strength, which is their influence (*Nyoze sa*), their fundamental causes (*Nyoze in*), along with their karmic circumstances (*Nyoze en*), the effects they produce (*Nyoze ka*), and their apparent and karmic consequences (*Nyoze hō*). Also in any way dharmas make themselves perceptible to any of our six sense organs – eyes, ears, nose, tongue, body, and mind – has a coherence with their 'apparent karmic consequences', which are present in every instant of life (*Nyoze hon makku kyō tō*)."

[Nam Myōhō Renge Kyō means to devote our lives to and found them on (*Nam*[*u*]) the Utterness of the Dharma (*Myōhō*) (entirety of existence, enlightenment and unenlightenment) permeated by the underlying white lotus flower-like mechanism of the interdependence of cause, concomitancy and effect (*Renge*) in its whereabouts of the ten (psychological) realms of dharmas (*Kyō*).]

What is the meaning of this sutric text?

The answer given is that the substance or what they really are and their subjectivities and the dependent environments of the ten [psychological] realms of dharmas from hell at the bottom, ascending to the Buddha realm at the top – all of them without leaving out a single dharma – is what the text of the *Sutra on the White Lotus Flower-like Mechanism of the Utterness of the Dharma* (*Myōhō Renge Kyō*) is concerned with. If there is a karmic consequence on the dependent environment, then there is certainly a corresponding karmic consequence on its subjectivity. This is explained by, "The karmic requital on the dependent environment and the karmic requital on its subjectivity are always the affirmation of life or *Myōhō Renge Kyō*, which means the Utterness of the Dharma (*Myōhō*) [entirety of existence, enlightenment and unenlightenment] permeated by the underlying white lotus flower-like mechanism of the interdependence of cause, concomitancy and effect (*Renge*) in its whereabouts of the ten [psychological] realms of dharmas (*Kyō*)."

It is also explained as, "The real aspect must imply all dharmas. All dharmas must imply the ten such qualities. The ten ways in which dharmas make themselves perceptible to any of our six organs of sense – eyes, ears, nose, tongue, body, and mind – must imply the ten [psychological] realms of dharmas. And the ten [psychological] realms of dharmas have to have a subjective body and an environmental terrain."

It also says, "The subjectivity and its dependent environment of the hell of incessant suffering are completely present in the minds of the supremely enlightened, and likewise the person and the environmental terrain of such a Guardian Deva King of the North (*Birushana, Vairochana*) does not go beyond the bounds of the universe that is contained in the instant of mind of ordinary people."

These explanations are understandably clear. Who would have any doubts about them? Therefore, the configuration of the realms of dharmas differs in no way from the five ideograms for *Myōhō Renge Kyō*.

Even when the two Buddhas, Tahō Prabhūtaratna Tathāgata and Shākyamuni, who, as functions of the Buddha wisdom (which is represented by Shākyamuni) and its objective reality (represented by Tahō), bestowed the benefit of the application of the five ideograms *Myōhō Renge Kyō*, they manifested it in its practical aspect as the two Buddhas in the stupa made of precious materials, nodding to each other in assent.

No one other than Nichiren could have revealed such gateways to the Dharma. Tendai (*T'ien T'ai*), Myōraku (*Miao-lo*), and Dengyō (*Dengyō Daishi*) knew them in their hearts but never spoke about them aloud. Instead, they kept them hidden within the innermost recesses of their minds. There is a reason for this. Since they had not been entrusted with this particular assignment, the time had not yet come. And also they were not the disciples of the Buddha of the primordial infinity.

From among the bodhisattvas who spring up from the earth, no one except the principal leaders of the chant, such as the Bodhisattvas Jōgyō and Muhengyō, can appear during the first five hundred years of the final phase of the Dharma of Shākyamuni (*mappō*), in order to propagate the five ideograms for *Myōhō Renge Kyō*, of the fundamental substance of the Dharma, or reveal the two Buddhas sitting next to each other [on both sides of the seven ideograms for *Nam Myōhō Renge Kyō*], carrying out the ceremony inside the stupa made of precious materials. This is on account of it being none other than a concrete revelation of the one instant of mind containing three thousand existential spaces (*ichinen sanzen*) in the *Sixteenth Chapter on the Lifespan of the Tathāgata* that belongs to the original gateway.

[This is the essence of the Fundamental Object of Veneration (*gohonzon*).]

Even though the two Buddhas Shākyamuni and Tahō are carrying out their roles of Buddhas who are suspended in time and place, still it is the *Nam Myōhō Renge Kyō* – which means to devote our lives to and found them on (*Nam*[*u*]) the Utterness of the Dharma (*Myōhō*) [entirety of existence, enlightenment and unenlightenment] permeated by the underlying white lotus flower-like mechanism of the interdependence of cause, concomitancy and effect (*Renge*) in its whereabouts of the ten [psychological] realms of dharmas (*Kyō*) – that is really the original Buddha and the workings of existence. This ceremony is referred to in the *Dharma Flower Sutra* as, "the esoterically inaccessible extent of the reaches of the mind of the Tathāgata". The Tathāgata's esoteric inaccessibility refers to the Dharma (middle way), the reward (relativity), and the corresponding (phenomenon) bodies of all dharmas. This is the original Buddha.

However, the extent of the reaches of the mind of the Tathāgata are what the Dharma, reward, and corresponding bodies can do within the limits of place and temporality and therefore are Buddhas suspended in time and place. Albeit it is thought that Shākyamuni was endowed with the three virtues of lord, parent, and teacher for the sake of sentient beings such as us, this is not the case. Instead, it was ordinary people who invested the Buddha with these three virtues.

It is for this reason that Tendai's (*T'ien T'ai*) explanation for the word Tathāgata is defined as, "The Tathāgata is the general title for all the Buddhas of the ten directions and of the past, present, and future, the two Buddhas Shākyamuni and Tahō, the three Buddhas of the Dharma, which are the reward, and corresponding entities, the original Buddha, and the Buddhas who are suspended in time and place." In this explanation, the original Buddha is an ordinary person, whereas the person whom we refer to as 'the Buddha' is a Buddha who is suspended in time and place.

Nonetheless, the difference between being deluded or being enlightened is in accordance with the distinction between a sentient being and a Buddha. But what sentient beings are ignorant of is the fact that they too have a Dharma body, which is the highest aspect of the threefold body of the enlightened. It is ineffable, unmanifested, and relativity (*kū*) and can only be conceived through wisdom. This is the part of us that lives all space, all time, simultaneously and effortlessly. The reward body is the inherent wisdom of the Buddha. The corresponding body is how we appear as ordinary human beings. All three are endowed with the fundamental substance of the original Buddha (that is the triple body devoid of all karma) and also the ability to carry out its functions.

This is why when we put all dharmas and the ten [psychological] realms of dharmas together we are talking about the real aspect. The real aspect is an alternative name for *Myōhō Renge Kyō, the Sutra on the White Lotus Flower-like Mechanism of the Utterness of the Dharma* (*Myōhō Renge Kyō*), which is what all dharmas are.

[This real aspect (*Myōhō Renge Kyō*) could be understood as Nam Myōhō Renge Kyō, which means to devote our lives to and found them on (*Nam*[*u*]) the Utterness of the Dharma (*Myōhō*) (entirety of existence, enlightenment and unenlightenment) permeated by the underlying white lotus flower-like mechanism of the interdependence of cause, concomitancy and effect (*Renge*) in its whereabouts of the ten (psychological) realms of dharmas (*Kyō*).]

Hell, when shown to be in the form of hell, then that is its real aspect. But when it turns into the realm of hungry demons, it is no longer in its real form. The Buddha is seen as the shape of a Buddha image and the Common Mortal in the form of an ordinary human being.

The actual fundamental substance of all existence that appears to us is what the actual fundamental substance of *Myōhō Renge Kyō, the Sutra on the White Lotus Flower-like Mechanism of the Utterness of the Dharma* (*Myōhō Renge Kyō*), really is. This is what is referred to as the real aspect of all dharmas. "The recondite intrinsicality of the real aspect is the inherently and infinitely existing *Nam Myōhō Renge Kyō*."

The significance of this explanation implies that these well-known words, 'the real aspect', dominate the teachings that refer to events in time and place, but the inherently and infinitely existing *Myōhō*

Renge Kyō is a gateway to the Dharma superior to that of the original gateway. What I ask of you is to please ponder very thoroughly over these explanations in the depths of your mind.

I Nichiren, being born in the final phase of the Dharma of Shākyamuni, was the first to go ahead and roughly spread abroad the teaching of the Utterness of the Dharma (*Myōhō, Saddharma*), which was meant to be propagated by the Bodhisattva Jōgyō, and also to have what must be the privilege of drawing up the Fundamental Object of Veneration (*gohonzon*), that reveals Shākyamuni as the primordial Buddha of the *Sixteenth Chapter on the Lifespan of the Tathāgata* of the original gateway, along with the Buddha Tahō who rose up from the earth at the time of the *Eleventh Chapter on Seeing the Vision of the Stupa made of Precious Materials* of the temporary doctrine. Furthermore, I was also the first to reverently show, by setting out in order on the Fundamental Object of Veneration (*gohonzon*), the bodhisattvas who sprang up from the earth, at the time of the *Fifteenth Chapter on the Bodhisattvas who Swarm up out of the Earth*.

My appointed lot is something splendid. However much they may hate Nichiren, how can they possibly measure up to his inner substantiation?

Be that as it may, still the sin of having Nichiren exiled on this island is one I do not think will be expiated even after boundless *kalpas*. In the *Third Chapter on Similes and Parables*, it says this: "If we were to discuss this sin until the *kalpa* expires, it would not be the end of the matter." On the other hand, should one make offerings to Nichiren or become his disciple and supporter, then, even in terms of the wisdom of the Buddha, this merit could not exhaustively be measured. In the *Twenty-Third Chapter on the Bodhisattva Sovereign Medicine* (*Yaku' ō, Bhaishajya-rāja*) in the *Dharma Flower Sutra*, it says, "Even if its extent were to be fathomed according to the Buddha's wisdom, it would be without bounds."

Nichiren alone is the forerunner of the bodhisattvas who sprang up from the earth, even though it is improbable that he is entered among their numbers. But should we suppose that Nichiren was listed in the count of the bodhisattvas who sprang up from the earth, then how can it be that the disciples and supporters of Nichiren are not rated among those bodhisattvas? In the *Tenth Chapter on the Dharma as a Teacher* in the *Dharma Flower Sutra*, it says, "Should someone painstakingly and in private explain to another individual just one phrase of the *Dharma Flower Sutra*, then without doubt it must be known that this person is indeed the envoy of the Tathāgata and has been dispatched by him in order to carry out the Tathāgata's work." How could this possibly refer to anyone else?

For all that, when people praise me beyond measure, anything whatsoever that my will desires to bring about can be made to happen. This indeed is what springs from words of praise. Being born during the final phase of the Dharma of Shākyamuni, the practitioners who are to spread abroad the *Dharma Flower Sutra* will, on account of the three kinds of enemy, be exiled and even sentenced to death.

[The three kinds of enemy are *i*) those lay people practically ignorant of everything concerning the Buddha teaching, who denigrate those who do the practices of the *Dharma Flower Sutra* and attack them in various manners, or *ii*) arrogant monks who claim to be superior or even enlightened who vilify the people that do the practices of the Buddha teaching seriously, or even *iii*) monks and other religious leaders who, fearing the loss of their established reputations and fortunes, incite the authorities in power to persecute those who follow the practices of the *Dharma Flower Sutra*.]

Yet, the Buddha Shākyamuni [that is to say, the Fundamental Object of Veneration (*gohonzon*)] will give protection like a garment to those who insist on its propagation. All the *deva* (*ten*) will make offerings to them, place them on their shoulders, and carry them on their backs. By being people with great roots of good, they will have to be great teachers and guides for the sake of all sentient beings. Accordingly, they will be praised by the Buddha Shākyamuni, the Buddha Tahō, all the Buddhas and bodhisattvas of the ten directions, the seven ranks of Heavenly Divinities, and the five ranks of Earthly Divinities, Mother Numen of the Demonic Children (*Kishimojin, Hārītī*) and her cannibalistic demon daughters (*rasatsu, rakshasi*), the Four Heavenly Guardians of the Universe, the Deva Kings Bonten (*Brahmā*) and Taishaku, the Dharma King Emma, the spirits of the waters, the spirits of the wind, the spirits of the mountains, the spirits of the sea, the Buddha of Universal Sunlight (*Dainichi, Mahāvairochana Tathāgata*), the Bodhisattva Universally Worthy (*Fugen, Samantabhadra*) and the Bodhisattva Mañjushrī (*Monjushiri*), the *deva* of the sun, the moon, and all those who are venerated, who make it possible for the practitioner of the *Dharma Flower Sutra* to endure countless hardships.

On being commended, one can risk personal harm without even looking back. And, when adversely criticised, one unwittingly may bring about one's own damnation. Such behaviour is the implicit karma of the common mortal [Nichiren].

Whatever happens, you must now exert a mind of faith as a practitioner of the *Dharma Flower Sutra* and keep on being a disciple of Nichiren. If you are in agreement with Nichiren, then would you not be a bodhisattva who swarmed up out of the earth? Then, if you have decided that you are a bodhisattva who sprang up from the earth, how can you doubt that you were a disciple of the Shākyamuni of the primordial infinity? This is what it says in the *Fifteenth Chapter on the Bodhisattvas who Swarm up out of the Earth* in the *Dharma Flower Sutra*, "Ever since the primordial infinity in time, I have been teaching and converting these people."

In the final phase of the Dharma of Shākyamuni, there should be no discrimination between the men and women who are to spread abroad the five ideograms for *Myōhō Renge Kyō*, the *Sutra on the White Lotus Flower-like Mechanism of the Utterness of the Dharma*. For, if they were not all manifestations of the bodhisattvas who sprang up from the earth, then the theme and the title (*daimoku*) would be hard for them to recite.

At first, only Nichiren chanted Nam Myōhō Renge Kyō, but then two or three people followed and recited and transmitted it to others. Moreover, it will also be the same way in the future. How can this not be the meaning of swarming up out of the earth?

Besides, at the time of the broad propagation, humankind as a whole will recite Nam Myōhō Renge Kyō [which means to devote our lives to and found them on (Nam[u]) the Utterness of the Dharma (Myōhō) (entirety of existence, enlightenment and unenlightenment) permeated by the underlying white lotus flower-like mechanism of the interdependence of cause, concomitancy and effect (Renge) in its whereabouts of the ten (psychological) realms of dharmas (Kyō)], as surely as the whole earth is an unmissable target for an arrow.

Whatever happens, by setting your reputation in the *Dharma Flower Sutra*, you have to dedicate the whole of yourself to it. When the two Buddhas, the Buddha Shākyamuni and the Buddha Tahō, surrounded by all the Buddhas and Bodhisattvas of the ten directions, in the stupa made of precious materials in the relativity without space, nodded to each other, it was because what they agreed upon could have been no other concern, but solely to make the teaching they had established last in eternity, throughout the final phase of the Dharma of Shākyamuni (*mappō*).

The moment the Buddha Tahō had courteously shared half the throne with the Tathāgata Shākyamuni, the standard of the Myōhō Renge Kyō was already exposed to view. Then, Shākyamuni and Tahō, as the two great Buddha generals, made their decision. How could there be any deception about it? After all is said and done, it was a dialogue on how we sentient beings could be made to open up our inherent Buddha nature.

Even though Nichiren was not present at that gathering, on looking at the sutric text, there is absolutely nothing obscure about it. Yet, had I even been at that ceremony, by being an ordinary human being, I cannot know the past. Looking at the present, I am the practitioner of the *Dharma Flower Sutra*, and, furthermore, in the future it is certain that I will arrive at the site of the place of enlightenment [under the bodhi tree]. By this we can infer that I could have been at the ceremony in the spaceless relativity. The past, present, and future cannot be separated from each other.

Because I keep on thinking this way, even though I am an exile, I feel a gladness and joy that cannot be measured. There are tears of happiness, as well as tears for things that are hard to bear. Tears are something that communicates both the good and the bad. A thousand *arhats* – people who had attained the supreme reward of the individual vehicle – shed their tears as they recalled to mind things about the Buddha. The Bodhisattva Monjushiri (*Mañjushrī*) was in tears as he recited Nam Myōhō Renge Kyō, and, out of those thousand *arhats*, the Honoured One Anan (*Ānanda*) was crying as he replied, "Thus I heard." Then the remaining nine hundred and ninety-nine arhats, using their tears as water for their ink slabs, wrote down Nam Myōhō Renge Kyō.

Nichiren is now feeling exactly the same emotion. I have become the person that I am on account of my propagation of the seven ideograms for Nam Myōhō Renge Kyō, because what I heard was this particular Myōhō Renge Kyō that was left by the Buddha Shākyamuni and the Buddha Tahō for the sake of all the sentient beings of the world of humankind in the times to come.

There are tears as I ponder over my enormous difficulties. And, as I think of the bliss of opening up my inherent Buddha nature in the future, the tears cannot be stopped. Birds and insects cry, but they do not shed tears. Nichiren does not cry, but the tears are incessant. These tears are not for mundane affairs, but solely on account of the *Dharma Flower Sutra*. Since it is so, they must be tears of the nectar of immortality.

In the *Sutra on the Buddha's passing over to Nirvana*, it says that the tears shed at the separation and parting of all the fathers and mothers, brothers and sisters, wives and children, and relatives and friends would be more than all the water in the four great seas. But it seems that not a drop was shed for the sake of the Buddha Dharma. One becomes a practitioner of the *Dharma Flower Sutra*, due to an entrenched karmic habit. In the same way, it is due to karmic circumstances that some trees of the same kind are made into Buddha images. And, again, the reason why some Buddhas are suspended in time and place is also due to their entrenched karmic relationships.

In this letter Nichiren has written out Dharma gateways of universal concern. Look into them, understand them thoroughly, and receive them into your heart. Have faith in the foremost Fundamental Object of Veneration (*gohonzon*) of the world of humankind. Pay single-minded attention, and fortify your mind of faith, so that you receive the protection of Shākyamuni, Tahō, and all the Buddha emanations of the ten directions. You must apply yourself to the two paths of practice and study. Should practice and study die out, then the Buddha Dharma would no longer exist.

Do as I do, by teaching and converting others. Practice and study come about through a mind of faith. If you have the strength, you must tell others about the single ideogram "*Myō*" in the one and only title. Nam Myōhō Renge Kyō, Nam Myōhō Renge Kyō.

With awe and respect,
Nichiren

The 17th day of the fifth month

A Reply to the Venerable Sairen

I will follow by saying that Nichiren has on previous occasions written out and passed on various gateways to the Dharma that he has inherited. Those that are mentioned in this letter are of especial universal concern. Is there not a wonderful agreement between us? Are you not a manifestation of one of the Four Bodhisattvas who were headed by the Bodhisattva Superior Practice (*Jōgyō, Vishishtachāritra*), leader of the bodhisattvas who swarmed up out of the earth whose number was sixty thousand times the number of grains of sand of the Ganges? Certainly there is a reason.

Generally speaking, I have passed on to you Dharma gateways that apply to the person of Nichiren. Would you not suppose that Nichiren was of the following of the bodhisattvas who swarmed up out of the earth, whose number was sixty thousand times the grains of sand in the Ganges?

I have been reciting Nam Myōhō Renge Kyō, because of my desire to lead all the men and women of the world of humankind onto the path of enlightenment. Does it not say in the *Fifteenth Chapter on the Bodhisattvas who Swarm up out of the Earth* in the *Dharma Flower Sutra*, "The first is named Bodhisattva Superior Practice (*Jōgyō, Vishishtachāritra*)?" Then the text continues, until, "the teachers and guides of the chant". As a matter of fact, it is the sequel of an entrenched karmic relationship that made you my disciple.

Keep this letter secret and with the greatest of care. I have written down the Dharma gateways of my own substantiation. I will end here.

Nichiren

Treatise on the Fundamental Object of Veneration For Contemplating the Mind Instigated by the Bodhisattva Superior Practice (Jōgyō, Vishishtachāritra) For the Fifth Five-hundred-year Period After the Tathāgata's Passing over to Nirvana

Kanjin no Honzon shō
Goshō Shimpen, pp. 644-662

The 25th day of the fourth month of the tenth year of Bun.ei [1273], at 52 years of age

In the fifth fascicle of the *Universal Desistance from Troublesome Worries in order to See Clearly (Maka Shikan)*, it says, "The one mind is endowed with ten [psychological] realms of dharmas, and, since each dharma realm is again endowed with all of the others, it becomes a hundred dharma realms. Each dharma realm is provided with thirty kinds of existential space. So we then have a hundred dharma realms, which become three thousand kinds of existential spaces. These three thousand are contained in a single instant of mind. If there is no mind, then that is the end of it. But even the minutest existence of mind is endowed with the three thousand [existential spaces]." The text continues until, "Because it becomes what is called the objective realm of Utterness, it is here where the meaning lies." Whether you have three thousand existential spaces or three thousand ways in which we perceive dharmas, the result is the same, even if the way of going about it is different. Another text says that each realm is endowed with the three kinds of existential space.

A question is asked: Does the *Recondite Significance of the Dharma Flower Sutra* specify the term "the one instant of mind containing three thousand existential spaces (*ichinen sanzen*)"?

The answer given is that Myōraku (*Miao-lo*) says, "It is not specified."

The question is asked: Does the *Textual Explanations of Dharma Flower Sutra* (*Hokke Mongu*) mention the term "the one instant of mind containing three thousand existential spaces (*ichinen sanzen*)"?

The answer is given: Myōraku (*Miao-lo*) says, "It is not mentioned."

The question is asked: How does Myōraku (*Miao-lo*) explain this?

The answer is given: "Neither of the two texts has yet mentioned the one instant of mind containing three thousand existential spaces (*ichinen sanzen*)."

The question is asked: Do the first, second, third, and fourth fascicles of the *Universal Desistance from Troublesome Worries in order to See Clearly* (*Maka Shikan*) mention the term "the one instant of mind containing three thousand existential spaces (*ichinen sanzen*)"?

The answer is given: "No, not at all."

The question is asked: How can you prove this?

The answer is given: Myōraku (*Miao-lo*) states, "On coming to the exposition on how to correctly contemplate the dharmas in the *Universal Desistance from Troublesome Worries in order to See Clearly* (*Maka Shikan*), he particularly uses the three thousand existential spaces as a guide."

Then there is a query: In the second fascicle of the *Recondite Significance of the Dharma Flower Sutra*, it says, "Again, each dharma realm contains the nine other dharma realms. In those hundred dharma realms, there are a thousand ways in which we perceive dharmas." In the first fascicle of the *Textual Explanations of Dharma Flower Sutra (Hokke Mongu)*, it says, "As each one of the senses and its object is endowed with the ten [psychological] realms of dharmas, each one is again equipped with its own ten respective realms of dharmas. Then, in each one of these ten [psychological] realms of dharmas, there are ten ways in which we perceive dharmas, which bring it to one thousand." In the *Recondite Significance of Kannon*, it says, "If the ten dharma realms are so mutually endowed, which makes them come to a hundred realms of dharmas, then there are a thousand kinds of the ways in which we perceive dharmas and inner qualities along with any way they make themselves perceptible to any our six sense organs – eyes, ears, nose, tongue, body, and mind – obscurely hidden in the mind. They may not be before our eyes, but the mind is fully endowed with them."

The question is asked: Is the term "the one instant of mind containing three thousand existential spaces (*ichinen sanzen*)" mentioned in the first four volumes of the *Universal Desistance from Troublesome Worries in order to See Clearly (Maka Shikan)*?

The reply is given: Myōraku (*Miao-lo*) says, "It is not."

The question is asked: How does he explain this?

Answer: In the fifth fascicle of the *Broad Elucidation*, it says, "If you aspire to a correct contemplation, the complete practice has not yet been fully discussed. Moreover, there are twenty-five dharmas to work through, which in practice give rise to understanding. In all conscience, they are to be endured as an expedient means for correct observance. For this reason, the first six fascicles all may be counted as bringing about understanding." Also in the same text, it says that it is for this reason that when the *Universal Desistance from Troublesome Worries in order to See Clearly (Maka Shikan)* comes to explain how one should contemplate the dharmas correctly, the three thousand existential spaces were particularly cited as a guide. Therefore, it is the final superlative of the ultimate discourse. This is why Shōan [Chang-an, 561-632 CE], in the middle of his introduction, affirms that it is Tendai's (*T'ien T'ai*) discourse on the gateway to the Dharma, which he himself practised in his innermost being. Indeed he had a reason for this and asks those who seek to read this work not to seek karmic relations elsewhere.

That wise person Tendai (*T'ien T'ai*) widely disseminated the Dharma for thirty years. During twenty-nine years, he expounded all the implications of the *Recondite Significance of the Dharma Flower Sutra* and the *Textual Explanations of Dharma Flower Sutra* (*Hokke Mongu*). He also made clear the five periods and eight teachings, as well as the hundred realms of dharmas and the thousand such qualities. Not only did he refute the fallacies of the previous five hundred years, but he also brought to light that which had not yet been expounded by the Indian teachers of dogma. The Universal Teacher Shōan said, "Even the Indian Nāgārjuna (*Ryūju*) is not of the same calibre of Tendai (*T'ien T'ai*), so why should we go as far as to trouble ourselves talking about the scholars of China? This is not boastful arrogance. The nature of his Dharma is just as it is."

What hopelessness it was that the latter scholars of Tendai (*T'ien T'ai*) chose to let those thieves, the founders of the Kegon [Flower Garland] and the Shingon [Mantra] Schools, steal and spirit away the weighty treasure of the one instant of mind containing three thousand existential spaces (*ichinen sanzen*), and then, ironically, they became fellow disciples of those schools. The Universal Teacher Shōan already knew this, when he commented with grief, "Should this principle fall away in the future, it will be bleak indeed."

The question is asked: What is the difference between the hundred realms, the thousand ways in which dharmas make themselves perceptible to any of our six organs of sense – eyes, ears, nose, tongue, body, and mind, and the one instant of mind containing three thousand existential spaces (*ichinen sanzen*)?

The reply is given: The hundred realms and the thousand ways in which dharmas make themselves perceptible to any of our six organs of sense – eyes, ears, nose, tongue, body, and mind – are limited to the realm of sentient existence, whereas the one instant of mind containing three thousand existential spaces (*ichinen sanzen*) comprises both the sentient and the non-sentient.

Not quite understanding, it is asked: If the ten such qualities extend to the non-sentient, then do you mean to say that plants and trees are endowed with mind and are able to become Buddhas like sentient beings?

The reply is given: This is a matter that is difficult to believe and difficult to understand.

With Tendai (*T'ien T'ai*), there are two things that are difficult to believe and difficult to understand. One is the difficulty of believing and understanding in regards to the gateway of the teaching. The other is the difficulty of believing and understanding in regards to the gateway to meditation. The difficulty of believing and understanding, with regard to the gateway of the teaching, is that the Buddha taught, in all the sutras prior to the *Dharma Flower*, that people of the two vehicles and people of incorrigible disbelief will not ever become Buddhas in the future, and that the Lord of the Teaching, Shākyamuni, became correctly enlightened initially during his historical lifetime. However, when we come to both the temporary and original gateways of the *Dharma Flower Sutra* (*Myōhō Renge Kyō*), both of these arguments are demolished. A Buddha with two contradictory statements like fire and water, can anyone believe him? This is what is difficult to believe and difficult to understand, as regards the gateway of this teaching.

What is difficult to believe and difficult to understand, concerning the gateway to meditation, is the hundred realms of dharmas, the thousand ways in which dharmas make themselves present to our six sense organs, and the one instant of mind containing three thousand existential spaces (*ichinen sanzen*), as well as the two dharmas of mind and materiality of the ten such qualities, in regards to that which is insentient. Nevertheless, the two kinds of image, both those that are painted and those carved in wood, have been permitted in the canons, within and outside the Buddha teaching, as fundamental objects of veneration. But what lies behind the significance of this comes solely from the school of Tendai (*T'ien T'ai*). If the cause and fruition of mind and materiality were not placed upon plants and trees, it would be of no advantage to reverently depend on wooden and painted images as fundamental objects of veneration.

Mistrustfully, it is asked: In which texts are the two dharmas of the cause and fruition of the ten such qualities being in plants, trees, abode and terrain, to be found?

The answer is given: In the fifth fascicle of the *Universal Desistance from Troublesome Worries in order to See Clearly* (*Maka Shikan*), it says, "The existential space of abode and terrain is again endowed with the ten kinds of dharma [such qualities]. Therefore, an evil abode and terrain has its appearance, nature, substance, and strength." In the sixth fascicle of the *Explanatory Notes*, it says, "Appearance (*sō*) only exists as materiality. Substance (*tai*), strength (*riki*), action (*sa*), and karmic relations (*en*) take on the combined significance of materiality and mind. Cause and fruition only exist as mind, and karmic consequences (*hō*) only as materiality." In the *Discourse of the Vajra Scalpel*, it says, "Accordingly, a blade of grass, a tree, a pebble, or a speck of dust, each one has the Buddha nature, the cause to bring about its fruition, as well as being endowed with the concomitancies and karmic consequences (*hō*) for becoming a Buddha."

The question is asked: Now having heard where these teachings come from, what is the meaning of contemplating the mind?

The answer is given: Through contemplating the mind, we observe that we may see the ten [psychological] realms of dharmas within it. This is what is called contemplating the mind. It is as though we may see the six organs of sense of other people, but because, we do not see these six sense organs on our own faces, we do not know they are there. However, on being confronted with a clear mirror, we then see for the first time that we too have these six organs. For instance, even though all the sutras in various places refer to the six paths of the unenlightened and the four more enlightened tendencies, without looking into the clear mirrors of either the *Dharma Flower Sutra* (*Myōhō Renge Kyō*) or the *Universal Desistance from Troublesome Worries in order to See Clearly* (*Maka Shikan*), which was expounded by the Universal Teacher Tendai (*T'ien T'ai*), we cannot know about our being endowed with the ten [psychological] realms of dharmas, the thousand such qualities, and the one instant of mind containing three thousand existential spaces (*ichinen sanzen*).

The question is asked: In what text of the *Dharma Flower Sutra* (*Myōhō Renge Kyō*) is "the one instant of mind containing three thousand existential spaces (*ichinen sanzen*)" to be found, and how does Tendai (*T'ien T'ai*) explain this?

The answer is given: In the first fascicle of the *Dharma Flower Sutra* (*Myōhō Renge Kyō*) in the *Chapter on Expedient Means*, it says, "By being a sentient being, I wish to open their Buddha knowing and perception." This is the nine realms of dharmas being endowed with the realm of the Buddha. In the *Chapter on the Lifespan of the Tathāgata*, it says, "It is a universally primordial infinity of time, since I became a Buddha. My allotted lifespan comprises incalculable billions of *kalpas* and dwells in eternity without coming to an end. All you good people, even now the allotted lifespan of when I originally attained to the practice of the bodhisattva path has yet to be exhausted. It will be again twice that number." This sutric text is the Buddha being endowed with the nine realms.

In the sutra it says, "Daibadatta (*Devadatta*), after going through boundless *kalpas* in various hells, finally reaches the state of becoming a Buddha, whose title and name is the Tathāgata 'Buddha Sovereign of the Deva' (*Tennō Butsu*)." This is the realm of the dharmas of hell being endowed with the Dharma realm of the Buddha. In the sutra it says, "The first was named Ramba", and continues until, "Only those of you who ably hold on to and protect the name of the Dharma Flower will have immeasurable happiness." This is the realm of dharmas of hungry demons being endowed with the ten [psychological] realms of dharmas. In the sutra it says, "The Dragon King's daughter"; the text continues until, "became universally and correctly enlightened". This is the realm of animality being endowed with the ten [psychological] realms of dharmas. In the sutra it says, "Baji the Ashura King"; the text continues until, "On hearing the one metrical hymn or the one phrase, they will attain to the universal and correct awakening."

This is the realm of dharmas of the *shura* (*ashura*) being endowed with the ten [psychological] realms of dharmas. In the sutra it says, "Supposing that people for the sake of the Buddha"; the text continues until, "All of them have already attained to the Buddha path." This is the realm of dharmas of humanity being endowed with the ten [psychological] realms of dharmas. In the sutra it says, "Daibon the Deva King"; the text continues until, "just like us, will certainly attain the Buddha harvest." This is the *deva* (*ten*) realm of dharmas being endowed with the ten [psychological] realms of dharmas.

In the sutra it says, "Sharihotsu (*Shariputra*)"; the text continues until, "the Tathāgata Kekō". This is the realm of dharmas of the hearers of the voice being endowed with the ten [psychological] realms of dharmas. In the sutra it says, "Those who seek to be enlightened by concomitancies, monks and nuns"; the text continues until, "by putting your palms together with a mind of reverence and wishing to hear the path to complete fulfilment." This is the realm of dharmas of those enlightened due to concomitancies being endowed with the ten [psychological] realms of dharmas. In the sutra it says, "The countless numbers of Bodhisattvas who swarm up out of the earth"; the text continues until, "the truly pure universal Dharma". This is the bodhisattva realm of dharmas being endowed with the ten [psychological] realms of dharmas. In the sutra it says, "Sometimes I speak of my own person, and sometimes I talk about others", which is to say that the Buddha realm is endowed with the ten [psychological] realms of dharmas.

The question is asked: If, on looking at the six organs of sense on my own face or on somebody else's, I cannot see the ten [psychological] realms of dharmas, how can I believe in them?

The answer is given: It says in the *Tenth Chapter on the Dharma as a Teacher in the Dharma Flower Sutra* (*Myōhō Renge Kyō*), "It is difficult to believe and difficult to understand." In the *Eleventh Chapter on Seeing the Vision of the Stupa made of Precious Materials*, it refers to "the six difficult and nine easy acts". The Universal Teacher Tendai (*T'ien T'ai*) says, "Because both the temporary and original gateways contradict the past sutras, they are difficult to believe and difficult to understand." The Universal Teacher Shōan (*Chang-an*) says, "In view of this fact, the Buddha makes it his overriding concern. How could you take this to be easy to understand?"

The Universal Teacher Dengyō (*Dengyō Daishi*) says, "The *Dharma Flower Sutra* (*Myōhō Renge Kyō*) is by far the most difficult to believe and difficult to understand, because it is according to his own enlightened mind. Those who had the correct disposition of being in the world during the Buddha's lifetime had, in addition, their deeply entrenched karmic relationship with him, the Lord of the Teaching Shākyamuni, the Buddha Abundant Treasure (*Tahō Nyorai, Prabhūtaratna*), all the Buddha emanations of the ten directions, the countless numbers of bodhisattvas who swarmed up out of the earth, as well as the Bodhisattva Universally Worthy (*Fugen, Samantabhadra*) and Maitreya (*Miroku*), to help goad them into understanding. Yet, even then, there were people who failed to believe. Five thousand left their seats. *Deva* (*ten*) and men moved elsewhere. If it was like this during the correct and formal phases of the Dharma of Shākyamuni, how is it going to be at the beginning of its final phase? Were you to glibly believe, then it would not be the correct Dharma."

The question is asked: As regards the sutric texts and the explanations of Tendai (*T'ien T'ai*) and Shōan, there are no ensnaring doubts. Only, what is being said is that fire is water and black is white. Supposing that even these are things that were said by the Buddha, it is difficult to believe and accept them. Every now and then I take a look at other people's faces. But they are limited to the realm of humanity, and I cannot see any of the other realms. And again it is the same with my own face. How can I bring about a mind of faith?

Answer: If you look at other people's faces, sometimes there is joy; sometimes there is anger; and sometimes equanimity. Sometimes there appears greed; at other times, they reveal stupidity, or even flattering deceit. Anger is hell. Greed is the hungry demon. Stupidity is animality. Flattering deceit is the *shura* (*ashura*). Joy is the *deva* (*ten*). And equanimity is the quality of humankind.

In the physical aspect of the faces, the six paths of the unenlightened are altogether present. In contrast, the four sage-like tendencies are latent, but not manifest. So, you do not see them. However, if you look carefully for details, they become apparent.

The question is asked: Even though my understanding about the six paths of the unenlightened is not entirely clear, on the whole, I must agree that it seems to be that we are furnished with them. But how is it that the four sage-like tendencies are not apparent at all?

The answer is given: Previously you doubted the six paths of the unenlightened being within the realm of humanity. Nevertheless, you agreed with me, through my emphasising this point, by putting forward analogies. So should it not be the same with the four sage-like tendencies?

In an endeavour to add some justification, I will recapitulate a ten thousandth part.

The transitory nature of what we call our existential space is right before our eyes. So how can you say that the realm of the two vehicles does not exist in the realm of dharmas of humanity?

A wicked man with no regrets can love and show affection to his wife and children. This is an aspect of the bodhisattva realm.

Only the Buddha realm is difficult to discern. However, by the fact that we are endowed with the nine other realms, you must emphatically believe it and have no doubt.

In the text of the *Dharma Flower Sutra* (*Myōhō Renge Kyō*), where it explains the realm of humanity, it says, "By being a sentient being, I wish to open their own Buddha knowing and perception." In the *Sutra on the Buddha's Passing over to Nirvana*, it says, "Even though the people who study the universal vehicle (*daijō, mahāyāna*) only have eyes of flesh, when they study the Buddha teaching, they become the eyes of the Buddha." The common mortal born in the final era in the realm of dharmas of humanity, with faith in the

Dharma Flower Sutra (*Myōhō Renge Kyō*), is because the realm of dharmas of humanity is also endowed with that of the Buddha.

The question is asked: What the Buddha says about each of the ten [psychological] realms of dharmas being mutually furnished with the same ten realms is understandably clear. Nonetheless, naturally it is difficult for our inferior minds to believe and accept that we are endowed with the Dharma realm of the Buddha. Now, this time if I do not acquire faith, I shall become a person of incorrigible disbelief. I beg you to show your universal loving-kindness and make me believe, so that I may be saved from the hell of incessant suffering.

The answer is given: If you do not already believe, after having seen and heard the sutric text of the sole reason for the appearance of the Buddha in this world of cause and concomitancies, then how can anyone, from Shākyamuni to the bodhisattvas of the four dependencies, save and protect you from disbelief? Still, by all means I will try to tell you.

[These four dependencies are the four important principles, on which the practitioner relies – *i*) to practise according to the Dharma and not according to the person who expounds it, *ii*) to practise according to the intended significance of the Dharma, and not the superficial meaning of the words that are used, *iii*) to practise according to one's inner wisdom and not according to one's acquired knowledge, *iv*) to practise according to the real aspect of the middle way as it is expounded in the *Sutra on the Implications Without Bounds* (*Muryōgi-kyō*), and none other.]

There were people who could not be enlightened through meeting the Buddha, but, on hearing Anan (*Ānanda*) and others, they were able to attain to the path. There exist two opportunities. One is by seeing the Buddha and attaining to the path through the Dharma Flower. The second is without seeing the Buddha and attaining to the path through the Dharma Flower.

Besides, before the Buddha teaching, many of the Taoists and Confucianists in China, as well as the Brahmins and followers of the four Vedas in India, were able, through these karmic relationships, to come to the correct view of life. Again, there were many bodhisattvas and common mortals, who, by listening to the sutras of the universal vehicle (*daijō, mahāyāna*) of the Flower Garland, the equally broad (*hōdō, vaipulya*) and wisdom (*hannya, prajña*) periods, came to be aware of their karmic relationship with the seeds sown in the primordial distance by the Buddha Daitsū (*Mahābhijnajnanabhibhu Buddha*). One might suppose these were the people who were enlightened on their own, through the scattering of blossoms and the falling of leaves, or those who attained to the path outside the Buddha teaching.

Then there are those people who did not have a karmic relationship with the seeds sown in the past and became attached to the provisional teachings or the individual vehicle (*sanzō*). Even if they find the *Dharma Flower Sutra* (*Myōhō Renge Kyō*), they are unable to escape their vision of these provisional and individual vehicles (*shōjō, hīnayāna*). Because they accept their individual viewpoint to be the correct meaning, they take the *Dharma Flower Sutra* (*Myōhō Renge Kyō*) to be the same as the teachings of the individual vehicle (*sanzō*), or the *Flower Garland Sutra* (*Kegon, Avatāmsaka*), or the *Sutra on the Buddha Dainichi*, or place it even lower. All these teachers are inferior to the wise men of the Confucian and Brahmanic doctrines.

For the time being, let us put this aside. To formulate the mutual possession of the ten [psychological] realms of dharmas is like fire in a stone or flowers within a tree. Still, even though this is hard to believe, these things do happen on meeting with the right karmic affinities and are quite credible. Nevertheless, dragon fire comes out of water, and dragon water is produced from fire, even though it is not known why. But, because there is this manifest evidence, it becomes believable. Already you believe that the realm of humanity contains another nine realms. Then why are you not able to include the realm of the Buddha?

The Emperors Gyō (*Yao*) [2357-2255 BCE] and Shun (*Shun*) [2255-2205 BCE], as sage-like men, were impartial to all people. This is a part of the Buddha realm within that of humanity. What the Bodhisattva Not Holding Anyone or Anything in Contempt Ever (*Jōfukyō, Sadapāribbhūta*) saw in mankind was the person of the

Buddha. And Prince Sitta became the person of the Buddha, out of the realm of humanity. Surely this manifest evidence should make you believe.

(From here on, keep this strictly to yourself.)

The question is asked: Shākyamuni, Lord of the Teaching, was the Buddha who cut off the three delusions [greed, stupidity, and anger] and is lord of the abodes of all the realms of dharmas of the ten directions, as well as being lord and prince of all the bodhisattvas, people of the two vehicles, *deva* (*ten*), and humankind. Whenever he went about, there was Bonten (*Brahmā*) on the left and Taishaku (*Indra*) in attendance on the right. Monks, nuns, laymen, and laywomen, as well as the eight kinds of nonhumans with human intelligence followed behind, and the Vajra Holders led the way in front. Through the teaching of the Dharma store of eighty thousand teachings, he made all attain enlightenment. How could a Buddha such as this dwell in the individual minds of common mortals such as us?

Again, if we are to discuss the meaning of the former teachings and those of the temporary gateway, then the Lord of the Teaching Shākyamuni became correctly enlightened for the first time in his historical lifetime. But, when we look into his causal practices, either he was Prince Nōse, the Bodhisattva Judō, King Shibi, or Prince Satta. It was during this period of either three *asōgi kalpas*, a hundred *kalpas*, or for a period of *kalpas* that are liable to exceed the grains of dust, or for the incalculable *asōgi kalpas*, or from the time when he first resolved to attain to the bodhi mind, or even three thousand *kalpas* of grains of dust. He made offerings to seventy thousand, five thousand, six thousand, or seven thousand Buddhas, and, with the completion of the practices of accumulated *kalpas*, he has now become Lord of the Teaching Shākyamuni. Do you mean to say that the individual minds of all of us are endowed with the meritorious virtue of a Dharma realm of a bodhisattva, whose causal position is all those practices?

If we discuss the effective position, then the Lord of the Teaching Shākyamuni is the Buddha who became correctly enlightened for the first time in his historical life. Over a period of forty years, he displayed and revealed his sublime and solemn physical Buddha manifestations. And, during the four teachings and through the articulate expounding of the former teachings, the temporary gateway, and the *Sutra on the Buddha's Passing over to Nirvana*, he was able to benefit all beings.

When it comes to the periods of the Flower Garland and the Teachings of the Three Receptacles, we have Birushana Buddha (*Vairochana*) on the dais of the ten directions. In the sutras of the period of the teachings of the individual vehicle (*sanzō*), the Buddha cut the knots of misleading views and through the thirty-four states of mind, in order to attain to enlightenment. In the Equally Broad (*hōdō, vaipulya*) and Wisdom (*hannya, prajña*) teachings, we have thousands of Buddhas, and, in the *Sutra on the Buddha Dainichi* and the *Sutra on the Vajra Apex*, there are one thousand two hundred or so World Honoured Ones.

Then, there are the sublime and solemn physical Buddha manifestations of the four Buddha abodes – which are *i*) the dwelling place of humankind, *deva* (*ten*), and Buddha disciples, *ii*) the abode of hearers of the Buddha's voice or intellectual seekers and the people who are partially enlightened due to a profound search for the meaning of life, *iii*) the abode of partially enlightened bodhisattvas, and *iv*) the abode of silence and enlightenment – all of which are mentioned in the *Eleventh Chapter on Seeing the Vision of the Stupa made of Precious Materials*, which belongs to the temporary gateway. In the *Sutra on the Buddha's Passing over to Nirvana*, the Buddha is seen as sixteen feet high, or, alternatively, he reveals himself in either his large or small manifestations, or even as Birushana (*Vairochana*), and even as an embodiment that is not different from empty space. From the four kinds of body up to his entering nirvana at the age of eighty, he leaves his relics behind, for the effective benefit of the correct, formal, and final phases of his Dharma.

If you are to have doubts about the original gateway, Shākyamuni was a Buddha, prior to a length of time that would amount to the grains of dust would that go into the making of five hundred *kalpas*. Also, it is the same with his causal position. Since then, he has emanated his person in the existential spaces of the ten directions. In a lifetime of an articulate exposition of enlightened teaching, he taught and converted as many sentient beings as there are grains of dust.

If we compare those who were converted through the original gateway to those who were converted through the temporary, then it could be likened to a drop of water in the great sea, or a speck of dust to a huge mountain. One bodhisattva, of the original gateway, confronted with the Bodhisattva Universally Worthy (*Fugen, Samantabhadra*) or Kannon (*Avalokiteshvara*), of the existential spaces of the ten directions, would not even compare with the disparity between Taishaku (*Indra*) and a monkey.

Apart from this are the people of the two vehicles of the realms of dharmas of the ten directions who have destroyed delusion and witnessed fruition, Taishaku (*Indra*), the *deva* (*ten*) of the sun and moon, the Four Deva Kings, the Four Wheel Turning Deva Kings, down to the great flames of the hell of incessant suffering – are all the ten [psychological] realms of dharmas of our instant of thought or the three thousand existential spaces in our own minds? Even though this is what the Buddha taught, I find it hard to believe.

Then, we must take into consideration that all the sutras of the former teachings are real facts and words of truth. The *Flower Garland Sutra* (*Kegon, Avatāmsaka*) says, "Being the final superlative, it is free from empty delusion and without contamination, like the empty space of relativity (*kū*)." In the *Sutra on the Benevolent King*, it says, "When one has exhausted the source of troublesome worries (*bonnō, klesha*) and terminated at the fundamental nature, there remains the wisdom of Utterness." In the *Sutra on the Vajra Wisdom that Ferries Beings to the Shores of Nirvana*, it says, "There is nothing but immaculately pure goodness." In the *Awakening of Faith* by the Bodhisattva Memyō (*Ashvaghosha*), it says, "In the store of the Tathāgata, there is only immaculately pure and meritorious virtue." In the *Discourse on Consciousness Only* by the Bodhisattva Tenjin (*Vasubandhu*), we have, "It is said, when the remaining tainted and inferior tainted seeds appear in front of you during a *samādhi* like the vajra, you draw upon the chastely immaculate all round and clear original cognition. And, since it has no dependent environment, everything is relinquished and cast off forever."

If you measure the former teachings against the *Dharma Flower Sutra* (*Myōhō Renge Kyō*), the former sutras are without number, and the time it took to expound them is so much longer. Since the Buddha has two arguments, you should stay with the former teachings. Memyō (*Ashvaghosha*) was the eleventh successor to the Dharma store, whose advent was foretold by the Buddha. Tenjin was the teacher of dogma of a thousand volumes and a universal scholar of the four dependencies. The Universal Teacher Tendai (*T'ien T'ai*) was an inconsequential monk from an obscure border town who did not write a single treatise. Who could believe him?

[These four dependencies are *i*) to practise according to the Dharma and not the person who expounds it, *ii*) to practise according to the intention of the Dharma and not just the words that are used to express it, *iii*) to practise according to one's inner wisdom and not according to acquired knowledge, *iv*) to practise according to the real aspect of the middle way, as it is expounded in the *Sutra on Implications Without Bounds* (*Muryōgi-kyō*), and none other.]

Furthermore, I could even discard the many former teachings and adhere to the one, if there were a passage in the *Dharma Flower Sutra* (*Myōhō Renge Kyō*) that was understandably clear and on which one could at least depend. In which place in the text of the *Dharma Flower Sutra* (*Myōhō Renge Kyō*) is the clear and understandable textual proof of the mutual possession of the ten [psychological] realms of dharmas, the thousand such qualities, and the one instant of mind containing three thousand existential spaces (*ichinen sanzen*)?

In the sutra we have, "He cut off the evil in all dharmas." Neither Tenjin's *Discourse on the Dharma Flower* nor the Bodhisattva Kenne's *Discourse on the Precious Nature* has anything concerning the mutual possession of the ten [psychological] realms of dharmas. Not even the great Chinese teachers of dogma of the southern and northern schools, nor even any of the later teachers of the seven temples of Japan, have this concept. It is only Tendai

(*T'ien T'ai*) who has this biased view that was solely passed on in error by Dengyō (*Dengyō Daishi*). This is what the Teacher of the State Shōryō meant when he said, "It is the mistake of Tendai (*T'ien T'ai*)."

The Dharma Teacher Eon said, "However, when Tendai (*T'ien T'ai*) called the individual vehicle (*shōjō, hīnayāna*) the teaching of the Three Receptacles, he inadvertently got the names mixed up." Ryōkō said, "It is only Tendai (*T'ien T'ai*) who has not yet fathomed the meaning of the *Flower Garland Sutra* (*Kegon, Avatāmsaka*)." Tokuichi said, "Aren't you ashamed, Chi, you brat? Whose disciple do you think you are, with your tongue that is less than three inches? You slander the teachings of the time that were expounded with the Buddha's long, broad tongue that covered his face!"

The Universal Teacher Kōbō said, "The scholars of China wrangled with each other, in order to steal the ultimate, all-inclusive doctrine, which is the teaching of the one instant of mind containing three thousand existential spaces (*ichinen sanzen*), each one naming it as that of their own school." The Dharma gateway of the one instant of mind containing three thousand existential spaces (*ichinen sanzen*) is a term that is lacking in the provisional and the original teaching of the Buddha's lifetime. None of the masters of the four dependencies refer to this concept, and, since the scholars of China and Japan do not advocate it, how can one believe it?

Your criticism is indeed most harsh. However, it is understandably clear that what comes out of the sutric texts is the disparity between the *Dharma Flower* and all the other sutras – what is not yet revealed and that which has already been revealed, the demonstration of the proof by the long, broad tongue of the Buddha, whether the people of the two vehicles become Buddhas or not, or whether the Buddha became enlightened in his historical lifetime, or if he was enlightened in the primordial infinity of time.

With regard to the teachers of dogma, the Universal Teacher Tendai (*T'ien T'ai*) says, "Tenjin and Nāgārjuna (*Ryūju*) inwardly knew the truth, but withheld it, so as to properly conform to the times which were based upon the temporary doctrines. Nevertheless, the teachers of men, who came after, were biased in their understanding, and scholars invariably held on to their personal views, which finally led to stone throwing and abuse. Each clung to his own particular position and generally contravened the path of enlightenment." The Universal Teacher Shōan (*Chang-an*) said, "Even the Indian *Universal Discourse* is not of the calibre of Tendai (*T'ien T'ai*). So why should we go as far as to trouble ourselves talking about the scholars of China? This is not boastful arrogance. The nature of the Dharma is just as it is."

Tenjin (*Vasubandhu*), Nāgārjuna (*Ryūju*), Memyō (*Ashvaghosha*), and Kenne had inwardly known the truth but withheld it, because the time had not yet arrived, and it was not right to propagate it. Among the teachers of humankind, before Tendai (*T'ien T'ai*), some kept such thinking to themselves, whereas others knew nothing of it. Of those teachers who came after, some at first refuted this concept, but later compliantly committed themselves to it, while others made no use of it whatsoever.

But you have to understand the sutric text, "He cut off the evil in all dharmas." Here, the Buddha is referring to a sutric text that came before the *Dharma Flower Sutra* (*Myōhō Renge Kyō*). On taking a closer look at it, in this text, he is understandably and clearly about to discuss the mutual possession of the ten [psychological] realms of dharmas, where he says, "By being a sentient being, I wish to open their own Buddha knowing and perception." Tendai (*T'ien T'ai*), inspired by this sutric phrase, said, "If sentient beings had no Buddha knowing and perception, then why would he want to discuss their opening? As indeed you ought to know, sentient beings do have the knowing and perception of the Buddha inherently." The Universal Teacher Shōan (*Chang-an*) said, "If it were assumed that sentient beings did not have the knowing and perception of the Buddha, then why would he be about to open their awareness of it? If a poor woman did not have a treasure store, then why would he want to reveal it to her?"

The points that are difficult to understand are these enormous problems concerning the Lord of the Teaching Shākyamuni that we have just been discussing. As these problems are an impediment to our understanding of the Buddha, it says in the sutra, "Of all the sutras I have expounded, am expounding, and will expound, this *Dharma Flower Sutra* (*Myōhō Renge Kyō*) is the most difficult to believe and understand." We next come to the six difficult and nine easy acts. The Universal Teacher Tendai (*T'ien T'ai*) said, "Because the temporary and original gateways contradict the past sutras, they are difficult to believe and to understand. It is a matter that is as hard as facing the tip of a halberd." The Universal Teacher Shōan (*Chang-an*) said, "In view of this fact that the Buddha makes it his overriding concern, how could you take this to be easy to understand?" The Universal Teacher Dengyō (*Dengyō Daishi*) said, "This *Dharma Flower Sutra* (*Myōhō Renge Kyō*) is by far the most difficult to believe and most difficult to understand, because it is according to the Buddha's own enlightened mind."

From the one thousand eight hundred or so years since the Buddha's demise into nirvana, throughout the three countries of India, China, and Japan, there were only three people who were enlightened to and perceived this correct Dharma. They were Shākyamuni of India, the Universal Teacher Tendai (*T'ien T'ai*) of China, and Dengyō (*Dengyō Daishi*) of Japan. These three are the enlightened men of the Buddhist scriptures.

The question is asked: What of Nāgārjuna (*Ryūju*) and Tenjin (*Vasubandhu*)?

The answer is given: These enlightened men knew it, but out of unselfishness, they did not talk about it. Instead, they expounded a portion of the temporary gateway, but said nothing of the original gateway, nor the contemplation of the mind. Perhaps the propensity of the hearers was right, but the time was not. Or it could be that neither their propensity nor the time was appropriate.

After Tendai (*T'ien T'ai*) and Dengyō (*Dengyō Daishi*), many, many people understood it, through applying the wisdom of these two sages. Among these were Kashō of the Sanron School and the hundred or so persons from the three southern and seven northern schools of China, Hōzō and Shōryō of the Kegon School, Genjō

Tripitaka and the Universal Teacher Ji.en of the Hossō School, Zenmui Tripitaka, Kongōchi Tripitaka and Fukū Tripitaka of the Shingon, and Dōsen of the Ritsu School. At first, they were in opposition to the teaching of the one instant of mind containing three thousand existential spaces (*ichinen sanzen*), but later they wholeheartedly and obediently committed themselves to it.

Now, in order to restrain your harsh criticism, the *Sutra on Implications Without Bounds* (*Muryōgi-kyō*) says, "Let us imagine that the king of the realm and his queen had just had a prince born to them, and that he is only one day, two days, or seven days old, or that he is one month, two months, or seven months old, or one year, two years, or seven years old. Even though he is not able to administer the affairs of state, already he is honoured and respected by the ministers and citizens, and the children of all the great sovereigns are his companions. The king and queen attentively and with great love show him kindness and always speak to him gently. What is the reason for this? It is because of his being a little child.

"Good people, those who hold to this sutra are just like this child. The king of the realm is all the Buddhas, and this sutra is the queen who in union gave birth to the bodhisattva prince. Let us suppose that this bodhisattva hears of this sutra, and then he reads and recites the one phrase or the one metric hymn, then reads and recites all the sutra once, twice, ten times, a hundred times, a thousand times, ten thousand times. Or shall we assume he reads it a billion times, the number of grains of sand of the Ganges, or incalculable and numberless times? And yet, even though he is unable to realise the ultimate, true principle," the text continues, "he will already be held in esteem and honoured by all the monks, nuns, laymen, laywomen, the eight categories of the non-human beings with human intelligence, and all the great bodhisattvas will keep him company." The text continues until, "He will always be protected and borne in mind by all the Buddhas, and they will earnestly shelter him with their care and love, because he is a neophyte who is learning."

In the *Sutra on Practising Meditation on the Bodhisattva Universally Worthy* (*Fugen, Samantabhadra*) [*Butsu Setsu Kan Fugen Bosatsu*

Gyōhō Kyō], it says, "This sutric canon of the universal vehicle (*daijō, mahāyāna*) is the treasure store of all the Buddhas and is the eye of all the Buddhas of the ten directions of the past, present, and future." The text continues until, "...and is the seed from whence all the Tathāgatas of the past, present, and future come into being." The text continues until, "through your practice of the universal vehicle (*daijō, mahāyāna*), your Buddha seeds will not expire." Also, it says, "This sutra of the Equally Broad (*hōdō, vaipulya*) teachings is the eye of all the Buddhas. It is through this cause that all the Buddhas attain the five kinds of vision. The three kinds of body of the Buddha come into being out of the Equally Broad (*hōdō, vaipulya*) teachings. It is this gesture (*mudrā*) of proof of the universal Dharma that is substantiated in the sea of nirvana. Such an ocean as this is able to engender the immaculately pure three bodies of the Buddha. These three kinds of body are the fields of happiness of mankind and the *deva* (*ten*)."

Now we should think about the lifetime of the Tathāgata Shākyamuni. We have the exoteric and the esoteric, the two teachings of the universal and the individual vehicle (*sanzō*), as well as the dependent sutras of all the schools, such as the Kegon and the Shingon. Then, taking all this into further consideration – the Buddha Birushana, on the lotus throne with petals pointing to the ten directions, the cloud of all the assembled Buddha Tathāgatas gathered together from all over the universe, the apparition of the thousand Buddhas whose defilements are fused into the nothingness of the relativity (*kū, shūnyatā*) of the Wisdom (*hannya, prajña*) sutras, and the twelve hundred world honoured ones of the *Sutra on the Buddha Dainichi* and the *Sutra on the Vajra Apex* – all these sutras articulately expound the causes and fruition that are close at hand. But they do not reveal the cause and fruition in the primordial infinity.

Even though the Buddha talks about prompt, swift, and sudden attainment, his realisation in the immeasurability of the time span, like the grains of dust that make up three or five thousands *kalpas*, is missing, and the indications of the beginning and end of his converting and guidance are visibly lacking. On the one hand, the *Flower Garland Sutra* (*Kegon, Avatāmsaka*), or the *Sutra on the Buddha Dainichi* of the four teachings, that came before the Dharma

Flower, appear to be similar to the particular teachings or the all-inclusive teaching. But, on the other hand, if you think it over, they are comparable to the Equally Broad (*hōdō, vaipulya*) teachings or the Three Receptacles doctrine, without approaching a comparison to those of the particular or the all-inclusive doctrines. As the fundamentally existing three causes for Buddhahood are absent in these sutras, then how should we determine what the Buddha seeds are?

All the same, the day when the translators of the new editions returned to China, they saw and heard about Tendai's (*T'ien T'ai*) one instant of mind containing three thousand existential spaces (*ichinen sanzen*) and added it to the sutras that they would be bringing back with them. Or, they pretended it was, because they had received and committed this teaching to memory in India. Some of the scholars of Tendai (*T'ien T'ai*) were delighted that these teachings were the same as their own schools. Or they venerated the doctrines that had come from far away and showed contempt for those close at hand. Or they discarded the older teachings and embraced the new.

This was an outcome of wicked and stupid thinking. However it may be, if the point to which we refer did not have the Buddha seed of the one instant of mind containing three thousand existential spaces (*ichinen sanzen*), then sentient beings becoming Buddhas, along with both carved and painted images becoming fundamental objects of veneration, would just be words without substance.

I have not yet heard your perceptive understanding with regard to my great difficulties concerning the one instant of mind containing three thousand existential spaces (*ichinen sanzen*).

The answer is given: In the *Sutra on Implications Without Bounds* (*Muryōgi-kyō*), it says, "Even though you have not attained to the six practices (*pāramitā*) that ferry one beyond the sea of mortality to the shore of nirvana, the benefit of all six will surely be in front of you." In the *Dharma Flower Sutra* (*Myōhō Renge Kyō*), it says, "wishing to hear the path to complete fulfilment". In the *Sutra on the Buddha's passing over to Nirvana*, it says, "*Sat* is the name for complete fulfilment." The Bodhisattva Nāgārjuna (*Ryūju*) says, '*Sat* is six." In the *Annotations on the Profound Significance of the Four Treatises of the Universal Vehicle on the Wisdom that is Unqualified and Unobtainable by being Dependent on its own Relativity*, it says, "When *sat* is made clear, it means six, and, in the Dharmas of India, six has the implication of complete fulfilment." In the commentary referred to as the *Auspicious Treasury*, it says, "In translation, *sat* becomes complete fulfilment." The Universal Teacher Tendai (*T'ien T'ai*) said, "*Sat* is a Sanskrit word which is translated here as Utterness."

Were I to add any perceptive explanation, it would be sullying the original texts. In all events, the two dharmas of the causal practices and the culminating virtue of Shākyamuni were completely fulfilled through the seven ideograms for *Nam Myōhō Renge Kyō*, which means to devote our lives to and found them on (*Nam*[*u*]) the Utterness of the Dharma (*Myōhō*) [entirety of existence, enlightenment and unenlightenment] permeated by the underlying white lotus flower-like mechanism of the interdependence of cause, concomitancy and effect (Renge) in its whereabouts of the ten [psychological] realms of dharmas (*Kyō*). Then, should we receive and commit to memory these seven ideograms, we would naturally inherit the culminating virtue of those causal practices.

When the four great hearers of the voice apprehended this, they said, "We inadvertently acquired this peerless cluster of jewels, without even looking for it." This is the realm of the hearers of the Buddha's voice [or intellectuals] in our own minds. "Equal to myself without any difference whatsoever, just as that which I vowed in ancient times, has already been entirely fulfilled. All sentient beings, through their conversion, will be led onto the Buddha path." If the utterly enlightened Shākyamuni is our flesh and blood, then should not his causal practices be the marrow of our bones?

In the *Eleventh Chapter on Seeing the Vision of the Stupa made of Precious Materials*, it says, "Those people who protect the *Dharma Flower Sutra* (*Myōhō Renge Kyō*) are precisely those who make offerings to the Buddha Abundant Treasure (*Tahō Nyorai*,

Prabhūtaratna) and myself." The text continues until, "Moreover, they make offerings to the radiant brightness that majestically sublimates all the dharma realms of all the Buddha emanations that are present." Shākyamuni, Buddha Abundant Treasure (*Tahō Nyorai, Prabhūtaratna*), and all the Buddhas of the ten directions are the Buddha realm within. By inheriting and following this path, we will receive and attain their meritorious virtue. This is illustrated by, "If you listen to this sutra for only a moment, you will realise the ultimate, universal, and correct awakening."

In the *Sixteenth Chapter on the Lifespan of the Tathāgata*, it says, "However, since I really became a Buddha it is incalculable, boundless, hundreds of thousands, ten thousands, hundred thousands, uncountable *kalpas* ago." The Shākyamuni in our individual minds is the primordial Buddha without a beginning who manifested his three bodies, prior to a time span equal to the grains of dust that go into the making of five hundred *kalpas*. In the sutra it says, "The allotted lifespan of when I originally attained to the bodhisattva path has yet to be exhausted. It will be again twice that number." This is the bodhisattva realm in our own individual minds.

The countless numbers of bodhisattvas who swarmed up out of the earth are the retinue of the Shākyamuni in our minds, just as the Dukes Tai and Shū were ministers of King Bu [*Wu*, c. 1020 BCE] of Shū (Chou) and later were part of the court of the infant King Sei, or like the great minister Take-no-uchi, who was the supporting pillar of the Empress Jingū and afterwards became a minister of the Crown Prince Nintoku. The Bodhisattva Superior Practice (*Jōgyō, Vishishtachāritra*), Infinite Practice (*Muhengyō, Anantachārita*), Pure Practice (*Jyōgyō, Vishuddhachārita*), and Firmly Established Practice (*Anryūgyō, Supratishthichārita*) are the bodhisattvas of our individual minds. The Universal Teacher Myōraku (*Miao-lo*) said, "Really, you should know that the body and its terrain is the one instant of mind containing three thousand existential spaces (*ichinen sanzen*), because when one attains to the path, this fundamental principle, being substantiated in the one body and its one instant of mind, ubiquitously permeates through the realms of all the dharmas."

During the fifty or so years, which began at the site of Shākyamuni's attainment to the path of silence and extinction and the Dharma realm of the lotus flower – which is the abode of the Tathāgata Dainichi in the *Flower Garland Sutra* (*Kegon, Avatāmsaka*) – until his demise in the Grove of the Sal Trees, this Buddha taught that the three esoteric and majestically sublime terrains and the three or four transformations of abodes and terrains, expounded in the *Eleventh Chapter on Seeing the Vision of the Stupa made of Precious Materials*, are all manifestations of a transitory nature of expedient means, such as a terrain of real reward and of silence and enlightenment. The terrains of peaceful nourishment, immaculate lapis lazuli, and the majestically sublime are the coming into being, the duration, the decline, and their disappearance into the nothingness of relativity (*kū, shūnyatā*). When the Lord of the Teaching, who was able to produce these various emanations of the Buddha, entered into nirvana, all these Buddhas who were his emanations passed into extinction. And naturally it was also the same regarding their respective terrains.

The world in which we live at present is the time of the *Sixteenth Chapter on the Lifespan of the Tathāgata* of the original gateway and is free from the three calamities that come about with the collapse of a *kalpa*. It is an immaculate terrain that dwells in eternity. In times gone by, the Buddha has never ceased to be, nor does he come into being in the future. Those who are converted by him are of the same substance, which is the full endowment of the three thousand existential spaces in the one instant of mind in our individual minds. The reality of this had not yet been discussed in the fourteen chapters of the temporary gateway, because, even within the bounds of the *Dharma Flower Sutra* (*Myōhō Renge Kyō*), the propensity of the hearers and the time had not yet matured.

The Buddha did not even entrust the essence of the original gateway [the seven ideograms for Nam Myōhō Renge Kyō, the consecration and founding of one's life on the *Sutra on the White Lotus Flower-like Mechanism of the Utterness of the Dharma*] to the Bodhisattva Mañjushrī (*Monjushiri*), the Bodhisattva Universally Worthy (*Fugen, Samantabhadra*), and the Bodhisattva Sovereign Medicine (*Yaku' ō, Bhaishajya-rāja*), let alone anyone else. But he did entrust it, during his teaching of the eight vital chapters, to the countless numbers of bodhisattvas who swarmed up out of the earth at his summons.

As for the real appearance of the Fundamental Object of Veneration (*gohonzon*), the original teacher is seated in the *stupa* made of precious materials in empty space above the world in which we live. And on the left and right of the [Nam] Myōhō Renge Kyō, there are Shākyamuni Buddha and the Buddha Abundant Treasure (*Tahō Nyorai, Prabhūtaratna*), flanked by the Four Bodhisattvas led by the Bodhisattva Superior Practice (*Jōgyō, Vishishtachāritra*). Then we have Mañjushrī (*Monjushiri*), Maitreya (*Miroku*), and others of the following of the Four Bodhisattvas, placed on seats nearby. All the bodhisattvas great and small from other regions, who were converted by the temporary teachings, are placed upon the ground, like commoners looking up to court officials and executives of state. All the Buddhas of the ten directions are also on the ground, so as to express the idea of temporary Buddhas on temporary terrains.

Such an Object of Veneration (*gohonzon*) did not exist during the first fifty years when the Buddha was in the world. Its confines are only the final eight years of the eight vital chapters. During the two thousand years of the correct and formal phases of the Dharma of the Shākyamuni of the individual vehicle (*shōjō, hīnayāna*), Kashō (*Mahākashyapa*) and Anan (*Ānanda*) were in attendance on either side. The Shākyamuni of the provisional universal vehicle (*daijō, mahāyāna*), in the *Sutra on the Buddha's Passing over to Nirvana* and the teachings derived from the external events of the Buddha Shākyamuni's life and work of the *Dharma Flower Sutra* (*Myōhō Renge Kyō*), was flanked on either side by the Bodhisattva Mañjushrī (*Monjushiri*) and the Bodhisattva Universally Worthy (*Fugen, Samantabhadra*).

Even though there were sculptures and paintings of these Buddhas throughout the correct and formal phases of the Dharma, the Buddha of the *Sixteenth Chapter on the Lifespan of the Tathāgata* had not yet been portrayed. Now that we have entered the final phase of the Dharma (*mappō*), should we not begin to reveal the representation of this Buddha?

A question is posed: In the course of the two thousand years of the correct and formal phases of the Dharma, the bodhisattvas of the four dependencies, as well as the teachers of men, set up images and temples for various Buddhas and for the Shākyamuni of the individual vehicle (*shōjō, hīnayāna*), for the provisional universal vehicle (*daijō, mahāyāna*), the former teachings, and the teachings derived from the external events of the Buddha Shākyamuni's life and work.

Yet, there is no instance of the Fundamental Object of Veneration (*gohonzon*) of the *Sixteenth Chapter on the Lifespan of the Tathāgata* of the original gateway and the four great bodhisattvas being venerated and honoured by rulers and their ministers, either in India, China, or Japan. I can understand most of what you say, but, because it has never been heard by former generations, my eyes and ears are taken aback, and my mind and thoughts are bewildered. Please explain this once more. I would like to hear it in detail.

[These four dependencies are *i*) to practise according to the Dharma and not the person who expounds it, *ii*) to practise according to the intention of the Dharma and not just the words that are used to express it, *iii*) to practise according to one's inner wisdom and not according to acquired knowledge, *iv*) to practise according to the real aspect of the middle way, as it is expounded in the *Sutra on Implications Without Bounds* (*Muryōgi-kyō*), and none other.]

The answer is given: The eight fascicles and twenty-eight chapters of the *Dharma Flower Sutra* (*Myōhō Renge Kyō*) really begin with the four flavours [fresh milk, cream, curds, and butter, used as metaphors for the Flower Garland (*Kegon*), the teachings of the individual vehicle (*sanzō*), the equally broad (*hōdō, vaipulya*), and that of the wisdom (*hannya, prajña*) periods], and are all the sutras of a lifetime along with the *Sutra on the Buddha's Passing over to Nirvana*. The period that begins at the site of the attainment to the path of silence and extinction and ends at the Wisdom (*hannya, prajña*) sutras, is the introduction. The ten fascicles that make up the *Sutra on Implications Without Bounds* (*Muryōgi-kyō*), the *Dharma Flower Sutra* (*Myōhō Renge Kyō*), and the *Sutra on the Bodhisattva Universally Worthy* (*Fugen, Samantabhadra*) are the essential doctrine, and the *Sutra on the Buddha's Passing over to Nirvana* is the transmission.

[Nearly all the sutras can be divided into an introduction, an essential doctrine, and a transmission to be propagated widely. However, these divisions are often different, due to the conflicting viewpoints of the various schools.]

Within the ten fascicles, which make up the essential doctrine, there is an introduction, an essential doctrine, and a transmission that is to be propagated widely. The *Sutra on Implications Without Bounds (Muryōgi-kyō)* and the *Introductory Chapter of the Dharma Flower Sutra (Myōhō Renge Kyō)*, are the introduction. The fifteen and a half chapters, from the *Second Chapter on Expedient Means* to the nineteenth line of the metric hymn in the *Seventeenth Chapter on Discerning the Meritorious Virtues*, are the essential doctrine. The eleven and a half chapters and the one fascicle, from the four ways of believing for the present time of the *Chapter on Discerning the Meritorious Virtues* to the *Sutra on the Bodhisattva Universally Worthy (Fugen, Samantabhadra)*, are the transmission to be propagated widely.

Moreover, within the ten fascicles of the *Dharma Flower Sutra (Myōhō Renge Kyō)* there are again two sutras, each one having its own introduction, essential doctrine, and a transmission to be propagated widely. The *Sutra on the Implications Without Bounds (Muryōgi-kyō)* and the *Introductory Chapter of the Dharma Flower Sutra (Myōhō Renge Kyō)* are the introduction. The eight chapters, from the *Second Chapter on Expedient Means* to the *Eighth Chapter on the Prediction of Enlightenment for Five Hundred Disciples*, are the essential doctrine, and the five chapters from the Tenth, on the *Dharma as a Teacher*, to the *Fourteenth Chapter on Practising in Peace and with Joy*, make up the transmission that is to be propagated widely.

When we come to talk about the Lord of these teachings, then it was the Buddha, first correctly enlightened in his historical lifetime, whose correct Dharma was difficult to believe and difficult to understand. This is so, because it was expounded according to his own enlightened mind. He was able to reach beyond the past, present, and future, through expounding the previously nonexistent, but now existing, hundred realms of dharmas and the thousand such qualities.

If we look into the karmic circumstances that bound this Buddha with his disciples in the past, it was when he was the sixteenth son of the Buddha Daitsū (*Mahābhijnajnanabhibhu Buddha*) that he sowed the seeds of enlightenment in their lives. On proceeding further, it was through his karmic relationship with the four periods of teachings that came before the *Dharma Flower Sutra* (*Myōhō Renge Kyō*), the *Flower Garland* (*Kegon, Avatāmsaka*), the teachings of the individual vehicle (*shōjō, hīnayāna*), the equally broad (*hōdō, vaipulya*), and the wisdom (*hannya, prajña*) periods, which brought about the awakening and perception of the seeds of enlightenment planted by the Buddha Daitsū (*Mahābhijnajnanabhibhu Buddha*). This was not the fundamental intention of the Buddha Daitsū. Rather, it was to clear away some of the poison. Ordinary people and those of the two vehicles, through their karmic relationship with the first of the four periods of teachings that came before the *Dharma Flower Sutra* (*Myōhō Renge Kyō*), were gradually able to approach the Dharma Flower and discover the seeds that were sown in the primordial infinity and the propensity to free themselves from the teachings derived from the external events of the Buddha Shākyamuni's life and work and to discover the real teaching.

Moreover, when the Buddha was in the world, the eight vital chapters, or the one phrase, or the metric hymn, that were heard for the first time by humankind and *deva* (*ten*), became the seeds of their Buddhahood, which either grew towards maturity or became the seeds of the Buddha fulfilment. Some were liberated when they came to the *Sutra on the Bodhisattva Universally Worthy* (*Fugen, Samantabhadra*) and the *Sutra on the Buddha's Passing over to Nirvana*. Then again, for others, it was during the correct, formal, and final phases of the Dharma that the individual and provisional doctrines became the karmic relationship whereby they were able to enter into the *Dharma Flower Sutra* (*Myōhō Renge Kyō*), in the same way as the people who were familiar with the teachings of the first four periods and were able to discover their seeds of enlightenment during the lifetime of the Buddha.

Again, the fourteen chapters of the original gateway possess an introduction, an essential doctrine, and a transmission to be propagated widely. The first half of the *Fifteenth Chapter on the Bodhisattvas who Swarm up out of the Earth* is the introduction. The remaining half that comes just before the *Sixteenth Chapter on the Lifespan of the Tathāgata* and the first half of the *Seventeenth Chapter on Discerning the Meritorious Virtues* is the essential doctrine. The remaining chapters are the transmission that is to be widely propagated. When we come to discuss the lord of these teachings, it is not the Buddha Shākyamuni, first correctly enlightened in his historical lifetime. The Dharma gateways that he expounded contrast with the gateway to enlightenment of the teachings derived from the external events of the Buddha Shākyamuni's life and work, as much as the earth differs from sky.

In addition to the ten [psychological] realms of dharmas and the primordial infinity, he made the existential spaces and the differentiation of abode and terrain apparent and provided the one instant of mind containing three thousand existential spaces (*ichinen sanzen*) with an envelope, just as a husk encloses the pith of bamboo. Furthermore, the gateway to enlightenment of the teachings derived from the external events of the Buddha Shākyamuni's life and work, as well as the first four periods of the teachings prior to the *Dharma Flower Sutra* (*Myōhō Renge Kyō*), the *Sutra on Implications Without Bounds* (*Muryōgi-kyō*) and the *Sutra on the Buddha's Passing over to Nirvana*, were all taught according to the minds of others and therefore easy to believe and easy to understand. But the discourse of the original gateway is difficult to believe and difficult to understand, because it is according to the enlightened mind of the Buddha.

In the original gateway, there is also an introduction, an essential doctrine, and a transmission that is to be propagated widely. From the *Dharma Flower Sutra of the Buddha Daitsū* (*Mahābhijnajnanabhibhu Buddha*) of the past to the *Flower Garland* (*Kegon, Avatāmsaka*) of the present time – including the fourteen chapters of the teachings derived from the external events of the Buddha Shākyamuni's life and work gateway and the *Sutra on the Buddha's Passing over to Nirvana*, as well as all the sutras of the fifty or so years of a lifetime's teaching, along with all the sutras of all the Buddhas of the past, present, and future of the ten directions, which are as countless as the grains of dust – these comprise the introduction to the *Sixteenth Chapter on the Lifespan of the Tathāgata*.

Apart from the second half of the *Fifteenth Chapter on the Bodhisattvas who Swarm up out of the Earth*, the whole of the *Sixteenth Chapter on the Lifespan of the Tathāgata*, and the first half of the *Seventeenth Chapter on Discerning the Meritorious Virtues*, the remainder can be referred to as the teachings of the individual vehicle (*sanzō*) that are distorting and incomplete and have not yet attained to enlightenment, or teachings that conceal the real intention of the Buddha. If we are to discuss the natural inclination of those who follow these teachings derived from the external events of the Buddha Shākyamuni's life and work, then they are heavily sullied, with little virtue. They are immature and feel like unwanted orphans or birds and beasts who cannot appreciate the love of their parents.

Besides the former teachings and the all-inclusive teachings of the teachings derived from the external events of the Buddha Shākyamuni's life and work gateway, such teachings do not possess the cause for becoming a Buddha and cannot even match the *Sutra on the Buddha Dainichi* and all the sutras of the individual vehicle (*shōjō, hīnayāna*). They are of even less value than the instructions of the teachers of men and the teachers of dogma of the seven schools, such as the Kegon and the Shingon Schools.

Putting it strongly, the spirit of these teachings is not different from the teachings of the three receptacles, the interrelated teachings, or the particular teaching. For instance, even though these Dharmas are said to be extremely profound, they have not yet discussed the seeds of enlightenment of Nam Myōhō Renge Kyō, as opposed to those seeds that were implanted by a Buddha in a distant past that nurtured and ultimately brought about emancipation. Instead, they propose that the body be reduced to ashes and that the mind and intellect be annihilated, as in the individual vehicle (*shōjō, hīnayāna*). In these doctrines, there is no suggestion of when the Buddha began and ended his teachings and guidance. Should such a person as a queen be made pregnant by an animal's seed, the offspring would be even inferior to an outcast. For the time being, we will put this aside.

On taking a first glance at eight chapters of the essential doctrine of the fourteen chapters of the gateway to enlightenment of the teachings derived from the external events of Shākyamuni's life and work, the people of the two vehicles are in the forefront, and the bodhisattvas and common mortals are set to one side. But, on thinking it over a second time, it is the common mortal who comes to the fore during the correct, formal, and final phases of the Dharma. In these three periods of the correct, formal, and final phases, it is the beginning of the final phase that becomes the correct phase.

The question is asked: What evidence do you have for this?

The answer is given: In the *Tenth Chapter on the Dharma as a Teacher*, it says, "Nevertheless, with this sutra, at present, the Tathāgata is much begrudged and envied. So how will it be after his passing over to nirvana?" In the *Eleventh Chapter on Seeing the Vision of the Stupa made of Precious Materials*, it says, "In order that the Dharma may be protracted unendingly," continuing in the text until, "the Buddha emanations must be aware that this is his intention." You should look at the *Thirteenth Chapter on Exhorting the Disciples to Receive and to Hold to the Buddha Teaching* and the *Fourteenth Chapter on Practising in Peace and with Joy*. This is indeed what the gateway to enlightenment of the teachings derived from the external events of Shākyamuni's life and work is about.

Now we come to consider the original gateway, which was destined solely for the people of correct propensities at the beginning of the final phase of the Dharma of Shākyamuni (*mappō*). That is to say, we first take a look at the period when the seeds are those of the primordial sowing. Nurtured by the Buddha Daitsū (*Mahābhijnajnanabhibhu Buddha*), and, afterwards through the first four periods of teachings prior to the *Dharma Flower Sutra* (*Myōhō Renge Kyō*) and the gateway to enlightenment of the teachings derived from the external events of Shākyamuni's life and work, they ripened. On coming to the original gateway, these seeds were brought to the attainment of both the Universal

Enlightenment [*Tōgaku*] and the Enlightenment to Utterness [*Myōgaku*].

On taking a second look, the original gateway is quite unlike the temporary gateway, the introduction, the essential doctrine, as well as the transmission to be widely propagated of the original gateway, in that they all refer to the beginning of the final phase of the Dharma (*mappō*). The original gateway, when the Buddha Shākyamuni was in the world, and that of the beginning of the final phase of his Dharma (*mappō*) are a pure circle, but the former is his teaching of the harvest [the fulfilment of the seeds of enlightenment that were implanted by a Buddha in the distant past, which matured, and brought about emancipation].

However, this is the Buddha teaching of the seeds situated in the interdependence of cause and effect of the Utterness of the Dharma (*Myōhō, Saddharma*). The former doctrine is based on the second half of the *Fifteenth Chapter on the Bodhisattvas who Swarm up out of the Earth*, the whole of the *Sixteenth Chapter on the Lifespan of the Tathāgata*, and the first half of the *Seventeenth Chapter on Discerning the Meritorious Virtues*. This later doctrine is the teaching of the seven ideograms for *Nam Myōhō Renge Kyō* only.

The question is asked: What proof do you have for this?

The answer is given: In the *Fifteenth Chapter on the Bodhisattvas who Swarm up out of the Earth*, it says, "At that time, all the bodhisattvas who had relinquished their entry into nirvana for the sake of the Buddha enlightenment of all sentient beings (*bosatsu makasatsu, bodhisattva mahāsattva*), who had come from other abodes and terrains and whose number exceeded eight times the grains of sand of the Ganges, stood up in the great assembly, placed their palms together in obeisance, and said to the Buddha, 'World Honoured One, when, after the passing of the Buddha into nirvana, we are to be born into the Dimension that must be Endured (*shaba sekai, sahā-lokadhātu*), if you will allow us to guard, hold, read, recite, copy, and make offerings to this sutric canon, with zealous and unfailing progress, then surely we will broadly expound it throughout this terrain.'

"Then the Buddha said to the assembly of bodhisattvas who had relinquished their entry into nirvana for the sake of the Buddha enlightenment of all sentient beings (*bosatsu makasatsu, bodhisattva mahāsattva*), 'Desist! Good people, there is no need for you to guard and hold to this sutra.'"

The sutric content of the preceding five chapters, that follow the *Tenth Chapter on the Dharma as a Teacher,* are as contradictory as fire and water. At the end of the *Eleventh Chapter on Seeing the Seeing the Vision of the Stupa made of Precious Materials*, it says, "With a great voice, the Buddha addressed the monks, nuns, laymen, and laywomen: 'Is there anyone who is able to broadly propagate the *Sutra on the White Lotus Flower-like Mechanism of the Utterness of the Dharma* throughout the abode and terrain that we live in and endure?'"

There is the instance when the lord of the teaching, being but one single Buddha, encouragingly raised this question. The bodhisattvas who had relinquished their entry into nirvana for the sake of the Buddha enlightenment of all sentient beings (*bosatsu makasatsu, bodhisattva mahāsattva*), such as the Bodhisattva Sovereign Medicine (*Yaku' ō, Bhaishajya-rāja*), the *deva* (*Brahmā*) and Taishaku (*Indra*), the *deva* (*ten*) of the sun and moon, and the Four Deva Kings, took this to be a matter of grave concern, whereupon the Buddha Tahō and the Buddhas of the ten directions, as invited guests, added to their consternation. All the bodhisattvas, on hearing this generous collaboration, made the vow, "We will not begrudge our lives", because they wholeheartedly wished to comply with the Buddha's will.

Nevertheless, within the space of an instant, Shākyamuni contradicts himself, by forbidding the crowd of bodhisattvas – whose count exceeded eight times the number of grains of sand of the Ganges – to propagate the *Dharma Flower Sutra* (*Myōhō Renge Kyō*). Going forwards and backwards like this decidedly goes against ordinary understanding.

The wise Universal Teacher Tendai (*T'ien T'ai*) led us to comprehend the six explanations of three previous reasons, as to why the Buddha prohibited the bodhisattvas who had relinquished their entry into nirvana for the sake of the Buddha enlightenment of all sentient beings (*bosatsu makasatsu, bodhisattva mahāsattva*) from propagating the sutra throughout the world in which we live, and three subsequent reasons for his summoning the bodhisattvas who swarm up out of the earth. What was implied is that the bodhisattvas who had relinquished their entry into nirvana for the sake of the Buddha enlightenment of all sentient beings (*bosatsu makasatsu, bodhisattva mahāsattva*) from all other directions, along with those who were converted through the temporary teachings derived from the external events of Shākyamuni's life and work, did not have the substantiation of the Shākyamuni, who is the essence of the *Sixteenth Chapter on the Lifespan of the Tathāgata*, bestowed upon them [i.e., the indestructibility of existence]. These bodhisattvas were forbidden to propagate the *Dharma Flower Sutra* (*Myōhō Renge Kyō*), because of the fundamentally evil qualities of the abodes and terrains, where the Dharma would be vilified at the beginning of the final phase of the Dharma of Shākyamuni (*mappō*).

Then, he summoned the bodhisattvas who had relinquished their entry into nirvana for the sake of the Buddha enlightenment of all sentient beings (*bosatsu makasatsu, bodhisattva mahāsattva*) of the thousand realms of dharmas who swarmed up out of the earth, in order to confer upon the sentient beings of the world of humankind the five ideograms for Myōhō Renge Kyō, which are the essence of the *Sixteenth Chapter on the Lifespan of the Tathāgata*. Moreover, the great assembly of bodhisattvas, converted through the temporary teachings, were not the disciples of Shākyamuni when he first resolved to attain a mind of enlightenment. The Universal Teacher Tendai (*T'ien T'ai*) cites the *Dharma Flower Sutra* (*Myōhō Renge Kyō*), "These are my disciples who are destined to propagate my Dharma." Myōraku (*Miao-lo*) called to mind, "The sons who spread abroad the Dharma of the father are a benefit to the world." In the *Supplementary Adjustments and Annotations of the Textual Explanations*, it says, "Since this is the Dharma of the primordial infinity, it was to be entrusted to the people who were enlightened in that primordial infinity."

In the sutra it says that, when the Bodhisattva Maitreya (*Miroku*) wished to clear his doubts, he remarked, "Even though we believe that what the Buddha says is correct, the words that he utters are never empty delusions, and his wisdom is completely pervasive and penetrating. Nevertheless, after the Buddha's passing over to nirvana, bodhisattvas who are newly resolved to attain to enlightenment may not accept with faith that the Bodhisattvas who swarmed up out of the earth are the Buddha's original disciples and that will give rise to the cause and karmic circumstances of the sin of negating the Dharma. It is only natural, World Honoured One, that we ask you to explain and take away our doubts, so that all good people, in generations to come, will not be sceptical when they hear of this matter." The meaning of this text is that Maitreya (*Miroku*) implored the Buddha to expound the Dharma gateway of the *Chapter on the Lifespan of the Tathāgata*, for those who are to come after his passing over to nirvana.

It says in the *Sixteenth Chapter on the Lifespan of the Tathāgata*, "Some lost their original minds and others did not." The text continues until, "Those who did not lose their minds saw that this medicine was good both in appearance and flavour, whereupon they took it and were completely cured and relieved of their sickness." All the bodhisattvas, people of the two vehicles, and *deva* (*ten*) – whose Buddha seeds had been planted in the primordial infinity of time, were later nurtured through their karmic relationship with the Buddha Daitsū (*Mahābhijnajnanabhibhu Buddha*), and through the four periods of teachings, that came before the *Dharma Flower Sutra* (*Myōhō Renge Kyō*) and the temporary gateway – attained the way when they heard the original gateway.

In the sutra it goes on to say, "Those who had lost their minds were filled with joy when they saw that their father had arrived, and they earnestly begged him to cure their sickness. But, even though they were given the medicine, they did not take it. This was because the spirit of the poison had penetrated deeply, and, having lost their original minds, they found the attractive and delicious preparation unpalatable." The text continues until, "I really must contrive an expedient means, in order to make them take this medicine." The text further explains, "'I will now place this good and estimable medicine here. And you must take and make use of it, without worrying that it may not cure you.' After giving these instructions, he again went off to another country, where he sent back a messenger to announce that he was dead." In the *Chapter on Discerning the Meritorious Virtues*, it says, "For those of the time of the evil age of the final phase of the Dharma (*mappō*)."

The question is asked: What is meant by "he sent back a messenger to announce"?

The answer is given: Within the four dependencies of the Buddha teaching, there are four categories.

[These four dependencies are the four important principles, on which the practitioner relies. They are *i*) to practise according to the Dharma and not the person who expounds it, *ii*) to practise according to the intention of the Dharma and not just the words that are used to express it, *iii*) to practise according to one's inner wisdom and not according to acquired knowledge, *iv*) to practise according to the real aspect of the middle way, as it is expounded in the *Sutra on Implications Without Bounds* (*Muryōgi-kyō*), and none other.]

Those of the first of the four dependencies of the individual vehicle (*shōjō, hīnayāna*) appeared for the most part during the first five hundred years of the correct era of the Dharma. Those of the second of the four dependencies of the universal vehicle (*daijō, mahāyāna*) appeared for the most part during the latter five hundred years of the correct phase of the Dharma. Those of the third of the four dependencies of the temporary gateway mostly appeared during the thousand years of the formal phase of the Dharma, but a smaller number appeared during the beginning of its final phase. Those of the fourth of the four dependencies of the original gateway are the countless numbers of bodhisattvas who swarm up out of the earth and must certainly appear at the beginning of the final phase of the Dharma (*mappō*).

The "messenger sent back to announce" is now the bodhisattvas who swarm up out of the earth. "This good and estimable medicine" is the theme and title, the substance, the purpose, the function, and the influence of Nam Myōhō Renge Kyō, which comprises the essentials of the *Chapter on the Lifespan of the Tathāgata*. The Buddha did not even confer this good medicine upon the bodhisattvas who were converted by the temporary teachings, let alone those from other directions.

In the *Chapter on the Reaches of the Mind of the Tathāgata*, it says, "At that time, as many bodhisattva great beings as there are particles of dust that comprise a thousand existential spaces swarmed up out of the earth in front of the Buddha, and, with a single mind, put their palms together, looked up with reverence at his venerable countenance, and said, 'World Honoured One, after the Buddha's passing over to nirvana, we must certainly propagate widely this sutra in the abodes and terrains where your emanations exist and in the places where you pass over to nirvana.'"

Tendai (*T'ien T'ai*) said, "It appears that only the bodhisattvas who swarmed up out of the earth made this vow." Dōsen said, with regard to the assignment, "This sutra was solely entrusted to those who swarmed up out of the nether directions. What is the reason for this? It is because the primordial Dharma was assigned to the people of the primordial attainment."

The Boddhisattva Mañjushrī (*Monjushiri*) was the disciple of the Buddha Fudō of the Golden Coloured Realm of the Eastern Direction. Kannon (*Avalokiteshvara*) was the disciple of the Buddha Muryōju of the Western Direction. The Bodhisattva Sovereign Medicine (*Yaku' ō, Bhaishajya-rāja*) was the disciple of the Buddha Nichigetsu Jōmyotoku. The Bodhisattva Universally Worthy (*Fugen, Samantabhadra*) was the disciple of the Buddha Ho.i. In general terms, these bodhisattvas came to the existential realm that has to be endured (*shaba sakai, sahāloka*), in order to help Shākyamuni with his activity of converting people. But, as they were bodhisattvas of the former, temporary teachings and not in possession of the original Dharma, they were not qualified to propagate it during the final phase of the Dharma (*mappō*).

In the sutra it says, "At that time, the World Honoured One," and the text continues until, "in front of the assembly, he displayed the immensity of the reaches of his mind, by extending his long and broad tongue as far as the realm of Bonten (*Brahmā*)." Again, the text continues until, "all the Buddhas of the ten directions seated on their lion thrones did likewise, extending their long and broad tongues."

Now, in none of the sutras, whether they are of the universal (*daijō, mahāyāna*) or the individual vehicle (*shōjō, hīnayāna*) or whether they are exoteric or esoteric, is there a passage that describes Shākyamuni and all the other Buddhas seated and extending their tongues to the heaven of Bonten (*Brahmā*). The *Sutra on the Buddha Amida* (*Amitabha Buddha*) has the Buddhas extending their tongues and covering three thousand great thousand existential spaces, but they are words without substance. In the *Wisdom Sutra* (*hannya, prajña*), the Buddha's tongue also covered three thousand great thousand existential spaces and emitted boundless light when he began to expound this sutra. But, this is completely without substance, since both of these texts are only the Pure Land and Wisdom (*hannya, prajña*) teachings, whose partial role was to obscure the Buddha's enlightenment in the primordial infinity.

After the Buddha revealed his ten immense reaches of his mind, as told in the *Chapter on the Reaches of the Mind of the Tathāgata*, he then entrusted and implicated the bodhisattvas who swarmed up out of the earth with the seven ideograms of the Utterness of the Dharma (*Nam Myōhō Renge Kyō*). As it is recounted in the sutra, "At that time the Buddha said to Superior Practice's (*Jōgyō, Vishishtachāritra*) great assembly of bodhisattvas, 'Thus are the reaches of the minds of all Buddhas. They are incalculable, boundless, and cannot be thought through or deliberated upon. In order to entrust and implicate people in this sutra by means of these spiritual powers, if I were to recount its meritorious virtues, for incalculable and boundless hundreds, thousands of *nayuta kalpas*, I would not be able to explain them fully. So, I will mention these crucial points. They are all the dharmas that are in the possession of the Tathāgata, all the unrestricted reaches of the mind of the Tathāgata, all the esoterically essential stores of the Tathāgata, and all the extremely profound concerns of the Tathāgata. All these are proclaimed, shown, revealed, and expounded in this sutra.'"

Tendai (*T'ien T'ai*) says, "In this chapter, from the line, 'At that time, the Buddha said to Superior Practice (*Jōgyō, Vishishtachāritra*),' and onwards, is the third stage of entrusting the bodhisattvas who swarmed up out of the earth with the assignment of binding together the essentials." Dengyō (*Dengyō Daishi*) says, "Again, in the *Chapter on the Reaches of the Mind of the Tathāgata*, from, 'So, I will mention these crucial points; it is all the Dharmas that are in possession of the Tathāgata,' and continuing until, 'All these are proclaimed, shown, revealed, and expounded in this sutra,' – what we can clearly infer from this is that all the Dharmas that are in the possession of the Tathāgata are those of the karmic dimension of utter enlightenment. All the unrestricted reaches of the mind of the Tathāgata are also those of the karmic dimension of utter enlightenment, as well as the esoterically essential store of the Tathāgata. All are proclaimed, shown, revealed, and expounded in the *Dharma Flower Sutra* (*Myōhō Renge Kyō*)." These immense reaches of his mind were, through the five ideograms of the *Sutra on the White Lotus Flower-like Mechanism of the Utterness of the Dharma*, (*Myōhō Renge Kyō*), conferred upon the four Great Bodhisattvas Superior Practice (*Jōgyō, Vishishtachāritra*), Firmly Established Practice (*Anryūgyō, Supratishthichārita*), Pure Practice (*Jyōgyō, Vishuddhachārita*), and Infinite Practice (*Muhengyō, Anantachārita*).

[The ten reaches of his mind are the following: *i*) to show that the Buddha does not tell fantastic untruths, *ii*) the emission of light from all the pores of the Buddha's body shining into all existence of the ten directions, demonstrating where the wisdom of the Tathāgata can penetrate. *iii*) The Buddha clears his throat, in order to speak with gentleness that will be heard by all his hearers and also to be able to teach the truth without hindrance. *iv*) The Buddha snaps his fingers to show that he is expounding according to his own enlightenment. *v*) The Buddha brings about six earth tremors, so that the six organs of sense of sentient brings may be purified and that every stage of enlightenment may be awakened. *vi*) The great assembly and the Buddha are universally manifested to all sentient beings of the ten directions, in order to give them joy and also to show that the paths of all the Buddhas are identical. *vii*) The Buddha in the empty space of all the heavens, facing the great assembly that had come from the ten directions, announced in a strong voice that they should wholeheartedly venerate the *Dharma Flower Sutra* (*Myōhō Renge Kyō*), so that it will be propagated to future generations. *viii*) The sentient beings who heard the Buddha's voice from out of the empty space took refuge in his teaching, in order that all abodes and terrains would be filled with people who could hold to his teaching. *ix*) All the offerings made to the Buddha by all the sentient beings from the ten directions form a cloud-like canopy over all the assembled Buddhas, to show that only this sutra will be practised in the future. *x*) Since all the realms of existence of the ten directions are the Buddha terrain, this means that in the future all sentient beings will be able to open up and reveal their own Buddha nature and will understand the true nature of their abodes and terrains. According to the *Textual Explanations of Dharma Flower Sutra* (*Hokke Mongu*), the first five of these reaches of his mind were for the time when Shākyamuni was in the world, and the last five were for the benefit of sentient beings in the future.]

The first five of the reaches of his mind were for when the Buddha was in the world and the second five for when the Buddha had passed over to nirvana. However, if one were to discuss this more fully, then all these reaches of his mind were for the period after the Buddha's passing over to nirvana. Hence, further on in the text, it says, "After the Buddha's passing over to nirvana, because of their being able to hold to this sutra, all the Buddhas, by way of rejoicing, reveal their limitless spiritual powers."

In the following *Chapter on the Assignment of the Mission*, it says, "At that time the Buddha Shākyamuni stood up from his Dharma throne and revealed the universal reaches of his mind. With his right hand, he touched the tops of the heads of incalculable bodhisattva beings," continuing until, "I entrust you with this assignment."

At first the bodhisattvas who swarmed up out of the earth, followed by those converted by the teachings derived from the external events of Shākyamuni's life and work, and those who came from other directions, as well as Bonten (*Brahmā*), Taishaku (*Indra*), and the four Deva Kings, were all entrusted and implicated in this sutra – "All of the Buddha Emanations who came from the ten directions returned to their original terrains," until, "The Stupa of the Buddha Abundant Treasure (*Tahō Nyorai, Prabhūtaratna*) had to be returned to its original place as well." From the *Chapter on the Bodhisattva Sovereign Medicine (Yaku' ō, Bhaishajya-rāja)* as far as the *Sutra on the Buddha's Passing over to Nirvana*, after the bodhisattvas who swarmed up out of the earth had departed, the Buddha once again entrusted the assembly of bodhisattvas converted by the temporary teachings derived from the external events of Shākyamuni's life and work and the bodhisattvas from other regions with the commission of propagating the *Dharma Flower Sutra (Myōhō Renge Kyō)*. This is the entrustment and implication and a final ordering of the details.

It is asked doubtfully: During the two thousand years of the correct and formal era of the Dharma, did the thousands of realms of bodhisattvas, who swarmed up out of the earth, appear in the world of mankind to propagate this sutra widely?

Naturally, they did not.

The questioner having been taken aback, it is then asked: If the *Dharma Flower Sutra (Myōhō Renge Kyō)* and the original gateway were to become the fundamental doctrine for when the Buddha had passed over to nirvana, and had been first conferred to the thousands of realms of bodhisattvas who swarmed up out of the earth, why did they not appear during the correct and formal eras of the Dharma to propagate them? Why is it?

The answer is given: If I were to tell you, it would be as it was for all the people of all the existential realms [who refused to believe and slandered] in the final phase of the Dharma of the Buddha Ionnō. Or, if I were to vaguely disclose it to my disciples, it would degenerate into backbiting slander. Therefore, I desist and remain silent.

Still, to pursue the question further, it is said that by not discussing it with you, I will fall into the error of holding back the truth.

Then, the answer given is that, whether I advance or retreat, I shall fall into the chasm, so I will try to expound it to you.

In the *Chapter on the Dharma as a Teacher*, it says, "So how will it be after his passing over to nirvana?" In the *Sixteenth Chapter on the Lifespan of the Tathāgata*, it says, "I now leave it here." In the *Chapter on Discerning the Meritorious Virtues*, it says, "the time of the evil generations of the final phase of the Dharma (*mappō*)". And, in the *Chapter on the Bodhisattva Sovereign Medicine* (*Yaku' ō, Bhaishajya-rāja*), "After the fifth five hundred years, there will be broad propagation throughout the world of mankind." In the *Sutra on the Buddha's Passing over to Nirvana*, it says, "For example, there are seven children who are all equally loved by their parents. Nevertheless, they are particularly concerned for one that is sick."

By the clear mirror of the passages just quoted, we can infer and realise what the intentions of the Buddha are. The Buddha did not come into the world just for the people who were on Spirit Vulture Peak (*Ryōjusen, Gridhrakūta*) during the eight years of teaching, but for humanity during the correct, formal, and final phases of the Dharma. It was not merely for the people of the two thousand years of the correct and formal phases of the Dharma, but for those at the beginning of the final era of the Dharma, like myself. The so-called "one that is sick" points to those who revile and slander the *Dharma Flower Sutra* (*Myōhō Renge Kyō*) after the Buddha's passing over to nirvana. "I now leave it here," refers to the phrase, "They found this attractive and tasty remedy unpalatable."

The thousands of realms of bodhisattvas and their realms of dharmas that swarmed up out of the earth did not appear during the correct and formal phases of the Dharma, as the propensities of the people and the time were not right.

The thousand years of the correct Dharma was for the individual vehicle (*shōjō, hīnayāna*) and the provisional universal vehicle (*daijō, mahāyāna*). The great bodhisattvas of the four dependencies had karmic relationships with these provisional and individual teachings (*shōjō, hīnayāna*), which became their implanted seeds that were liberated whilst the Buddha was in the world. If the bodhisattvas who swarmed up out of the earth had appeared at that particular time and taught the *Dharma Flower Sutra* (*Myōhō Renge Kyō*), they would have been greatly slandered. This would have destroyed the benefit of the emancipation of the great bodhisattvas of the four dependencies, whose basic capacities and dispositions were for the first four periods of teachings, prior to the *Dharma Flower Sutra* (*Myōhō Renge Kyō*).

[These four dependencies are *i*) to practise according to the Dharma and not the person who expounds it, *ii*) to practise according to the intention of the Dharma and not just the words that are used to express it, *iii*) to practise according to one's inner wisdom and not according to acquired knowledge, *iv*) to practise according to the real aspect of the middle way, as it is expounded in the *Sutra on Implications Without Bounds* (*Muryōgi-kyō*), and none other.]

In the middle and towards the end of the formal phase of the Dharma, the Bodhisattva Kannon (*Avalokiteshvara*) was reborn as Nangaku (*Nan-yüeh*), and the Bodhisattva Sovereign Medicine (*Yaku' ō, Bhaishajya-rāja*) as Tendai (*T'ien T'ai*). The temporary gateway was taught in the open, and the original gateway held in reserve. Tendai exhaustively expounded the significance of the hundred realms and the thousand thousand ways in which dharmas make themselves present to any of our six sense organs – eyes, ears, nose, tongue, body – and the one instant of mind containing three thousand existential spaces (*ichinen sanzen*), teaching everything as being its own intrinsicality and aspects of the whole. But he did not actually put into practice nor propagate the seven ideograms for Nam Myōhō Renge Kyō, nor the Fundamental Object of Veneration (*gohonzon*) of the original gateway. In the final analysis, he had propensities for the all-inclusive teachings, but it was not the right time.

Now, at the beginning of the final phase of the Dharma (*mappō*), the followers of the individual vehicle (*shōjō, hīnayāna*) attack the universal doctrine, and the people who follow the provisional teachings demolish those of the real universal vehicle (*daijō, mahāyāna*). East and west are muddled together, and heaven and earth are turned upside down. The people of the four dependencies, converted by the temporary teachings, are hidden away and no longer before us. And the *deva* (*ten*) have abandoned their abodes, no longer guarding and protecting them.

This is the time when the bodhisattvas, who swarm up out of the earth, begin to appear, solely to administer to the immature sentient beings the ideograms for Nam Myōhō Renge Kyō. This is in fact the implication of, "By slandering, they fall into evil, and it is on account of this that they seek to acquire meritorious virtues."

My disciples, take this into account: The thousands of bodhisattvas who swarmed up out of the earth are the disciples of the Lord of the Teaching Shākyamuni, when he first resolved to attain to the mind of enlightenment. They did not come to the site of the attainment to the path of silence and extinction. Nor did they visit the grove of sal trees at the end, thereby falling into the error of lacking filial piety. They were not even present during the fourteen chapters of the temporary teachings, and left their seats before the last six chapters of the original gateway. They remained only for the first eight chapters of the original gateway, then left.

Such noble and honourable bodhisattvas made their promise to Shākyamuni, the Buddha Abundant Treasure (*Tahō Nyorai*, *Prabhūtaratna*), and all the other Buddha emanations and received the teaching of the Utterness of the Dharma (*Myōhō*, *Saddharma*). So are they not supposed to appear at the outset of the final phase of the Dharma (*mappō*)? Indeed you must know that when the Four Bodhisattvas appear, propagating the Buddha teaching by refuting erroneous concepts, they will become like the wise king who admonishes and goads the foolish people. And, when they proselytise, refuting the misconceptions of others, they will be like the monks who hold to and spread the correct Dharma.

The question is asked: What does the text of the *Sixth Chapter on the Disclosure of the Future Record of Those who Will Attain Enlightenment* say about the final phase?

The answer is given: After the fifth of the five five-hundred-year periods, there will be the broad propagation throughout the world of humankind. When the Universal Teacher Tendai (*T'ien T'ai*) forecast the future, he said, "The fifth five hundred years will be irrigated by the path that is Utterness." Myōraku (*Miao-lo*) says in his predictions, "The beginning of the final phase of the Dharma will not be without its deep-rooted advantages." The Universal Teacher Dengyō (*Dengyō Daishi*) said, "The correct and formal phases of the Dharma have almost slipped by, and the final phase of the Dharma (*mappō*) is terribly close."

His explanation of "terribly close" implies that his time was not the correct period. The Universal Teacher Dengyō (*Dengyō Daishi*) was in Japan, when he made the prophecy concerning the beginning of the final phase of the Dharma (*mappō*): "In regard to the age, it will be the end of the formal phase and the beginning of the final phase of the Dharma. If we enquire about the country, then it will be to the east of Kara [China] and to the west of Matsukatsu [Korea], that is to say Japan. And, when we take a look at the people, they will be the beings of the five pollutions of a *kalpa* in decay [i) when it suffers deterioration, which brings about the impairment of views, ii) such as selfishness, cynicism, etc., in which iii) the troublesome worries (*bonnō*, *klesha*) of wanting, anger, pride, and doubts prevail; as a result, iv) human miseries increase, and happiness wanes, v. causing our bodies to be polluted and the quality of our lives reduced; it will be a time of war and strife]." As it says in the sutra, "So much begrudged and envied, so how will it be after his passing over to nirvana?" There is a good reason for these words.

The explanation of war and strife points to the two present calamities of treachery within our boundaries and the threat of invasion from the Western Sea. This is the time when the thousands of realms of bodhisattvas, who swarm up out of the earth, are to appear, in order to give support to the Shākyamuni of the original gateway and to establish in this country the Fundamental Object of Veneration (*gohonzon*) for the world of humankind. This Object of Veneration (*gohonzon*) has never been seen in India or China.

Even though it was Prince Shōtoku of Japan who established Shitennōji Temple, the time had not yet come, so the fundamental object of veneration was the Buddha Amida (*Amitabha Buddha*), whose world was elsewhere. The Emperor Shōmu built the Tōdaiji

Temple, whose lord of the teaching was that of the *Flower Garland Sutra* (*Kegon, Avatāmsaka*), but he did not reveal the real significance of the *Dharma Flower Sutra* (*Myōhō Renge Kyō*). It was the Universal Teacher Dengyō (*Dengyō Daishi*) who divulged its true meaning in general terms. But, as the time had not arrived, he did not make manifest the Four Bodhisattvas of the original gateway and instead set up an image of the sovereign of the eastern direction with webbed hands and feet.

What really transpired was that this Fundamental Object of Veneration (*gohonzon*) of our school was bequeathed to the thousands of realms of bodhisattvas who swarmed up out of the earth. These bodhisattvas, bound to the Buddha's command, are close at hand underground. They did not appear in the correct and formal phases of the Dharma. But, if they do not appear in the final phase of the Dharma (*mappō*), they will be bodhisattvas whose words are nothing but barefaced lies. And the same applies for the predictions of Shākyamuni, the Buddha Abundant Treasure (*Tahō Nyorai, Prabhūtaratna*), and all the other Buddha emanations, whose prophecies will be no more than frothy bubbles.

On taking these facts into consideration, there have been earthquakes, comets, and other calamities, unlike those of the correct and formal phases of the Dharma. These were not violent changes brought about by *karura* (*garuda*), *shura* (*ashura*), or dragon spirits. So are these not the particular presages that announce the appearance of the Four Great Bodhisattvas?

Tendai (*T'ien T'ai*) said, "On seeing the intensity of the downpour, we know the size of the dragon that makes it. On seeing the bloom of the lotus flowers, we can judge the depth of the pond." Myōraku (*Miao-lo*) said, "Wise men know what the future holds, as serpents know their own nature." When the sky is clear, the earth brightens. Shouldn't the person who knows the Dharma Flower derive benefits from worldly dharmas?

The person who is unaware of the one instant of mind containing three thousand existential spaces (*ichinen sanzen*) is what causes the universal loving-kindness of the Buddha to wrap this idea into a jewel of seven ideograms and hang it around the neck of foolish people of the final era of the Dharma of Shākyamuni. The Four Great Bodhisattvas will guard and protect such a person, in no way differently from the Dukes Tai and Shū's assistance and support for King Bun [*Wen*, *c.*1050 BCE], or the way the four white-haired elders waited upon and served the Emperor Kei [r. 194-188 BCE].

The 25th day of the fourth month of the tenth year of Bun.ei [1273]
This was written down by Nichiren

Postscript to the Treatise
On the Fundamental Object of Veneration
For Contemplating the Mind

The 26th day of the fourth month of the tenth year of Bun.ei [1273], at 52 years of age

I respectfully acknowledge your gift of one summer kimono, three sticks of ink, and five writing brushes.

I have written down some notes concerning the Dharma gateway for the contemplation of the mind and present them to you, Lord Ōta, the Venerable Kyōshin, and the others. This matter is the all-embracing concern of the very person of Nichiren. This letter ought to be kept secret. But, should it be seen by people not doubly motivated, it may help to open new ground.

This treatise criticises a great deal and offers few answers, as it contains things that have never been heard of previously. No doubt it will startle and move the ears and eyes of those who read it, or hear it being read. For instance, even if you do show it to other people, you must not read it to three or four people at the same sitting.

Since the two thousand two hundred twenty years after the Buddha's passing over to nirvana, what the heart is of this treatise has never been put forward. I now proclaim it, in spite of the persecutions by the state, and wait expectantly for the fifth five-hundred-year period. I earnestly beg that the people who come to read it will exert strong faith, so that both master and disciple together will pay their respects to the Immaculate Terrain of Spirit Vulture Peak (*Ryōjusen, Gridhrakūta*), and reverently gaze upon Shākyamuni, the Buddha Abundant Treasure (*Tahō Nyorai, Prabhūtaratna*), and all the Buddha emanations.

With awe and respect,
Nichiren [formal signature]

A reply to Lord Toki

Treatise on the Significance of the Actual Fundamental Substance

Tōtai Gi Shō
Goshō Shimpen, pp. 692-703

The tenth year of Bun.ei [1273], at 52 years of age

Question: What indeed are the items that embody *Myōhō Renge Kyō*, the *Sutra on the White Lotus Flower-like Mechanism of the Utterness of the Dharma*?

[This refers to the *Utterness of the Dharma* (the entirety of existence, both the enlightened and unenlightened aspects of it) permeated by the underlying white lotus flower-like mechanism of the interdependence of cause, concomitancy and effect (in its whereabouts of the ten (psychological) realms of dharmas.]

Answer: It is the actual fundamental substance of the white lotus flower-like mechanism of the Utterness of the Dharma (*Myōhō Renge Kyō*), which is namely the subjectivity and the dependent environment of the ten psychological realms of dharmas.

Question: If it is so, then should we not say that all the living beings such as us are also the total embodiment of the Utterness of the Dharma (*Myōhō, Saddharma*)?

Answer: Of course. In the sutra it says, "what is referred to as all dharmas". The text continues until "also in any way dharmas make themselves perceptible to any of our six sense organs – eyes, ears, nose, tongue, body, and mind –.has a coherence with their apparent karmic circumstances which are present in every instant of life".

The Universal Teacher Myōraku (*Miao-lo*) explains this by saying, "The true aspect must imply all dharmas; all dharmas must imply the ten ways dharmas make themselves perceptible to any of our six sense organs – eyes, ears, nose, tongue, body, and mind; the ten ways dharmas make themselves perceptible to any of our six sense organs must imply the ten [psychological] realms of dharmas; and the three realms of dharmas imply the body and its terrain." Tendai (*T'ien T'ai*) said, "It is only in the present sutra that all the dharmas which they make themselves perceptible by means of any of our six sense organs – eyes, ears, nose, tongue, body, and mind – along with the ten psychological realms of dharmas of the three thousand are correctly put together." The Universal Teacher Nangaku (*Nan-yüeh*) said, "Why is it called *Myōhō Renge Kyō*, the *Sutra on the White Lotus Flower-like Mechanism of the Utterness of the Dharma*? The answer is because the Utterness is the Utterness of all beings and because the Dharma is not separate from the dharmas of all beings." Tendai (*T'ien T'ai*) also makes this clear by saying, "The Dharma of all beings is their Utterness."

Question: If the actual fundamental substance of all sentient beings is not separate from the total substance of the Utterness of the Dharma (*Myōhō, Saddharma*), then are all the karmic causes and effects, from hell to the nine other realms, the makeup of the entity of the Utterness of the Dharma (*Myōhō, Saddharma*)?

Answer: In the utterly imponderable, underlying principle of the Dharma nature, there are the two dharmas of defilement and purity. When defiled dharmas seep through, they become our delusions, and when pure dharmas do the same, they become enlightenment. Enlightenment is the Buddha realm, whereas delusion is the characteristic of ordinary people. Even though these two dharmas of enlightenment and delusion are two, they are nevertheless the single principle of the real way the Dharma nature functions.

For instance, if a lens made of quartz is held up to the sun's disc, it draws down fire, but if it is held up to the full moon, it draws down water. Even though the lens is a single entity, the effect produced is not the same, on account of the circumstances. It is, moreover, just the same with the principle of Utterness of the real suchness. Although it may be the principle of the real suchness of the single Utterness, it becomes a delusion when it meets with evil karmic circumstances. And, on meeting with good karmic circumstances, it becomes enlightenment. Enlightenment is namely the Dharma nature, and delusion is unenlightenment.

To give an example, it would be as though someone were to dream about various kinds of good and bad karma, but, on waking, he would think that it was like a dream that he saw from his place in the oneness of mind. The oneness of mind is the single principle of the real suchness of the Dharma nature. The good and evil are the delusions of unenlightenment and the enlightenment to the Dharma nature. If it can be understood like this, then one must cast away the evil delusions of unenlightenment and make one's foundation the good awakening to the Dharma nature.

In the *Sutra Containing the Exhaustive Significance of the Universally and Perfectly Awakened Sutra*, it says, "The beginningless imaginings and unenlightenment of each and every living being are built from the all-inclusive and enlightened mind of each and every Tathāgata." In the *Universal Desistance from Troublesome Worries in order to See Clearly* (*Maka Shikan*) of the Universal Teacher Tendai (*T'ien T'ai*), it says, "Unenlightenment and being perplexed and misled by appearances is fundamentally the nature of dharmas. It is because of that perplexity that causes appearances to beguile us into making the nature of the Dharma turn into unenlightenment."

[Tathāgata (*Nyorai*) signifies the following: one who has gone; one who has followed the Path and arrived at the real suchness; one of the ten titles of a Buddha. Tathāgata can be explained as a person who comes from the real suchness of existence, which is Nam Myōhō Renge Kyō – which means to devote our lives to and found them on (*Nam[u]*) the Utterness of the Dharma (*Myōhō*) (entirety of existence, enlightenment and unenlightenment) permeated by the underlying white lotus flower-like mechanism of the interdependence of cause, concomitancy and effect (*Renge*) in its whereabouts of the ten (psychological) realms of dharmas (*Kyō*) – and that person will return to it.]

The Universal Teacher Myōraku (*Miao-lo*) says, "The intrinsicality of the nature of dharmas is without substance; it is entirely due to unenlightenment. Unenlightenment is without substance; it is entirely due to the Dharma nature." Unenlightenment is the delusion to be cast away; the Dharma nature is the intrinsicality that we are to substantiate.

How can you have doubts and ask if the fundamental substance is a oneness? You should know what these texts mean. The example of the dream in the ninety-fifth fascicle of the *Universal Discourse* and the example of the lens of the Tendai School are really fascinating. Evidently, the proof of unenlightenment and the Dharma nature being a single entity is in the *Dharma Flower Sutra* (*Hokke-kyō*), where it says, "The Dharma state is the way dharmas are and is always present in the appearances of existential spaces." In the *Universal Discourse*, it says, "Enlightenment and unenlightenment are neither different, nor are they separate from each other. When things are understood this way, it is called the middle way."

[Only the principle of the Utterness of the absolute reality, which transcends the multitude of forms in the phenomenal world, is in possession of the two dharmas of purity and defilement.]

But even though there are many textual proofs with regard to the two dharmas of defilement and purity in the true suchness of the utterly imponderable, underlying principle, the sentence in the *Flower Garland Sutra* that says, "Mind, the Buddha, and ordinary living beings' purity and defilement are not three separate entities," does not surpass the text of the real aspect of all dharmas in the *Dharma Flower Sutra* (*Hokke-kyō*).

The Universal Teacher Nangaku (*Nan-yüeh*) said, "Albeit that the fundamental substance of mind is completely endowed with the two dharmas of defilement and purity, still mind is devoid of different aspects and is consistently equable as a uniform state." Again the example of the clear mirror is indeed precise, just as it is explained in the *Universal Desistance from Troublesome Worries in order to See Clearly* (*Maka Shikan*) of the Universal Vehicle. For an effective explanation, it says in the sixth fascicle of the *Explanatory Notes on the Recondite Significance of the Dharma Flower* (*Hokke Gengi*), "When the [one instant of mind containing] three thousand exists in theory, it is said to be the same as unenlightenment. When the fruition of the three thousand is accomplished, everything everywhere can be referred to as eternal joy. When the three thousand existential spaces are devoid of change, then enlightenment is not separate from unenlightenment. And when the [one instant of mind containing] three thousand is aligned with eternity, it is both the original substance and the way it works." This explanation is understandably clear.

Question: If all living beings, all of them and everywhere, are the actual fundamental substance of the *Sutra on the White Lotus Flower-like Mechanism of the Utterness of the Dharma*, then are stupid, misguided, benighted, dull and common mortals such as us also the actual substance of the Utterness of the Dharma (*Myōhō, Saddharma*)?

Answer: Even though there are many people in the present age, there are two sorts that come to the fore – that is to say, those of the provisional teachings and those of the real teachings. However, the people who have faith in the provisional teachings as an expedient means, such as the school that recites the prayer formula of the Buddha Amida (*Amitābha*) [by reciting *Namu Amida Butsu*, i.e., Nembutsu], cannot be said to be the actual original substance of the white lotus flower-like mechanism of the Utterness of the Dharma (*Myōhō, Saddharma*). The people who have faith in the real teachings of the *Dharma Flower Sutra* are the actual fundamental substance of the embodiment of the Utterness that is the true suchness of the lotus flower.

In the *Sutra on the Buddha's Passing Over to the All-embracing Extinction of Nirvana*, it says, "Because of all the living beings that have faith in the universal vehicle (*daijō, mahāyāna*), they are referred to as the people of the universal vehicle (*daijō, mahāyāna*)."

The Universal Teacher Nangaku (*Nan-yüeh*), in his *Implications of the Chapter on Practising with Peace and Joy*, quotes from the *Sutra on the Universally Vital Zeal*, where it says that "living beings and the Tathāgata have in common the same Dharma body which is incomparably wonderful, immaculately pure, and is called the *Sutra on the White Lotus Flower-like Mechanism of the Utterness of the*

Dharma (Myōhō Renge Kyō)." It also says, "Since all the fruitions are simultaneously endowed in this oneness of mind and the single discipline of the practice of the *Dharma Flower Sutra*, it is not entered into by stages, in the same way as a single bloom of the lotus flower is furnished with all of its fruitions contemporaneously. This is what is meant by the living beings of the single vehicle."

Again, it says, "People of the two vehicles and bodhisattvas whose propensities are dull practise and study by stages. The bodhisattvas with keen propensities simply cast aside the expedient means and do not cultivate practices that evolve by degrees. These people are called the living beings of the single vehicle. With the substantiation of the *samādhi* of the Dharma Flower, there is the full endowment of all the fruitions everywhere."

What Nangaku (*Nan-yüeh*) means by these explanations is that "the three words 'practising by degrees' are intended for the present-day scholars of the particular teaching (*bekkyō*). It is because, naturally, this explanation is to emphasise the path of complete fulfilment of cause and fruition of the Dharma Flower that it stands in contrast to the paths of the expedient means that are referred to as 'practising by degrees'. These are the All-inclusive Doctrines (*enkyō*) of the former teachings, all the sutras of the universal vehicle (*daijō, mahāyāna*) of the former teachings, as well as all the direct and gradual doctrines in the sutras of the universal and individual vehicles."

The proof is in the *Sutra on the Implications Without Bounds (Muryōgi-kyō)*, where it says, "Then, through the exposition of the twelve sections of the Equally Broad (*Hōdō, vaipulya*) Sutras, the *Sutra on the Wisdom that Carries Sentient Beings to the Shores of Nirvana (Mahāprajñāpāramitā)*, and the sea of relativity of the *Flower Garland (Kegon, Avatāmsaka) Sutras*, the cultivation of practices that perpetuate through *kalpas* were proclaimed and discussed."

The usage of the two ideograms for the concepts of "having in common" and "the same", in the *Sutra on the Universally Vital Zeal*, became an inherited transmission. The people who have in common and the same belief in the *Dharma Flower Sutra* are the substance of the sutra on Utterness. Those who have nothing in common and are not the same are those who bear in mind the formula of the Buddha Amida (*Amitābha*) [by reciting *Namu Amida Butsu*, i.e., Nembutsu]. And, since they turn their backs on the Buddha nature and the Dharma body of the Tathāgata, they are not the substance of the Sutra on Utterness.

What the implication of these texts suggests is that all the common mortals and sage-like persons of the provisional teachings – of the three vehicles [*i*) the hearers of the Buddha's voice, *ii*) those who are partially enlightened due to a profound search for the meaning of existence, *iii*) bodhisattvas], the five vehicles, which are the same as the above but with the inclusion of the realms of dharmas of humankind and the *deva* (*ten*), the people within the seven grades of expedient means, the people within the nine realms of dharmas, the people who are practising within the bounds of the doctrines of the Flower Garland (*Kegon*), the Teachings of the Individual Vehicle (*Agon*), the Equally Broad (*Hōdō, vaipulya*), or the Wisdom Doctrines (*Hannya, prajña*), or even the Teachings of the Three Receptacles, the Interrelated or the Particular – cannot be designated as the living beings of the actual fundamental substance of the white lotus flower-like mechanism of the Utterness of the Dharma (*Myōhō Renge Kyō*) of the single vehicle.

It is like this. Even though the Buddha of the provisional teachings is a Buddha, we cannot apply to him the illustrious term of the Buddha realm, because the three bodies of the provisional teachings have not yet eluded transience. So how could we apply this illustrious term to the remaining existential spaces?

These explanations imply that those of the 'inhuman kind' of the final phase of the Dharma inspire greater veneration than the rulers of state and great ministers of the two thousand years of the correct and formal phases of the Dharma. What it comes down to is that the actual fundamental substance of the white lotus flower-like mechanism of the Utterness of the Dharma (*Myōhō, Saddharma*) is the disciples and supporters of Nichiren. Their bodies of flesh and blood are born of their parents, and they believe in the *Dharma Flower Sutra*.

Nangaku (*Nan-yüeh*) explains this, by saying, "All living beings are fully endowed with the store of the Dharma body, which is at one with the Buddha without any discrepancy whatsoever. This is the reason why it says in the *Dharma Flower Sutra*, 'Again, the immaculately pure and eternal eyes, ears, nose, tongue, body, and mind are just like this'." It also says, "The question is asked: In which sutra is it expounded that the eyes and all the organs of sense are referred to as being the Tathāgata?" The answer is given: "In the *Sutra on the Universally Vital Zeal*, both sentient beings and the Tathāgata, by having the same Dharma body in common, are defined as the incomparably pure and immaculate Utterness of *Myōhō Renge Kyō*, the *Sutra on the White Lotus Flower-like Mechanism of the Utterness of the Dharma* (*Myōhō Renge Kyō*)."

Even though this sentence comes from a provisional text, it is possible to provide references from that which was revealed in the text of the *Dharma Flower Sutra* that came later. The persons who straightforwardly abandon the expedient means and hold faith solely in the *Dharma Flower Sutra* have their troublesome worries, karma, and three paths of bitterness transformed into the three virtues of the Dharma body, wisdom, and deliverance. Then the triple insight of relativity, phenomena, and the middle way are revealed as not being separate from the oneness of mind, so that the place where such a person dwells is the Terrain of Eternal Silence and Enlightenment.

The Buddha of the Lotus Flower of the actual original substance of the *Chapter on the Lifespan of the Tathāgata* of the original gateway is able to abide in the place of abode and is the body and terrain, the materiality and mind which is endowed with the original substance, and the function of the triple body independent of all action. This is the concern that involves the disciples and supporters of Nichiren and is indeed the actual original substance of the Dharma Flower as well as the manifestation of the meritorious power of the reaches of a mind free from resistance. In all events, this is something about which you should have no doubts at all.

Question: The Universal Teacher Tendai (*T'ien T'ai*) is said to have expounded the meaning of the metaphorical white lotus flower-like mechanism of the Utterness of the Dharma (*Myōhō, Saddharma*) and the lotus flower of the actual fundamental substance. If this is so, then what is intended by the metaphorical lotus flower and that of the actual fundamental substance?

Answer: The metaphorical lotus flower is the threefold explanation of bestowing the truth through the provisional teachings, clearing away the provisional teachings in order to reveal the truth, and then discarding all else of a provisional nature in order to establish the truth. This should be thoroughly examined.

As for the Lotus Flower of the actual fundamental substance, it says, in the seventh fascicle of the *Recondite Significance of the Dharma Flower* (*Hokke Gengi*), "When the lotus flower is not a metaphor, it acquires the name of the actual fundamental substance. It is just like it was at the outset of *kalpas*, when all things were without a name. At that time, the sage-like Man [*Shōnin*], contemplating their intrinsicality, set up exact rules and made up words for each."

It also says, "Now for argument's sake, let us take the metaphorical aspect away from the concept of lotus flower, so that it becomes the Dharma gateway of the Dharma Flower. Since the Dharma gateway of the Dharma Flower is immaculately pure, it is therefore the meticulousness and Utterness of cause and effect. If we are to attach a name to this Dharma gateway, it becomes the lotus flower. Then, by applying a name to the actual substantiation of this *samādhi* of the Dharma Flower, it is by no means a simile or a metaphor."

Again the text continues, "Question: Is the lotus flower decisively the *samādhi* of the Dharma Flower, or is it conclusively the botanical lotus flower? Decidedly, it is the Dharmic lotus flower. As the Dharmic lotus flower is difficult to understand, the lotus flower as a plant is used as a metaphor. Those with sharp propensities, by understanding the principle that the name implies, have no need for similes or metaphors. All they need is to apprehend the Dharma Flower. Those of middling and lesser propensities do not yet have this awareness, but the use of metaphors can make them realise it. By drawing a comparison with the lotus flower that is easy to understand, they can relate it to the lotus bloom that is difficult to know. For this reason, the Dharma was taught in three stages. So as to correspond to the needs of the superior, this was expressed in terms of the Dharma. For those of middling and lower propensities, the language of parables and metaphor was used. With the three propensities being jointly discussed, the Dharma and the metaphor are designated as one. Who could possibly contradict the person who explains it in this way?"

The meaning of this explanation is that the ultimate intrinsicality is without a name. When the sage-like man (*shōnin*) contemplated the intrinsicality, he attached a name to a myriad of things, as well as perceiving an interdependence of cause, concomitancy and effect of the unthinkably unutterable single Dharma. If we name it, it is *Myōhō Renge Kyō*, the *Sutra on the White Lotus Flower-like Mechanism of the Utterness of the Dharma*. This single Dharma of *Myōhō Renge Kyō*, the *Sutra on the White Lotus Flower-like Mechanism of the Utterness of the Dharma* (*Myōhō Renge Kyō*) is furnished with all the dharmas of the ten realms and their three thousand existential spaces, without leaving anything out. Those who cultivate themselves in this practice acquire both the Buddha cause and the Buddha fruition simultaneously.

When the sage-like Man (*shōnin*) became the teacher of this Dharma, by cultivating himself in the practice, he became enlightened [*satori*] to the Buddha Path. He felt his attainment to the interdependence of the Utterness of the cause and the Utterness of its fruition, because he had become the utterly enlightened and completely realised Tathāgata.

For this reason, the Universal Teacher Dengyō (*Dengyō Daishi*) said, "The *Myōhō Renge Kyō* of the oneness of mind grows simultaneously with the bloom of cause and the calyx of fruition. It is the Lotus Flower of the actual fundamental substance. In each one of the three stages of the Buddha's explanation of the Dharma [first straightforwardly in its own technical language, secondly by means of a parable, or thirdly when the Buddha makes a reference to one of his former lives], at each one of these junctures, we have both the metaphorical lotus flower and that of the fundamental substance. Generally speaking, the *Dharma Flower Sutra* contains all the similes and metaphors, as well as the actual fundamental substance. But when we come to the details, all these are contained in the lotus flower of the actual fundamental substance.

"These are such details as the seven parables in the *Dharma Flower Sutra*. Also, we have the three simultaneous qualities of the interdependence of cause, concomitancy and effect, not to mention the ten insuperable gateways to the Dharma."

[The seven parables in the *Dharma Flower Sutra* are *i*) the burning house and the three kinds of vehicles in the *Third Chapter on Similes and Parables*, *ii*) the elder and the impoverished son in the *Fourth Chapter on Faith leading to Understanding*, *iii*) the three plants and two trees in the *Fifth Chapter on the Parable of the Medicinal Herbs*, *iv*) the imaginary city and the place of precious things in the *Seventh Chapter on the Parable of the Imaginary City*, *v*) the jewel in the lining of the clothes in the *Eighth Chapter on the Prediction of Enlightenment for Five Hundred Disciples*, *vi*) the jewel in the chignon in the *Fourteenth Chapter on Practising with Peace and with Joy*, *vii*) the good doctor who cures his sick children in the *Sixteenth Chapter on the Lifespan of the Tathāgata*.]

[The three simultaneous qualities are *i*) the vehicles that lead to the Buddha enlightenment, *ii*) the simultaneous quality of the existential realms and nirvana, *iii*) the simultaneous quality of the entities of the Buddhas Tahō and Shākyamuni.]

[The ten insuperable gateways to the Dharma are *i*) the insuperability of the seeds of enlightenment of the *Dharma Flower Sutra*, since they are the implantations of the ever-present primordial infinity; *ii*) the insuperability of its practice, since from the time of the Buddha Daitsū it has always been the virtue of the practice to be the All-inclusive replenished whole of the one instant of mind containing three thousand existential spaces; *iii*) the insuperability of the extent of the Dharma Flower. Because of its All-inclusiveness, this sutra is the culmination of all the other sutras; *iv*) the insuperability of what the *Dharma Flower Sutra* involves, because this sutra imparts the real principle of existence to sentient beings; *v*) the insuperability of the immaculate purity of its abode and terrain, because the Dharma realm of the *Dharma Flower Sutra* is the Utterness of the abode and terrain of all the Buddhas; *vi*) the insuperability of the theme of the Dharma Flower, since this sutra is said to be the paramount of all the discourses of the Tathāgata, the most profound, and therefore insuperable; *vii*) the insuperability of the *Dharma Flower Sutra* to convert and teach that all sentient beings will be brought to the Buddha path through this sutra; *viii*) the insuperability of the *Dharma Flower Sutra* to bring about total enlightenment; *ix*) the insuperability of nirvana, since the fundamental of the Dharma Flower is inherently infinite, which is the essential characteristic of nirvana and therefore insuperable; *x*) the insuperability of the reaches of Utterness, because when the *stupa* of the Tathāgata Abundant Treasure (*Tahō Nyorai, Prabhūtaratna*) first appeared, he said that the sutric power of the *Dharma Flower Sutra* (*Myōhō Renge Kyō*) was beyond all other Dharmas, since it was imponderably inexplicable and utter.]

"On putting a name to what the intrinsicality of this teaching implies, it is the *Sutra on the White Lotus Flower-like Mechanism of the Utterness of the Dharma* (*Myōhō Renge Kyō*)."

The Universal Teacher Myōraku (*Miao-lo*) said, "Most certainly it is through the seven parables that the provisional or the true significance of each lotus flower is to be compared." The text continues until, "Whatever way one looks at it, the lotus flower is none other than the bestowing of the provisional for the sake of truth, as well as opening the provisional so that the truth can be revealed. It is likewise with all the seven parables."

Again, at the outset of *kalpas*, this flowering plant existed. The sage-like man (*shōnin*), on seeing its intrinsicality, called it by the word "lotus flower". The flowering plant was endowed with the interdependence of cause, concomitancy and effect and was similar to the white lotus flower-like mechanism of the Utterness of the Dharma (*Myōhō, Saddharma*); hence the plant that flowers is called the lotus flower. The red lotus flowers and the white lotus flowers that grow in the ponds – this botanical lotus flower, is the lotus of simile and metaphor. Thus, it is through the flowering plant that the difficulty in understanding the white lotus flower-like mechanism of the Utterness of the Dharma (*Myōhō, Saddharma*) is overcome. The Universal Teacher Tendai (*T'ien T'ai*), when explaining this concept, said, "The Utterness of the Dharma (*Myōhō, Saddharma*) is hard to understand. But, by using a simile for the sake of argument, the explanation is made easier."

Question: Who, since the outset of *kalpas*, has attained to the substantiation of the lotus flower of the actual fundamental substance?

Answer: Shākyamuni, since his attainment to the substantiation of the lotus flower of the actual fundamental substance of the Utterness of the Dharma (*Myōhō, Saddharma*) prior to a period of time that would be the same amount of grains of dust that would go into the making of five hundred *kalpas*, has, from existence to existence, recited the attainment to the path and revealed the fundamental principle of being able to substantiate that which is to be substantiated.

Again, when the Buddha was in the world, he was born in the Kingdom of Magadha in central India. His desire was to reveal this lotus flower, but neither the propensities of the people nor the time were appropriate. Because in the single lotus flower of the Dharma he had to differentiate three flowering plants in order to impart the provisional dharmas of the three vehicles, over a period of forty years he had to carefully protract his intentions, so as to attract and induce people towards the truth. Since there was a myriad of diversities in the propensities and characters of the sentient beings of this period, he formulated several variations of the flowering plant, but in the end was unable to impart the Lotus Flower of the Utterness of the Dharma. This is why it says in the *Sutra on Implications Without Bounds*, "At first I sat at the site of the path under the bodhi tree." The text continues until, "After some forty years of teaching, I had not yet revealed the truth."

On arriving at the *Dharma Flower Sutra*, Shākyamuni cast aside the various flowering plants of the lesser vehicle and the expedient means of the first four periods of his teaching.

[The first four periods are *i*) the Flower Garland (*Kegon*), *ii*) the teachings of the individual vehicle (*Agon*), *iii*) the equally broad (*hōdō, vaipulya*) doctrine, and *iv*) the period of the wisdom (*hannya, prajña*) teachings.]

Then he expounded only the single Lotus Flower of the Utterness of the Dharma (*Myōhō, Saddharma*). When he had cleared away the three flowering plants and revealed the single Lotus Flower of the Utterness of the Dharma (*Myōhō, Saddharma*), the faithful of the provisional doctrines of the three teachings of the first four periods arrived at the lotus flower of the cleared away proximity, so as to reveal the distance, rather than receiving the lotus flower of the first of the ten stages of the bodhisattva. Instead, they attained to the second, third, or tenth stage, or even attained to the lotus flower of the supreme fruition of the overall awakening or the awakening to Utterness.

Question: In which phrase in which chapter of the *Dharma Flower Sutra* are the lotus flowers of the actual fundamental substance and the one that is metaphorical unmistakably pointed-out and discussed?

Answer: If we briefly discuss this from the viewpoint of the hearers of the three stages of the Buddha's explanation of the Dharma –*i*) in terms of the Dharma, *ii*) by parables, and *iii*) by means of a story of the life of a past Buddha – then the whole of the *Chapter on Expedient Means* is entirely an exposition of the lotus flower of the actual fundamental substance. The *Chapter on Similes and Parables* and the *Chapter on the Parable of the Imaginary City* discuss the metaphorical lotus. However, the *Chapter on Expedient Means* is not devoid of the metaphorical lotus flower, and the other chapters are not in default of the Lotus Flower of the actual fundamental substance.

Question: If that is so, then which text is it that strictly accounts for the lotus flower of the actual fundamental substance?

Answer: It is the text of "The way all dharmas make themselves perceptible to any of our six senses– eyes, ears, nose, tongue, body, and mind", in the *Chapter on Expedient Means*.

Question: By what means can I ascertain that this is in fact the text of the lotus flower of the actual fundamental substance?

Answer: Myōraku (*Miao-lo*) and Tendai (*T'ien T'ai*), on quoting this particular text, explained it as the fundamental substance of the present sutra. Also, the Universal Teacher Dengyō (*Dengyō Daishi*) said in his explanations, "Nowadays scholars keep this explanation secret and do not reveal its name. However the name of this text is *Myōhō Renge Kyō* [the *Sutra on the White Lotus Flower-like Mechanism of the Utterness of the Dharma*]."

Question: What is regarded as the fundamental substance of the *Dharma Flower Sutra*?

Answer: "The way all dharmas make themselves perceptible to any of our six senses" is regarded as its fundamental substance. This explanation is understandably clear. There is also the manifest evidence of the triple body in the *Chapter on Seeing the Vision of the Stupa made of Precious Materials*; in this we have an immediate proof. Then there are the bodhisattvas who swarm up out of the earth, or the Dragon King's daughter becoming aware of her own Buddha nature without changing her personality. This is why the sutric text of the bodhisattvas that swarm up out of the earth and become an immediate proof is referred to as "like a lotus flower in the water". Then the actual fundamental substance of these bodhisattvas was made known. Because of this, the proof of the Dragon King's daughter's enlightenment is explained as, "On her arrival at the Spirit Vulture Peak (*Ryōjusen, Gridhrakūta*), she seated herself upon a thousand-petalled lotus flower as big as the wheel of a cart."

Again, in the matter of the thirty-three or four bodies of the Bodhisattva Sound of Utterness (*Myō.on, Gadgadasvara*) and Kannon (*Avalokiteshvara*) the explanation is [that] "If it were not due to their attainment to the substantiation of the karma of actions and thoughts that are free from delusion of the imponderably inexplicable *samādhi* of the Dharma Flower, then how were they able to manifest these thirty-three forms?", or even the phrase "the manifestations of the existential spaces are ever-present and eternal". All these quotations are textual evidence and are studied by scholars of the present age.

Nevertheless, it is needless to say that Nichiren's real proof of the lotus flower of the actual fundamental substance comes from the text in the *Chapter on Expedient Means* and the part of the *Chapter on the Reaches of the Mind of the Tathāgata*, where it says, "all the dharmas that are possessed by the Tathāgata". The Universal Teacher Tendai (*T'ien T'ai*), by quoting these texts, explained the present sutra in terms of the five layers of recondite significance. This single text in particular is the textual proof.

Question: The immediate proof that you have just quoted is particularly outstanding. How is it then that you adhere to the text from the *Chapter on the Reaches of the Mind of the Tathāgata*?

Answer: This single text, being endowed with the deepest of implications, is particularly inspiring.

Question: What are these deepest implications?

Answer: This is because this text deals with Shākyamuni entrusting his original following, who are the bodhisattvas that swarm up out of the earth, with the conclusive essential of the transmission of the five ideograms of the actual fundamental substance, *Myōhō Renge Kyō*, and to the Bodhisattva Superior Practice (*Jōgyō, Vishishtachāritra*) in particular.

The desire of the Tathāgata Shākyamuni of the real attainment in the primordial infinity was completed, when he said, "Just as I had wished in the past and now is already fulfilled, all sentient beings on conversion will be set upon the Buddha Path." This is because this is the passage where the Tathāgata, in order to expound the broad propagation during the fifth five-hundred-year period after his passing over to nirvana, called up the bodhisattvas who swarmed up out of the earth and entrusted them with the lotus flower of the actual fundamental substance as its crucial point.

This is also the passage where the Tathāgata expressed his devoutest wish, which was that the esoteric dharma, to which he had attained at the site of enlightenment, should be accomplished, by people such as us of the present and future of the final phase of the Dharma of Shākyamuni, to the genuine substantiation of the lotus flower of the actual fundamental substance.

Of all people, the emissary of the Tathāgata cannot be anyone else other than the person who comes forth knowing this passage of the textual proof of the lotus flower of the actual fundamental substance.

By being the truth, it is an esoteric text. By being the truth, it is a matter of universal concern. By being the truth, it is to be venerated. Nam Myōhō Renge Kyō, Nam Myōhō Renge Kyō.

[Nam Myōhō Renge Kyō is the consecration of founding one's life on the Utterness of the Dharma (entirety of existence, enlightenment and unenlightenment) permeated by the underlying white lotus flower-like mechanism of the interdependence of cause, concomitancy and effect in its whereabouts of the ten (psychological) realms of dharmas.]

Question: What is the meaning of the present school? When all those people of the other schools come along, what is the textual evidence for the Lotus Flower of the actual fundamental substance? Which particular passage of the *Dharma Flower Sutra* should we point out?

Answer: At the beginning of the twenty-eight chapters, there is the title, *Myōhō Renge Kyō*, the *Sutra on the White Lotus Flower-like Mechanism of the Utterness of the Dharma*. These are the words you must point out.

Question: How are we able to know that the title and theme of the twenty-eight chapters is the lotus flower of the fundamental substance – because when the Universal Teacher Tendai (*T'ien T'ai*) was explaining the title by saying that the lotus flower was a simile and a metaphor, is not his explanation that of the metaphorical lotus flower?

Answer: In the lotus flower of the title and theme, both its actual fundamental substance and the similes and metaphors are expounded simultaneously. The explanations that Tendai (*T'ien T'ai*) gave during his lifetime were at the time for illustration, in terms of simile and metaphor. In the first fascicle of his *Recondite Significance of the Dharma Flower* (*Hokke Gengi*), Tendai (*T'ien T'ai*) gives the six similes of the original and temporary gateways. In the seventh fascicle, the actual fundamental substance is explained in the same way. Because Tendai (*T'ien T'ai*) accounted for both the viewpoints of the actual fundamental substance and that of the similes and metaphors in the theme and title of the lotus flower, on this account he does not fall into error.

Question: How are we able to know that the lotus flower of the theme and title is the simultaneous exposition of its similes and metaphors, as well as its being the fundamental substance? When the Universal Teacher Nangaku (*Nan-yüeh*) gave an explanation of the five ideograms for *Myōhō Renge Kyō*, he said, "Because Utterness is the Utterness of sentient beings and its dharmas are the dharmas of sentient beings, the lotus flower [which is the interdependence of cause, concomitancy and effect] is provisionally applied to them as a simile and metaphor." How is it then that, until now, the explanations given by Nangaku (*Nan-yüeh*) and Tendai (*T'ien T'ai*) are those of the metaphorical lotus?

Answer: Both the explanations of Nangaku (*Nan-yüeh*) and Tendai (*T'ien T'ai*) are similar. Nevertheless, even though the simultaneous exposition of the actual fundamental substance and the similes and metaphors is not distinctly apparent in the sutric text, Nangaku (*Nan-yüeh*) and Tendai (*T'ien T'ai*) actually based their judgment and explanation of the implications of the simultaneous exposition on the arguments of Tenjin (*Vasubandhu*) and Nāgārjuna (*Ryūju*).

In Tenjin's (*Vasubandhu*) *Discourse on the Dharma Flower*, it says, "In the *Sutra on the White Lotus Flower-like Mechanism of the Utterness of the Dharma* (*Myōhō Renge Kyō*), there are two different references. One has the meaning of the lotus coming out of the water." The text continues until, "...coming out of the mud. All the hearers of the voice and all the Tathāgatas who took part in the great assembly were seated upon lotus flowers like all the bodhisattvas. On hearing the Tathāgata discourse on the unexcelled wisdom and its immaculately pure environment determined by its own karma, this was a metaphor for the substantiation of the Tathāgata's repository of teachings that had not yet been disclosed. Secondly, when the lotus flower burst into bloom, because of all those people within the universal vehicle (*daijō, mahāyāna*) whose minds are cowardly, weak, and unable to give rise to a mind of faith, the Tathāgata opens and reveals the purity and Utterness of his Dharma body, in order to make them believe."

The words "all the bodhisattvas" imply all the bodhisattvas of the individual and universal teachings that came prior to the Dharma Flower. On their reaching the *Dharma Flower Sutra*, their perception of the lotus flower of the Buddha becomes understandably clear, as in the *Discourse on the Dharma Flower*. Because of this, one should understand that "the attainment of the bodhisattvas to the various stages of practice" was just an expedient means.

The Universal Teacher Tendai (*T'ien T'ai*) explains this text from the *Discourse on the Dharma Flower* in his *Recondite Significance of the Dharma Flower* (*Hokke Gengi*). "In order to understand the meaning of the present discourse, if one is to say that, as a sentient being, the Buddha made manifest the immaculate Utterness of his Dharma body, then by opening and proclaiming this Utterness of cause, it becomes the lotus flower-like mechanism of the interdependence of cause, concomitancy and effect in its whereabouts of the ten [psychological] realms of dharmas. If one is to say that, in the midst of the great assembly, the Tathāgata was seated upon a lotus flower, which, by being the abode and terrain of the reward of Utterness, becomes the lotus flower of the interdependence of cause, concomitancy and effect, then, if the hearers of the voice attain an entrance to this dimension, it would immediately become the abode and terrain of the reward of Utterness and become the lotus flower of the interdependence of cause, concomitancy and effect."

Again, when Tendai justified in a detailed manner the simultaneous exposition of the actual fundamental substance and its similes and metaphors, he took the phrase from the *Sutra on the Great Assembly*, "I now bow in veneration to the lotus flower of the Buddha." As a statement to prove the point of the sentence from the *Discourse on the Lotus Flower* just quoted, he explains it as, "Because, according to the *Sutra on the Great Assembly*, the cause and effect of the practice of the Dharma is in itself all the implications of the lotus flower, then, since the bodhisattvas are seated upon it, it must be the flower of causation. Because they bow to the Lotus Flower of the Buddha, it must then be the flower of effect. If according to the *Discourse on the Lotus Flower* the dependent abode and terrain and reward become the lotus flower of the interdependence of cause and effect, then again the bodhisattvas, through their cultivation of the practice of the lotus flower of the interdependence of cause and effect, attained to the abode and terrain of this particular lotus flower as a reward. As indeed you should know, everything to do with subjectivity and its environment, as well as its cause and effect, are entirely the dharmas of this lotus flower. Then why should we indeed use metaphors to demonstrate it? It is for those people who are less sharp-witted, who cannot understand the lotus flower. So we show them the mundane flower as an illustration. Why indeed should there be any objection to it?"

Again, it goes on to say, "If it were not for the lotus flower, what means would there be to account for all the dharmas that come into being everywhere? It is because both the Dharma and the metaphor are dealt with equally that it is called *Myōhō Renge Kyō*, the *Sutra on the White Lotus Flower-like Mechanism of the Utterness of the Dharma*."

In the *Universal Discourse* of the Bodhisattva Nāgārjuna (*Ryūju*), it says, "Both the Dharmic and the metaphorical lotus flowers were presented at the same time." When the Universal Teacher Dengyō (*Dengyō Daishi*) was explaining the two texts of the treatise of Tenjin (*Vasubandhu*) and Nāgārjuna (*Ryūju*), he said, "The texts in these discourses say that although the title is only *Myōhō Renge Kyō*, the *Sutra on the White Lotus Flower-like Mechanism of the Utterness of the Dharma* (*Myōhō Renge Kyō*), there are two categories of meaning. Although it is only referred to as the lotus flower, one cannot say that there are not two meanings. However, to make them entirely identical with the Dharma and the metaphor would be quite in order. If they were not identical, then what else would one use for an explanation? This is why in the explanation of these discourses both the Dharma and the metaphor are demonstrated conjointly. The *Sutra on the White Lotus Flower-like Mechanism of the Utterness of the Dharma (Myōhō Renge Kyō)* of the oneness of mind grows simultaneously with the flower of cause and the calyx of fruition. The significance of this is hard to understand, but by making use of an illustration it becomes easier. This teaching that is within the limits of the three realms where sentient beings have organs of sense as well as desires, where there is a physical dimension and realms where there is only mental activity, is called *Myōhō Renge Kyō*, the *Sutra on the White Lotus Flower-like Mechanism of the Utterness of the Dharma*."

The explanations and the meaning of the expository texts are understandably clear. You must look at what is written down. On account of the fact that it is neither wrapped up nor concealed, the significance of the interdependent exposition becomes the ultimate meaning of these explanations, which are understandably clear.

Generally speaking, the meaning of the *Dharma Flower Sutra (Myōhō Renge Kyō)* implies that the simile and metaphor are not separate from the reality of dharmas and that the reality of dharmas is not separate from their metaphors and similes. Because of this, the Universal Teacher Dengyō (*Dengyō Daishi*) said, "Even though there are many metaphors and similes in the present sutra, the overall metaphor consists of seven parables. These seven parables are not separate from their dharmic reality, nor is the reality of the Dharma separate from its metaphors and similes. Outside of its metaphors and similes, there is no reality of the Dharma. Outside the reality of the Dharma, there are no metaphors or similes. However, the reality of dharmas is the intrinsic reality of the Dharma nature. The metaphors and similes are therefore the practical side of the reality of the Utterness of the Dharma (*Myōhō, Saddharma*). Hence, we say that the Dharma and its metaphors are a single reality. The practical side is not separate from its intrinsic reality, and its intrinsic reality is not separate from its practical side. It is on these premises that the Tendai school argues that all explanations with regard to the *Dharma Flower Sutra* have to be both dharmic and metaphoric at the same time."

What these explanations imply is distinctly clear, so I will not go over them again.

Question: When the Tathāgata was in the world, who was able to attain to the substantiation of the Lotus Flower of the actual fundamental substance?

Answer: One can generally say that during the periods of the direct, gradual, and undetermined teachings – of *i*) the Flower Garland (*Kegon*) period, *ii*) the period that was by and large composed of the individual vehicle (*Agon, Āgama*) doctrines, *iii*) the equally broad (*Hōdō, Vaipulya*) period, and *iv*) the period of the wisdom (*Hannya, Prajña*) teachings – the three and five vehicles for imparting the Dharma to men, *deva* (*ten*), hearers of the Buddha's voice and people partially enlightened due to a profound search for the meaning of life, also people who adhere to the seven categories of expedient means, and sentient beings who dwell within the nine realms of dharmas, as well as the bodhisattvas, and the Lord of the all-inclusive teachings that were implicit in the provisional doctrine, and the Lord of the teaching of the Dharma Flower of the temporary gateway – none of them, with the sole exception of the Lord of the teaching of the *Chapter on the Lifespan of the Tathāgata* of the original gateway, had even heard of the expression of the lotus flower of the actual fundamental substance of the original gateway, let alone had attained to its substantiation.

The lotus flower of the unsurpassed enlightenment, of clearing away the three vehicles in order to reveal the one, was not divulged until after some forty years of teaching. Hence, the reason for the phrase, "Finally, he was able to achieve unsurpassed enlightenment in the *Sutra on Implications Without Bounds*." The lotus flower of clearing away the three vehicles in order to reveal the one, of the temporary gateway, was not expounded in the teachings prior to the Dharma Flower, let alone the clearing away of the proximity of the thousand realms of dharmas in order to reveal the distance of the one instance of thought containing three thousand existential spaces, or the subtle integration of the objective realm and the subjective insight of the original terrain that is so hard to understand. So should Maitreya (*Miroku*), who was converted by the temporary teachings, have known that the lotus flower of the actual fundamental substance is fundamentally existing and is independent of all action?

Question: How is one able to know that the bodhisattvas of the all-inclusive teachings prior to the Dharma Flower or the bodhisattvas of the all-inclusive teachings of the temporary gateway did not attain to the substantiation of the original gateway?

Answer: The bodhisattvas of the all-inclusive teachings prior to the Dharma Flower did not know the lotus flower of the temporary gateway, and the bodhisattvas of the all-inclusive teachings of the temporary gateway were ignorant of the lotus flower of the original gateway. Tendai (*T'ien T'ai*) said, "Those who succeeded to the place of the provisional teachings did not know the colleagues that were converted through the temporary gateway, and those who were converted through the temporary gateway did not know the colleagues who were converted through the teachings of the original gateway to the Dharma."

It is said that the eighty thousand bodhisattvas of the former and the teachings derived from the external events of the Buddha Shākyamuni's life and work that made up the great assembly of the present sutra wanted to hear about the path of fulfilment. The Universal Teacher Dengyō (*Dengyō Daishi*) said, "Even though this is the direct path, it is not the universally direct path." The meaning of this is made clear where he goes on to say, "…because they were not yet aware of the universally direct path to enlightenment."

Albeit that the bodhisattvas of the teachings prior to the Dharma Flower and the temporary gateway had attained to their rightful share of partially destroying delusion and realising the principle in part, when they were confronted with the teachings of the original gateway with the destruction of their delusion being only partial, it was not a destruction of delusion that could "bestride upwards over the joints of the bamboo" as in stages to the level of these highest teachings, as it was still only fragmentary. Consequently, the explanation for the phrase, "In various places in the teachings prior to the Dharma Flower and those of the teachings derived from the external events of the Buddha Shākyamuni's life and work, bodhisattvas were able to attain access to the path", gave rise to the expression, "attaining access to the path directly", at a time when the people of the two vehicles were discredited.

But it was at the time of the original gateway when the great bodhisattvas of the teachings prior to the Dharma Flower and the temporary gateway attained to the substantiation of the lotus flower of the Buddha. The genuinely true destruction of delusions came about at the time of their hearing the single *Chapter on the Lifespan of the Tathāgata*.

When the Universal Teacher Tendai explained the following text from the *Chapter on the Bodhisattvas who Swarm up out of the Earth*, "On account of the reaches of the mind of the Buddha, he made fifty small *kalpas* seem to all those at the great assembly as though they were half a day," he said that this was "because for the person who is aware of the primordial infinity in time, shortness is not separate from length, so that it appears to be fifty small *kalpas*. The bewildered, who are unaware that, in the primordial infinity in time, length is based on shortness, think of these *kalpas* as though they were half a day."

Myōraku (*Miao-lo*), taking up this argument, said, "The bodhisattvas, by having already broken through their unenlightenment, are referred to as people who are aware of the primordial infinity. But the great assembly, by only being seated in the places of people of wisdom, are spoken of as those who are not yet aware of the primordial ever-present infinite in time (*kuon ganjo*)."

This explanation is understandably clear. It can be said that the bodhisattvas of the teachings prior to the Dharma Flower and those of the temporary gateway of the teachings derived from the external events of the Buddha Shākyamuni's life and work were yet bewildered and unaware of the primordial ever-present infinite in time (*kuon ganjo*). But, apart from the bodhisattvas who sprang up from the earth, there were no other persons who were aware of it.

However, when the people of the present-day Tendai School discuss the similarities and differences of the temporary and original teachings, they say that there is no contradiction between the two. When they come to interpret this text, they distort the truth, by saying that there were people who were aware of the primordial ever-present infinite in time (*kuon ganjo*) among those who were converted by the teachings of the temporary gateway. The sutric texts and the explanatory commentaries are understandably clear. How could they come to make such a distorted statement?

According to the sutric text, the bodhisattvas who sprang up from the earth praised and extolled the Tathāgata for a period of fifty *kalpas*, whereas it is recounted that the assembly on the Spirit Vulture Peak (*Ryōjusen, Gridhrakūta*) that had been converted by the temporary gateway of the teachings derived from the external events of the Buddha Shākyamuni's life and work thought of this period as though it were half a day. When Tendai (*T'ien T'ai*) made the confrontation with those who were aware of the primordial infinity and those who were not, he explained that the assembly of those who had been converted by the temporary teachings derived from the external events of the Buddha Shākyamuni's life and work were those who were unaware, on account of their thinking of this time span as half a day. This is nothing but a prejudiced viewpoint.

The bodhisattvas who sprang up from the earth were aware of the primordial infinity, because their viewpoint of a time span of fifty small *kalpas* was the correct way of understanding it. Myōraku (*Miao-lo*), on following this argument, explained that the bodhisattvas who had broken through their unenlightenment were those who were aware of the primordial ever-present infinite in time (*kuon ganjo*), and those who were unaware of it were the bodhisattvas who had not yet broken through their own benightedness.

[Clocks move, planets move, but time stays where it is.]

What is in the text is intelligibly apparent. There are those who would suggest that, even though there were bodhisattvas who were converted through the former and temporary teachings derived from the external events of the Buddha Shākyamuni's life and work, the bodhisattvas of the higher abodes had already broken through their unenlightenment. This is the kind of scholar who would make all the sutras that do not attain to enlightenment read as those that do.

Even though the teachings prior to the Dharma Flower and those of the temporary gateway were of a preparatory nature, there is also the Buddha who is utterly awakened. And when the people yearned for the true Buddha of the *Chapter on the Lifespan of the Tathāgata* of the original gateway, it is said that those who were not yet aware of the primordial ever-present infinite in time (*kuon ganjo*) were still placed in the seats of the wise. Since the triple body of the provisional teachings derived from the external events of the Buddha Shākyamuni's life and work had not yet thrown off his transitory nature, he was therefore but an empty Buddha in a dream.

When the people of the former teachings and those who were converted through the temporary gateway of the teachings derived from the external events of the Buddha Shākyamuni's life and work came to the original gateway, they were still people who had not yet destroyed their delusions. Correctly speaking, their state would correspond to the first bodhisattva stage in the process of the fifty-stages of becoming a Buddha.

Myōraku (*Miao-lo*) said in his explanations, "When the gateway of the teachings derived from the external events of the Buddha Shākyamuni's life and work was cleared away so as to reveal the original, they all entered into the first bodhisattva stage in the process of becoming a Buddha." He also argued that "they were still placed in the seats of the wise". You should think about these two quotations at the same time.

The people of the teachings prior to the Dharma Flower or those of the temporary gateway are said to be like a Buddha and bodhisattvas who were still unaware of the ever-present infinite in time (*kuon ganjo*), and who had not yet broken from their unenlightenment. This is an outright true fact.

As you know, because of the exposition and revelation of the *Chapter on the Lifespan of the Tathāgata* of the original gateway, everyone in the whole assembly on the Spirit Vulture Peak (*Ryōjusen, Gridhrakūta*) attained to the substantiation of the lotus flower of the actual fundamental substance [i.e., Nam Myōhō Renge Kyō, which means to devote our lives to and found them on (*Nam[u]*) the Utterness of the Dharma (*Myōhō*) (entirety of existence, enlightenment and unenlightenment) permeated by the underlying white lotus flower-like mechanism of the interdependence of cause, concomitancy and effect (*Renge*) in its whereabouts of the ten (psychological) realms of dharmas (*Kyō*)]. The people of the two vehicles, those of incorrigible unbelief, and those of a self-opinionated mentality, as well as women, and people of an evil disposition, attained to the substantiation of the original Buddha.

The Universal Teacher Dengyō (*Dengyō Daishi*), on explaining the lotus flower of the universal and essential purpose of the appearance of the Buddha [Shākyamuni] in this world, said, "The universal and essential Dharma Flower being the justification and the circumstances for the sole purpose of the appearance of the Buddha in this world is in order that the lotus flower can be revealed. 'Sole' implies the sole true practice; 'universal' implies that its nature is universally extensive; and 'purpose' refers to the nature of the Dharma. When it comes to the final superlative, it is none other than the wisdom, the practice, and the all-embracing quality of the teaching that is within the three realms where sentient beings have organs of sense as well as desires, where there is a physical dimension and the realms where there is only mental activity. If the one vehicle can be reached, then the people of the three vehicles, those of a self-opinionated mentality, those within the path and those who are outside it, those with unhappy desires and those who are hard-hearted, all of them everywhere will arrive at the stage of the enlightened wisdom of understanding all dharmas. This sole purpose of the appearance of the Tathāgata in this world is his clearing the way, so as to reveal and enlighten people to enter into the wisdom and perception of the Buddha." This means that women, people of incorrigible unbelief, those of a self-opinionated mentality, the people of the two vehicles, and extremely evil people who were on Spirit Vulture Peak (*Ryōjusen, Gridhrakūta*) attained to the substantiation of the lotus flower of the actual fundamental substance.

Question: At the present time of the final phase of the Dharma, who has attained to the substantiation of the Dharma Flower of the actual fundamental substance?

Answer: On looking at the realities of the present age, there are many people who have come to the realisation of the fundamental substance of the hell of incessant suffering. Yet there is not one who has attained to the substantiation of the Lotus Flower of the Buddha. This is due to beliefs in the expedient means of the provisional teachings that do not attain to the path, and also on account of negative criticism with regard to the Lotus Flower of the actual fundamental substance, which is the one that is genuine and true.

The Buddha said, in his teaching, "If a man in his disbelief destructively vilifies this sutra, he will thereupon cut off the Buddha seeds from all his existential spaces." The text continues until, "At the end of this person's life, he will fall into the hell of incessant suffering." Tendai (*T'ien T'ai*) said, "This sutra opens up the Buddha seeds everywhere in the six paths of unenlightenment. If one were to slander this sutra, it would mean that those seeds would be cut off."

Nichiren says that this sutra disseminates the Buddha seeds throughout the ten [psychological] realms of dharmas. If one were to slander this sutra, it would correspondingly imply that the Buddha seeds throughout those ten realms would be cut off. This person will decidedly fall into the hell of incessant suffering. How could he expect to get release?

On the other hand, the sole gateway to the Dharma of Nichiren is that one simply cast aside the erroneous implications of the fallacious dharmas of the false teachers of the teachings derived from the external events of Shākyamuni's life and work and straightaway put faith in the true significance of the correct Dharma and the proper teacher, so as to attain to the substantiation of the lotus flower of the actual fundamental substance, which is the revelation of the actual fundamental substance of the utterly imponderable, underlying principle of eternal silence and illumination.

This comes about through believing the golden words of the Lord of the teaching of the *Chapter on the Lifespan of the Tathāgata* and by reciting Nam Myōhō Renge Kyō, which means to devote our lives to and found them on (Nam[u]) the Utterness of the Dharma [entirety of existence, enlightenment and unenlightenment] (*Myōhō*) permeated by the underlying white lotus flower-like mechanism of the interdependence of cause, concomitancy and effect (*Renge*) in its whereabouts of the ten [psychological] realms of dharmas (*Kyō*).

Question: Albeit that the Universal Teachers Nangaku (*Nan-yüeh*), Tendai (*T'ien T'ai*), and Dengyō (*Dengyō Daishi*) widely transmitted the *Dharma Flower Sutra* as the sole vehicle of the Dharma teaching of the school of the all-inclusive doctrine, how is it that they had not yet recited *Nam Myōhō Renge Kyō*? If this should be the case, were these Universal Teachers unaware of the actual fundamental substance, or should we say that they had not attained to its substantiation?

Answer: It is said that the Universal Teacher Nangaku (*Nan-yüeh*) was the bodhisattva incarnation of Kannon and the Universal Teacher Tendai (*T'ien T'ai*) was the bodhisattva incarnation of the Bodhisattva Sovereign Medicine (*Yaku' ō, Bhaishajya-rāja*). However, even though they attained to their substantiation, when they heard the teaching of the *Chapter on the Lifespan of the Tathāgata* of the original gateway on the Spirit Vulture Peak (*Ryōjusen, Gridhrakūta*), the period in which they lived was one in which the influence of the teachings of the Buddha Shākyamuni was still valid and not in the time for the propagation of the

Utterness of the Dharma (*Myōhō, Saddharma*). Therefore, we could exchange the name and ideograms of the Utterness of the Dharma (*Myōhō, Saddharma*) for the term "the desistance from troublesome worries", which consists in the meditation of sitting still, so as to set the mind at rest and to stop every thought that arises, in order to dwell on the thought that nothing exists independently from the one instant of mind containing three thousand existential spaces or that an instant of mind contains simultaneously phenomena, relativity, and the middle way.

Nevertheless, as to those Universal Teachers reciting *Nam Myōhō Renge Kyō*, it could be thought of as the genuineness and truth of the inner substantiation of their own practice. The Universal Teacher Nangaku (*Nan-yüeh*) says, in his *Confession of the Doctrine of the Dharma Flower*, "Nam Myōhō Renge Kyō, to consecrate and found one's life on the *Sutra on the White Lotus Flower-like Mechanism of the Utterness of the Dharma* (*Myōhō Renge Kyō*)". The Universal Teacher Tendai says, "I consecrate my life to the single vehicle of impartial wisdom of the *Sutra on the White Lotus Flower-like Mechanism of the Utterness of the Dharma* (*Myōhō Renge Kyō*)." He also says, "I touch my head on the ground and make obeisance to the *Sutra on the White Lotus Flower-like Mechanism of the Utterness of the Dharma* (*Myōhō Renge Kyō*)." And again he says, "To devote one's life to, and found it on the *Sutra on the White Lotus Flower-like Mechanism of the Utterness of the Dharma* (*Myōhō Renge Kyō*)". The Universal Teacher Dengyō (*Dengyō Daishi*), in his writings on the very last ten earthly wishes at one's dying hour, uses "*Nam Myōhō Renge Kyō*".

Question: This textual evidence is understandably clear. But why was it not propagated abroad, just as it is?

Answer: There are two reasons for this. Firstly, it was because the time was not yet ripe, and, secondly, the Universal Teachers Tendai (*T'ien T'ai*) and Nangaku (*Nan-yüeh*) were not entrusted with this assignment. Broadly speaking, the five ideograms for the Utterness of the Dharma (*Myōhō, Saddharma*) are the universal white dharma, which is to be disseminated during the final phase of the Dharma of Shākyamuni (*mappō*). It is the mission that was given to the countless numbers of great bodhisattvas who sprang up from the earth. This is why Nangaku (*Nan-yüeh*), Tendai (*T'ien T'ai*), and Dengyō (*Dengyō Daishi*) did not propagate this teaching, but remained aloof, keeping their enlightenment to themselves, since it was bequeathed to teachers and guides of the final phase of the Dharma of Shākyamuni (*mappō*).

Nichiren [formal signature]

Postscript to the Treatise on the Significance of the Actual Fundamental Substance

Question: Because the lotus flower of the actual fundamental substance is difficult to understand, a metaphor is provisionally used to make it clear. What proof is there in the sutric text?

Answer: In the sutra, it says, "untainted by worldly affairs, just like a lotus flower in the water that has grown up through the mud". You should know the simile of the bodhisattvas that spring up from the earth being the lotus flower of the actual fundamental substance.

At some later date, I must write this all out again. As this gateway to the dharma is the intrinsic element of what is implied in the Sutra on Utterness, it was also the fundamental intention of the Tathāgata Shākyamuni to entrust the great bodhisattvas who sprang up from the earth with the assignment of broadly propagating the essential of this sutra, during the final phase of his Dharma. Even after the sovereign of the state is shown to have a mind of faith, this gateway to the Dharma, from the very outset, must be the treasury of esoteric wisdom. Nichiren has ended this transmission to the Venerable Sairen.

Nichiren

The Oral Transmission on the Significance of the Dharma Flower Sutra

Ongi kuden,
Nam Myōhō Renge Kyō
Goshō Shimpen, p. 1719

The first day of the first month of the first year of Kō,an [1278], at 57 years of age

Nam Myōhō Renge Kyō

The Oral Transmission on the Meaning of the Dharma Flower Sutra (Ongi Kuden) states that *Namu* is a word that comes from Sanskrit *(Namas)*; here, when rendered into Chinese, it means "upon what we establish our lives and devote them to". The Fundamental Object of Veneration *(gohonzon)*, whereupon we establish our lives and to which we devote them, is both the person of Nichiren and the Dharma, which is characterised by the one instant of thought containing three thousand existential spaces. The person is the Eternal Shākyamuni who is contained within the text of the *Sutra on the White Lotus Flower-like Mechanism of the Utterness of the Dharma (Myōhō Renge Kyō)*. The Dharma is the *Sutra on the White Lotus Flower-like Mechanism of the Utterness of the Dharma (Myōhō Renge Kyō)* as the recitation of its title and subject matter [*Daimoku*, which is Nam Myōhō Renge Kyō] and its Fundamental Object of Veneration *(gohonzon)*, both of which we dedicate our lives to and establish them on.

Again, devotion means to turn to the principle of the eternally unchanging, fundamental quality of existence *(fuhen shinnyo no ri)* [the fixed principle of the true nature of existence], as it was expounded in the teachings derived from the external events of Shākyamuni's life and work *(shakumon)*. The establishment of one's life means that it is founded on the wisdom of the original archetypal state (*honmon*), which is reality as it changes according to karmic circumstances (*zuien shinnyo no chi*).

We in fact establish our lives on and devote them to Nam Myōhō Renge Kyō, which means to devote our lives to and found them on (*Nam[u]*) the Utterness of the Dharma [entirety of existence, enlightenment and unenlightenment] (*Myōhō*) permeated by the underlying white lotus flower-like mechanism of the interdependence of cause, concomitancy and effect (*Renge*) in its whereabouts of the ten [psychological] realms of dharmas (*Kyō*).

There is an explanation by the Universal Teacher Dengyō (*Dengyō Daishi*), who states, ". . . . both the wisdom of the teachings of the original archetypal state (*honmon*), which implies reality as it changes according to karmic circumstances (*zuien shinnyo no chi*), and the principle of the eternally unchanging, indispensable quality of existence at the same time (*fuhen shinnyo no ri*) [the fixed principle of the true nature of existence], as it was expounded in the teachings derived from the external events of Shākyamuni's life and work (*shakumon*) . . . . ."

This refers to the silence and the shining light that are in fact the real and fundamental nature of life itself. Also, devotion is the manifestation of our physical selves, whereas establishing our lives on something is a dharma of the mind. The ultimate teaching of the *Sutra on the White Lotus Flower-like Mechanism of the Utterness of the Dharma* (*Myōhō Renge Kyō*) points out that both mind and materiality are not separate from each other.

There is an explanation that says, "We take refuge in this ultimate teaching [i.e., the *Dharma Flower Sutra* (*Hokke-kyō*)], because it is the vehicle to enlightenment that the Buddha himself relied on."

The Oral Transmission on the Meaning of the Dharma Flower Sutra (*Ongi Kuden*) then goes on to say that the *Nam(u)* of Nam Myōhō Renge Kyō is derived from Sanskrit (*Namas*) and that *myōhō, renge,* and *kyō* are words of Chinese origin. This makes *Nam(u) Myōhō Renge Kyō* both Sanskrit and Chinese at the same time.

[At the time of the Daishōnin, these two languages were the main tongues of humankind.]

Also, Myōhō Renge Kyō in Sanskrit is *Saddharma Pundarīka Sutram*. *Sad* [the phonetic change of *Sat*] is Utterness in English and *Myō* in Japanese. The nine ideograms that are a substitute for the Sanskrit lettering are the five Buddhas and four bodhisattva entities on the eight petals and the centre of the lotus flower that lies in the breast of all sentient beings.

[This eight-petalled lotus with five Buddhas (one in the centre) and four bodhisattva entities is a Shingon or Tantric concept that is the central court of the mandala that represents the underlying Buddha nature that runs through the whole of both physical and mental existence.]

This concept implies that the nine realms of dharmas of ordinary existence are not separate from the oneness of the enlightened realm of the Buddha. *Myō* or the Utterness is the Dharma realm of enlightenment, which is Nam Myōhō Renge Kyō and all its implications. [This is the real nature and the original state of the world of phenomena (the content of the Buddha enlightenment being a full understanding of what dharmas really are).] *Hō* or dharmas stands for unclearness and unenlightenment [that is, the way we perceive things in our ordinary lives]. So, when unclearness and enlightenment become a single entity, it is called the Utterness of the Dharma (*Myōhō*). The lotus flower (*Renge*) stands for the three dharmas of cause, concomitancy and effect. This is the interdependence of cause, concomitancy and effect. *Kyō* or sutra is the expression of the words, speech, voices, and sounds of all sentient beings. This is explained as when the voice is in the service of the Buddha enlightenment; then this is what is called a sutra.

A sutra may also be described as that which is constant and unchanging throughout the past, present, and future. The Dharma realm of the Buddha or all the realms of dharmas of ordinary people is the Utterness of the Dharma (*Myōhō*, *Saddharma*). The Dharma realm or the realms of dharmas of ordinary people is the location where they occur (*Kyō*). The eight-petalled lotus with five

Buddhas and four bodhisattvas is the substantiation of the Buddha enlightenment in all of us. You should think this over thoroughly.

The Eight-petalled Lotus with Five Buddhas and Four Bodhisattvas

The eight-petalled lotus shows five Buddhas and four bodhisattvas [one Buddha in the centre and four others in the cardinal directions], the other four quarter points being occupied by bodhisattvas. This is the same as the mandala of the womb treasury (*taizōkai, garbhadātu*) that is used by the Tantric and Mantra School (*Shingon*) in Japan.

The womb treasury (*taizōkai, garbhadātu*) is the fundamental source of enlightenment, as well as life itself. This matrix is comparable to a womb in which a child is conceived. It is both the container and its contents which entail the fundamental of enlightenment and wisdom in its purest state. It also represents the human heart (mind) in its essential innocence and purity, which is seen as the compassion of the Buddha and his moral awareness.

The central Buddha of this mandala is the Tathāgata of the Universal Sun (*Dainichi-nyorai, Mahāvairochana-Tāthagata*), who emanates his light onto all the other manifestations of wisdom and enlightenment. It is the enlightenment of the original archetypal state (*honmon*), which induced the teachings of Shākyamuni that were derived from the external events of his life and work (*shakumon*).

On the eastern petal is the Buddha Jewelled Banner (*Hōtō, Ratnaketa*); on the southern petal sits the Buddha Sovereign of the Flowering of the Whole Surface [to be enlightened] (*Kaifuka'ō*). On the western petal is the Buddha of Boundless Light (*Amitābha Buddha, Amida Butsu*), and on the northern petal sits the Buddha who represents the *Dharma-kāya* or the universal entity of the Buddha (*Tenkurai'on, Amoghasiddhi*).

The remaining petals represent the four bodhisattvas. On the southeastern petal is the Bodhisattva Universally Worthy (*Fugen,*

Samantabhadra); on the northeastern petal sits the Bodhisattva Perceiving the Sounds of the Existential Dimensions (*Kanzeon, Avalokiteshvara*); on the northwestern petal is the Bodhisattva Maitreya (*Miroku*); and on the southwestern petal sits the Bodhisattva Mañjushrī (*Monjushiri*).

All these Buddhas and bodhisattvas are seen as the nine honoured ones. Also, the lotus flower in this context is thought of as a symbol for the heart or mind of sentient beings. In *The Oral Transmission on the Meaning of the Dharma Flower Sutra* (*Ongi Kuden*), the nine honoured ones are understood as the principle of the nine realms of dharmas not being separate from the Dharma realm of the Buddha. They are the following:

1. The Tathāgata of the Universal Sun (*Dainichi-nyorai, Mahavairochana-Tāthagata*)
2. The Buddha who represents the *Dharma-kāya* (*Tenkurai'on*)
3. The Bodhisattva Perceiving the Sounds of the Existential Dimensions (*Kanzeon, Avalokiteshvara*)
4. The Buddha Jewelled Banner (*Hōtō, Ratnaketa*)
5. The Bodhisattva Universally Worthy (*Fugen, Samantabhadra*)
6. Buddha Sovereign of the Flowering of the Whole Surface (*Kaifuka'ō*)
7. The Bodhisattva Mañjushrī (*Monjushiri*)
8. The Buddha of Boundless Light (*Amitābha-Buddha*)
9. The Bodhisattva Maitreya (*Miroku*)

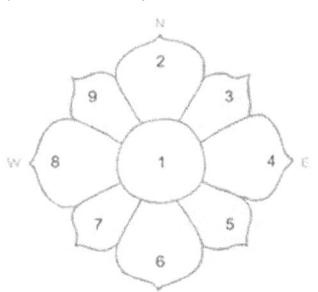

Treatise on Questions and Answers Concerning the Fundamental Object of Veneration Addressed to the Lay Practitioner Jōken

Honzon Mondō Shō
Goshō Shimpen, pp. 1274-1283

The ninth month of the first year of Kō.an [1278], at 57 years of age

The question is asked: What has been decided as to what should be the Fundamental Object of Veneration (*gohonzon*) for the common mortals during the dissolute era of the final period of Shākyamuni?

The answer is given: The title and theme of the *Dharma Flower Sutra* (*Myōhō Renge Kyō*) must be the Fundamental Object of Veneration (*gohonzon*).

The question is asked: From which sutric text does this explanation derive?

The answer is given: In the fourth fascicle of the *Dharma Flower Sutra* (*Myōhō Renge Kyō*) in the *Chapter on the Dharma as a Teacher*, it says, "Bodhisattva Sovereign Medicine (*Yaku' ō, Baishajya-raja*), in every place wherever the Dharma Flower is expounded, read, recited, or written out, or wherever this sutra is placed, it should be decided that a *stupa* made of the seven precious materials be erected, as high as it is wide, and solemnly decorated. Again, there is no further need to be contented with just a reliquary. Why is this so? It is because inside this is placed the whole person of the Tathāgata."

In the fourth fascicle of the *Sutra on the Buddha's passing over to Nirvana*, in the *Chapter on the Nature of the Tathāgata*, it says, "What is more Kashō (*Kāshapa*), what was taught by the teacher of all the Buddhas is referred to as the Dharma. This is why the Tathāgata venerates and makes offerings to it. The reason why the Dharma is eternal is because all the Buddhas are also eternal."

The Universal Teacher Tendai (*T'ien T'ai*) says this about the perfect absorption into the *Dharma Flower Sutra* (*Myōhō Renge Kyō*) as a single object of meditation: "In the sites where Buddhas attained to the path, set up a good high pedestal and enshrine the whole of the *Dharma Flower Sutra* (*Myōhō Renge Kyō*). There is no need to place any Buddha images or any other sutra. Only the *Dharma Flower Sutra* (*Myōhō Renge Kyō*) needs to be enclosed within the *stupa*."

It is said without doubt that the Universal Teacher Tendai (*T'ien T'ai*), in the second chapter of his *Universal Desistance from Troublesome Worries in order to See Clearly* (*Maka Shikan*), says that the fundamental object of veneration for the four kinds of practice of perfect absorption into the one object of contemplation (*samādhi*) is the Buddha Amida (*Amitābha*). In Tripitaka Fukū's (*Amoghavajra*) translation of the *Ceremony of the Sovereign Yoga Practices for Contemplating the Wisdom of the Dharma Flower Sutra* (*Myōhō Renge Kyō*), the fundamental object of veneration is the eternal Shākyamuni and Tathāgata Abundant Treasure (*Tahō Nyorai, Prabhūtaratna*) of the Dharma Flower. Do you really refute the argument of these two?

[Here, Tripitaka is a title. Fukū, in Chinese Pu k'ung (*Amoghavajra*), (705-774 CE) was the sixth master in the lineage of the Tantric School. He was born in Northern India and came to China in 720 CE He assisted his master Vajrabodhi (*Kongōchi*) in translating sutras. After Vajrabodhi's death, he went to Southern India to get original Sanskrit manuscripts. Apart from having translated many sutras, he strongly encouraged the Tantric and Mantra School.]

The answer is given: This is not my intended meaning. What you have just mentioned now are quotations from the sutras and the explanations of the Universal Teacher Tendai (*T'ien T'ai*). However, with regard to the Buddha Amida (*Amitābha*) being the fundamental object of veneration for the four kinds of *samādhi* in the *Universal Desistance from Troublesome Worries in order to See Clearly* (*Maka Shikan*), there are three kinds of image of this Buddha that correspond to the *Sutra on the Buddha's Answers to Monjushiri's Questions*, the *Sutra on the Samādhi in which the Buddhas of the Ten Directions are Seen as Clearly as the Stars at Night*, and the *Sutra on the Invocations [dhāranîs] to Entreat the Bodhisattva Kannon to Destroy and Suppress Poisonous Harm*.

Nevertheless, these sutras are from among those that were expounded prior to the *Dharma Flower Sutra* (*Myōhō Renge Kyō*) and had not yet revealed the true reality. The images of the Buddha Amida (*Amitābha*) in their role as fundamental objects of veneration are depicted as either being seated in perpetual contemplation, or in a stance of perpetual practice, or in his manifestation of being in the *samādhi* of his own awakened mind.

There are two kinds of *samādhi*, one of which consists in half practice and half contemplation and whose fundamental object of veneration for contemplation is made up of the Seven Buddhas and Eight Bodhisattvas in the *Sutra on the Invocations [dhāranîs] of the Universal and Equally Broad Teachings*. The *samādhi* that is made up of two halves consists of the two practices of walking round the Buddha images to show reverence and also sitting in quietude in order to meditate upon them. The other *samādhi* synthesises the full meaning of the Shākyamuni and Tathāgata Abundant Treasure (*Tahō Nyorai, Prabhūtaratna*) in the *Dharma Flower Sutra* (*Myōhō Renge Kyō*).

It would seem that, since we are referring to the *samādhi* of the Dharma Flower, then the *Dharma Flower Sutra* (*Myōhō Renge Kyō*) ought to be its fundamental object of veneration. In the *Ceremony of the Sovereign Yoga Practices for Contemplating the Wisdom of the Dharma Flower* of the Tripitaka Fukū (*Pu-k'ung, Amoghavajra*) took this concept from the *Chapter on the Appearance of the Stupa made of Precious Materials*. But using this as the Fundamental Object of Veneration (*gohonzon*) of the Lord of the teaching of the *Dharma Flower Sutra* (*Myōhō Renge Kyō*) was not the meaning that was intended. The Fundamental Object of Veneration (*gohonzon*) that I mentioned previously is the one that has Shākyamuni, Tathāgata Abundant Treasure (*Tahō Nyorai, Prabhūtaratna*), and all the Buddhas of the ten directions inscribed upon it, which is what the practitioner of the *Dharma Flower Sutra* (*Myōhō Renge Kyō*) really intends.

The question is asked: In Japan there are ten schools – the Kusha School, the Jōjitsu School, the Ritsu School, the Hossō School, the Sanron School, the Flower Garland School, the Tantric School, the Jōdo School, the Zen School, and the Hokke School – all of which have conflicting fundamental objects of venerations. For instance, the three Schools of the Kusha, Jōjitsu, and the Ritsu use the lesser manifestation of the corresponding body of Shākyamuni, which Shākyamuni used to entice future believers. Both the Hossō and Sanron Schools use the superior manifestation of the body which was used to encourage bodhisattvas that is sixty feet high. The Flower Garland School uses the image of the Tathāgata Shākyamuni as the manifestation of Birushana [*Vairocana*] enthroned upon the calyx of the Lotus Flower. The Tantric School has the image of the Tathāgata of the Universal Sun (*Dainichi-Nyorai, Mahāvairochana-Tāthagata*). The Jōdo School venerates the Buddha Amida [*Amitābha*]. The Zen School uses the image of Shākyamuni himself. But why does the Hokke or Tendai School use the *Dharma Flower Sutra* (*Myōhō Renge Kyō*) as its fundamental object of veneration?

Answer: They use the content of their sutra as an object of veneration instead of an image of the Buddha, which is significant.

Question: What does this mean, and why is this sutra paramount?

The answer is given: You must use the Fundamental Object of Veneration (*gohonzon*) that is paramount. For instance, when the Confucian teachings were the supreme doctrine, the Three August Rulers and the Five Emperors were used as fundamental objects of veneration. But with the advent of the Buddha teaching, the images of Shākyamuni in turn became the fundamental objects of veneration.

The question is asked: How is it that you do not use the image of the Buddha as your fundamental object of veneration, but only use the theme and title of the *Dharma Flower Sutra* (*Nam Myōhō Renge Kyō*) instead?

[Nam Myōhō Renge Kyō means to devote our lives to and found them on (*Nam*[*u*]) the Utterness of the Dharma (*Myōhō*) (entirety of existence, enlightenment and unenlightenment) permeated by the underlying white lotus flower-like mechanism of the interdependence of cause, concomitancy and effect (*Renge*) in its whereabouts of the ten (psychological) realms of dharmas (*Kyō*).]

Answer: Take another look at the sutric quotation from the *Chapter on the Dharma as a Teacher* at the beginning of this treatise. But this is not what I mean. Shākyamuni and Tendai (*T'ien T'ai*) decided that the fundamental object of veneration had to be the *Dharma Flower Sutra* (*Nam Myōhō Renge Kyō*). Therefore, just like Shākyamuni and Tendai (*T'ien T'ai*) in the past, Nichiren in the present final era takes the *Dharma Flower Sutra* (*Nam Myōhō Renge Kyō*) as being the Fundamental Object of Veneration (*gohonzon*). This is because the *Dharma Flower Sutra* (*Nam Myōhō Renge Kyō*) is the father and mother of Shākyamuni and the eyes of all the Buddhas. Broadly speaking, Shākyamuni, the Tathāgata of the Universal Sun (*Dainichi-Nyorai, Mahāvairochana-Tāthagata*), and all the Buddhas of the ten directions are brought into being through the *Dharma Flower Sutra* (*Myōhō Renge Kyō*). Hence, it is the Fundamental Object of Veneration (*gohonzon*) that can give birth to all existence.

It is asked: What evidence do you have for this?

The answer is given: In the *Sutra on the Bodhisattva Fugen*, it says, "This sacred book of the universal vehicle (*daijō, mahāyāna*) is the treasure store of all the Buddhas. It is the means of seeing of all the Buddhas of the ten directions and of the past, present, and future. It is also the seed from which all the Tathāgatas of the past, present, and future are born." Furthermore, it says, "This *Dharma Flower Sutra* (*Myōhō Renge Kyō*) is the one that is the eyes of all the Buddhas and is the means whereby all the Buddhas acquire the five kinds of vision of *i*) humankind, *ii*) the *deva* (*ten*), *iii*) the wisdom of the individual vehicle (*shōjō, hīnayāna*), *iv*) of the bodhisattvas, and *v*) that of the wisdom of the Buddhas. It is the sutra out of which the three kinds of entity of the Buddha come into being in a universally all-embracing manner. Through this universal gesture of the Buddha truth, it proves that this sutra is the sea of nirvana. Therefore, it is this sea that gives rise to the three kinds of immaculately pure embodiments of the Buddha. These three bodies are the fields of happiness of humankind and the *deva* (*ten*). Also these three bodies are worthy of the utmost veneration."

This text from the sutra shows that the spirit of the *Dharma Flower Sutra* (*Myōhō Renge Kyō*) is able to give rise to the Buddha, and also it is from whence the Buddha comes into being. It is the embodiment of the Buddha himself. However, one has to be precise. It is only the *Dharma Flower Sutra* (*Nam Myōhō Renge Kyō*) that can be applied to the ceremony of making offerings, in order to open the eyes of either painted or wooden images of the Buddha. In any case, nowadays with regard to these ceremonies concerning painted or wooden Buddha images, there are the mantras and the hand gestures [*mudrā*] that are carried out by the Tantric School to make offerings for the opening of the eyes of the Tathāgata of the Universal Sun (*Dainichi-Nyorai, Mahāvairochana-Tāthagata*). But this is extremely unproductive.

The question is asked: Between the *Dharma Flower Sutra* (*Nam Myōhō Renge Kyō*) being the fundamental object of veneration and the Tathāgata of the Universal Sun (*Dainichi-Nyorai, Mahāvairochana-Tāthagata*) being the fundamental object of veneration, which is the superior?

The answer is given: If it were to be the significance that was intended by the Universal Teachers Kōbō, Jikaku, and Chishō, then the Tathāgata of the Universal Sun (*Dainichi-Nyorai, Mahāvairochana-Tāthagata*) would be the superior, and the *Dharma Flower Sutra* (*Nam Myōhō Renge Kyō*) would be the lesser.

Question: What do you mean by this?

Answer: In the Universal Teacher Kōbō's work, *The Precious Key to the Esoteric Storehouse*, in the part where it deals with the ten stages of firm ground, it says, "The eighth is the *Dharma Flower Sutra* (*Myōhō Renge Kyō*). The ninth is the Flower Garland Sutra. And the tenth is the Sutra on the Tathāgata of the Universal Sun (*Dainichi-*

Nyorai, Mahāvairochana-Tāthagata)." From the point of view of these Universal Teachers, this is starting from the shallows and going towards the deep. In the Universal Teacher Jikaku's *Commentary on the Sutra on the Vajra Apex* and his *Commentary on the Sutra on Excellent Achievement*, as well as the Universal Teacher Chishō's *Taking refuge in the Significance of the Sutra on the Tathāgata of the Universal Sun* (*Dainichi-Nyorai, Mahāvairochana-Tāthagata*), they all say, "The *Sutra on the Tathāgata of the Universal Sun* (*Dainichi-Nyorai, Mahāvairochana-Tāthagata*) is first, and the *Dharma Flower Sutra* (*Myōhō Renge Kyō*) comes second."

Question: What do you think about this?

Answer: According to the evaluation of the Tathāgata Shākyamuni, the Tathāgata Abundant Treasure (*Tahō Nyorai, Prabhūtaratna*), and all the Buddhas of the ten directions in general, all say, "Out of all the sutras of the past, present, and future, the *Dharma Flower Sutra* (*Myōhō Renge Kyō*) is preeminently the foremost."

Question: Throughout present-day Japan, all the monks of the Tendai and Tantric Schools, as well as the sovereign, his ministers, and all the common people say questioningly, "How can Nichiren, that wrangler of the Dharma, be superior to the Universal Teachers Kōbō, Jikaku, and Chishō?"

Answer: Nichiren reproachfully replies, "Should the Universal Teachers Kōbō, Jikaku, and Chishō be superior to Shākyamuni, Tathāgata Abundant Treasure (*Tahō Nyorai, Prabhūtaratna*), and all the Buddhas of the ten directions?"

Point number one: In present-day Japan, from the sovereign of the realm down to the common people, all are the children of Shākyamuni. Shākyamuni, in his very last testament, stated, "It should be according to the Dharma, and not according to the person who expounds it."

The *Dharma Flower Sutra* (*Myōhō Renge Kyō*) in the first place conforms to the Dharma. So are these three universal teachers really so superior? Should not the sovereign, his ministers, the people, right on down to the horses and oxen who trail behind, be considered unfilial brats? This is point two.

Question: Did not the Universal Teacher Kōbō take a look at the *Dharma Flower Sutra* (*Myōhō Renge Kyō*)?

Answer: The Universal Teacher read through all the sutras. Among these were the *Dharma Flower Sutra* (*Myōhō Renge Kyō*), the *Flower Garland Sutra*, and the *Sutra on the Tathāgata of the Universal Sun* (*Dainichi-Nyorai, Mahāvairochana-Tāthagata*). All of them were read from the point of view of starting from the shallows and proceeding towards the depths, as well as taking into consideration which sutra was the superior and which was the less profound. On reading the *Dharma Flower Sutra* (*Myōhō Renge Kyō*) after his own fashion, he said, "The *Dharma Flower Sutra* (*Myōhō Renge Kyō*) of the Bodhisattva Mañjushrī (*Monjushiri*) is the esoteric and secret store of All the Buddha Tathāgatas. But the one that was expounded by Shākyamuni is not of the same category." Again, after reading further on, according to his own way of understanding the *Dharma Flower Sutra* (*Myōhō Renge Kyō*), he said, "Bodhisattva Sovereign Remedy (*Yaku' ō, Bhaishajya-rāja*), I must now tell you that, out of all the sutras I have expounded, there is nevertheless, among them the *Dharma Flower Sutra* (*Myōhō Renge Kyō*), which is the third in rank." Again, when both the Universal Teachers Jikaku and Chishō read this sutra according to their own perception, they said, "Out of all the sutras that exist, this is the most mediocre." Also they said, "It is by far the most second-rate."

When Shākyamuni, Tathāgata Abundant Treasure (*Tahō Nyorai, Prabhūtaratna*), the Tathāgata of the Universal Sun (*Dainichi-Nyorai, Vairochana-Tāthagata*), and all the other Buddhas compared the *Dharma Flower Sutra* (*Myōhō Renge Kyō*) with all the other sutras, they said, "The Dharma Flower is the highest of all the sutras." What this comes down to is the question: "Have Shākyamuni and all the Buddhas of the ten directions, as well as the three Universal Teachers Kōbō, Jikaku, and Chishō considered what the fundamental of the object of veneration should be?" In any case, the way Nichiren would settle the matter would be that, since these three Universal Teachers have turned their backs on all the Buddhas of the ten directions for such a long time, could they themselves not become the fundamental of the object of veneration instead?

Question: The Universal Teacher Kōbō [774-835 CE] came from the county of Sanuki. He was the disciple of Gonsō, who had received the title 'Highest of Monks'. The Universal Teacher Kōbō also had the highest understanding of the doctrines of the six Sanron and Hossō schools. In the fifth month of the twenty-third year of the historical reign called Enryaku [804 CE], Kōbō was commanded by the Emperor Kammu to go to China, where, under the tutelage of the Chinese sovereign Junsō [805 CE], Kōbō entered the Seiryūji Temple and there under the Master Keika he received the whole of the Dharma teaching of the Shingon School. Later, the Master Keika made Kōbō the seventh in the line of the Dharma heritage that stems from the Tathāgata of the Universal Sun (*Dainichi-Nyorai, Vairochana-Tāthagata*). His concept is based on the idea that, even though human beings may live and die, the Dharma remains constant, in the same way as water can be poured from one vessel into another. Even though the Tathāgata of the Universal Sun (*Dainichi-Nyorai, Vairochana-Tāthagata*), Kongōsatta, Ryūmyō, Ryūchi, Kongōchi, Fukū (*Amoghavajra*), Keika, and Kōbō may have been different vessels, the water of the wisdom that was passed from one vessel to the next remains the same Shingon teaching.

After this Universal Teacher had studied the doctrines of the Shingon School, he then crossed over three thousand waves and billows, before he finally arrived in Japan. The three successive sovereigns Heizei, Saga, and Junna all conferred honours upon him. On the nineteenth day of the first month of the fourteenth year of the historical reign Kōnin [823 CE], he received the imperial command to build the Tōji [Eastern Temple]. From then on, the esoteric teachings of the Shingon School were propagated everywhere. Throughout the five home provinces, the seven districts, the sixty-six provinces of both islands, how could anybody not have been caught up in the latest of fashions of taking up the bell and twirling the *vajra* of the Shingon rites?

Again, the Universal Teacher Jikaku was from the county of Shimotsuke and was a disciple of Kōchi Bosatsu. In the third year of the reign Daidō [809 CE] at the age of fifteen, Jikaku became the disciple of the Universal Teacher Dengyō (*Dengyō daishi*). He then spent the following fifteen years on Mount Hiei, during which he studied the teachings of the Sanron, Hossō, Kegon, Ritsu, and Kusha Schools. But in particular he studied the teachings of the Dharma Flower School [Tendai] and those of the Shingon School, in order to be able to transmit them. In the fifth year of the reign Shōwa [838 CE], Jikaku went to China at the time of the reign of Crown Prince Bu Sō [*Wu Tsung*, 841 CE], where he met Hassen, Gensei, Gishin, Hōgetsu, Shuei, Jion, and others of the Tendai School. He also met the Shingon School's Sekigaku. In China, Jikaku mastered the two paths of the exoteric and esoteric doctrines. Furthermore, he studied the Shingon secret doctrines for a period of ten years to the fulfilment of his merits. He then became the ninth in the line of the Dharma heritage that stems from the Tathāgata of the Universal Sun (*Dainichi-Nyorai, Vairochana-Tāthagata*).

In the first year of the reign entitled Kashō [848 CE], the Emperor Ninmyō became Jikaku's disciple. Throughout the reigns Ninju [851-54 CE] and Saikō [854-57 CE], this Universal Teacher wrote commentaries on the *Sutra on the Vajra* (Scalpel) and *the Sutra on Excellent Achievement* [*susiddhi*]. Among other things, he built the Sōji.in Monastery on Mount Hiei and became the third patriarch of the Tendai School. This was the beginning of the intermixture of the Shingon teachings with those of Tendai (*T'ien T'ai*).

Now we come to the Universal Teacher Chishō, who was from the county of Sanuki. In the fourth year of the reign Tenchō [827 CE], he became a novice on Mount Hiei and then became the disciple of the Master Gishin. In Japan, Chishō studied under the meritorious auspices of the Abbots Gishin, Jikaku, and Enchō with whom he studied the doctrines of eight schools. In the first year of the historical reign Ninju [851 CE], the Emperor commanded that Chishō should go to China for further study. Throughout the Emperor of China Sensō's rule, whose reign was called Taichū [847-59 CE], Chishō studied under the Universal Teachers the Masters Hōzen and Ryōsho for seven years, during which he became thoroughly versed in both the exoteric and esoteric doctrines. In the course of the reign that was given the name of Tennan [857-59 CE], Chishō returned to Japan. Both the Emperors

Montoku and Seiwa became his disciples. Whether they did it for their present lives or for their lives to come, illustrious nobles, whose heritages were as stable as the sun and moon, and also ministers, as well as the common people, regularly became believers who diligently looked towards Chishō's teachings and took refuge in them. The reason for this was that all of these people were silly and misguided enough to simply take Chishō at his word. Indeed, apart from contradicting the words of the Buddha, "according to the Dharma and not according to the person who expounds it", should we then suppose that the Dharma is according to Kōbō and not according to the Buddha?

Question: In the last analysis, what does this all mean?

Answer: The thousand years that came after the Lord of the Teaching Shākyamuni had entered into the extinction of nirvana was the appropriate time for the broad propagation of the Buddha teaching in India. The first five hundred years consisted of the individual vehicle (*shōjō, hīnayāna*), and the five hundred years that followed were for the propagation of the universal vehicle (*daijō, mahāyāna*). Even though there might have been disputes over the individual (*shōjō, hīnayāna*) and the universal (*daijō, mahāyāna*) vehicles or over the provisional and the real teachings, there was decidedly very little mention of the esoteric and exoteric teachings. Fifteen years after the debut of the formal era of the Dharma, the Buddha teaching had already spread as far as China. It was certain that in the beginning there were violent disputes between those who followed the teaching of Shākyamuni and the Confucianists and Taoists.

Nevertheless, the Buddha Dharma which was not different from that of India gradually spread, in spite of all the occasional disputes over the individual (*shōjō, hīnayāna*) and universal (*daijō, mahāyāna*) vehicles or over the provisional and the real teachings. After the Buddha teaching had been established in China for six hundred years, at the time of the Emperor Gensō [r.713-55 CE], three Indian monks who all held the title of being well-versed in the tenets of Buddha teaching (*Tripitaka*) – Zenmui, Kongōchi, and Fukū (*Amoghavajra*) – came to China and established the Shingon school, whereupon they set about demolishing the arguments of the Flower Garland school, the Dharma Flower school, and any other school that was not their own. From the sovereign to the common people, everybody thought that the dissimilarity between the Shingon teachings and those of the *Dharma Flower Sutra (Myōhō Renge Kyō)* were like clouds and mud. Later, during the reign of the Chinese Emperor Tokusō [780-804 CE], there was a person called the Universal Teacher Myōraku (*Miao-lo*) of the Dharma Flower School who had a strong desire to topple the Shingon School in debate. However, the arrangements for such an occasion never came about, so that there was nobody who could make it clear as to which of these two schools was the superior.

In Japan, during the reign of Kinmei [539-71 CE] who was the thirtieth of sovereigns who were humankind, the Buddha Dharma started to cross over to Japan from Korea. At first, for a period of thirty or so years, there were terrible disputes between the followers of the Buddha and those who followed the local Shinto deities. During the reign of the Empress Suiko [592-628 CE], Prince Shōtoku set about spreading the Buddha teaching, at about the same time the Senior Monks Ekan and Kanroku from Korea were busy propagating the doctrines of the Sanron School. In the course of the reign of the Emperor Kōtoku [645-54 CE], the teachings of the Zen School were brought over by Dōshō, and, when the Emperor Tenmu was on the throne [673-86 CE], Chikō, who came from the northernmost Korean kingdom Shiragi, brought over the teachings of the Hossō School.

At the time when the Emperor Genshō was on the throne [715-24 CE], the Tripitaka Zenmui brought the *Sutra on the Tathāgata of the Universal Sun (Dainichi-Nyorai, Vairochana-Tāthagata)* to Japan, but he did not propagate it. During the time when the Emperor Shōmu ruled Japan [724-49 CE], the Universally Virtuous Shinjō and the Highest of the Order Rōben came over to Japan with the *Flower Garland Sutra*. Then, when the forty-fourth in the line of sovereigns who were humankind Kōken [749-58 CE] was the Empress of Japan, the Chinese Tō [*Tang*] Dynasty Master Ganjin (*Jianzhen*) arrived with the teachings of the Ritsu School and the *Dharma Flower Sutra (Myōhō Renge Kyō)*. They did propagate the rules for monks and nuns according to the Ritsu School, but the *Dharma Flower Sutra (Myōhō Renge Kyō)* was not circularised.

During the seventh month of the twenty-third year of the reign entitled Enryaku [804 CE] of the Emperor Kanmu who was the fiftieth in the line of sovereigns of Japan, the Universal Teacher Dengyō (*Dengyō daishi*) was given permission to cross over to the shores of China, where he met two disciples of the Universal Teacher Myōraku (*Miao-lo*), Dōsui and Gyōman, from whom he was transmitted the wisdom and the contemplative practice of the perfect absorption into the one object of contemplation of the Dharma Flower School. Also, the Universal Teacher Dengyō (*Dengyō daishi*) received the bodhisattva precepts from the Teacher of Monastic Rules Dōsen (*Tao Hsüan*) and studied the esoteric teachings of the Shingon school under Master Jungyō as well. When the Universal Teacher Dengyō (*Dengyō daishi*) came back to Japan, he had difficulty in demonstrating the superiority of the Dharma Flower School to the Shingon School in the same way as he had learned from his Chinese teachers. But, by quoting and comparing explanations from the *Sutra on the Tathāgata of the Universal Sun* (*Dainichi-Nyorai, Mahāvairochana-Tāthagata*) and the *Dharma Flower Sutra* (*Myōhō Renge Kyō*), not only did he show that the *Sutra on the Tathāgata of the Universal Sun* (*Dainichi-Nyorai, Vairochana-Tāthagata*) was inferior to the Dharma Flower, but he also considered taking Tendai's (*T'ien T'ai*) insight and understanding of Zenmui's *Commentary of the Sutra on the Tathāgata of the Universal Sun* (*Dainichi-Nyorai, Vairochana-Tāthagata*) and making it a part of the teaching of the Hokke School.

With regard to the Shingon School's attempts to impose itself, it seems more than likely that, after the sutras of the Shingon School of the Universal Teacher Kōbō had been refuted, there must have been a lot of bad feeling. Not only was the *Sutra on the Tathāgata of the Universal Sun* (*Dainichi-Nyorai, Vairochana-Tāthagata*) proven to be inferior, but also the *Flower Garland Sutra* was shown to be subordinate. What a shame it is that neither Jikaku of the Temple on Mount Hiei nor Chishō of the Onjōji Temple could accept Tendai's (*T'ien T'ai*) view concerning the *Commentary of the Sutra on the Tathāgata of the Universal Sun* (*Dainichi-Nyorai, Vairochana-Tāthagata*). However, in order that the prejudiced views of the Universal Teacher Kōbō should not spread throughout Japan, both of the Universal Teachers were in agreement over the Dharma Flower being superior to the *Flower Garland Sutra*. But, since these two were of the same mind as the Universal Teacher Kōbō with regard to the Shingon doctrine being superior to the Dharma Flower, it is not surprising that they became the bitter enemies of the Universal Teacher Dengyō (*Dengyō daishi*).

Nevertheless, after these events, there were in Japan persons of great virtue who had reached the highest level of wisdom. But there was nobody who could surpass these three Universal Teachers Kōbō, Jikaku, and Chishō. At that time, in an interval of four hundred years, the whole of Japan had finally decided that the teachings of the Shingon School were superior to the *Dharma Flower Sutra* (*Myōhō Renge Kyō*). Now and then, one came across people who had studied Tendai (*T'ien T'ai*), who could give reasons why the *Dharma Flower Sutra* (*Myōhō Renge Kyō*) was superior to teachings of the Shingon School. However, the pavilions of the enthroned Lord Tendai (*T'ien T'ai*) were so high and venerated that there was no need to be afraid of anything that was argued. On the other hand, there were other people who did not uphold the significance of the Tendai (*T'ien T'ai*) doctrine. But when they vainly said that they mean the same thing, they then scoffed derisively, as though they thought they were not on the same level as the teachers of the Shingon School.

Albeit throughout Japan there were some hundred thousand temples and Shinto shrines, practically all of them were in the sway of the Shingon School. Occasionally, there were temples of the Dharma Flower School standing alongside, giving the impression that the Shingon temples were the masters and those of the Dharma Flower were servants. If there were people who were versed in more than one teaching, who in their hearts felt they were at one with the Shingon teachings, then all the enthroned lords, heads of temples, temple surveyors who were the directors of nuns, as well as the directors of temple affairs, would all earnestly look up towards the Shingon School. So when the people did likewise in order to please their superiors, there was not a single person who could get away from the teachers of the Shingon School.

Although there were people who read and gave lip service to the *Dharma Flower Sutra* (*Myōhō Renge Kyō*) being paramount, in their innermost thoughts this teaching would only be second or third in rank, or they believed it to be so in their bodies, speech, and minds. As for practitioners reading the *Dharma Flower Sutra* (*Myōhō Renge Kyō*) as being paramount and who practised and venerated it with perfect sincerity of body, speech, and mind, there was not a single person, during a time period of some four hundred years. What is more, you should not even try to imagine that there was anybody who was a practitioner who was able to hold to this sutra. This is because, from the one sovereign person down to the myriads of ordinary people, they were all "full of jealousy while the Tathāgata was present in this world, not to mention after his passing over to nirvana" and also bitter enemies of the *Dharma Flower Sutra* (*Myōhō Renge Kyō*).

For all that, Nichiren is the son of a person in the fishing industry, from a seaside village of Tōjō that is in the district of Nagasa, which is in the twelfth out of the fifteen counties [*Kuni*] of Tokaidō and goes by the name of Awa. At the age of twelve, I was sent up to the village temple that was called Seichōji. Apart from being far away in the provinces, and even though it was called a monastery, there was nobody who had really studied. Nevertheless, the level of learning and practice in all the provinces was considerably high. But for my part, I felt incompetent. Nobody taught me, and it was not easy to see the difference between the degrees of importance or unimportance in the original concepts of the ten schools of the Buddha teaching.

From time to time, I prayed to the Buddha and bodhisattvas, imploring them to help me. I collated all the sutras and discourses, so as to apply them to the ten schools. The Kusha School teachings were close at hand and shallow in meaning, but it seemed that a part of them coincided with the individual vehicle (*shōjō, hīnayāna*). The Jōjitsu teachings had mistakes and fallacies, due to their being a rough-and-ready combination of the universal (*daijō, mahāyāna*) and individual (*shōjō, hīnayāna*) vehicles. Originally, the teachings of the Ritsu School were those of the individual vehicle (*shōjō, hīnayāna*), but, somewhere along the line, their doctrines became those of the universal vehicle (*daijō, mahāyāna*), and nowadays they wholeheartedly belong to it.

The Ritsu School teachings were commented upon by the Universal Teacher Dengyō (*Dengyō daishi*), who saw them as an unessential study. It is more than likely that the source of the Hossō School's teachings were from the shallow and easy Dharma gateways of the provisional universal vehicle. Gradually, these teachings were extended and assimilated the real universal vehicle (*daijō, mahāyāna*) also. As a result, the reasons for demolishing this school are already known.

A comparison could be made with the rebellions of Masakado or Sumitomo against the Shogunate. This is an example of a subordinate bringing down his superior. Again, the Sanron School has a portion of its teaching that is the relativity (*kū*) of the provisional universal vehicle's doctrine. This school also considered its teachings to be those of the real universal vehicle (*daijō, mahāyāna*). Whereas the Flower Garland School is said to be founded on the teachings of the provisional universal vehicle, it also takes advantage of the other schools, rather in the same way as an overbearing regent subjugates the heir to the throne. However, because they became a school that was hostile to the *Dharma Flower Sutra* (*Myōhō Renge Kyō*), they can be alluded to as being the yes-men who would follow a powerful sovereign.

The doctrines of the Jōdo School are also partially made up from the teachings of the provisional universal vehicle. Due to skilful scheming on the part of Zendō and Hōnen, nearly all the sutras were held high. But the *Dharma Flower Sutra* (*Myōhō Renge Kyō*) that was used for its insight in order to see the truth or by its role as a fundamental object of veneration was degraded. Those who had propensities for the correct and formal eras of the Dharma were glorified, but those whose propensities were for the final period of the Dharma (*mappō*) of Shākyamuni were held in contempt. Those who did have propensities for this final period were picked out for the Nembutsu School. Whatever propensities people had for other teachings, the corresponding sutras were demolished. A lifetime of the Buddha's enlightened instruction was lost, and only the single gateway of the Nembutsu School remained. This is rather like the marginalisation of a person of excellent virtues, due to a sharp-witted, nasty individual getting himself raised to a higher position, because people respect the short-lived qualities of his brain.

As for the Zen School, it is said to be the real Dharma which stands apart from the lifetime of Buddha enlightened teaching. This could be compared to killing the parent and adopting the child, or having the ruler killed so that the successor may take his position. The so-called Shingon School, by being simply an arbitrary play of words, allows its followers to hide the original source of their doctrine, so as to make it difficult to reveal to people whose propensities are less profound. For many years now, their followers have been deluded by this madness.

The Shingon School was not originally from India, even though its adepts say so. But the evidence for this should be looked into. What it all comes down to is due to the fact that the *Sutra on the Tathāgata of the Universal Sun* (*Dainichi-Nyorai, Vairochana-Tāthagata*) was brought over to Japan. One can confront the *Sutra on the Tathāgata of the Universal Sun* (*Dainichi-Nyorai, Vairochana-Tāthagata*) by quoting certain excerpts from the *Dharma Flower Sutra* (*Myōhō Renge Kyō*), in order to show precisely where it is superior. It is due to seven important implications that the *Sutra on the Tathāgata of the Universal Sun* (*Dainichi-Nyorai, Vairochana-Tāthagata*) is inferior to the *Dharma Flower Sutra* (*Myōhō Renge Kyō*). The evidence in support of the *Dharma Flower Sutra* (*Myōhō Renge Kyō*) is understandably clear.

At this point, I am not going to make quotations. However, there are people who say that the *Dharma Flower Sutra* (*Myōhō Renge Kyō*) is sovereign lord only due to two or three important implications. Outside these inferences, any other viewpoint is distorted. For example, it is like Ryūsō who was a humble personage that led the Emperor Bin's horse by the bridle, and then, by being an exceptionally outstanding person of the people, he manoeuvred his way up to the position of emperor through his dirty tricks. Again, this is comparable to the Brahman called Self Conceit, who sat upon Shākyamuni as though he were a couch. In China, there does not seem to have been anybody like this. Also, I doubt if there was anyone similar in Japan, albeit it is already four hundred years since these Shingon and other intrigues took place.

Since there was such dubiousness over what was right and what was wrong in the Buddha Dharma, this meant that the laws of the realm were gradually affected. In time, this would certainly bring about another country destroying our own, and we would become a vanquished nation. I, Nichiren, through having pondered over these matters, was the only person who really understood this. For the sake of the Dharma and the laws of the realm, I collected all the relevant texts and wrote them out onto a scroll. This document I presented to Hōjō Tokiyori, and the name of this document was *Securing the Peace of the Realm through the Establishment of the Correct Dharma* (*Risshō Ankoku ron*). So what is in this text has been written out in detail.

The eighty-second monarch in the line of sovereigns who were humankind was the Emperor Go-Toba. He was also called by the nickname the Dharma King of Oki. On the fifteenth day of the fifth month of the third year of the reign called Kenkyū [1192 CE], forces in favour of the Emperor Go-Toba attacked, captured, and put to death Iganotarō Hangan Mitsue, who was closely related to the Shogunate regency. Then, when the fervour of the troops who supported the emperor was aroused to attack the regent Yoshitoki, in Kamakura, the emperor before long was scouring the five home provinces and the seven districts for sturdy men to become his soldiers. Just as three forces were about to attack Yoshitoki, the emperor was unexpectedly defeated by his opponent. This led to the Emperor Go-Toba being exiled to the island of Oki. One of the two princes was exiled to the island of Sado, and the other to the county of Awa. Also, seven of the court nobles were summarily beheaded.

How is it that these people were defeated? As unexpectedly as a hawk seizes a pheasant or like a cat pouncing on and biting a mouse, a commoner becomes the sovereign of the realm. In fact, this is just the same as a cat devouring a mouse or a pheasant being snatched away by a hawk. Albeit it is only through the harmonious adjustment of body, speech, and mind, all these evils can be exorcised and be done with.

The so-called Highest of the Order and Enthroned Lord of the Tendai School Ji.en, the Shingon Elder of the Ninnaji Temple that had once been the retreat of the fifty-eighth Emperor Uda after he had taken enlightened orders, and also the Head of the Onjōji Temple, held sway over the seven and fifteen major temples of Nara where the wisdom, precepts, and practice of these three high dignitaries were like the sun and moon. Their profound and barely accessible esoteric teachings were centred around that of the three Universal Teachers Kōbō, Jikaku, and Chishō. This Dharma culminated in the esoteric teachings of the fifteen altars [which was the ritual of exorcism ordered by the retired Emperor Go-Toba for the defeat of the Kamakura Shogunate]. Bathed in rivulets of sweat and overburdened with mental stress, they carried out this ritual from the nineteenth day of the fifth month to the fourteenth day of the sixth month [of 1221 CE]. The conclusion of this great Dharma ceremony was observed both in the Ninnaji Temple in Nara and the Purple Imperial Hall [*Shishinden*] in Kyōto, which involved crossing the Realm of Japan three times.

These rituals started on the eighth day of the sixth month. On the fourteenth day, the army of the Shogunate was at Ujisata near Kyōto, broke into the capital, and took the three ex-emperors alive. The interior of the palace was set ablaze, and it burned to ashes within an hour. The three ex-emperors were exiled to the three outlying counties. Again, seven of the court nobles were summarily beheaded. But this was not all. The warriors of the regent forced their way into the royal apartments and set about tormenting the emperor's most beloved younger brother's child who was called Seitaka. In the end, they cut his head off. His Royal Highness, without giving it a second thought, decided to end his life, since both the child and the mother were dead. All the people who were relying on this exorcism, which comprised some tens of thousands of individuals, all died without even knowing why. Those few who did survive lived on in vain.

The prayers of the Royal Household started on the eighth day of the sixth month and ended on the fourteenth day of the same month. When you count the days in between, there are only seven full days. In the composition of the Dharma ritual referred to as the Fifteen Altars, there were the Gold Circle of the One Syllable (*Bhrūm*), the Four Heavenly Kings, the Ferocious Sovereign of Enlightenment Fudō the Immoveable, the Ferocious Sovereign of Enlightenment Mahātejas of Awe-inspiring Virtue, The Dharma Wheel-turning Bodhisattva, the manifestation of Kannon who holds the wheel that symbolises a response to every prayer, the Ferocious Sovereign of Enlightenment Aizen Tainted with Amorous Desire, the eyes of the Buddha that see everything correctly, and the six ideograms for *An Da Ri Han Da Ri* which are associated with the Bodhisattva Kannon, the Ferocious Manifestation of the Vajra Prince (*Vajrakumāra*), the Venerated Stellar Kings, and the Ferocious Sovereign of Enlightenment Taigen, and the All-embracing Origin and the Guardian of the Sutras. The object of this Dharma ceremony was to bring down the enemies of both the sovereign and the realm, as well as to call up and compel the spirits (*kon, animus*) of the dead to be sent over to the Immaculate Terrain of Birushana (*Vairochana*).

Furthermore, those who were carrying out this ceremony were not unprofound people. There was the Enthroned Lord of the Tendai School Ji.en, the Highest of the Order Jōjūin with forty-one monks and a hundred or so monks to accompany them from the Eastern Temple, which was the main temple of the Shingon School, and the Ninnaji Temple in Nara. Those who took part in this ritual were a generation that suffered the same fate as the previous one. Then why was it that they were defeated?

For instance, without ever having had some gain, they had to face the humiliation of being wiped out completely. Nobody seems to know what the cause was of all this. As Lord of the realm, Yoshitoki set upon these people like a hawk swooping down onto a smaller bird. Although the emperor's forces were beaten, it was something that had to be endured for one, two, ten, or twenty years. It all started on the fifteenth day of the fifth month. Then they were vanquished on the fourteenth day of the sixth month, which is hardly thirty days. This is because these powerful great lords do this sort of thing without realising or even caring about it.

Nevertheless, with what little wisdom Nichiren possesses, he was able to ponder out the reason for all this. It was due to the perverse teachings of the Shingon School. Although it is the soured prejudiced view of one person, it becomes the affliction of all the provinces. Although it may have only been one man carrying out the Shingon practices, still it was that that destroyed two counties, not to mention the lives of three hundred or so people. The lords of the realm have become the bitter enemies of the *Dharma Flower Sutra* (*Myōhō Renge Kyō*). Why is it they have not destroyed it?

As the years go by, such universally evil teachings will gradually bring about the downfall of the Shogunate, which in turn will involve the directors of religious affairs and the monks who assist in the rites of every temple. Since samurai that do not serve in the capital have always known little about what is correct or wrong in the teaching of the Dharma, they think that they only need to pay reverence to the Buddha, the Dharma, and the clerical community (*sō, sangha*). It goes without saying that, as the years gradually pass by and the samurai still have recourse to these [Shingon and other] practices, another nation will attack and do harm to our country and then try to destroy it. Not only the eight counties ruled by the Shogunate, but Mount Hiei, the Eastern Temple, the Onjōji Temple, as well as the enthroned lords and directors of temple affairs of the seven temples in Nara, due to their dealings with the Shogunate, will become like the Dharma Emperor of Oki (*Go-Toba*) and will decidedly turn into supporters of this universally evil teaching.

To become a lord of the realm means to be a part of the scheme of all the greater and lesser Brahmanic Deva Kings (*Bonten*), Taishaku (*Indra*), the sun and the moon, and the Four Heavenly Kings. So when somebody becomes a bitter enemy of the *Dharma Flower Sutra* (*Myōhō Renge Kyō*), the *deva* (*ten*), on account of the *Dharma Flower Sutra* (*Myōhō Renge Kyō*) and on account of their vow to uphold this sutra, should subdue and punish the offender. Hence, during the reign of the Emperor Antoku [1180-85 CE] who was the eighty-first in the line of sovereigns who were humankind, the Chancellor Kiyomori, for the sake of the Emperor and the Taira clan, went into monkish orders. In order to bring Yoritomo Hyōenosuke into submission through exorcist rites, it was decided that Mount Hiei should adhere to his clan. Even though Kiyomori relied on this king of monasteries and his guardian household gods, the Emperor Antoku was drowned in the western sea. Myō.un was killed by Yoshinaka. The whole clan was destroyed in one sweep.

There was a second time when this happened, and the present event would be the third. By ignoring the admonition of Nichiren, the rulers of the state will try to exorcise the Great Mongolian Empire through the evil teaching of the Shingon School. But Japan will be the one that is cursed instead. It is said that a malediction returns to the person who invoked it. In that case, rather than creating advantages in life through revenge, the Dharma Flower can be the unexcelled path to becoming a Buddha. The prayers and exorcisms of the present age are manifest evidence for the reading and reciting of the sutras of Sir Yoritomo Hyōenosuke.

I am aware of the principle that one should requite the kindness and effort of one's parents and teacher. However, both my father and mother have passed away. But there was still my teacher the Venerable Dōzen who had uneasy doubts about the lord of the manor's attitude towards the *Dharma Flower Sutra* (*Myōhō Renge Kyō*). I think that the Venerable Dōzen was an unhappy person at heart, and on the outside he was detestably nasty. I did hear later on that he seemed to have a little faith in the *Dharma Flower Sutra* (*Myōhō Renge Kyō*), but I have doubts about it. I wonder how it was at the moment when death pressed upon him. It is not likely he went to hell. Again I do not think he has freed himself from the cycles of living and dying. Unfortunately, he is most likely drifting somewhere in that space between dying and being reborn again.

At the time when the lord of the manor was full of rage, you, the Lay Practitioner Jōken and the Venerable Gijō were sent away from the Seichōji Temple. In some way or another, you are people who obey and carry out the Buddha teaching for the benefit of others. Also, you will be able to shake off the fetters of the cycles of living and dying.

After the Buddha had explained and laid down what the Fundamental Object of Veneration (*gohonzon*) should be, it would be after a period of two thousand two hundred and some twenty or so years, before it was revealed to anybody in the world of humankind. Both Tendai (*T'ien T'ai*) of China and Dengyō (*Dengyō daishi*) of Japan were roughly acquainted with it, but they did not divulge it. Indeed, it is this day and age that is the proper time for its propagation.

Although what we see in the *Dharma Flower Sutra* (*Myōhō renge kyō*) is that Bodhisattva Superior Practice (*Jōgyō, Vishishtachāritra*), Muhengyō (*Anantachārita*), and the other bodhisattvas are to appear to do the propagating, as yet they have not been seen. Even though Nichiren is not one of these persons, he does have some understanding [of the Fundamental Object of Veneration (*gohonzon*)], so that until these bodhisattvas come forth, he can still effusively ramble on. Putting it roughly, this is what was brought about by "there being still a lot of envy and jealousy, not to mention after his passing over to nirvana".

What I really wish and pray for is to be able to repay my parents, teacher, and all sentient beings, by means of this meritorious virtue. In order that you may progress in your understanding of what this is all about, I am sending you a Fundamental Object of Veneration (*gohonzon*) that I have written out for you. Cast away all other matters and earnestly pray in front of this Fundamental Object of Veneration (*gohonzon*) for your existence to come. As you know, I will talk about this again. Whatever happens, do use your discretion when it comes to other monks.

Nichiren [formal signature]

The Essential of the Teaching of Nichiren Daishōnin

A Collation of the Layers of the Various Teachings of all the Buddhas of the Past, Present and Future as to Which Specific Doctrines are to be Discarded or Established

Sō Kan Mon Shō
Goshō Shimpen, pp. 1408-1426
Translator's Note

The tenth month of the second year of Kō.an [1279], at 58 years of age

The whole of Shākyamuni's lifetime of Buddha enlightened instruction was expounded over a period of fifty years. This is said to be all the sutras. All these sutras are divided into two categories. One was for the instruction and development of other people, and the second was teachings from the Buddha's own enlightened viewpoint.

The teachings for the instruction and development of other people were expounded over the period of forty-two years prior to his teaching the *Dharma Flower Sutra*. These sutric doctrines entail various kinds of teachings, and all of them are referred to as the teachings derived from the external events of Shākyamuni's life and work doctrine or as expedient means.

Out of the four different means of instruction for the growth of other people, there are these three – 1) The Three Receptacles (*Sanzō, Tripitaka*) that contain the teachings of the individual vehicle (*shōjō, hīnayāna*), 2) The Interrelated Teachings (*tsūgyo*) that serve as a bridge between the doctrines of the individual vehicle and those of the universal vehicle (*daijō, mahayana*), and 3) The Particular Teaching (*bekkyō*) that was expounded for the benefit of bodhisattvas.

335

In terms of the five periods that represent the order in which the major sutras were taught, there is the *Flower Garland Sutra* (*Kegon, Avatāmsaka*), the teachings of the individual vehicle (*Agonji*), the Equally Broad (*Hōdō, Vaipulya*), and the Wisdom (*Hannya, Prajña*) periods. These are the four periods of the teaching of the sutras that came before the *Dharma Flower Sutra*.

If we look at these provisional teachings from the point of view of the ten [psychological] realms of dharmas (*jippokai*), then, in contrast to the Buddha realm (*Bukkai*), all these provisional doctrines refer to the first nine only [1) hell (*jigokukai*), 2) hungry demons (*gakikai*), 3) animality (*chikushōkai*), 4) shura (*shurakai*), 5) humanity (*jinkai*), 6) deva (*tenkai*), 7) hearers of the Buddha's voice (*shōmonkai*), 8) partially enlightened due to a profound search for the meaning of life (*engakukai*), 9) bodhisattvas (*bosatsukai*)].

Again, if we look upon these provisional teachings in terms of dreaming and being wide-awake, then the teachings derived from the external events of Shākyamuni's life and work are like the good and evil events in a dream. Dreams are what they are, as long as they last, and therefore provisional. Being wide-awake is reality. Since dreams are for the time being only, they have no real substance in themselves; nor do they have any real nature. This is why they are said to be provisional. The essence of mind is completely awake and is forever-present. This is why its substance is permanent. It is also referred to as reality.

In the forty-two years of Shākyamuni's teaching, the sutras were instructions for dealing with the good and bad things that happen in the dream of living and dying. These are the provisional sutric teachings, which were an enticement and guidance for the sentient beings who were involved in the dream.

In order to lead these people into the thoroughly awakened dimension of the *Dharma Flower Sutra* (*Myōhō Renge Kyō*), the Buddha Shākyamuni expounded the teachings of the sutras as a preparatory expedient means, and they are designated as the provisional teachings. It is on this account that we have to be clear about our understanding of the words "real" and "provisional".

The contents of the provisional teachings are made clear, when Shākyamuni, in his *Sutra on Implications Without Bounds* (*Muryōgi-kyō*), states, "I have not revealed the truth for forty years." All these sutras are preparatory teachings for the dream world, where the truth has not yet been revealed.

This is why Myōraku (*Miao-lo*), in his *Explanatory Notes on the Recondite Significance of the Dharma Flower*, says, "Whether we are in a dream, or whether we are wide-awake, there is no difference in the essence of the mind itself."

A dream exists because it is something imagined, which immediately suggests that the Buddha, who is to get through to the illusory conditions of the people to whom he teaches, with their illusory feelings, their illusory interaction with the Buddha, and their illusory propensities to grow – both the Buddha and his listeners are together in an illusion that was only for the time being. Reality does not yet exist. As a result, all these sutras are those that had not yet revealed what the truth is. All were expounded as an expedient means, for the illusory situation of the people in the dream.

Myōraku (*Miao-lo*) says, "Whether we are in the dream or whether we are wide-awake, there is no difference in the essence of mind itself." His intention in this statement is that, even if we are involved in the dream, or even if we are completely awake, the essential mind that is capable of perceiving these two situations is one and the same.

A dream is just something imagined. But, when we are wide-awake, existence becomes an objective truth. Still, in each case, it is only the revelations of the various perceptions of the mind. This has been explained as seeing the truth as our own individual minds.

Myōraku (*Miao-lo*), in his *Commentary and Explanations of the Universal Desistance from Troublesome Worries*, says, "Three of the teachings that came before the *Dharma Flower Sutra* – 1) the three receptacles (*sanzō, tripitaka*), 2) the interrelated teachings (*tsūgyō*), and 3) the particular teaching for bodhisattvas (*bekkyō*) with their four universal vows – are all a complete fantasy. So, both the Buddha who teaches and those who are taught mutually cease to exist, because both are wrapped up in a dream."

The four universal vows are 1) to save all living beings without limit, 2) to put an end to troublesome worries however numerous, 3) to study the endless gateways to the Dharma, and 4) to attain perfection in the Buddha path.

So, it can be assumed that all the sutras that were expounded during the forty-two years before the Dharma Flower (*Myōhō Renge Kyō*) were provisional teachings and various expedient means that had not yet revealed the truth. This is because they were a way of leading people towards the *Dharma Flower Sutra*. They were never teachings that referred to bare-faced reality.

With regard to this, the Buddha himself collected all the teachings of forty-two years, in an effort to propound the doctrine of the interdependence of cause and effect that runs throughout the whole of existence (*Myōhō Renge Kyō*). He went on to teach the *Sutra on Implications Without Bounds* (*Muryōgi-kyō*), which was to serve as an introduction to the *Dharma Flower Sutra*. The Buddha, having made up his mind as to what the content of the *Dharma Flower Sutra* would be, decided not to make use of ordinary human talk, in order to avoid any space for doubts.

In the *Explanatory Notes on the Recondite Significance of the Dharma Flower*, Myōraku states, "The provisional teachings were taught for the propensities of the people who are trapped in the first nine realms of dharmas, but it was the real teachings that revealed the Dharma realm of the Buddha, which is the ultimate truth. The provisional teachings that were for the benefit of the people in the nine realms of dharmas were taught over a period of forty-two years. The ultimate truth of the Buddha's own enlightenment (*bukkai*) only took eight years to expound. This was the *Dharma Flower Sutra*."

It is for this reason that the *Dharma Flower Sutra* (*Nam Myōhō Renge Kyō*) is referred to as the Buddha vehicle for attaining enlightenment. The provisional teachings refer to the existential reality of the living and dying of the people in the nine realms of dharmas (things or anything else they might perceive), whereas the Dharma teaching of the timeless eternity of life, in its most wide-awake sense, refers to the Dharma realm of the Buddha (*bukkai*).

The lifetime of fifty years of teaching and instruction of Shākyamuni is his whole life of Buddha enlightened guidance. The concept of all the sutras is the combination of the forty-two years of provisional teachings, along with the eight years of real teachings that manifest the Buddha's own enlightenment.

As a result, when we shine onto the two words "provisional" and "real" as if they were spotlights onto all the sutras, then these discrepancies become evidently clear, without the slightest haziness whatsoever.

Accordingly, if someone were to do the bodhisattva practices of the three receptacles that contain the teachings of the individual vehicle (*sanzō, tripitaka*), for the astronomically long period of three *asōgi* (*asamkhyeya*) [which means countless or innumerable and is said to be a huge number that is represented by one digit and fifty-one zeros] major *kalpas*, with the aim of becoming a Buddha, this person's body and mind would come out of the fire of total annihilation, his body would be turned to ashes, and his wisdom would be extinguished altogether. This is because the aims of the teachings of the individual vehicle were for the personal attainment of nirvana, which means ceasing to exist.

If someone else were to think of fulfilling all the bodhisattva practices of the interconnecting teachings (*tsūgyō*) over another astronomically long period of seven *asōgi* (*asamkhyeya*) [which means countless or innumerable and is said to be a huge number that is represented by one digit and fifty-one zeros] and an uncountable hundreds of *kalpas*, then, in the same way as the person who had completed the practices of the individual vehicle, his body and mind would be reduced to fine ashes, which would finally disappear without a trace. This is because the aims of the interconnecting teachings were also the attainment of nirvana.

Then again, if another individual were to try to complete all the practices of the particular teaching for bodhisattvas (*bekkyō*) with the intention of becoming a Buddha, for an even more interminable period of twenty major *kalpas*, this person would ultimately become a Buddha of the provisional teachings in the midst of the dream of living and dying. From the point of view of the wide-awake awareness of the original enlightenment (*hongaku no utsutsu*) of the *Dharma Flower Sutra*, there is no real Buddha of the particular teachings for bodhisattvas. This can only be a Buddha within the dream.

The path for the attainment of the truth through personal experience, by means of the particular teachings (*bekkyō*) for bodhisattvas, would only arrive at the first of the ten stages of firm ground (*juji*), from among the fifty-two bodhisattva stages in the process of becoming a Buddha. A portion of the delusions that hinder enlightenment would be cut away and replaced with the same portion of awareness of the principle of the Buddha teaching of the middle way of reality.

The teachings of this path are isolated from the main body of the four classifications of the teachings of Shākyamuni, according to their content – 1) the three receptacles (*sanzō, tripitaka*), 2) the interconnecting teachings (*tsūgyo*), 3) the particular teaching (*bekkyō*), 4) the all-inclusive teaching (*engyō*) – as well as the five teaching periods of the Buddha's lifetime, in terms of doctrinal advancement. These are 1) the period of the teachings of the *Flower Garland Sutra* (*Kegon, Avatāmsaka*), 2) the period of the teachings of the individual vehicle (*Agon*), 3) the period of the equally broad teachings (*hōdō*), 4) the period of the *Dharma Flower* and *Nirvana Sutra* doctrines (*hokke nehan*).

Furthermore, in the practice of the particular teachings for bodhisattvas, the three bodies of the Buddha, as well as the three inseparable aspects of reality (*santai*), are considered separate entities.

The three bodies are 1) the Dharma body, i.e., the enlightened body of the Buddha that involves the whole of existence (*hosshin*),

2) the embodiment of the Buddha's wisdom (*hōshin*), 3) the body that corresponds to the needs of the unenlightened people (*ōjin*).

The three inseparable aspects of reality (*santai*) are 1) its appearance and its material aspect (*ke*), 2) what it seems to be in terms of our experience and what goes on in our heads [which is ultimately Nam Myōhō Renge Kyō and means to devote our lives to and found them on (*Nam[u]*) the Utterness of the Dharma (*Myōhō*) (entirety of existence, enlightenment and unenlightenment) permeated by the underlying white lotus flower-like mechanism of the interdependence of cause, concomitancy and effect (*Renge*) in its whereabouts of the ten (psychological) realms of dharmas (*Kyō*)] (*kū*), the combination of both 1 and 2 together, which is reality as it is perceived every moment of our lives (*chū*). In the particular teachings for bodhisattvas, these three inseparable aspects of existence are considered to be three separate entities.

Nonetheless, if any of these people who do the practices of the provisional vehicle were to move on and become faithful to the all-inclusive teachings (*engyō*), then this would mean that these people would no longer be held back by the limitations of the particular teachings for bodhisattvas. Among bodhisattvas, there are three different levels of propensity – those of superior propensities, medium propensities, and those who are less capable. Regarding those who have risen above the first, second, or third of the fifty-two stages in becoming a Buddha (*gojūni'i*), or even those who have become universally enlightened (*tōgaku*), which is the last but one of the fifty-two stages, every one of these people is a follower of the all-inclusive teachings.

Therefore, outside the text of the *Flower Garland Sutra* (*Kegon, Avatāmsaka*), which is the text for the particular teaching for bodhisattvas, there is no real Buddha; nor has anyone become a Buddha through these doctrines.

The Universal Teacher Dengyō (*Dengyō Daishi*) wrote, in connection with this problem, in his *Essays on Safeguarding and Protecting the Frontiers of the State* (*Shugo Kokkai Shō*), "Even though he was a Buddha of transitory nature who came into being through various karmic causes and relationships (*u'i mujō*), his wisdom body was that of a provisional enlightenment in the midst of a dream."

What this implies is that, even if his Buddha enlightenment was only manifest in terms of the three receptacles (*sanzō, tripitaka*) that contain the teachings of the individual vehicle, the interconnecting teachings, as well as the particular teaching for bodhisattvas, it is due to the Buddha's own observation of his mind, which is the practice of the all-inclusive teachings, that made him the real Buddha, who was consciously aware of the profoundest reality of the triple body, independent of all karma.

Again, Dengyō (*Dengyō Daishi*) writes, "The Dharma, wisdom, and corresponding bodies (*hosshin*), (*hōshin*), and (*ōjin*) of the Buddha of the provisional teachings could not avoid being impermanent." But, by evolving into the Buddha who was able to observe mind for what it is, which is reciting the title and theme (*daimoku*) in front of a written representation of the one instant of thought containing three thousand existential spaces (*ichinen sanzen*), Shākyamuni became both the entity and the role (*kutaikuyū*) of the Dharma, wisdom, and corresponding bodies of the real teachings. You must keep this explanation firmly in your mind.

The provisional teachings are comparable to the sort of thinking that, if someone were to practise painful and difficult austerities, that person might, by a stroke of luck, become a Buddha. Nevertheless, such a Buddha's enlightenment would only be in the makeshift world of dream. When the time comes to be thinking in terms of being consciously aware of the inherent enlightenment that is the fundamental of all existence, then the Buddhas of the provisional teachings are not real at all. They are not even Buddhas who have arrived at the ultimate realisation of the practice to become enlightened. The provisional teachings do exist, but nobody ever becomes a Buddha through such doctrines.

Furthermore, if somebody were to say to people that the teachings derived from the external events of Shākyamuni's life and work were the truth, so that those people were to do the practices of these provisional teachings, then such people would be somewhat confused about the original intention of Shākyamuni's lifetime of Buddha enlightened teaching.

I shall put aside what I was saying about the evidence that nobody was able to become a Buddha through the teachings of the *Flower Garland Sutra* (*Kegon, Avatāmsaka*), the three receptacles that contain the teachings of the individual vehicle (*sanzō, tripitaka*), as well as the interconnecting doctrines (*tsūgyō*). The main point for the people living in the final period of Shākyamuni's teaching (*matsudai*) is to open up their wisdom to understand the aim of the Buddha teaching and to live with a constant awareness if it.

The ordinary people, who inhabit the nine realms of dharmas (*kyūkai*), are wholeheartedly immersed in the sleep of the unenlightenment of not wanting to know. They are drowned in the dream of living and dying, as well as having forgotten what the wakefulness of the enlightenment of the original state is all about. They cling at all costs to what is going on in the dream. And they stray from one darkness to the next.

As a result, this becomes the reason why the Tathāgata decided to enter the dream, so as to be in the same karmic situation as the ordinary people, who are full of wild fantasies that prevent them from seeing reality for what it is.

[Tathāgata (*Nyorai*) signifies the following: one who has gone; one who has followed the Path and arrived at the real suchness; one of the ten titles of a Buddha. Tathāgata can be explained as a person who comes from the real suchness of existence, which is Nam Myōhō Renge Kyō – which means to devote our lives to and found them on (*Nam[u]*) the Utterness of the Dharma (*Myōhō*) (entirety of existence, enlightenment and unenlightenment) permeated by the underlying white lotus flower-like mechanism of the interdependence of cause, concomitancy and effect (*Renge*) in its whereabouts of the ten (psychological) realms of dharmas (*Kyō*) – and that person will return to it.]

Then, with the idea of leading these people towards the truth, the Buddha tells them about the truth and misguided conceptions within the dream. When it comes to explaining the truth, the misguided concepts within the dream are embedded layers upon layers, in boundless and countless numbers.

With regard to expounding the truth, the Buddha had to establish three levels of instruction – the highest, a middle one, and another grade for the less capable. These three levels then become the three categories of instruction or the three vehicles (*sanjō, tripiṭaka*). These are 1) those who listen to the Buddha's voice (*shōmon, shrāvaka*), 2) those who are partially enlightened due to a profound search for the meaning of life (*engaku, hyakushibutsu, pratyekabuddha*), and 3) the bodhisattvas who practise not only for themselves but also for others. Again, the Tathāgata put the people who do the practices of the three vehicles into three categories according to their propensities – 1) superior, 2) average, and 3) those with less ability. This teaching is referred to as the nine separate levels within the doctrines of the three vehicles.

After the Buddha had finished expounding in this manner, he established the correct way of understanding existence. This was the view of the people with the highest propensities, out of nine separate levels within the teachings of the three vehicles. This is also understood as the teaching for the people of the separate levels, within the doctrines of the three vehicles.

Nevertheless, these teachings were on all accounts the correct way of understanding existence, as well as the delusions to be avoided by the people within the dream of living and dying. Here it might be worthwhile mentioning that the Universal Teacher Myōraku (*Miao-lo*), in his *Record of Essential Gleanings from the Universal Desistance from Troublesome Worries* (*Maka Shikan Sōyōki*), puts all these provisional doctrines outside the Buddha teaching, since they all gave rise to distorted views.

Because it was seen that the people with the highest propensities – out of the nine separate levels within the doctrines of the three vehicles – were capable of understanding that, at this point, Shākyamuni's teachings were based on the principle of the wide-awake awareness of the original enlightenment, this doctrine was also expounded, so that people could understand that this way of thinking corresponded to the realities of being alive.

Therefore, with the Buddha's ability to establish, for the benefit of the people within the dream, the distinction between thinking in terms of the wide-awake awareness of the original enlightenment and the world of bewilderment and fantasies, the real aspect of the originally awakened mind was made known for the first time.

At this juncture, the Buddha pointed out that, even though dreaming and being awake may have the difference between fantasy and reality, all dharmas or anything whatsoever that may touch upon any of our senses or mental faculties, either imagined or real, and the mind that perceives them are both one and the same.

When we are tired, we go to sleep, and sometimes we dream. When we have finished sleeping, our minds become wide-awake. However, we realise that, whether we are dreaming or whether we are wide-awake, both mind and dharmas are the same, or rather it is one and the same mind that is having two kinds of experiences. When this concept was fully understood, the Buddha used it as a foundation for many teachings that were used as an expedient means. This was how people considered the middle way of reality, in the particular teachings for bodhisattvas (*bekkyō*).

It was on these grounds that Shākyamuni did not reveal the doctrine of each one of the ten [psychological] realms of dharmas being mutually endowed with the same ten realms (*jikkai gogu*), or the identities of objects and living beings not being separate from their appearance and behaviour (*ke*), the space that accommodates them, along with what goes on in their minds (*kū, shūnyatā*), as well as the combination of these two factors. This forms the middle way of reality. As a result, nobody attained enlightenment or became a Buddha.

Hence, it took the Buddha forty-two years of instructing in the teaching of the three receptacles to reach the level of the particular doctrine for bodhisattvas. All the eight classifications of Shākyamuni's teaching, which are divided into four kinds of teaching and four modes of instruction, are progressive guidances to enable his disciples to fully understand the teaching of the fundamental state of the *Dharma Flower Sutra*.

The four kinds of teaching are, firstly, the teaching of the three receptacles that contain all the teachings of the individual vehicle (*sanzō, tripitaka*); secondly, the interrelated teachings (*tsūgyō*), which act as an individual step between the individual vehicle (*shōjō, hīnayāna*) and the universal vehicle (*daijō, mahayana*); thirdly, the particular teaching for those people who were bodhisattvas (*bekkyō*), and, fourthly, the all-inclusive teaching (*engyō*), which is the perfect doctrine of the *Dharma Flower Sutra* as well as the real intention of the Buddha.

All these teachings were taught in four different manners – 1) directly and the whole truth, 2) graded and in stages, 3) esoteric teachings that were only understood by certain people in the assembly, and 4) general and indeterminate teachings, from which various people would derive a benefit according to the depth of their understanding.

However, regardless of what these teachings may involve, all these teachings were only different kinds of expedient means. All these provisional teachings refer to the correct insights and the distorted views within the dream. The object of such teachings was as a preparation, as well as a means to draw people towards the truth of the *Dharma Flower Sutra*.

In all of these provisional teachings, there are both strategic improvisations and the truth about what life really is. Each one of the four teachings at first shows us that all things exist (*umon*). The dharmas are shown to be the relativity, or rather, since only our faculties and minds perceive them, then they don't exit. This leads to the concept that things both really exist and don't really exist at the same time. And, finally, things are neither material nor immaterial. They are neither existing, nor simply the emptiness of relativity.

None of these concepts are untruths. They are just as the words indicate. [Existence is Nam Myōhō Renge Kyo, which means to devote our lives to and found them on (*Nam*[*u*]) the Utterness of the Dharma (*Myōhō*) (entirety of existence, enlightenment and unenlightenment) permeated by the underlying white lotus flower-like mechanism of the interdependence of cause, concomitancy and effect (*Renge*) in its whereabouts of the ten (psychological) realms of dharmas (*Kyō*).] But it is due to a misunderstanding of what the words mean that gives rise to confusion as to which teaching is provisional and which teaching is real.

When it comes to the teachings that are an expedient means, they only exist in places like this impure and imperfect world of ours. They are not present in the immaculate terrains that only consist of a Buddha realm. In the *Second Chapter on Expedient Means* in the *Dharma Flower Sutra*, it says, "In the Buddha lands in the ten directions – which are east, west, south, and north, southeast, southwest, northeast, northwest, as well as above and below – there are neither two vehicles to enlightenment, nor even the three [1) the vehicle to enlightenment for bodhisattvas, 2) those people who are partially enlightened due to a profound search for the meaning of life ((*engaku, hyakushibutsu, pratyekabuddha*), 3) those who have listened to the Buddha (*shōmon*)] because all these three vehicles to enlightenment have been done away with."

According to this text, the teaching in these Buddha terrains can only be that of the one vehicle to enlightenment, which is the *Dharma Flower Sutra*. This text also implies that there are no provisional teachings that serve as an expedient means.

The Pure Land School that recites the Nembutsu, which is *Namu Amida Butsu*, does not have a concept of the Buddha terrains of the ten directions. So there is no doubt that these Pure Land teachings are an expedient means and therefore only temporary. The Daishōnin remarks that the adepts of this school dislike the *Dharma Flower Sutra*, which is the only conveyance to enlightenment. So, should we consider this a Buddha teaching or not?

In order to instruct people and to get them to think along the lines of the Buddha teaching, Shākyamuni expounded various doctrines. But later he taught the single vehicle of the Dharma, which is the Buddha teaching that makes no distinction between the differences of the ten [psychological] realms of dharmas, since each one is its own experience of the truth of the whole of existence.

All the Buddhas of the past, present, and future expounded, expound, or will expound the Dharma, in exactly the same way as Shākyamuni. The teachings that are an expedient means lead people into the doctrine that makes no distinction between the ten [psychological] realms of dharmas, because each realm of dharmas is its own reality. Each and every dharma entails the whole of phenomenal and noumenal existence. All of them are stored away in our own minds. This is the enlightenment of the Utterness of the Dharma (*Myōhō, Saddharma*).

The Buddha expounded his teachings, which treat the people enmeshed in the ten [psychological] realms of dharmas from hell to the Buddha realm as being on the same footing, since each and every one of these realms is its own reality – hence, Shākyamuni's desire to make people in this impure and imperfect world of ours open up their own Buddha enlightenment.

The Buddha concluded by saying that the sutras he had taught previously were for the benefit and instruction of other people, in order to make them grow towards the *Dharma Flower Sutra*. This becomes clearer when we affirm what the Buddha originally practised for himself. All of this is implicit in the *Sixteenth Chapter on the Lifespan of the Tathāgata* and the theme and title *Nam Myōhō Renge Kyo*, which means to devote our lives to and found them on (*Nam[u]*) the Utterness of the Dharma (*Myōhō*) [entirety of existence, enlightenment and unenlightenment] permeated by the underlying white lotus flower-like mechanism of the interdependence of cause, concomitancy and effect (*Renge*) in its whereabouts of the ten [psychological] realms of dharmas (*Kyō*). In present-day language, this would be "basing and founding our lives on the place where the interdependence of cause and effect of the whole of existence occurs".

The Buddha teaching which Shākyamuni practised for himself consists of the *Dharma Flower Sutra*, which was practised over a period of eight years. This is also the sutra that gives meaning to the Buddha's own awareness of the original mind that lies deep within all of us. But since people are used to imagining that this is what produces all things both on the outside and within us, the Buddha appropriated the way things were expressed in the words of the dream, in order to teach them about being awakened to the deepest part of their own psyches.

However, even though Shākyamuni used words that really belong to the dream of living and dying, his intention was to teach and throw light on the original mind. He knew that if the text and the explanations were not absolutely clear, people would become confused as to their real meaning.

Nevertheless, even those gateways to the Buddha teaching that were expounded for the instruction and benefit of other people were also based on the wide-awake enlightenment that is the original mind. When these teachings were applied to the people in the dream, they had enormous benefits.

Because the awareness of the original mind lay as a foundation of the teachings for the people within the dream, this meant that the foundation was *Myōhō Renge Kyō,* which means the Utterness of the Dharma (*Myōhō*) [entirety of existence, enlightenment and unenlightenment] permeated by the underlying white lotus flower-like mechanism of the interdependence of cause, concomitancy and effect (*Renge*) in its whereabouts of the ten [psychological] realms of dharmas (*Kyō*). And it meant that, beyond the meaningfulness of this concept, there is no existence.

Rather in the same way as all waterways flow towards the sea, the Buddha mind must include every single item imagined or real, as well as the minds of ordinary people who are capable of embracing the whole of existence. This means that these two concepts of Utterness or the whole, *Myō*, are stored away in our minds. Outside and beyond our individual minds, there is no existence whatsoever.

Therefore, our individual minds, which go on functioning from day to day in the midst of concrete reality – the essence of mind or its fundamental quality, and the entity of mind itself, which is inseparable from our bodies or the whole of life – are in fact the three bodies of the originally enlightened Tathāgata. In the *Second Chapter on Expedient Means* in the *Dharma Flower Sutra*, these bodies are expressed as three ways in which existence makes itself apparent to our six organs of sense– eyes, ears, nose, tongue, body, and mind – which are 1) such an appearance (i.e., the corresponding or incarnate body of the Tathāgata), 2) such an essential quality [what goes on in our minds] (i.e., the wisdom body of the Tathāgata), 3) what we conceive of as the Tathāgata's life which is the whole of existence. These are referred to as three of the qualities of suchness.

The text says the following: "This real aspect of all dharmas is said to be (*Sho'i shohō*) in any way they make themselves present to any of our six sense organs – eyes, ears, nose, tongue, body, and mind [e.g., a carrot is orange; it tastes sweetish and may have a smell] (*Nyoze sō*), their various inner qualities which in any event must lead up to all the implications of Nam Myōhō Renge Kyō [e.g., which include all the words associated with carrots, i.e., zanahoria, carotte, carota, ninjin, and all our memories of carrots and all the way up to their essence which is Nam Myōhō Renge Kyō; when we see this carrot, we unconsciously see a carrot, and both what we see and the associations in our heads automatically come together] (*Nyoze shō*), their substance or what they really are (*Nyoze tai*)."

These three qualities of the suchness of the originally enlightened Tathāgata are the embodiment of all the realms of existence in all the ten directions. This means the fundamental, pure mind that exists on its own that underlies the whole of life, as well as all the Buddha marks and signs of physical existence throughout the ten directions.

It is for this reason that our persons consist of the originally awakened Tathāgata and are alive and present in every dharma everywhere. This is the enormous benefit of the virtue and role of the Buddha, as well as all dharmas being those of the Buddha.

When Shākyamuni expounded this, all the people who were in attendance at this teaching, all the monks, nuns, as well as all the men and women who were devotees, the eight categories of humanlike beings, i.e., *deva* (*ten*), dragons, *yasha* (*yaksha*), *kendabba* (*gandharva*), *karura* (*garuda*), *kinnara* (*kimnara*), and *magoraga* (*mahorāga*), along with those people outside the Buddha teaching – all of them, without leaving a single person out, were mythomaniacs, dirty-minded, and with prejudiced views. Every one of them was stopped from becoming a scatterbrained numskull and took refuge in the wide-awake awareness of the original enlightenment. Every one of them was able to arrive at the full practice of the Buddha path.

The Buddha is a person who is wide-awake. Sentient beings such as us are immersed in the dream. All those people who were wrapped up in living and dying woke up from the dream of illusions and took refuge in the original enlightenment. They became aware that their own Buddha nature was not separate from their respective personalities. Also, they became fully conscious of the impartial universal wisdom, as well as the Buddha understanding that treats the ten [psychological] realms of dharmas from hell to the Buddha realm with equality (*mufunbetsu*), since each is its own experience of the truth of the whole of existence. All sentient beings arrive at the path of the Buddha, because there is only a single gateway to the Dharma.

Although the various Buddha lands may be thought of as divergent regions, the Buddha teaching that is taught in all these Buddha lands is the Dharma of the single vehicle. In the various Buddha lands, there are no teachings that are an expedient means, since it is the Buddha teaching that treats the ten [psychological] realms of dharmas from hell to the Buddha realm equally, because each is its own experience of the truth. Although the sentient beings of the ten [psychological] realms of dharmas (*jikkai*) may be different from each other, but because the principle of the real aspect of all dharmas is only one, it is the Buddha teaching that treats all realms of dharmas equally.

Although the gateways to the hundred realms of dharmas, the thousand ways in which dharmas make themselves present to any of our six organs of sense – eyes, ears, nose, tongue, body, and mind, and the three thousand spaces where existence takes place, i.e., the teaching of the one instant of thought containing three thousand existential spaces (*ichinen sanzen*), may all differ from each other, because each of the ten [psychological] realms of dharmas is endowed with the other ten, all these gateways to the Dharma treat the ten [psychological] realms of dharmas, from the realm of hell to the Buddha realm, equally. Although dreaming and being awake, falsehood and truth are different from each other and exist as separate items, but because these dharmas are all dharmas of the oneness of mind, they are all inseparable from one another, each being a single aspect of life. Although we conceive the past, future, and present as separate points in time, they are all a part of the instants in our own minds. The past, present, and future are simply the oneness of time and life.

In all the teachings prior to the *Dharma Flower Sutra*, the words used were the modes of expression from inside the dream. For instance, a fan that is held up to hide the moon is used to suggest our unenlightenment. In the Buddha teachings, the full moon is often used as a symbol for enlightenment. A finger is pointed to the wind blowing a tree, to suggest the wisdom that blows away our erroneous delusions. But the words used to express the broad insight of the *Dharma Flower Sutra* are direct, such as "the moon" and "the wind." The full moon of the originally awakened mind shines through our unenlightenment. The wind of the wisdom of the real aspect of all dharmas blows away the dust of strange and wild ideas.

The reason for this is that, by using the concepts of the fan and tree, it becomes possible to make people aware of the moon and wind in the mind that is to be awakened, so that the last remains of the dream can be scattered, and the mind is able to return to the broad insight of its original state.

In the *Desitance from Troublesome Worries in order to see Clearly* (*Maka Shikan*), it says, "When the moon is hidden by layers of mountain ranges, we then hold up a fan and use it as a metaphor. When the wind stops blowing out of the sky, we then teach people about the wind making the trees move."

In Myōraku's (Miao-lo) *Support for the Practices of the Desistance from Troublesome Worries* (*Maka Shikan Bugyō Dengu Ketsu*), it says, "When the moon that alludes to the true reality of the essence of the Buddha nature that dwells in eternity is hidden by the mountain ranges of our troublesome worries (*bonnō, klesha*), and since these troublesome worries (*bonnō, klesha*) come in layers, they are referred to as mountain ranges. When the winds of the teaching of the all-inclusive, unobstructed accommodation of phenomena (*ke*), noumena or relativity (*ku*), and the middle way (*chū*), (i.e., the *Dharma Flower Sutra*) cease to teach and convert people, they return to the principle of silence. There is nothing that can hinder the Dharma principle of silence and extinction; hence it is just like the sky. When the winds of the teaching of the all-inclusive, unobstructed accommodation of phenomena (*ke*), noumena (*ku*), and the middle way (*chū*), (i.e., the *Dharma Flower Sutra*) stop teaching and converting people, these gusts return to the principle of silence and extinction, in the same way as the sky. The bodhisattvas who were dependent on rags for clothing, begging for food, sitting under trees, and purgatives, as a moral and spiritual means, used fans and pointed to trees as metaphors to propagate their doctrines. Their object was so that people could get to know the deeper implications of the moon and the wind."

Again, there was somebody who said, "In the dream, the clouds of troublesome worries are gathered in layer upon layer, like mountains in a mountain range. Since there are eighty-four thousand particles of bodily and mental suffering, they hide the moon of the original awakening of the essence of mind. The analogies of fans and trees were taught according to the texts, ideograms, and wording of the provisional sutras and their commentaries. The moon and the wind are used as symbols for the Buddha enlightened teaching of the perception and awakening to the concept of the original enlightenment. The reason for this is that both a fan and a tree are simply devices to illustrate the provisional doctrines."

This somebody whom I have just quoted gives only a rough explanation and not the real meaning. In order to understand the moon as the enlightenment of the essence of mind and the

Utterness of the Dharma (*Myōhō*) or the wind as the wisdom to understand all things, we now use *Myōhō Renge Kyō* [which means the Utterness of the Dharma (*Myōhō*) (entirety of existence, enlightenment and unenlightenment) permeated by the underlying white lotus flower-like mechanism of the interdependence of cause, concomitancy and effect (*Renge*) in its whereabouts of the ten (psychological) realms of dharmas (*Kyō*)]. Hence it says, in Myōraku's (*Miao-lo*) *Explanatory Notes on the Recondite Meaning of the Dharma Flower* (*Hokke Gengi Shakusen*), "If you look for the appropriate expression for all physical manifestations as well as sounds, then you have to go as far as the ultimate principle of the absolute truth as having no differentiated perceptions."

There is another explanation that says that the appropriate names for all physical manifestations as well as sounds are like the fan and the tree of the dreamland of all the sutras and their commentaries, whereas the ultimate principle of the absolute truth that has no differentiated perceptions is comparable to our being enlightened to the moon and the wind of the ultimate joy of silence and illumination of the essence of our own minds.

This ultimate joy is the subjectivity of the sentient beings of the dharma realms of the ten directions, along with their dependent abodes and terrains of reward, all combined together in a single entity. This would indicate the objective realm of the Dharma, wisdom, and corresponding bodies of the Buddha, all put into one.

This ultimate joy is also the non-differentiation of the four abodes of the Buddha. They are 1) the dwelling place of humankind, *deva* (*ten*), disciples of the Buddha and the people who are not disciples, 2) hearers of the Buddha's voice (*shōmon, shrāvaka*) and people who are partially enlightened due to a profound search for the meaning of existence (*engaku, hyakushibutsu, pratyekabuddha*), 3) partially enlightened bodhisattvas, and 4) the space of silence and illumination. All these abodes are therefore installed in the Dharma body of the single Buddha.

The realms of dharmas seen as a whole entity are the body of the Dharma. These ten [psychological] realms of dharmas seen in terms of our minds and body are the reward, or wisdom. When the ten [psychological] realms of dharmas take on our personal shapes, they then become the corresponding body. There is no Buddha outside of the ten [psychological] realms of dharmas. Outside of the Buddha, there are no ten [psychological] realms of dharmas. There is only the non-duality of our subjectivity and its dependent objective environment; that is to say, our persons and their environmental terrains are not separate entities.

Since the realms of dharmas of the ten directions are the embodiment of the one Buddhahood, these realms of dharmas can also be seen as the terrain of silence and illumination. This means the oneness of the ultimate principle of the absolute truth, without any differentiated perceptions. It is far removed from the impermanency of things, such as coming into being, lasting as long as they should, and later disintegrating into nothingness. Hence, it is the ultimate reality which cannot be conceived as having any particularisation whatsoever.

Here is the principle of the recondite meaning at the very bottom of the profoundest depth of the Dharma nature. It is also the place from whence the bodhisattvas who swarmed up out of the earth came, as well as being the absolute truth. The absolute truth has no particularisation at all and is the essence of the mind of sentient beings. It is the immaculately pure and karmically determined environment that is entirely free from troublesome worries. If we were to give a name to it, it would be the calyx of the lotus of the mind of the Utterness of the Dharma (*Myōhō, Saddharma*).

Therefore, outside of mind there is not a single item (dharma) that exists independently. So when we realise this, it is the perception and understanding that all existence (dharmas) is the Dharma of the Buddha.

It is then that the two polarisations of life and death change and become the concept of the dream of living and dying, and that both of these two are only a hallucination and a flurry of mental images. When we see our persons correctly in the light of the original awakening, our births are not the beginning, and our deaths are not the end. We are not killed by swords, nor are we shot by arrows. If we are put inside a mustard seed, the mustard seed doesn't get any bigger, nor do our minds and material worlds shrink. If we were to fill the empty sky, the empty sky would not get any bigger, nor can the mind and things be reduced in size.

The opposite of good is bad. The opposite of bad is good. But due to the fact that outside our own minds nothing exists whatsoever, there is no real such thing as good, nor is there any real such thing as bad. What exists apart from the qualifications of good and bad is something that is morally neutral. Both good and bad are unrecordable, as neither being one thing nor another. There cannot be any mind that is separated from any experience whatsoever. Hence good and bad, pure and defiled, common mortals or the enlightened, heaven and earth, great and small, east and west, north and south, the four points of the compass as well as above and below are all judged by the words that describe them.

Everything that comes into our minds and all actions produced by our minds fade away and cease to exist. Thoughts are discriminated and expressed in words, so that outside of our minds there cannot be a differentiation of things, or one concept and another, nor can there be either any perception or any understanding of the fundamental identity of all things. Words are the expression in the sounds of speech of the echoes of our mental processes.

The ordinary person being unenlightened and unaware of the reality of things is confused about the mind in his own body. The Buddha who is enlightened to the nature of mind is referred to as having the power to penetrate the reaches of the mind. The power to penetrate the reaches of the mind (*shinzū shi riki*) is to be able to see into it all dharmas, without any hindrance whatsoever. Sentient beings are also endowed with the power of the mind to see into all dharmas at will. Badgers and foxes (who in Japanese folklore are said to have special powers) are able to reveal them, but this is only the partial enlightenment that is common to all beings that are sentient.

Mind flows out automatically to depict the spaces and terrains that we depend on for an existence. (But mind does not create.) This was explained throughout the Buddha's lifetime of enlightened teaching that is made up of the treasury of the Dharma of eighty-four thousand sutras. Each and all of these teachings are gateways to the Dharma, in the body of the single person of Shākyamuni.

Nevertheless, this Dharma treasury of eighty-four thousand sutras is the text of a diary for each one of us as a single individual.

[In other words, even though this treasury of eighty-four thousand sutras is the makeup of the body of the Buddha, it is the same life as the ordinary person. The number of particles in the human body is supposed to be eighty-four thousand. Hence this term is used for a number of things, often in the general sense of a great number. There are said to be eighty-four thousand physical signs of a Buddha, as well as the same number of troublesome worries and mortal distresses.]

This store of eighty-four thousand dharmas is brought about and cherished within the mind in our own bodies. As a result, to think of the Buddha, his Dharma, and his immaculate terrain as being anywhere outside the mind in our own bodies, or to call upon them as being somewhere else, is completely misguided.

The mind, on its encounters with good or evil karmic relationships, conjures up good or evil dharmas. In the *Flower Garland Sutra* (*Kegon, Avatāmsaka*), it says, "Just as a skilled painter depicts and shows the different five aggregates that darken the awareness of our original enlightenment (*go'on*), so are all the dharmas, in the spaces where existence takes place (*seken*), entirely dreamt up by the mind. So it is the same with the Buddha and ordinary people."

[The five aggregates (*go'on*) are 1) bodily form, matter, physicality related to the five organs of sense, 2) reception, sensation, feeling as a psychological process, 3) thought, discerning, and turning things over in the mind, 4) the mental process of deciding what is good or bad, right or wrong, and deciding whether to act on those decisions, 5) the mental faculty that makes us think we are who we are on account of our experiences and what we know.]

"Also, the three realms of dharmas are only the manifestation of mind. Outside of the mind there are no separate dharmas. Between the mind, the Buddha, and ordinary people there is no distinction, since all three are in the mind."

[The three realms of dharmas are where 1) sentient beings have appetites and desires, 2) which are incarnated in a subjective materiality with physical surrounding, 3) who are, at the same time, endowed with the immateriality of the realms of thoughts and ideas (*sangai, triloka*).]

In the *Sutra on Implications Without Bounds* (*Muryōgi-kyō*), it says, "Both the absolute truth as having no differentiated perceptions (*musō*) and the inexplicable quality of the one instant of thought containing three thousand existential spaces that is inherent in all life (*fusō*) are born out of the single Dharma that has boundless implications." The absolute truth as having no differentiated perceptions and also the inexplicable quality of the one instant of thought containing three thousand existential spaces are both included in the mind of each instant of thought of all sentient beings.

In explaining this sutra, *The Textual Explanations of the Dharma Flower* (*Hokke Mongu*) says, "Existing or turning into nothing are not the appearance of impermanency, but the absolute truth as having no differentiated perception that is common to everything. The aspects of the two nirvanas of the people of the two vehicles (*nijō*) who have a remainder of karma to fulfil, along with those whose remains of karma are completely ended, are both not separate from the position of having attained nirvana and have become the inexplicable quality of the one instant of thought containing three thousand existential spaces that is inherent in all life."

The discussion and clarification of the imponderably inexplicable quality of mind is said to be the visceral essential of the sutras and their explanations. The person who is awakened to and realises this is referred to as a person who has arrived at what existence really is, which is Nam Myōhō Renge Kyō.

When we look into this and see what it amounts to, then the ten [psychological] realms of dharmas (*jikkai*) are our bodies, our minds, and the realities we live in. Hence, this is the originally awakened Tathāgata, in terms of our own bodies and minds.

[Tathāgata (*Nyorai*) signifies the following: one who has gone; one who has followed the Path and arrived at the real suchness; one of the ten titles of a Buddha. Tathāgata can be explained as a person who comes from the real suchness of existence, which is Nam Myōhō Renge Kyō – which means to devote our lives to and found them on (*Nam*[*u*]) the Utterness of the Dharma (*Myōhō*) (entirety of existence, enlightenment and unenlightenment) permeated by the underlying white lotus flower-like mechanism of the interdependence of cause, concomitancy and effect (*Renge*) in its whereabouts of the ten (psychological) realms of dharmas (*Kyō*) – and that person will return to it.]

When this is not understood, it is called unenlightenment. When we are aware of this as well as knowing it, it is called the inner nature of the Dharma (*hosshō*).

However, our minds just as they are do not become enlightened. Unenlightenment and the inner nature of the Dharma are different expressions for the oneness of mind. The words and names may be two, but there is only one mind. This is why we must not simply cut off our unenlightenment or just chop off the self-deceptive, illusionary qualities of our unenlightenment – because the general meaning of the all-embracing teachings is that we should not even sever a single hair of our bewilderment, since all dharmas are the Dharma of the Buddha.

In the *Second Chapter of the Dharma Flower Sutra on Expedient Means*, it says, "In any way dharmas make themselves present to any of our six organs of sense – eyes, ears, nose, tongue, body, and mind – implies the features and bodily characteristics of all sentient beings, as well as the manifest body of the originally enlightened Tathāgata. Suchness is such an inner nature, which is the essence of the mind of all sentient beings and hence the wisdom and reward body of the originally enlightened Tathāgata. Suchness is also such an entity, which includes the whole of life, as well as being the embodiment and life of the originally enlightened Tathāgata. Then we have another seven such qualities, which have their origins in these first three. All together there are ten ways in which dharmas make themselves present to any of our six organs of sense – eyes, ears, nose, tongue, body, and mind."

These ten ways in which dharmas make themselves present to any of our six organs of sense – eyes, ears, nose, tongue, body, and mind – run all the way through the ten [psychological] realms of dharmas. The Universal Teacher Myōraku (*Miao-lo*) states, in his *Vajra Scapel*, "The real aspect of all dharmas has to imply each and every dharma. All dharmas must include the ten ways in which dharmas make themselves present to any of our six organs of sense – eyes, ears, nose, tongue, body, and mind, and these ten qualities of suchness must include the ten [psychological] realms of dharmas – which are the inhabitants of hell, hungry ghosts, animality, titans (*ashura*), humanity, *deva* (*ten*), hence the transitory qualities of ecstasy and joy, the hearers of the Buddha's voice (*shōmon*), which means those people who wish to understand, those people who are partially enlightened due to a profound search for the meaning of existence (*engaku, hyakushibutsu, pratyekabuddha*), the bodhisattvas, and the Buddha. These ten [psychological] realms of dharmas must include their respective subjective lives, as well as their environments."

These ten [psychological] realms of dharmas all stem from the mind of one person. But these ten realms amount to the countless particles in the human body, as well as the same amount of incalculable gateways to the Dharma.

[This teaching, although it refers to the single person of the Buddha, also equally applies to all sentient beings. Shākyamuni was talking about himself. But the ten (psychological) realms of dharmas open up the concept of the one instant of thought containing three thousand existential spaces, which leads to the possible enlightenment of all people.]

This paragraph on the ten ways in which dharmas make themselves present to any of our six organs of sense – eyes, ears, nose, tongue, body, and mind – is signed and sealed to show that it is the current teaching that has been thought over and agreed upon by all the Buddhas of the past, present, and future. The seal of the Buddha is the single *mudra* (hand gesture) for the real aspect of all dharmas. A *mudra* is another word for a seal of judgment. Apart from the *Dharma Flower Sutra*, all the other sutras are devoid of the *mudra* of the real aspect of all dharmas and are not texts from the manuscripts that apply to reality. There is no real Buddha in these texts, and, since there is no real Buddha, these manuscripts belong to the dream. Furthermore, there is no immaculate terrain for the Buddha to dwell on.

Although there are ten times the ten [psychological] realms of dharmas, there is only a single one of the sequence of the ten ways in which dharmas make themselves present to any of our six organs of sense – eyes, ears, nose, tongue, body, and mind. In the same way, there is only one moon in the sky.

The ten such qualities of suchness in the nine realms of dharmas, from hell to that of the bodhisattvas, are the ten ways in which dharmas make themselves present to any of our six organs of sense – eyes, ears, nose, tongue, body, and mind – of the dream, rather like the moon reflected in water. The ten such qualities of suchness of the Buddha realm of the Dharma are the ten ways in which dharmas make themselves present to any of our six organs of sense – eyes, ears, nose, tongue, body, and mind – of wide-awake understanding of the original enlightenment, just like the real moon in the sky.

It is because of this that the one sequence of the ten ways in which dharmas make themselves present to any of our six organs of sense – eyes, ears, nose, tongue, body, and mind – reveals at the same time the whole entity and the role played by the Dharma realm of the Buddha, along with the nine other realms of dharmas which are comparable to the moon reflected in water. Sentient beings are all equal, on account of the ten realms dharmas being mutually contained in each other. Both the moon in the sky [which represents the Buddha realm as having been opened up through continual practice] and the moon reflected in water [which indicates the delusions of ordinary people] are present in each and every person, without leaving a single individual out. As a result, from "any way in which dharmas make themselves present to any of our six organs of sense – eyes, ears, nose, tongue, body, and mind" to "their apparent and karmic consequences", all these nine such qualities of suchness are all equal, without differentiation. From beginning to end, they are all the ultimate dimension of the real aspect of all dharmas (*hon matsu kukyō tō*).

The beginning is the sequence of the ten ways in which dharmas make themselves present to any of our six organs of sense – eyes, ears, nose, tongue, body, and mind – of ordinary people; the end is the sequence of the ten such qualities of suchness of all the Buddhas. All the Buddhas make their appearance out of the one instant of mind of ordinary people. It begins with ordinary people and ends with all the Buddhas.

The point is that this is expounded in the *Dharma Flower Sutra*, in the *Third Chapter on Similes and Parables*: "Now then, these three realms, where sentient beings have a physical dimension and organs of sense, where they have needs and desires and also purely mental activities, are all in my possession, and the people everywhere in these realms are all my children."

This Buddha having attained to the way, in order to save other people, manifested himself to them and encouraged them to arrive at the path of Buddhahood (i.e., to practise). Since he was already inside the dream of living and dying, he expounded the wide-awake quality of being aware of the original state.

Consequently, the Buddha taught the parable of a father as the Buddha wisdom and children as being stupid and silly.

Although sentient beings have the ten ways in which dharmas make themselves present to any of our six organs of sense – eyes, ears, nose, tongue, body, and mind – or being awakened to the original state, they are hidden away under the one instant of dropping off into an unenlightened slumber and drifting into the dream of living and dying, so that the dharmic principle of being awakened to the original state is forgotten.

Even a tiny scrap of unenlightenment, like cutting off a single hair, is enough to make common mortals lose their way from the past, present, and future in meaningless dreamlike states.

The Buddha is like a person who has woken up from the dream. He then goes back into the dream of living and dying, in order to wake up the people within it. The Buddha's wisdom is like a parent, and sentient beings such as us are like children – hence the truth of the Buddha's declaration, "They are all my children everywhere."

When we understand this principle of the Buddha teaching, then from the very beginning we are both parent and child, as well as at the very end we are both parent and child. Being both parent and child is the fundamental nature with which we are born. Thus, it is perceived that our own minds and the mind of the Buddha are not different, since waking up from the dream of living and dying and returning to the wakefulness of the enlightenment of the original state is said to be the inseparability of making our inherent Buddha nature manifest with our persons just as they are. To open up our inherent Buddha nature with our personal characteristics just as they normally are implies that this is a quality that we are born with, and, being our fundamental nature, it is not without troubles or obstacles. It is the destiny of sentient beings, their apparent karmic consequences and the effects they produce, as well as the unseen protection of the Buddha and the bodhisattvas.

When you come to think it over, our dreaming is an example of our minds in a state of perplexity, and our wakefulness is an example of the mind alert to reality. So if we look at these examples in terms of the lifetime of the enlightened Buddha teaching of Shākyamuni, we find it is a nasty experience when we are in the empty delusion of the dream devoid of footprints. Covered in perspiration, we wake up to find that we ourselves, our homes and beds, are still the same as they always were. Nevertheless, both the emptiness of the dream and the reality of being awake are there before our eyes. Even though we may think that both are taking place in the mind of one person, the difference between reality and fantasy exists.

Therefore, we must fully understand that whether our minds see the dream of the nine realms of dharmas of living and dying or the alertness of the eternal Dharma realm of the Buddha, there is no distinction (since these two experiences are only to be found in our respective minds). There is no difference in the place where the mind sees the dream of the nine realms of dharmas of living and dying and the alertness of the eternal Dharma realm of the Buddha. The mind and the dharmas in it do not change; nor is there any alteration in where they exist or take place. Dreams are always fictions of the mind, and being alert is always the real thing.

In the *Universal Desistance from Troublesome Worries in order to See Clearly* (*Maka Shikan*), it says, "During the Chou Dynasty 370 B.C., there was a person called Chuang Tzŭ who dreamt that he had turned into a butterfly for a period of a hundred years in which he suffered greatly and had little joy. Then, when he awoke streaming with perspiration, he found he had not turned into a butterfly; nor was it for a hundred years. He had not suffered; nor had he had any joy. None of it had ever happened at all. It was all an illusion."

Referring to the concept that has just been expressed, it says, in the *Broad Elucidation to Support the Practice of the Desistance from Troublesome Worries* (*Maka Shikan bugyō kuketsu*), "Unenlightenment is like the butterfly in the dream. The hundred years is an analogy for the one instant of thought containing three thousand existential spaces. Since the one instant of thought has no reality in itself, the butterfly did not really exist. Nor are there any three thousand existential spaces, so that there were no years for Chuang Tzŭ to experience."

This explanation is a way of saying that becoming a Buddha is not separate from one's person just as it is. When Chuang Tzŭ became a butterfly in his dream, he himself did not change at all. When he woke up, he no longer thought he was a butterfly, nor had he become any other Chuang Tzŭ. When we think we are just common mortals bound to the endless cycles of births and deaths, we become the butterflies of our dreams, which is a prejudice based on a wrong way of thinking. But when we see ourselves as the fundamentally enlightened Tathāgata – i.e., we see ourselves as life itself – then we are like Chuang Tzŭ who has returned to his original self. This is the awareness that our own inherent Buddha nature is not separate from our respective personalities.

Nonetheless, the body of the butterfly did not become enlightened. To think of oneself as a butterfly is nonsense and certainly not another word for Buddhahood. This, however, is beside the point.

When we understand that the butterfly of the dream is our unenlightenment and that our distorted way of thinking is a delusive, wild idea, like the inner nature and the entity of yesterday's dream, who on earth could have doubts so as to believe and accept the illusionary dream of living and dying, instead of the essence of the Buddha of the eternal nirvana?

["The essence of the Buddha of the eternal nirvana" signifies Nam Myōhō Renge Kyō, which means to devote our lives to and found them on (*Nam*[*u*]) the Utterness of the Dharma (*Myōhō*) (entirety of existence, enlightenment and unenlightenment) permeated by the underlying white lotus flower-like mechanism of the interdependence of cause, concomitancy and effect (*Renge*) in its whereabouts of the ten (psychological) realms of dharmas (*Kyō*).]

It says, in the *Desistance from Troublesome Worries in order to See Clearly (Maka Shikan)*, "When it comes to the stupid bewilderment of unenlightenment, then its origin lies in the essence of the Dharma, which is the very nature of life itself. It is on account of our stupid bewilderment that our perception of the fundamental nature of existence, that is the essence of the Dharma, is transformed into the multitude of dharmas, which bring about all our absurd ideas about what is good and what is bad.

"When it gets cold, water freezes into ice. When water becomes solid, it is like ice. Again, when we go to sleep, the mind turns into all sorts of different dreams and fantasies. Even at this very instant, all the ill-assorted and out of place ideas about life (*moro moro no tendō*) are nothing more nor less than the essence of the Dharma, which is life itself. Although these concepts of life are neither a oneness nor are they separate from each other, they all have to be felt deeply and accepted as real. It is said that, when all our deluded perceptions arise or when they cease to exist, they are like the conjurors' revolving wheel of fire, which gives the illusion of fire going round and round. But in fact such a thing does not exist.

"You should not believe in such absurdities. Instead, you should hold faith in the fundamental of life, which is the essence of the Dharma [that is, Nam Myōhō Renge Kyō, which means to devote our lives to and found them on (*Nam[u]*) the Utterness of the Dharma (entirety of existence, enlightenment and unenlightenment) (*Myōhō*) permeated by the underlying white lotus flower-like mechanism of the interdependence of cause, concomitancy and effect (*Renge*) in its whereabouts of the ten (psychological) realms of dharmas (*Kyō*)]. When things come into being, it is the essence of the Dharma coming into existence, and, when things cease to exist, it is the cessation of the essence of the Dharma. When we try to be enlightened to this, there is in fact no coming into being, nor is there any cessation of existence. It is only when we see this as a mental confusion that we perceive that fundamentally everything everywhere is the essence of the Dharma. It is on account of the essence of the Dharma that we can relate to the essence of the Dharma. It is on account of the essence of the Dharma that we are able to bear it in mind. Whatever exists, it is always the workings of the essence of the Dharma [that is, Nam Myōhō Renge Kyō, which means to devote our lives to and found them on (*Nam[u]*) the Utterness of the Dharma (entirety of existence, enlightenment and unenlightenment) (*Myōhō*) permeated by the underlying white lotus flower-like mechanism of the interdependence of cause, concomitancy and effect (*Renge*) in its whereabouts of the ten (psychological) realms of dharmas (*Kyō*)]. When there is no essence of the Dharma, it means that there is no existence whatsoever."

[Translator's note: With regard to this quotation from Tendai (*T'ien T'ai*), I shall translate the entry for the essence of the Dharma or the Dharma nature in the *Universal Dictionary of Buddhism and Philosophy* (*Bukkyō Tetsugaku Daijiten*).]

Although we may conceive the essence of the Dharma as nonexistent, so that there can be no instant for it to occur in – we may think that the butterfly of the dream is real – but to take the living and dying of our crazy, mixed-up unenlightenment as real is a bewilderment.

In the ninth fascicle of the *Universal Desistance from Troublesome Worries in order to See Clearly* (*Maka Shikan*), we have, "For instance, the dharma of sleep obscures the mind in such a way that, within an instant, we dream up countless existences. . . . So, what stage in Buddhist practice brings about the state of the eternal and indestructible nirvana that is free from all troubles and suffering? . . . . All sentient beings are inseparable from nirvana. Again, there is no such thing as extinction in nirvana. So what is this particular place in the stages of Buddhist practice that brings about this state of being? Is it high or low, or is it great or small?

"This principle of the Dharma is uncreated and indefinable. Yet it is endowed with the chain of the twelve causes and karmic circumstances that run through the whole of sentient existence – 1) a fundamental unenlightenment which leads to the 2) dispositions that are inherited from former lives, 3) the first consciousness after conception that takes place in the womb, 4) body and mind evolving in the womb, 5) the five organs of sense and the functioning of the mind, 6) contact with the outside world, 7) receptivity or budding intelligence and the making of distinctions from six or seven years onwards, 8) the urge for sensual existence that forms 10) the substance of future karma, 11) the completed karma ready to be born again 12) and facing in the direction of old age and death.

"All of this can be explained. The teaching of the chain of the twelve causes and karmic circumstances that run through the whole of sentient existence explains the reasons why sentient beings come about. This chain of the twelve causes and karmic circumstances is described as a picture of a painted tree that is planted in empty space. It is only an expedient device to explain how these causes and karmic circumstances come into being."

The karmic consequences that produce the objective and subjective environments of the ten [psychological] realms of dharmas of our lives is the Dharma body and the universal ultimate truth of the

Buddha. To know that this single entity is endowed with effectuality (*toku*) that comprises the three bodies – which are the Universal Dharma, wisdom, and manifest presence – as well as to be able to thoroughly understand and realise completely that all dharmas are the existence of the Buddha, is to arrive at the second stage, which is an intellectual understanding of the truth, in the six stages of practice.

Since the second in the six stages of practice is an intellectual understanding of the truth, it is also the stage in which our inherent Buddha nature is made manifest. Therefore, the direct teaching of the all-inclusive one instant of thought containing three thousand existential spaces has no grades of practice in a consecutive order.

It says, in the *Recondite Significance of the Dharma Flower* (*Hokke Gengi Shakusen*), "Many scholars of the final phase of the Buddha teaching of Shākyamuni will compete with each other and argue over the practices and attachments to the treatises and sutras that are an expedient means in order to cut off and suppress our troublesome worries. Even though the water is cold, you may still have to drink some, in order to find out if it is so."

Among the explanations of the Universal Teacher Tendai (*T'ien T'ai*), we have, "Regarding the general features and outlines of the concept of stages of practice, in a consecutive order coming from the *Sutra on the Benevolent Sovereign* and the *Sutra on the Bodhisattva's Necklace of Precious Stones*, the stage in the practice for cutting off and suppression of our troublesome worries is as pointed out in the full edition of the *Sutra on the Wisdom that Carries People over to the Shores of Nirvana* and Nagarjuna's *Universal Discourses on the Wisdom that Carries People over to the Shores of Nirvana*."

The *Sutra on the Benevolent Sovereign*, the *Sutra on the Bodhisattva's Necklace of Precious Stones*, the full edition of the *Sutra on the Wisdom that Carries People over to the Shores of Nirvana*, and Nagarjuna's *Universal Discourses on the Wisdom that Carries People over to the Shores of Nirvana* are all based on sutras and discourses that were taught during the doctrinal periods prior to the *Dharma*

Flower Sutra. Because, when it comes to the practices of the provisional teachings, people ascend through consecutive stages toward enlightenment over an uncountable number of aeons, hence the reference to a coherent order. Now, because of the all-inclusive teaching (*engyō*), we have gone beyond the eight doctrinal periods that came before the *Dharma Flower Sutra* and swiftly and speedily attain enlightenment without passing through the different levels of practice.

Mind, the Buddha, and sentient beings are all ensconced in each single instant within the mind. If one can see that there is nothing outside the mind, then even the practitioner with lesser propensities can, in a single lifetime, arrive at the stage of enlightenment of Utterness (*myōgaku*). The one and the many have a phenomenal identity – i.e., the one is just like the many, and the many are just like the one. Each stage of practice is fully endowed with all the other stages. Therefore, in a single lifetime of practice, one can reach the stage of the enlightenment of Utterness.

If this is valid for people of lesser propensities, then naturally it is the same for people of middling aptitude. So, with people who have superior propensities, it goes without saying. Beyond what we perceive as reality, there is no separate Dharma. Therefore, in our perception of reality there is no order; nor are there stages of enlightenment within it.

Generally speaking, the lifetime of the enlightened teaching is a Dharma based on the example of the one individual, so that we ought to know thoroughly what our own constituents are. The person who is aware of what his body consists of is called a Buddha, and those people who are confused about it are referred to as sentient beings or ordinary people.

The Universal Teacher Myōraku (*Miao-lo*) says, in the sixth chapter of his *Broad Elucidation to Support the Practice of the Universal Desistance from Troublesome Worries* (*Maka Shikan Bugyō Kuketsu*), "It is understood that our bodies are, inch by inch, a duplication of the sky and the earth. The roundness of our heads mirrors the dome of the sky, and the squareness of our feet emulates the quadrangular surface of the earth. The empty space in our bodies is in imitation of the empty space of the universe. The warmth of our stomachs is modelled after spring and summer, and the hardness of our spinal column is in conformity with the autumn and winter. Our four limbs are patterned after the four seasons. The twelve major joints in our bodies are an echo of the twelve months of the year, and the three hundred sixty lesser joints represent the number of days in a year. The breath coming in and out of our noses fits the pattern of the wind that blows over the marshes and through mountain valleys and dales. The breath that comes and goes through our mouths is the wind that blows through the empty space. Our two eyes are like the sun and the moon, and our blinking is comparable to the alternation of day and night. The hair on our head resembles the stars and constellations in the sky.

"Our bones are like the minerals and precious stones. Our skin is like the soil and earth. The clusters of hair on our bodies suggest the woods and forests. The five major organs in our bodies – which are 1) the spleen, 2) the liver, 3) the heart, 4) the lungs, and 5) the kidneys – take after the planets in the sky – 1) Saturn, 2) Jupiter, 3) Mars, 4) Venus, 5) Mercury. And also, on the Earth, the five major organs resemble the five great mountain peaks in China – 1) Mount Tai in the east, 2) Mount Hêng in the south, 3) Mount Hua in the west, 4) Mount Yu Hêng in the north, and 5) Mount Song in the centre. The two poles Yin and Yang connect the five elements – 1) earth, 2) wood, 3) fire, 4) metal, 5) water.

"In the world of humankind, the five elements correspond to the five principles in Confucian thought – 1) sincerity, 2) benevolence, 3) wisdom, 4) integrity, 5) propriety. In terms of the functions of the mind, the number five refers to its five aspects – 1) thought, 2) its spiritual nature, 3) the psyche, 4) its animal nature, 5) intention. In behaviour, there are the five Confucian virtues – 1) cordiality, 2) sincerity, 3) reverence, 4) economicalness, 5) deference. Then there are the five punishments of Ancient China – 1) tattooing the forehead, 2) cutting off the nose, 3) amputating the feet, 4) castration, and 5) death.

"There are the five heavenly tutelary rulers, whose concern is the five elements of earth, wood, fire, metal, and water. Along with these tutelary spirits, there are the five clouds – 1) the blue cloud, 2) the white cloud, 3) the red cloud, 4) the black cloud, 5) the yellow cloud. When these five clouds turn into the five Dragons, they become 1) Vermilion Sparrow who rules the heart, 2) Black Warrior who rules the kidneys, 3) Blue Dragon who rules the liver, 4) White Tiger who rules the lungs, and 5) the spleen which is ruled by Aquiline Constellation."

Again, in the same way, *The Broad Elucidation to Support the Practice of the Universal Desistance from Troublesome Worries* (*Myōraku, Miao-lo*) states, "The five notes in Ancient Chinese music, the five illuminating studies of Ancient India – which are 1) grammar, 2) linguistics, 3) engineering, 4) astronomy, and 5) medicine – as well as the five arts in Zhou Dynasty (China 1122-770 B.C.) – 1) court ceremony, 2) music, 3) archery, 4) horsemanship, 5) calligraphy – all come from the five visceral organs. Moreover, this also holds good for the control of what is inside us. The mind that is enlightened to this become a universal sovereign whose royal palace (i.e., person) is surrounded by a hundred walls and guarded on the outside by the five military officials. The lungs are guarded by Szŭ Ma, the liver by Szŭ Tu, the spleen by Szŭ Kung. The four limbs are watched over by the loyal people. The left is watched over by Si Ming, and the right Si Lu. The navel is guarded by Dai Yi Chün."

The Universal Teacher Tendai (*T'ien T'ai*), in his *Explanation of the Gateways to the Dharma of Graded Meditations in order to Cross over to the Shores of nirvana* (*Shaku Zen Haramitsu Shidai Hōmon*), makes this teaching clear in detail.

On looking into the human body meticulously, you will find that it is just as the preceding paragraphs say. If you think that the indestructible Vajra (Diamond) body is not subject to impermanency, then you are mistaken. It is rather like the butterfly in the dream of Chuang Tzŭ, or just as the Universal Teacher Myōraku (*Miao-lo*) explained, in his *Broad Elucidation to Support the Practice of the Universal Desistance from Troublesome Worries*.

The five elements that are the components of the universe are earth, water, fire, wind, and the void of relativity (*kū, shūnyatā*).

The five aggregates that overshadow our original enlightenment are 1) bodily form, matter, the physical form related to the five organs of sense, 2) receptivity, sensation, feeling, the functioning of the mind or the senses in connection with affairs and things, 3) conception, thought, discerning, 4) the functioning of mind in its processes with regard to likes, dislikes, good and bad, etc., as well as actions that inevitably pass on their effects, 5) the mental faculty that makes us think we are who we are on account of what we know.

The five precepts of the individual vehicles (*shōjō, hīnayāna*), for men and women who do not becomes monks or nuns, are 1) no killing whatsoever, 2) no stealing, 3) no wrongful sexual relationships, 4) no telling lies or make-believe, 5) no consumption of intoxicants. The five permanent values of Confucian thought are 1) trust, 2 benevolence, 3) wisdom, 4) righteousness, 5) courtesy. The five directions are east, west, south, north, and the centre.

The five kinds of wisdom of the Tathāgata are 1) to clearly understand that the fundamental elements of existence are earth, water, fire, wind, relativity (*kū*), and cognition, 2) the wisdom to perceive that all existence reveals itself as though it were in a mirror, 3) the wisdom to see that all differences between the dharmas are extinguished into their essential equality, 4) the wisdom to contemplate and observe in terms of Utterness and to be able to take away the doubts of sentient beings, 5) the wisdom to be able to accomplish all that is necessary in order to benefit others and oneself.

Also, the five periods of the teaching of the Buddha are 1) the Flower Garland (*Kegon*) period, 2) the period of the teaching of the individual vehicle (*Agon*), 3) the period of the doctrine that connects the heritage of the individual vehicle to the universal vehicle (*hōdō, vaipulya*), 4) the Wisdom (*hannya, prajña*) period, 5) the period of The *Dharma Flower Sutra*, (*Myōhō Renge Kyō*).

Originally, all these groups of five referred to one thing only. In the sutras there are various explanations. Within the Buddha teaching and outside of it, the subject matters of these groups of five have grown apart from each other.

In the *Dharma Flower Sutra*, the five elements that are the makeup of all existence are taken for granted. In the minds of all ordinary people, there are the five essentials of Buddhahood – 1) the Buddha nature as a direct cause for enlightenment, all beings being inherently endowed with this Buddha nature, 2) the enlightening or revealing cause that is associated with the Buddha wisdom, 3) the revelation of the Buddha nature that is brought about by the karmic circumstances, 4) the fruition of the Buddha nature which is enlightenment, 5) the fruition of enlightenment being the substantiation of nirvana. This refers to the five ideograms for *Myōhō Renge Kyō*.

Because the essence of our persons is composed of these five ideograms, our entities have always existed and are also the originally enlightened Tathāgata.

This was expounded as the ten ways in which dharmas make themselves present to any of our six organs of sense – eyes, ears, nose, tongue, body, and mind, in the *Second Chapter on Expedient Means* of the *Dharma Flower Sutra*, where the Buddha says, "Only Buddha and Buddha can exhaustively look into the real aspect of all dharmas."

When the Buddha taught this gateway to enlightenment, it was then not known to the bodhisattvas who were beyond the stage of any regression, nor those who had attained the supreme reward of the individual vehicle (*arhat, arakan*), nor even those intellectuals who were still studying or those who were partially enlightened (*nijō*). But because all those who could hold faith in this all-inclusive teaching that brought about an immediate realisation were ordinary people at the first stage of faith, they were able to become aware of the fact that their inherent Buddha natures were not separate from their respective personalities. Hence, they became comparable to the substance of the indestructible diamond (*vajra*).

In this way, my person, heaven and earth are a single, inseparable entity. If heaven crumbles, then I crumble with it. If the earth splits apart, then I also split apart. If earth, water, fire, and wind perish, then I will perish along with them. Even though these five principal elements pass through the three tenses of past, present, and future, these five elements do not change. Although the correct, formal, and final periods of the teaching of Shākyamuni are separate from each other, the five major elements remain the same. They simply flourish, decline, supplant each other, and swap places.

In one of the commentaries on the *Fifth Chapter on the Parable of the Medicinal Herbs* in the *Dharma Flower Sutra*, it says, "The Dharma principle of the all-inclusive teaching of the Dharma Flower is like the great earth. The all-inclusive direct teaching is like the rain that falls from the sky. Again, the three doctrines of the individual teaching, the interrelated teaching, and the particular teaching for bodhisattvas are like the three kinds of medicinal herbs and the two kinds of tree in this parable. The reason for this is that these medicinal herbs and trees grow out of the great earth of the Dharma principle of the all-inclusive teaching and are nourished by the rain from the sky of the all-inclusive teaching that brings about an immediate awakening to the Buddha truth.

"So the herbs and trees of the five vehicles that were taught, because they were suited to the propensities of 1) ordinary humankind, 2) *deva* (*ten*), 3) intellectuals who are still studying, 4) intellectuals who are partially enlightened due to a profound search for the meaning of existence, and 5) the bodhisattvas, were all able to flourish. Did you not think or realise that it is because of the grace and mercy of heaven and earth that our persons are able to thrive? The Buddha uses a metaphor for the three teachings for humankind, *deva* (*ten*), the two classes of intellectuals, and bodhisattvas. However, since these people are said to be ungrateful, they are referred to as plants and trees in a parable.

"The point is that, since these people began to listen to the *Dharma Flower Sutra*, the people of the five vehicles who were represented in the parable as the two trees and three herbs recognised that the principle of the all-inclusive, direct doctrine was their father. By becoming aware that they all grew out of the single great earth, they were able to know their mother's love. In the same way, by being watered by the one rain, they were able to know what a father's affection was."

This is the intended meaning of the *Fifth Chapter on the Parable of the Medicinal Herbs* in the *Dharma Flower Sutra*.

In the *Fourteenth Chapter on Practising in Peace and with Joy* in the *Dharma Flower Sutra*, it asserts that, during the final phase of the Dharma of Shākyamuni (*mappō*), even those ordinary people who have only begun to do the practice of the *Dharma Flower Sutra* will certainly become aware of their own inherent Buddha nature with their personalities just as they are.

1) These people practising in peace and with joy means that, if the persons of the final phase of the Dharma of Shākyamuni (*mappō*) avoid tempting distractions, they will find a suitable place to practise in peace and with joy. 2) Verbally practising in peace and with joy means that, after Shākyamuni's demise into nirvana, then these people will expound the implications of the *Dharma Flower Sutra*; but they will not be despised by other people, nor will they have their errors exposed. They will be able to proclaim and expound this teaching in peace. 3) Mentally practising in peace and with joy means that, when the Dharma of Shākyamuni has ceased to be effective, those people who hold faith in and recite Nam Myōhō Renge Kyō will not be jealous of other people who try to study the Buddha teaching. Nor will they seek to dispute with them. 4) To make the vow of practising in peace and joy means to have a heart of all-embracing loving-kindness and vow to try to save all sentient beings. These four references to the final phase of the Dharma of Shākyamuni (*mappō*) are recounted in the *Fourteenth Chapter on Practising in Peace and with Joy* in the *Dharma Flower Sutra*.

Apart from these references in the Fourteenth Chapter of the *Dharma Flower Sutra*, which is the chapter that alludes to the final phase of Shākyamuni's Dharma, we have, in the *Twenty-third Chapter on the Bodhisattva Sovereign Medicine* (*Yaku' ō, Bhaishajya-*

rāja), two more items that indicate this final phase. The first is the one that says, "Following the Buddha's demise into nirvana after the fifth period of five hundred years, we have a woman who on hearing this sutra practises just as it is taught." Then, there is the item that says, "During the fifth hundred year period after my demise into nirvana, there will be the broad propagation (*kōsen rufu*) throughout the world of humankind."

Also, in the *Twenty-eighth Chapter on the Persuasiveness and Quest [for Buddhahood] of the Bodhisattva Universally Good* (*Fugen, Samantabhadra*) in the *Dharma Flower Sutra*, there are again three more references to this final age (*mappō*): "In the polluted evil age that comes after the fifth five-hundred-year period subsequent to the Buddha's passing over to nirvana, there will still be people who hold faith in this (Dharma Flower) sutra." "In the latter age after the fifth five-hundred-year period of the polluted, evil generation, there will be monks and nuns, along with male and female believers, who seek the truth by holding faith, reading, and copying out, as well as desiring to do the practice of this *Dharma Flower Sutra*." "If there is a person after the fifth five hundred years after the Tathāgata's demise into nirvana who holds faith in the *Dharma Flower Sutra*, who also is seen to recite it and bears it in mind...."

What the Buddha has handed down to us clearly refers to present times. Other people have ignored the correct teachings and have attached their own mundane commentaries to them. The testament inherited from the Buddhas of the past, present, and future has been entrusted to stupidly foolish minds who contradict it in such a way that, should the Dharma be brushed aside, then how desperately regretful and how lamentably sad it would be for All those Buddhas of the past, present, and future.

In the *Sutra on the Buddha's Passing over to Nirvana*, there is the admonition that says, "It should be according to the Dharma and not in conformity with the persons who teach it." It is indeed painful and sad that the scholars of the final era through the work on their studies devastate the Dharma of the Buddha.

It is unhappily pointed out in Myōraku's (*Miao-lo*) *Broad Elucidation to Support the Practice of the Universal Desistance from Troublesome Worries*, "They listen to this all-inclusive teaching of the Dharma Flower that can bring about immediate enlightenment, yet they do not solemnly revere it. Indeed the people of recent times who study and practise the universal vehicle (*mahayana, daijō*) are confused about what is correct and what is distortion, not to mention those scholars of the formal period of the Buddha teaching (*zōbō*), who were with little common sense and weak faith. Even though the repository of the volumes on this all-inclusive teaching that brings about immediate enlightenment is full to overflowing, it never occurred to those scholars to have made the slightest attempt to consult them from time to time. Instead, they shut their eyes to what the Buddha Dharma really is. They led meaningless lives and had senseless deaths."

Indeed, it says in the fourth fascicle of the *Broad Elucidation to Support the Practice of the Universal Desistance from Troublesome Worries*, "The all-inclusive teaching of the Dharma Flower which brings about an immediate enlightenment is, from the very outset, a gateway to the Dharma that was expounded for ordinary people. If ordinary people cannot take advantage of this doctrine, then how can the Buddha stay in his own terrain of the essence of the Dharma? If the Buddha did not expound this all-inclusive teaching that brings about immediate enlightenment to all the Bodhisattvas by means of his entity of the essence of the Dharma, then, would it not be that the Buddha needed to appear in the three realms (*sangai*), where 1) sentient beings have appetites and desires, 2) which are incarnated in a subjective materiality, 3) who, at the same time, are endowed with the immateriality of the realms of thoughts and ideas (*sangai, triloka*)? Because ordinary people are given the life and destiny of the Buddha, this makes it possible for them to learn from and do the practice of the Tathāgata."

As a result, our individual minds and the person of the Buddha are seen as a single entity, and therefore we can readily become aware of our own inherent Buddha nature, which is not separate from our respective personalities. Once again, this is stated in the *Broad Elucidation to Support the Practice of the Universal Desistance from Troublesome Worries*. It says, "The Buddha essence of all the Buddhas is not thought of as something separate from the Buddha mind, so that we are able to become aware of our own Buddha natures."

This is what is referred to as contemplating the mind (*kanjin*). So, if we really become awakened to the fact that our own minds and that of the Buddha are the oneness of mind, even if we have to be obstructed by the moment of death being pressed upon us, there will probably be no bad karma. And if we are forced into the cycles of living and dying again, they will be no more than a series of illusory thoughts.

If we know that all dharmas are those of the Buddha, then there is no need for a good acquaintance to stimulate our minds to greater wisdom or give us instruction. So whatever people may say, or whatever people may do, or however they may behave, they are all the four respect-inspiring forms of behaviour of walking, standing, sitting, or lying down, which are all in harmony with the mind of the Buddha, as well as being a single embodiment that is independently free from the karma of actions, as well as having thoughts that are free from delusion and without any fault whatsoever or without any obstruction. This is thought of as the personal practice of the Buddha.

As a matter of course, the Tathāgata casts aside his conduct that is free from the karma of actions as well as having thoughts that are free from delusion, in order to be present, and yet not making his presence felt, or leaving any traces in the minds of unenlightened people with insane ideas. Those people who turn their backs on the teaching and explanations of all the Buddhas of the past, present, and future then drift from one benighted uncertainty to the next perplexity of not understanding, and the situation of those who continually oppose the Dharma of the Buddha is pitiful.

Now, those who can rectify their way of thinking can change their perplexities for enlightenment and realise that it cannot be any other way than to become aware that their own inherent Buddha nature is not separate from their personal traits just as they are.

Although the mirror of our minds and the mirror of the mind of the Buddha is only a single mirror, when we look into the mirror of our own minds, we do not see our respective Buddha nature. This is why this is referred to as our inherent bewilderment and not understanding.

The Tathāgata looks at the whole of the mirror as the one instant of thought containing three thousand existential spaces and perceives our inherent Buddha natures inside it. Therefore, enlightenment and unclearness are a single entity.

Even though there is only the one mirror, it is the way we see it for the difference between enlightenment and ignorance to come about.

Regardless of the mirror having its own depth, the whole is not an obstruction. It is only the way we look at it that makes us see what it does or does not reflect. Since both of these ways of looking are the coordination of our own minds and our surroundings, this makes them a single reality. Nevertheless, this is a single state of affairs with two different meanings.

The provisional Dharma that was expounded for the conversion of others is like staring right into the various reflections inside the mirror. But the Buddha's own practice of observing the mind is like looking at the mirror as a single whole.

The mirror of the provisional teachings that were expounded for the benefit of others and the mirror of the Buddha's own practice are not separate mirrors, but the single mirror of the essence of our own minds.

The word mirror is used as a metaphor for the concept of "not being separate from our persons just as they are". So, when we face the whole of the mirror, it becomes a metaphor for "opening up our inherent Buddha nature". Looking at the particulars of what is reflected inside the mirror is a metaphor for "the bewilderment of ordinary people (*shujō*)". This implies that we do not cut away the bad qualities of or personalities in the mirror of the mind. When we look into the mirror as a whole, it reflects various items, which in itself is not a virtue. Hence it is used as a metaphor for what the provisional teachings consist of. This is because the reflections in the mirror do not reveal the inherent Buddha nature of ordinary people like ourselves.

The Buddha's own practice and the practice he used in order to convert others have the strength and effectiveness of the discrepancy between gain and loss. In the first fascicle of the *Recondite Significance of the Dharma Flower*, Shōan (*Chang-an*) says, "When Sarvasiddharta, which was Shākyamuni's childhood name, took his grandfather's bow and drew it to the roundness of the full moon, this is referred to as strength. On releasing the string of the bow, the arrow tore its way through seven iron drums and the iron enclosing mountains that encircle the world, then perforated the earth and struck the wheel of water that is the third of the four wheels on which the world rests. This is called effectiveness. This is the strength and effectiveness of the Buddha's own practice.

"In contrast, the strength and effectiveness of the various teachings that are an expedient means are all flimsy and ineffective, just like an ordinary person who tries to shoot an arrow from the bow of the Buddha's grandfather. The reason is that for forty-two years those people who listened to the Buddha's instruction only received gateways to the Dharma that were a combination of the twofold wisdom of the provisional doctrines and the truth, since the principle of the Dharma of the one instant of thought containing three thousand existential spaces had not yet been broadly diffused. So those listeners had still not evolved a deep faith and had not yet exhausted all their remaining doubts.

"The above refers to the strength and effectiveness of the teachings that were for the conversion of other people. Nowadays ordinary people who have a karmic relation with the *Dharma Flower Sutra* can receive gateways to the Dharma that are a combination of the twofold wisdom of the provisional doctrines and the truth. And yet they can investigate thoroughly the karmic dimension of the Buddha, by giving rise to faith in the realm of the Dharma, by making headway on the path of the all-inclusive teaching of Utterness (*Myō*), by breaking off their fundamental perplexities, and by getting rid of fears of the changes and deviations of living and dying.

"Not only will they have the advantages and benefits of either those bodhisattvas born into mortal form who have not yet broken off their unenlightenment or the bodhisattvas who have through practice attained the patience to withstand the delusions of unenlightenment, but they will also have the advantages and benefits of either being a bodhisattva who had freed himself from pointless illusions or even a bodhisattva who is in his last incarnation who has freed himself from delusions and has attained the six universal powers acquired by the Buddha. The merit and influence of teaching and converting people is universally broad, and the advantages are deep and wide. But the power and effectiveness of the *Dharma Flower Sutra* is as powerful and effective as I have stated above."

The superiority or the inferior qualities of the power and effectiveness of the Buddha's own practice and the teachings he used in order to convert others are conspicuously clear. You should take a good look at this text from the *Recondite Significance of the Dharma Flower*. It reflects the extent of a lifetime's enlightened Buddha teaching, like a polished mirror.

"To investigate thoroughly the karmic dimension of the Buddha" points to the gateway to the Dharma of the ten ways in which dharmas make themselves present to any of our six organs of sense – eyes, ears, nose, tongue, body, and mind. These ten ways in which dharmas make themselves present to any of our six organs of sense – eyes, ears, nose, tongue, body, and mind – and the ten [psychological] realms of dharmas are mutually contained in each other. The cause and effect that lies within the ten [psychological] realms of dharmas and the ten ways in which dharmas make themselves present to any of our six organs of sense – eyes, ears, nose, tongue, body, and mind are the twofold wisdom of the individual vehicle (*hīnayāna*) and the universal vehicle (*daijō, mahāyāna*).

The nine objective realms determined by karma and the objective realm of the Buddha are all installed in our own persons. The ten [psychological] realms of dharmas are the nature of our minds. And, when the ten reams of dharmas take on a shape and form, then they become the originally enlightened Tathāgata. You must believe that all of this lies within our own persons.

"Making headway on the path of the all-inclusive teaching of Utterness (*Myō*)" means that the Buddha's own practice and the teachings he used in order to convert others are not separate from the all-inclusive accommodation of phenomenon (*ke*), relativity (*kū*), and the middle way (*chū*). In the same way as a jewel, its brilliance and its value are all the qualities of a single precious stone, which cannot be separated from it. The Dharma of the Buddha is furnished with the whole of existence, without leaving any items aside. By accepting and holding faith in the Dharma, people can open up their inherent Buddha nature within a single lifetime. Hence, people can make headway on the path of the all-inclusive teaching of Utterness, with joy and happiness.

"Cutting off our fundamental perplexities" means to wake up from the one instant of the sleep of unenlightenment and then return to the wide-awake state of the original enlightenment, so that the sufferings of living and dying and the joys of nirvana become the dream we had yesterday that leaves no trace whatsoever.

"Getting rid of the changes and deviations of living and dying" means that those people have passed over and were reborn in the three terrains of utmost joy – 1) the utmost joy of the terrain where the enlightened and ordinary people live alongside each other, 2) the utmost joy of the terrain of expedient means, and 3) the utmost joy of the terrain of real reward – where such people carry out the practices of the bodhisattvas and strive for the attainment of Buddhahood. Then, on their realisation of this attainment, they cross over from practices for the cause of enlightenment and move on to the effectiveness of ultimate fruition. They wait over many *kalpas* for the attainment of becoming a Buddha. This is referred to as the changes and deviations of living and dying.

The advancement from the practices that bring about enlightenment and the rejection of the lower stages that the practitioner has gone through implies death. The progress upwards to the various higher stages of practice is thought of as life. In this way, the changes and deviations of living and dying become the bitter worries in the immaculate terrains (i.e., the three terrains of utmost joy).

However, when we ordinary people cultivate ourselves in the practice of the *Dharma Flower Sutra* in this impure and imperfect world of ours, there is the mutual possession of the ten [psychological] realms of dharmas. Since the Dharma realm is of a single suchness, the alternating changes in the existence of the bodhisattvas of the immaculate terrains diminish, because when ordinary people intensify their practice on the Buddha path, the alternating changes of living and dying are condensed to a single lifetime, in which there exists the attainment to the way of the Buddha.

The two kinds of bodhisattvas of the temporary gateway, with human bodies, who have not broken off their unenlightenment, and those who have reached the forty-eighth or forty-ninth stages of the development of a bodhisattva into a Buddha and are also capable of perceiving the Dharma nature, on account of the increase of their wisdom of the middle way, are able to abandon their attachment to their lives that are made up of the alternating changes of living and dying. When those bodhisattvas whose entity is the Dharma, who at the same time have been able to reject a part of their troublesome worries and are also able to reveal something of their Buddha nature, relinquish the bodies they were born with, then they are able to dwell on the terrain of real reward. The bodhisattvas who are at the final stage of enlightenment are those who attained that stage of perfect and universal enlightenment.

However, the effective benefits of the temporary gateways are either to become a bodhisattva of the provisional teachings who has not yet broken off his unenlightenment or a bodhisattva who has attained through the dharma the patience to withstand the delusions of unenlightenment. The effective benefits of the original gateway are either to become a bodhisattva whose entity is the Dharma or a bodhisattva who is at the final stage before enlightenment. But now, through the temporary gateways being cleared away and the original gateway being replaced with the single teaching of the Utterness of the Dharma (*Myōhō, Saddharma*), then, according to the intensity of how we ordinary people carry out its practice in this impure and imperfect world of ours, our practice then becomes the effective benefit of the immaculate terrain of the ten stages of bodhisattva development into a Buddha and that of the perfect and universal enlightenment.

Furthermore, the merit of converting others is enormous. This refers to the virtue and benefits of proselytising. However, the vast, profound, and effective enrichment and also the enormous benefits are those derived from the personal practice of the Buddha who is the practitioner of the all-inclusive, direct teaching that is completely endowed with the one instant of mind containing three thousand existential spaces, without overlooking a single dharma. If we look at this concept horizontally, then it is as vast as the ubiquity of the dharma realms of the ten directions. From a perpendicular viewpoint, it is the utmost depth of the abyss of the Dharma nature that spans the past, present, and future. Such is the greatness of this sutra, when the personal practice of the Buddha is applied to it.

All the provisional sutras that were expounded for the conversion of others do not necessarily have the background of the Buddha's personal practice, which makes these sutras comparable to birds with only one wing, incapable of flying through the air, because fundamentally there is nobody who became a Buddha in any of these sutras. Now, by exposing and disposing of the teachings that were an expedient means for the conversion of others and then leaving them reintegrated as the temporary gateway into the one vehicle that is the Buddha's own practice, there can be nothing lacking in the Dharma whatsoever. Therefore, just as a bird with two wings can fly without hindrance, there can be nothing in the way of becoming aware that our own inherent Buddha nature is not separate from who we are now.

The Bodhisattva Sovereign Remedy (*Yaku' ō, Bhaishajya-rāja*) used ten comparisons to show the potential and effectiveness of the personal practice of the Buddha, as opposed to the teachings he used for the conversion of others.

[These ten comparisons are as follows: "Just as out of all watercourses, effluents, streams, rivulets, and great rivers the sea is the greatest, so it is the same with this *Dharma Flower Sutra*, which is the most embracing and profound out of all the sutras that the Tathāgata has expounded. Just as out of all the mountains, black mountains, the lesser inner ring of iron mountains that surround the world, and also the larger range of iron mountains that mark the boundary of this world, Mount Sumeru is the greatest, so it is the same with this *Dharma Flower Sutra* which is the highest peak among all sutras."]

["Just as, out of all the stars, the moon as prince of the *deva* is the first among the heavenly bodies at night, again it is the same with this *Dharma Flower Sutra*, which shines the brightest out of the thousands of myriads of millions of different kinds of sutric dharmas that exist. Again, just as the sun as prince of the *deva* can take away all darkness, so it is the same with this *Dharma Flower Sutra* that is able to reverse the darkness of everything that is not good."]

["Again in the same way an enlightened sovereign whose chariot wheels roll everywhere without hindrance (*tenrinnō, chakravartin*) is a monarch among all the lesser kings, it is the same with regard to this sutra, which is the most revered out of all the others. Just as Bonten (*Brahmā*) is the father of all sentient beings, it is the same with regard to this sutra, which is the parent of all those who aspire to the mind of a bodhisattva, all those who are enlightened and wise, and all those who are still studying to get rid of their delusions and those who have begun to cast them off."]

["Again, just as those whose practice is beyond the stream of transmigratory suffering, or those whose practice requires only one more lifetime before reaching nirvana, or those who have attained the supreme rewards of the individual vehicle, or those who realise nirvana for themselves and without a teacher are foremost among ordinary people, so it is the same with this sutra, whether it be expounded by the Tathāgata, or by a bodhisattva, or even by a person who has heard the Buddha's voice."]

["Out of the whole of the Dharma, this sutra is superior to all. Also the person who is able to receive and hold to this archetypal sutra takes first place among sentient beings. Just as the bodhisattvas are foremost among the hearers of the Buddha's voice and those who realise nirvana for themselves without a teacher, so it is the same with this sutra. Out of all the sutric dharmas (things), this sutra is superior to all. Just as the Buddha is the sovereign of all dharmas (things), so it is the same with this sutra that is the most important of all."]

The first of these comparisons says, "All the other sutras are like all the watercourses; the Dharma Flower is like the great sea." At least, this is the intended meaning of the quotation. In actual fact, all the watercourses of the sutras that were expounded for the conversion of others have been flowing ceaselessly day and night towards the great sea of the *Dharma Flower Sutra* that embodies the individual practice of the Tathāgata.

Nevertheless, even if these watercourses have been flowing into the great sea, the great sea itself neither diminishes nor increases, which reveals the imponderably inexplicable quality of the virtue and effectiveness of this sutra. But none of these watercourses of all the sutras, even for the slightest moment, add anything to the great sea of the *Dharma Flower Sutra*. Such is the superiority of the teaching that is derived from the Buddha's own practice, as opposed to those that were used as an expedient means.

Through the quotation of this one comparison, we have an example which covers the other nine. Yet all the comparisons are what the Buddha expounded, without any words inserted by humankind. When you have taken the meaning of this concept to heart, then the significance of the Tathāgata's lifetime of Buddha enlightened teaching will become as clear as daylight on a cloudless day. Who could have any doubts or confusion about this remark concerning the *Dharma Flower Sutra*?

Since this remark refers to the collation of the layers of teachings of all the Buddhas of the past, present, and future, I would not dare add a single word from the commentaries of the scholars of humankind. Also, this sutra is the ultimate aspiration and the reason of all the Buddhas of the past, present, and future for coming into this world. Furthermore, this sutra is the direct means for all sentient beings to become Buddhas.

The forty-two years of sutric teachings that were for the conversion of others led to the establishment of the Kegon School [the School of the *Flower Garland Sutra* (*Kegon, Avatāmsaka*)], the Shingon School [the Tantric and Mantra School], the Daruma School [the School of the teachings that were transmitted by Bodhidharma, i.e., Zen], the Jōdo School [the School of the Immaculate Terrain, i.e., Nembutsu], the Hossō School [the Consciousness-only School], the Sanron School [the School of the Three Treatises on the Middle Way], Risshū, the Ritsu School [the School of Monastic Discipline], the Kusha School [the School of the Doctrinal Store of the Dharma, *Abhidharma kosha*], and the Jōjitsu School [the School of the Establishment of the Real Meaning]. All the teachings of these schools belong to the four doctrinal periods of the eight classifications of Shākyamuni's teaching that were expounded prior to the *Dharma Flower Sutra*.

These first four doctrinal periods of the Buddha teaching the following: *i*) the combined doctrinal period in which the all-inclusive and the particular teaching were also taught during the Flower Garland period; *ii*) the teachings that were taught during the period of the individual vehicle were those of the three receptacles; *iii*) the comparative doctrinal period which corresponds to the period of the equally broad teachings, in which the doctrines of the three receptacles, the interrelated teachings, the particular teaching, and the all-inclusive teaching were contrasted with each other; and *iv*) the comprehensive doctrinal period, which is the period of the wisdom teachings that were the final preparation for the perfect teaching. These four doctrinal periods were all an expedient means to entice people towards the Dharma Flower.

This is the order in which all the Buddhas of the past, present, and future have expounded the Dharma. The fact that this order is the correct one makes this argument a discourse that is a gateway to the Dharma. If, however, the order is in some way divergent, then it cannot be the Buddha Dharma. The lifetime of instruction of the Lord of the Teaching, the Tathāgata Shākyamuni, was also founded on the precedence of doctrine, in which all the Buddhas of the past, present, and future expounded the Dharma without a single discrepancy of even one ideogram. I also expound the Dharma in exactly the same way.

In the sutra, it says, "In the same manner as all the Buddhas of the past, present, and future have expounded the Dharma, I now, in like fashion, expound the Dharma that is (a singularity) that is devoid of discrimination." If it were in any way otherwise, it would forever be in contradiction to the original intent of all the Buddhas of the past, present, and future. All the other teachers who have founded their own schools make the error of errors, by disputing the school of the Dharma Flower [the present teaching]. It is also the bewilderment of not knowing what the Buddha Dharma is about.

In the book called *A Probe into the Errors of other Doctrines*, where it refutes the arguments of these various schools, we have, "On the whole, if one were to look over the Dharma store of eighty thousand sutras, the special characteristics of the four categories of teachings that came prior to the Dharma Flower would not be at all apparent. The four categories of teachings are those of *i*) the three receptacles, *ii*) the interrelated teachings, *iii*) the particular teaching, and *iv*) the all-inclusive teachings. These four teachings first become noticeable in the sense that the three receptacles teachings were for the hearers of the Buddha's voice, the interrelated teachings were for those who were awakened due to a profound search for the meaning of life, the particular teachings were for the bodhisattvas, and the all-inclusive teachings were the Buddha vehicle.

How could the Shingon School, the Zen School, the Hossō School, the Ritsu School, the Jōjitsu School, go beyond the four categories of teaching just mentioned or any further than whatever their schools may have taught? How could they go beyond the teachings of their individual schools or their own theoretical concepts?

If I were to say that they do go beyond the four categories of teaching, then how could they not be distorting and incomplete practices outside the Buddha teaching? If I were to say that the teachings of these schools do not go any further than the four categories of teaching that came before the *Dharma Flower Sutra*, then did you have any other expectation through asking?

This is what the fruitions of the four vehicles amount to. Naturally, now that I have given you the answer, you must be sure of what you are inferring through your questioning. Through looking into the practice and study of the four categories of teaching that came prior to the Dharma Flower, I can decide what the anticipated fruitions will be. If you think I am wrong, then you must press for further answers.

In the meantime, I would like to say that, just like the *Flower Garland Sutra (Kegon, Avatāmsaka)*, each one of the five teachings of Shākyamuni's lifetime are those in which the cultivation and practice of the cause leads the practitioner towards the virtues of their fruition. [All the practices of the Buddha teachings prior to the *Dharma Flower Sutra* were conducted through fifty-two stages, right on from the first until the practitioner had reached the fifty-second stage, which was understood to be the Dharma realm of the Buddha. This quotation refers to these stages of practice as that] the first, middle, and later stages cannot become the oneness of the practice of the *Dharma Flower Sutra*.

Each single doctrine that came before the *Dharma Flower Sutra* (*Myōhō Renge Kyō*) has its own awaited fruition. If the three receptacle teachings, the interrelated teachings, the particular teachings, and the all-inclusive teachings did not have their respective causes and fruitions, they could not be the Buddha Teaching. It has to be decided as to which one of the three dharma wheels one is referring to – whether it is the dharma wheel of the basic fundamentals [the period of the teaching of the individual vehicle (*shōjō, hīnayāna*)], the dharma wheel of the branches and twigs [the period of the equally broad (*hōdō, vaipulya*) teachings], or the dharma wheel of removing the twigs and returning to the roots [the period of the wisdom (*hannya, prajña*) teachings].

By which vehicle of the Dharma are you aspiring to become enlightened?

If you say it is the Buddha vehicle, you have not yet seen the practice or the contemplation for becoming a Buddha. If you say you wish to become a bodhisattva, it is the difference between the practices of the middle way that are perpetuated over innumerable *kalpas*, whose teachings consider phenomena (*ke*), relativity (*kū*), and the middle way (*chū*) as separate entities, and the practice of the middle way, whose doctrine is based on the all-inclusive, unobstructed accommodation of phenomenon, relativity, and the middle way.

Are you able to choose the correct vehicle?

If you choose the practices of the middle way that are perpetuated over many *kalpas*, then you need not expect any fruition at all. If you make the practices of the all-inclusive, unobstructed accommodation of phenomenon, relativity, and the middle way your central point, then, with the Buddha Shākyamuni as a precedent, it is going to be difficult. Even if you were mistakenly going to start reciting mantras, you will probably not understand the destination of Utterness through perceiving the three axioms of relativity, phenomenon, and the middle way as not being separate from the oneness of the mind of sentient beings. Like many other people, I doubt that you will ever substantiate the underlying principle of Utterness.

Hence, it is a principle of our school to judge other teachings according to their ultimate aspirations. This is because, if you are looking in the direction of the wisdom sutras, the *Flower Garland*, and the *Sutra on the Buddha's Passing over to Nirvana*, you will find that these sutras are gateways to the Dharma that were used as an expedient means to entice people towards the real teaching. Such people become amenable through their propensities for the provisional teachings, which will ultimately lead them forward.

Since they are disciples who are following the individual vehicle or teachings that are distorting and incomplete, they should be brought to a level of insight that will bring them to the real teaching.

Therefore, when one is expounding, one should be aware of those people who relied on the four important principles of the practitioner These practitioners may have found it necessary in their instruction to keep the real teachings back, but they used various expedient means, until people were ready to hear what the real intention of the Buddha teaching was concerned with.

[The four principles are *i*) to practise according to the Dharma and not the person who expounds it, *ii*) to practise according to the intended significance and not the words used, *iii*) to practise according to one's inner wisdom and not according to acquired knowledge, *iv*) to practise according to the real aspect of the middle way (*chū*) as it is revealed in the *Sutra on Implications Without Bounds* and none other.]

Nevertheless, one must not become attached to these provisional doctrines. When people are inquiring into the significance of one's own school by means of the provisional teachings, one has to decide as to where these other teachings are right and where they are wrong. But on all accounts, one must not become a bigot.

Generally speaking, there are many direct, gradual, and undetermined doctrines, but only a very few have the implications of the all-inclusive teachings. This is what the virtuous universal teacher of the past had decided, when all the teachings of every school were held up to the bright light of day and set in order. The scholars of the final period are not aware of this. They are confused and cannot make judgements with regard to the gateways of the Buddha teaching. It is important that people make a thorough study of the three teachings that lead to the *Dharma Flower Sutra*.

There are three categories of teaching – the direct, the gradual, and the all-inclusive. Generally speaking, these three doctrinal categories were the three ways in which the truth was imparted during Shākyamuni's lifetime of the Buddha enlightened teaching. The direct and gradual doctrines were taught over a period of forty-two years, and, for the most part, the all-inclusive teaching was revealed during the last eight years of Shākyamuni's life. Altogether this makes the fifty years of teaching, outside of which there is no other Dharma.

How is it that people can get so mixed up about this fact?

As long as we are sentient beings, we talk in terms of the categories of teaching as representing the all-inclusive accommodation of phenomena (*ke*), relativity (*kū*), and the middle way (*chū*). But when we attain to the fruition of becoming Buddhas, we then talk about the three bodies of the Tathāgata. These are two different ways of saying the same thing.

To give a further explanation, what I have just said implies the lifetime of Buddha enlightened teaching of the Tathāgata. When we fully realise this, it becomes the total singularity of the all-inclusive accommodation of phenomena (*ke*), relativity (*kū*), and the middle way (*chū*).

This was taught in terms of the direct teaching of the *Flower Garland Sutra* as being the axiom of relativity, all the gradual teachings of the individual vehicle, the *Equally Broad* and *Wisdom Sutras* as being the axiom of phenomenon, and the *Dharma Flower Sutra* as being the axiom of the middle way. This is what the Tathāgata taught in conformity with his own enlightenment.

Furthermore, there are eight of the established schools outside our own that classify the three axioms of phenomena (*ke*), relativity (*kū*), and the middle way (*chū*) as being the constituents of the lifetime of the Buddha enlightened teaching of the Tathāgata. But according to the doctrine propounded by each of these schools, all of them lack the principle of being all-inclusive and completely filling the whole, thereby making it impossible for people to open up their inherent Buddha nature. This is the reason why all the other schools have no real Buddha.

What I dislike about these schools is their insufficiency of meaning. By taking the all-inclusive teaching, one can contemplate each and every dharma. Since the all-inclusive teaching is the unobstructed accommodation of phenomena (*ke*), relativity (*kū*), and the middle way (*chū*), as well as being the all-inclusive, replenished whole of the one instant of mind containing three thousand existential spaces (*ichinen sanzen*), it is like the full moon of the fifteenth night of every lunar month.

Because the all-inclusive teaching is the final superlative, it is absolutely perfect without any deficiency. It is beyond the dualities of good and bad, choosing the occasion, or seeking quiet places, or even personal qualities. Since you know that all dharmas (things) are entirely the Buddha Dharma, there is nothing that cannot be fathomed or understood. Therefore, even if you take the path of wrongdoing and injustice, (you will learn sooner or later through your negative experiences), through the fivefold wisdom of the Tathāgata, which is relativity, earth, water, fire, and wind.

This fivefold wisdom dwells in the minds of all sentient beings and is not separated from them, for even an instant. This fivefold wisdom exists harmoniously in our minds, both in the realms of existence or in the hereafter. Outside our own minds there are no dharmas whatsoever. Therefore, when you hear (or read) this, you will, just where you are standing at this very moment, attain the fruition of becoming aware of your own inherent Buddha nature and in no time will be able to reason your way through to the ultimate realisation.

This all-inclusive accommodation of phenomena (*ke*), relativity (*kū*), and the middle way (*chū*) was taught, in terms of the direct teaching of the *Flower Garland Sutra* (*Kegon, Avatāmsaka*), as being the doctrine of the axiom of relativity (*kū*), all the gradual teachings of the individual vehicle (*shōjō, hīnayāna*), the equally broad (*hōdō, vaipulya*) and wisdom (*hannya, prajña*) sutras as representing the axiom of phenomenon (*ke*), and the *Dharma Flower Sutra* (*Myōhō Renge Kyō*) as representing the middle way (*chū*).

These three categories of teaching could be compared to a gem, its brilliance, and the piece of jewellery in which it consists. On account of these three virtues, we talk of this all-inclusive accommodation of phenomena (*ke*), relativity (*kū*), and the middle way (*chū*) as the precious talismanic stone, capable of responding to every wish (*mani*) – hence, the metaphor of the three axioms. Were these three virtues to be separated from each other, then any effectiveness this gem possessed would be of no avail.

So it is the same with the schools whose teachings are the expedient means, which have to be practised over periods of separate *kalpas*. The gem is a metaphor for the Dharma body, its brilliance is analogous to the reward body, and the piece of jewellery itself is a metaphor for the corresponding body. If schools are founded upon partialities of the all-inclusive accommodation of phenomena (*ke*), relativity (*kū*), and the middle way (*chū*), one should have no use for them, due to their incompleteness. However, when all is said and done, the all-inclusive accommodation of the triple axiom is a oneness that is the inseparability of the three bodies from the single embodiment of the originally enlightened Tathāgata.

Furthermore, the terrain of silence and illumination is comparable to a mirror. The other three terrains –*i*) where the enlightened and ordinary people dwell alongside each other, *ii*) the terrain of expedient means, where its occupants still have the remains of misunderstanding to be cleared away, and *iii*) the land of the reward of enlightenment – in reality are the images that are reflected in that mirror. These four terrains are in fact a single terrain. The three bodies of the Tathāgata –*i*) the Dharma body, *ii*) the entity of wisdom, and *iii*) the person (i.e., manifestation) that corresponds to the needs of sentient beings – are the constituents of the one Buddha. Now, when these three bodies are joined in harmony with the four terrains, they become the virtue of the one entity of the Buddha that we refer to as the Buddha enlightenment of silence and illumination.

With the Buddha of silence and illumination becoming the Buddha of the all-inclusive teaching, then the Buddha of the all-inclusive teaching becomes the awakening to the enlightenment of the Buddha in reality. The Buddha in the three remaining terrains is the provisional Buddha in the midst of the dream.

But when all the Buddhas of the past, present, and future used the same modes of expression in collating their doctrines into a coherent definitive teaching, they did not use the terms of ordinary speech, nor did they give any discursive explanations that could be contradicted. If these definitive teachings had in any way been different from each other, then it would have been the enormous wrongdoing of someone who opposes the teaching of all the Buddhas of the past, present, and future – such as one of the Demonic Deva outside the Buddha path, who has for ages been opposed to the Buddha Dharma.

This esoteric treasure [the Fundamental Object of Veneration (*gohonzon*)] is to be kept hidden, so as not to let it be seen by profane people. If this esoteric treasure were not hidden, it would be bandied about in the open, and any substantiation of its intrinsicality through practice would be lost. Thus people would be left, in this present life and in their lives that are yet to come, to be eclipsed in an ever-increasing darkness. This is because both the people who vilify this Dharma and who turn their backs on all the Buddhas of the past, present, and future as well as those people who listen to these misguided concepts will fall into the paths of evil. It is on this account that I am letting you know and cautioning you against committing such an error.

You must make the effort to substantiate the intrinsicality of this esoteric treasure through your practice, since this is what all the Buddhas of the past, present, and future originally had in mind. The two enlightened persons, the Bodhisattva Sovereign Remedy (*Yaku' ō, Bhaishajya-rāja*) and the Bodhisattva Giver of Courage (*Yuze, Pradhānashura*), along with the two Universal Guardian Deva Kings, Jikoku and Bishamon, as well as the Rakshashi Kishimojin and her daughters, will watch over you and protect you. When you die you will be immediately reborn in the ultimate supreme terrain of silence and illumination.

But should you for the shortest while return to the dream of living and dying, your person [Dharma entity] will completely fill all the realm of dharmas of the ten directions, and your mind will be in the physical incarnations of all sentient beings. You will urge them on towards enlightenment from within, and on the outside you will show these sentient beings which path to take. Since there is a mutual correspondence between what is on the inside and what is on the outside, as well as there being a harmony between causes and karmic circumstances, you will busy yourself with the immense compassion that lies in the fullness of the reaches of your mind that is independently free to effectively benefit all sentient beings simultaneously.

What was in the mind of all the Buddhas of the past, present, and future, with regard to the one universal matter of the cause and karmic circumstances for making their appearance in the world [existential spaces], is that 'one' stands for the middle way and the *Dharma Flower Sutra* (*Myōhō Renge Kyō*); 'universal' represents the axiom of relativity and the *Flower Garland Sutra* (*Kegon, Avatāmsaka*); 'matter' refers to the axiom of phenomenon and the individual vehicle, the equally broad and wisdom (*hannya, prajña*) teachings.

What the above implies is that the all-inclusive accommodation of the axioms of relativity, phenomenon, and the middle way were taught throughout the lifetime of Shākyamuni, in terms of the direct teaching of the *Flower Garland Sutra* (*Kegon, Avatāmsaka*), as being the teaching of the axiom of relativity (*kū*), all the gradual teachings of the individual vehicle (*shōjō, hīnayāna*), the equally broad (*hōdō, vaipulya*) and wisdom (*hannya, prajña*) sutras as representing the axiom of phenomenon (*ke*), and the Dharma Flower as representing the axiom of the middle way (*chū*).

When you know and fully realise the implications of this all-inclusive accommodation of these three axioms, it means that your fundamental motive for coming into the world is to take the direct path for becoming enlightened. As for the 'cause', it is this all-inclusive accommodation of these three axioms that exist everlastingly and unchangingly in the midst of the incarnations of all sentient beings. This is generally referred to as the 'cause'.

Although 'karmic circumstances' may be said to be the triple aspect of the Buddha nature – which is *i*) the direct cause for becoming enlightened due to our innate Buddha nature, *ii*) the cause for becoming enlightened through being able to perceive the intrinsicality of the Dharma nature, and *iii*) the karmic circumstances that bring about the revelation of our own inherent Buddha nature – if the karmic circumstances do not exist for meeting a good friend who can stimulate you towards the Buddha wisdom, you will never be aware of it, or know it, or have it revealed to you.

On the other hand, due to the karmic circumstances of meeting a good friend who stimulates you towards the Buddha wisdom, you will certainly have it revealed to you as the Fundamental Object of Veneration (*gohonzon*) – hence, the use of the term 'karmic circumstances' or concomitancies being needed in the expression 'the one universal matter of the cause and karmic circumstances for the Buddha's coming into the world'. Nevertheless, by putting these five words of 'the one', 'universal', 'matter of', 'cause' and 'karmic circumstances' together, then you have met the difficultly-encountered good friend who stimulates you towards the Buddha wisdom.

Why are you still procrastinating?

When spring comes, due to the karmic circumstances of wind and rain, this season is when all the trees and plants whose minds are without consciousness start sprouting shoots and buds, which later become the blossoms and the carpet of flowers that greet the world with a feeling of light and colourfulness. When the autumn comes, it is due to the brightness of the moon that all the plants produce and all of the fruits of the trees become ripe, in order to sustain all sentient beings. Then, on account of the nourishing qualities of all of this produce, the lives of people are prolonged. In the end, they will reveal the enormous virtue of their role of having become Buddhas.

Is there anyone who doubts this or cannot believe it? If the plants and trees that are devoid of consciousness can do such things, then why not humankind, that is endowed with a natural sense of right and wrong?

Even though we are bewildered common mortals, at least we are endowed with enough mind and understanding to be able to know whether something is good or bad. However, with the entrenched karmic circumstances that have their origin in former lives, you were born in a country (terrain and abode) that has been receptive to the dissemination of the Buddha Dharma. Therefore, you should be able to discriminate the cause and fruition of having met the good friend who has urged you towards the Buddha wisdom.

Nevertheless, through having met this good friend, you ought to be a person who should be aware that your inherent Buddha nature is not separate from who you are now.

Do you mean to say you that are going to remain silent and show even less than what the plants and trees have of the threefold aspect of the Buddha nature that is within your own person?

This time you must, by all means, dissipate your illusions about the dream of living and dying and cut away the bonds of successive lives and deaths, by returning to the arousal of the original awakening. From now onwards, you must not get yourself taken in by the gateways to the dharmas (things) within the dream. You must open up an all-pervasive enlightenment, by cultivating yourself in the practice of reciting Nam Myōhō Renge Kyō, with your whole mind in perfect harmony with all the Buddhas of the past, present, and future.

[Nam Myōhō Renge Kyō means to devote our lives to and found them on (Nam[u]) the Utterness of the Dharma (Myōhō) (entirety of existence, enlightenment and unenlightenment) permeated by the underlying white lotus flower-like mechanism of the interdependence of cause, concomitancy and effect (Renge) in its whereabouts of the ten (psychological) realms of dharmas (Kyō).]

The difference between the teaching of the Buddha's own practice and the doctrines that the Buddha used for the conversion of others is as clear as the daylight on a cloudless day. The collation of the layers of the various teachings of all the Buddhas of the past, present, and future is precise about this point. This must be kept secret.

The tenth month of the second year of Kō.an [1279]
Nichiren

Translator's Note on the *Sō Kan Mon Shō*

Nichiren Daishōnin's Writing, here entitled, *A Collation of the Layers of the Various Teachings of all the Buddhas of the Past, Present and Future as to Which Specific Doctrines are to be Discarded or Established*, is also known as, *A General Collation of the Teaching of All the Buddhas of the Past, Present and Future so as to be able to Decide which Doctrines are to be Discarded or Established* (*Sanze Shōbutsu sō Kanmon Kyōsō hairyu*) [page 558 *Goshō Zenshū* & page 1408 *Goshō Shimpen*], as well as under the shorter title, "A General Collation of the Teachings of all the Buddhas of the Past, Present and Future" (*Sanze Shōbutsu sō Kanmon Shō*), or simply as a *General Collation of the Teachings* (*Sō Kan Mon Shō*).

This Writing was written in the tenth month of 1279, in Minobu, when Nichiren was fifty-eight. This was also the same year as the Dharma persecution in Atsuhara, when the people showed such a strong faith that Nichiren felt the time had come for him to realize his lifelong wish. On the twelfth day of the tenth month of that year, he inscribed the Fundamental Object of Veneration of the Altar of the Precept (*Kaidan no Gohonzon*).

Nevertheless, it is not definite that this writing was drawn up in 1279, and, even if some scholars insist that the recipient was Toki Jōnin, it is not recorded in *The Records of the Eternal Teacher of Enlightened Doctrine* (*Jōshi Seikyō Mokuroku*). No one has been pointed out as its recipient. Because of the quotations from Tendai, as well as the general discourse being comparable to the *Treatise on the Significance of the Actual Fundamental Substance* (*Tōtai Gi Shō*), this indicates that Sairenbō might have been the person to whom this Writing was addressed.

What the title of this treatise indicates is that, during the lifetime of Shākyamuni's teaching of the Dharma, the first forty-two years were the provisional teachings (*gonkyō*) that were an expedient means in order to convert other people, and that these should be discarded. But during the following eight years, Shākyamuni taught the real teaching of his own practice, which was the *Dharma Flower Sutra* (*Myōhō Renge Kyō*).

However, this doctrinal process is exactly the same as that of all the Buddhas of the past, present, and future. This is made clear in the *Second Chapter on Expedient Means of the Dharma Flower Sutra*, where it says, "It is the same method of the Buddhas in general – the Buddhas of the past, present, and future, the Buddhas of the present as well as Shākyamuni – to clear away the provisional teachings in order to reveal the truth."

Also, in the *Writing on Revealing Slander*, it says, "The Tathāgata Shākyamuni and the Buddhas of the past, present, and future all come into the world to expound each one of the sutras. So why should the *Dharma Flower Sutra* of the Buddhas not be the foremost?"

In the *General Collation*, the term "all the Buddhas" means that "all the Buddhas took into consideration all the texts and made a decision about them *in exactly the same way*. The word "general (*sō*)" has a dual significance. On the one hand, it refers to the person of the Buddhas and, on the other, it refers to the Dharma. When this word refers to the person of the Buddhas, it means all Buddhas of the past, present, and future, in exactly the same way.... In terms of the Dharma, it refers to the general principle of the Buddhas' three ways of teaching, which were either 1) directly, 2) gradually, or 3) neither one way nor the other, i.e., undetermined. Furthermore, in order to induce people to take refuge in the *Dharma Flower Sutra*, he generally arranged his teachings according to the triple axiom of existence – relativity (*kū*), phenomena (*ke*), or the middle way (*chū*).

By including both the Dharma as well as the person of the Daishōnin, we can begin to have a correct understanding of this Writing. Apart from the quotations from the *Dharma Flower Sutra*, Nichiren quotes the *Sutra on Implications Without Bounds* (*Muryōgi-kyō*), by saying, "For forty years I have not revealed the true reality."

Among the more relevant sentences from the *Dharma Flower Sutra*, Nichiren emphasizes this passage from the *Chapter on Expedient Means*: "As to the way in which all the Buddhas of the past, present, and future have expounded the Dharma, I also do the same, without any difference whatsoever." He then goes on to quote, "Among all the Buddha lands of the ten directions, there is the only one Buddha vehicle that leads to enlightenment; there are neither two, nor are there three." Further on, in another quote, it says, "There is only one reason and karmic circumstance for All the World Honoured Buddhas coming into and appearing in realms of existence."

As to "which of the Doctrines are to be Established or Discarded", obviously this refers to the content of the *Dharma Flower Sutra*. All the provisional teachings that are an expedient means are to be discarded, and the true reality is to be established.

Hence, on account of not having revealed the true reality for forty or so years, all these provisional teachings of Shākyamuni – that were those of the *Flower Garland Sutra* (*Kegon, Avatāmsaka*), those of the Individual Vehicle (*Agon*), the doctrines of the Equally Broad (*Hōdō, vaipulya*) period, as well as those of the Wisdom (*Hannya, prajña*) period – were either taught directly, or gradually, or in some way that is undetermined.

But since all these teachings were an expedient means specifically directed at people living in a dream state of existence that did not have the foundation of an awareness of the ever-present, original archetypal state (*hommon*), Nichiren said that all these teachings were to be set aside and people were to immediately start reciting the theme and title of the Dharma Flower (*daimoku*), which in itself is the original gateway to enlightenment (*hommon*). Nam Myōhō Renge Kyō implies devoting one's life to and basing it on the interdependence of cause and effect which is inherent throughout the whole of existence.

Returning to the point, the title of this Writing should be understood as Nichiren Daishōnin deciding, after examining the content of all the teachings of all the Buddhas of the past, present, and future, as to which of these doctrines should be abandoned and which should be established, whereupon Nichiren set up the Three Esoteric Dharmas, i.e., the Fundamental Object of Veneration of the Original Gateway (to enlightenment), the Altar of the Precept of the Original Gateway, and the Title and Theme of the Original Gateway.

The general subject matter of the Writing begins with the statement that the teachings of Shākyamuni can be divided into two parts – first, those that were taught for the forty-two years before the *Dharma Flower Sutra*, and, secondly, the eight years of the teaching of the *Dharma Flower Sutra* that followed. Again I will repeat that all the teachings of Shākyamuni that were expounded prior to those of the *Dharma Flower Sutra* were all expedient means designated for the conversion of others, whereas the *Dharma Flower Sutra* itself represents Shākyamuni's vision of the whole of existence, which stems from his practice and refers to actual reality. The sutras that came prior to the Dharma Flower refer to a dream world without any foundation; on the other hand, the *Dharma Flower Sutra* entails a wakefulness that is perfectly attuned to reality.

The teachings prior to the *Dharma Flower Sutra* are immersed in the nine realms of dharmas (*jikkai*), of 1) suffering, 2) wants, needs, and desires, 3) animality, 4) the ego trip, 5) human equanimity, 6) temporary joyfulness, 7) the intellectual seekers, 8) those who are partially awakened due to a profound search for the meaning of existence, and 9) the altruists (*bodhisattvas*). But the *Dharma Flower Sutra* itself expounds the indestructible and the eternal Dharma realm of the enlightened (*bukkai*). All this is simply because, in the *Sutra on Implications Without Bounds* (*Muryōgi-kyō*), it states, "I have not revealed the true reality (of things) for forty or so years."

The second part of this Writing goes on to explain the way things are in general, when it comes to the gateways to enlightenment in the teaching that were solely for the benefit of others. Nichiren comments upon the teachings that came before the *Dharma Flower Sutra* as teachings devoid of a person who has become enlightened through them and that these teachings are for a dream-world that is only for the time being. Shākyamuni's intention was that the provisional teachings were to prepare his listeners, before they were to take part in the assembly where he taught the *Dharma Flower Sutra*.

The third section of this Writing goes on to explain that the practice of the Dharma Flower was what the Buddha himself carried out. Then this Writing clearly establishes the position of the dream in contrast to being wide-awake, in order to explain the significance of Utterness (*Myō*) as understood by the assembly of the *Dharma Flower Sutra*.

Nichiren explains that no dharmas can exist outside the workings of the mind and its perceptions. He also discusses the real aspect (*jissō*) of the ten ways in which dharmas make themselves present to any of our six sense organs – eyes, ears, nose, tongue, body, and mind (*nyoze*), which must imply that all dharmas are the oneness of mind and that the Buddha and ordinary people are not two separate entities, which is the Utterness of the unimaginable. This is made somewhat clearer through the metaphors of the fan and the mountains that partially hide the moon. In addition to this, we have the story of Chuang Tzū being a butterfly for a hundred years.

This leads to each of the ten [psychological] realms of dharmas being endowed with the same three existential spaces (*jikkai gogu*). Then we have the evidence that bewilderment and enlightenment are not separate from each other, whereupon becoming aware of our own Buddha nature is not separate from who we are now and our respective personalities. This is followed by the dissertation on our persons not being in any way apart from heaven and earth or the whole of the Dharma realms, and that we should never doubt that we can open up our inherent Buddha nature with our personalities just as they are.

The fourth section of this Writing continues, with Nichiren saying that "beyond the depths in our own mind" was expressed in the India of Shākyamuni as the uncountable grains of dust that would amount to the granules that would be left over, if someone were to grind five hundred universes, starting with their respective beginnings and also their extinctions. This can also be understood as the ever-present infinite in time (*kuon ganjo*), or literally as the incredibly long period as described in the Sixteenth Chapter of the *Dharma Flower Sutra*, which points to the time before the original Buddha became enlightened (*gohyaku jintengo*).

He says, "When I was simply a common mortal, I realized that my body was composed of water, earth, fire, wind, and relativity (*kū*) (i.e., the components of the universe); thereupon I became enlightened." This action of the Daishōnin indicates that he became inseparable (*soku*) from the function of the self-received wisdom body of the Tathāgata in the ever-present infinite in time (*kuon ganjo*).

In the fifth paragraph, Nichiren talks about the power, as well as the advantages and disadvantages, of the teachings that were for the benefit of others and those which the Buddha practised for himself. Here he quotes and explains various sutric texts, encourages and gives incentives for ordinary people of the final era of the teachings of Shākyamuni (*mappō*) to practise the teaching that he propounds.

In the sixth part of this Writing, Nichiren discusses in general terms the triple axiom of phenomena (*ke*), noumena (*kū*), and the middle way of reality (*chu*), in the enlightened teachings of Shākyamuni's lifetime, stressing the point that one should know thoroughly the difference between the sutras through which one can attain enlightenment and those through which illumination is not possible. In particular, he reveals the merits and effectiveness of holding faith in the Utterness of the Dharma (*Myōhō, Saddharma*) of the all-embracing teachings.

In the seventh and last passage, Nichiren points out the reason and the karmic circumstances for bringing about the appearance of the Buddha in the world of humankind (*ichi daiji innen*). Defining himself as the ordinary person of the final period of the Buddha teaching of Shākyamuni (*mappō*), Nichiren rejoices at being able to be a good friend of the people of his own time.

Also, he says that, if people carry out the practice of reciting *Nam Myōhō Renge Kyō*, they will certainly be able to open up their inherent Buddha nature.

[Nam Myōhō Renge Kyō means to devote our lives to and found them on (Nam[u]) the Utterness of the Dharma (Myōhō) (entirety of existence, enlightenment and unenlightenment) permeated by the underlying white lotus flower-like mechanism of the interdependence of cause, concomitancy and effect (Renge) in its whereabouts of the ten (psychological) realms of dharmas (Kyō).]

"All the Buddhas of the past, present, and future, with a singularity of mind, practised the reciting of Nam Myōhō Renge Kyō and were able without any hindrance to open up their inherent illumination."

The difference between the teachings that the Buddhas themselves practised and these that they taught in order to entice other people is as clear as night and day. The consideration that all the Buddhas of the past, present, and future gave to all the sutric texts was done in this manner. Nichiren ends this Writing by saying that this is an esoteric teaching that is not to be bandied about to all and sundry.

Broadly speaking, this Writing has eight illustrative examples – which are that 1) the provisional teachings refer to the dream of living and dying, whereas the true doctrines refer to wide-awake reality; 2) all streams and rivers flow towards the great sea; 3) the metaphor of the fan, the trees, the wind, and the moon; 4) the reflection of the moon in the water and the moon in the sky; 5) the three kinds of plants, the two kinds of tree, and the one rain that nourishes the single earth; 6) the front and back of a mirror; 7) the wish-granting jewel, the gem, its shininess, and its value; 8) the substance and the use of the mirror.

These eight metaphors all go to show that the *Dharma Flower Sutra* (*Myōhō Renge Kyō*) is the only teaching that relates to reality. Again, towards the end of this Writing, Nichiren briefly describes the wisdom and the practical knowledge of what it means to be enlightened.

Martin Bradley

The Matter of Accepting and Undertaking to Serve the Three Esoteric Dharmas

San Dai Hihō Shō
Goshō Shimpen, pp. 1593-1596

The eighth day of the fourth month of the fifth year of Kō.an [1282], at 61 years of age

In the *Twenty-First Chapter on the Reaches of the Mind of the Tathāgata* that is in the seventh fascicle of the *Dharma Flower Sutra*, it says, "But if I should state the essentials, then all the dharmas in the possession of the Tathāgata, all the reaches of the mind at the will of the Tathāgata, the whole of the esoteric and quintessential ingredient [of the enlightenment] of the Tathāgata [Nam Myōhō Renge Kyō], as well as all the other extremely profound matters of the Tathāgata, would all be proclaimed, revealed, disclosed, and made clear in this sutra."

In the explanation, it says, "In the discourse of the essentials, in the *Dharma Flower Sutra*, the term 'essentials' is applied to four issues." In the *Twenty-First Chapter on the Reaches of the Mind of the Tathāgata* in the *Dharma Flower Sutra*, it says, "This is why after the Tathāgata's extinction into nirvana you must single-mindedly hold to this sutra, as well as reading, reciting, explaining its meaning, and copying it out, not to mention carrying out the practice as I have told you."

Question: What in fact are the essentials of the Dharma that was expounded?

Answer: An explanation involves starting from the time that the Honoured One of the Shakyas attained to the way for the first time in his historical lifetime, to the teachings of the three receptacles, the interrelated teachings, and the particular teaching of the fourth

409

flavour, up to the sitting where he established the broad clearance of the three vehicles, in order to reveal the one. Then, after generally clearing away the notion that he was first enlightened in his present lifetime, he showed that he had attained to the way in the primordial infinity of time, by summoning the hitherto hidden bodhisattvas who sprang up from the earth. The proof of this attainment to the real aspect through self-cultivation and practice in the primordial infinity is the Fundamental Object of Veneration (*gohonzon*), the altar of the precept, and the five ideograms of the title and the theme, Nam Myōhō Renge Kyō – which means to devote our lives to and found them on (*Nam[u]*) the Utterness of the Dharma (*Myōhō*) [entirety of existence, enlightenment and unenlightenment] permeated by the underlying white lotus flower-like mechanism of the interdependence of cause, concomitancy and effect (*Renge*) in its whereabouts of the ten [psychological] realms of dharmas (*Kyō*) – that belong to the *Sixteenth Chapter on the Lifespan*.

The Lord of the Teaching Shākyamuni, without concealing any of these esoteric dharmas during the past, present, and future, did not even transmit them to Fugen (*Samantabhadra*) or Mañjushrī (*Monjushiri*), let alone to any lesser beings. As a result, the way in which the ceremony of the exposition of these esoteric dharmas took place differs from the three teachings of the four flavours and the fourteen chapters of the provisional teachings of the *Dharma Flower Sutra*, because where it was possible to perform this ceremony could only be in the inherently infinite abode and terrain of silence and illumination.

The Lord of the Teaching who was able to perform this ceremony is the triple body that is inherently infinite and free from all karma, and those who are converted by this ceremony are also of the same fundamental substance. It was at this moment that the Tathāgata's highly praised followers, from the primordial infinity with Jōgyō at the head of the four Bodhisattvas, were summoned up all the way from the silence and illumination underneath the great earth and were entrusted with the assignment of the broad propagation of this teaching. Dōsen, the Teacher of Monastic Rules, said, "Because the Dharma is that which is grounded on the attainment in primordiality, it is the people who were enlightened in the primordial infinity who are those that belong to its teaching."

Question: With regard to the gateway to the Dharma of those who were entrusted with its propagation, at what period after the Buddha's passing over to nirvana should they broadly disseminate this teaching?

Answer: In the seventh fascicle in the *Twenty-third Chapter on the Bodhisattva Sovereign Medicine* (*Yaku'ō, Bhaishajya-rāja*), it says, "During the first five hundred years of the final phase of the Dharma of Shākyamuni (*mappō*), there will be throughout the world of mankind a wide diffusion, without ever letting it come to an end." If we with reverence conscientiously look at the sutric texts, we see that the period referred to after that Buddha's passing over to nirvana lies beyond the two thousand years of the correct and formal phases of the Dharma. The fifth five hundred years are referred to as the period of "fighting and quarrelling having become firmly established and the white Dharma having sunk into nothingness".

Question: Since the loving-kindness of all the Buddhas is like the moon in the sky and if the waters of circumstances and propensities are clear, then its life-transforming radiance is cast upon all the waters everywhere that are able to reflect it. How is it then that, out of the three eras of the correct, formal, and final phases of the Dharma of Shākyamuni (*mappō*), it is only in the final phase where the loving-kindness of the Buddha seems to be particularly apparent?

Answer: Even though the shining moon of all the Buddhas has harmonious beams that benefit all things and lighten up the darkness of the nine realms of dharmas, it cannot reflect its image upon the sludgy water of the person of incorrigible unbelief who slanders the Dharma.

Before people had the necessary capacities for the thousand years of the correct phase of the Dharma, there was only the individual vehicle and the teaching of the provisional universal vehicle to which they could really adapt. The thousand years of the formal phase were when the propensities of the people corresponded to the temporary gateway of the *Dharma Flower Sutra*.

Now, during the first five hundred years of the final phase of the Dharma of Shākyamuni (*mappō*), people who have the propensity to comply with this teaching should put aside all the chapters of the *Dharma Flower Sutra* that come before the *Sixteenth Chapter on the Lifespan of the Tathāgata*, as well as the thirteen chapters of the original gateway that come after it, and only spread abroad the one *Chapter on the Lifespan of the Tathāgata*.

Even during the last five hundred years of the formal phase of the Dharma, the propensities of mankind were not suited to this one *Chapter on the Lifespan of the Tathāgata* which belongs to the original gateway, not to mention the first five hundred years of this period. How is it then that, even if the propensities for the correct phase of the Dharma may have been only a temporary gateway, its power to do good has faded away?

It is also the same with the original gateway. Having already entered into the final phase of the Dharma of Shākyamuni, the teachings that came before the *Dharma Flower Sutra*, as well as those of the temporary gateway, are no longer a means to be free from the cycle of living and dying. However, I must stress that the one *Chapter on the Lifespan of the Tathāgata* that belongs to the original gateway is the only fundamental Dharma that will liberate us from the rotation of lives and deaths. All the Buddhas in their guidance and redemption are entirely without discrimination.

In the three periods of the correct, formal, and final phases of the Dharma, which followed the Buddha's passing over to nirvana, the assignments and affiliation of those who were converted by the original or temporary gateways are apparently clear. But the limitation of the one *Chapter on the Lifespan of the Tathāgata* as being for the benefit of the impure and evil people of the final phase does not seem to be very obvious in the sutric text. I would like to hear the passage in the sutra that reveals it. What do you have to say?

Answer: Just as you are forced to ask this question, then, when you hear the answer you must hold to a potent faith. It says, in the *Chapter on the Lifespan of the Tathāgata*, which I have just referred to, "This excellent medicine that will do you good, I will now leave it here so that you should accept it and take it. You must not torment yourselves in any way that it cannot cure you."

Question: The sutric text that particularises the benefits of the *Chapter on the Lifespan of the Tathāgata* as being limited to the evil age of the final phase of the Dharma is self-evident, so I will not trouble you further on that point. Nevertheless, what do you have to say about the substance of the three esoteric Dharmas?

Answer: In terms of the all-embracing concern of my own mind, it is the uttermost. Listen with undivided attention, and I will explain it in part.

The Fundamental Object of Veneration (*gohonzon*) of the *Chapter on the Lifespan of the Tathāgata* was set up in a past, prior to a period of time that would amount to the grains of dust that go into the making of five hundred *kalpas*. The infinitely existing triple body independent of all karma, by having a deep and close relation with this terrain, is therefore the Shākyamuni, Lord of this Teaching.

In the *Sixteenth Chapter on the Lifespan of the Tathāgata*, it refers to "the esoteric and inaccessible reaches of the mind of the Tathāgata". Also, in the *Preliminary Study of the Dharma Flower*, it says, "By putting a name to the one body not being separate from the three bodies, it would be 'esoteric'. Then, by putting a name to the three bodies not being separate from the one body, it would be 'inaccessible'. Again, to put a name to that which had never been expounded since time immemorial would be called 'esoteric'. To put a name to what only the Buddha himself knows would be called 'inaccessible'. The Buddha is equally in possession of the three bodies throughout the past, present, and future. Because this matter is esoteric, it is not transmitted in the other doctrines."

The theme and title have two implications. One refers to the correct and formal phases of the Dharma, and the other to the final phase. During the correct phase, the theme and title that was chanted by the Bodhisattva Tenjin (*Vasubandhu*) and the Bodhisattva Nāgārjuna (*Ryūju*) was solely for their own practice, so we will not go into it. During the formal phase of the Dharma, the *Nam Myōhō Renge Kyō* that was recited by Nangaku (*Nan-yüeh*) and Tendai (*T'ien T'ai*) was also for themselves. However, its meaning was barely taught for the conversion of others. These instances are the theme and title of the practice in theory.

Having entered into the final phase of the Dharma, the title and theme that is chanted by Nichiren is different from that of former ages. It is the *Nam Myōhō Renge Kyō,* which comprises both practising for oneself and for the benefit and the conversion of others. It is the five ideograms for the five recondite aspects that go to prove the superiority of the sutra [through *i*) precisely explaining the title, *ii*) defining what it ultimately embodies, *iii*) making clear what it implies, *iv*) discussing its merits and range of influence, *v*) by deciding as to which teaching the sutra belongs].

[Nam Myōhō Renge Kyō means to devote our lives to and found them on (*Nam*[*u*]) the Utterness of the Dharma (*Myōhō*) (entirety of existence, enlightenment and unenlightenment) permeated by the underlying white lotus flower-like mechanism of the interdependence of cause, concomitancy and effect (*Renge*) in its whereabouts of the ten (psychological) realms of dharmas (*Kyō*).]

When it comes to the altar of the precept, it will be when the laws of the state become subsidiary to those of the Dharma of the Buddha and the laws of the sovereign are in harmony with the Buddha teaching. The sovereign and his ministers will hold to the three esoterically inaccessible dharmas, so that King Utoku and the Bikkhu Kakutoku of ancient times will be transported to the future. Then, through a royal decree and an edict from the Patriarch, would they not then visit the most high and eminent slope, which resembles the pure land of Spirit Vulture Peak (*Ryojusen, Gridhrakūta*), and establish the altar of the precept?

It is only a matter of waiting for when the time is ripe. [This is what is called the Dharma of the altar of the precept in practical terms.] Not only in India, China, and Japan, but throughout the world of humankind, there has never been a Dharma of the altar of the precept where people could remorsefully repent and clear away their sins. It will be an altar of the precept where such Universal Deva Kings as Bonten (*Brahmā*) and Taishaku will descend to earth and place their feet upon the mountain where it stands.

After this altar has been set up, the altar of the precept in Enryakuji Temple will probably be a place that is of little advantage, since it is an altar of the temporary gateway and of the precept in principle only. Contrary to all expectation, the third and the fourth patriarchs Jikaku and Chishō, who came after the enthroned Lord and founder of the Tendai School on Mount Hiei, went against the teaching of their precursors Dengyō (*Dengyō Daishi*) and Gishin. Jikaku and Chishō evolved the ridiculous argument that both the theoretical and the practical were equally superior, thus holding in contempt the altar of the precept of the mountain of the school where it was taught. Through their slanderous and frivolous dissertations, the altar of the precept of Enryakuji Temple was left beyond the pale of their thoughts. It was to be the purely immaculate and unsullied altar of the precept of the middle way, but it would not be saying too much that the disciples had turned it into slush and mud.

What is there to do but lament? The monastery on Mount Mari (*Malaya*) in south India must be no more than tiles and stony rubble, and the groves of Sandalwood trees are reduced to a waste of thorns. Why should then those scholars who are able to see into the righteousness, the inappropriateness, the partiality, and the whole of a lifetime's enlightened teaching wish at the present time to set foot on the mount of the altar of the precept in Enryakuji Temple?

Since this particular gateway to the Dharma points only to the principle, I shall make its significance absolutely clear. At the time prior to the two thousand or so years in the past of the Buddha's lifetime, as the foremost leader of the Bodhisattvas who sprang up from the earth, I, Nichiren, solemnly received the orally transmitted instructions from the Universally Awakened World Honoured One. There is not the slightest discrepancy between what Nichiren practises today and what he accepted and undertook to serve on Spirit Vulture Peak (*Ryōjusen, Gridhrakūta*). Those are the all-embracing matters in the *Sixteenth Chapter on the Lifespan of the Tathāgata*, without any modification whatsoever.

Question: What is the precise textual proof for the one instant of thought containing three thousand existential spaces?

Answer: First I should tell you that there are two textual proofs. In the *Second Chapter on Expedient Means*, it says, "This real aspect of all dharmas is said to be in any way they make themselves present to any of our six sense organs – eyes, ears, nose, tongue, body, and mind." The text continues until, "with the desire to open the perceptive Buddha wisdom in all sentient beings". Is this not where the text refers to the fundamental principle of all sentient beings having been enlightened in the primordial infinity to the one instant of mind containing three thousand existential spaces (*ichinen sanzen*)?

In the *Sixteenth Chapter on the Lifespan of the Tathāgata*, it says, "Since I really became a Buddha, it is already up to countless and boundless and hundreds of thousands of myriads of billions of *nayuta asōgi kalpas* ago." [Existence has always existed and will continue to do so.] This is the evidence for the one instant of mind containing three thousand existential spaces (*ichinen sanzen*) of the real substantiation of the Buddha prior to the primordial infinity.

Nichiren feels that it is now time for this gateway to the Dharma to be widely propagated abroad. Even though for all these ages I have been keeping it hidden away in my heart, if I do not write it down so as to leave it behind, then the disciples that come after will vilify me for being heartless and devoid of compassion. Since I am aware that later it would be difficult to make amends, I am leaving this teaching written out for you. When you have read this through, you must keep it secret and not let other people read it. And, needless to say, you are not to discuss it.

The sole purpose of all the Buddhas coming into this world is to expound the *Dharma Flower Sutra*. Because this is the sutra that includes these three universal esoteric dharmas, it is the one that delivers us from the cycles of living and dying. You must keep this teaching to yourself.

The eighth day of the fourth month of the fifth year of Kō.an [1282]

Nichiren
A reply to Ōta Kingo, also known as, Ota Jomyo

The Essential of the Teaching of Nichiren Daishōnin

Explanations of Buddhist Terms and Concepts as Applied to the Teaching of Nichiren Daishōnin

Actual Fundamental Substance, the – Japanese: *Tōtai*
The actual fundamental substance is what the fundamental nature really is; it is what all dharmas (things) actually are. [See also *Treatise on the Significance of the Actual Fundamental Substance*.]

Ajase – Sanskrit: *Ajātashatru*
The son of King Bimbisāra of Magadha, an ancient kingdom in Central India. Urged on by Daibadatta (*Devadatta*), he killed his father, a devout follower of Shākyamuni, and ascended to the throne to become one of the most influential rulers of his time. Later, he contracted a terrible disease and, in remorse for his acts, became a follower of the Buddha teaching and supported the First Buddhist Council.

Amida Buddha – Japanese: *Amida Butsu* – Sanskrit: *Amitāyus Buddha*
The Buddha of Infinite Life or Amitābha Buddha the Buddha of Infinite Light. According to the Sutra on Universally Incalculable Longevity, the gist of the teaching of the Immaculate Terrain is that, many *kalpas* ago, there was a king who renounced his throne in order to become a monk by the name of Hōzō. At this time, there was a Buddha called Sejizai-ō, from whom Hōzō sought guidance in order to attain to enlightenment. He made a series of forty-eight vows and avowed to establish his own Buddha terrain. In his eighteenth vow, Hōzō promised to bring all sentient beings to his Immaculate Terrain, which he called Ultimate Bliss (*Gokuraku*), on the invocation of his name. After innumerable *kalpas* of austerities, he finally became enlightened as the Buddha Amida. In accordance with his eighteenth vow, all those people who bear in mind the Buddha Amida's formula with

sincerity can be reborn in his Immaculate Terrain. In the esoteric doctrine, the Buddha Amida is the Buddha of the western region.

Anan – Japanese: *Anan* – Sanskrit: *Ānanda*
One of Shākyamuni's ten major disciples, he was also one of Shākyamuni's cousins. He is said to have accompanied the Buddha wherever he went and therefore heard more of his teachings than any other disciple or bodhisattva. Anan was also said to have a perfect memory and played a central role in compiling the Sutras at the First Buddhist Council.

Arhat – Japanese: *Arakan*
The highest attainment in the teaching of the individual vehicle (*shōjō, hīnayāna*), in which all delusions and attachments are eradicated, and a state is reached where one is worthy of offering.

Arrive at the Path, to – Japanese: *Jōdō* [See also **Becoming a Buddha**.]

Ashura or **Shura** – Sanskrit: *Ashūra*
This category of mythological being is in many ways comparable to the Titans in Greek mythology, the mythological giants of Northern Europe, or the ogres in Northern European folklore. The *shura* are always fighting with the *deva* for supremacy; in one account, they stand in the midst of the ocean with the water coming up to their knees. There is no clear iconography, and they are seen as one of the dimensions of our mind. [See also "*shura*" in **Ten psychological realms of dharmas**.]

Asōgi – Sanskrit: *Asamkhya, Asamkhyeya*
This word is often understood as meaning countless or innumerable. It is said to be a huge number that is represented by one digit and fifty-one zeros.

Attain to the Path, to – Japanese: *Tokutō* [See also **Becoming a Buddha**.]

Becoming a Buddha, on – Japanese: *Jōbutsu*
This term is also used to refer to "attaining to the Path", "to arrive at the Path", "the Buddha harvest", and "to become universally and correctly awakened". Broadly stated, "to become a Buddha" indicates the result of the bodhisattva's practice over a long period of *kalpas*, in order to bring about a final severance and conclusion to his troublesome worries and finally to attain enlightenment. The individual vehicle (*shōjō, hīnayāna*) propounds attainment to the path, by cutting off and resolving thirty-four misleading views. The universal vehicle (*daijō, mahāyāna*) shows the gradual progressive ascent, through a sequence of forty-one or fifty-two stages. Nevertheless, in these teachings that came before the *Dharma Flower Sutra* (*Myōhō Renge Kyō*), it was clearly shown that people of an evil disposition, women, and people of the two vehicles could never become universally and correctly awakened. The contrary view comes with the *Dharma Flower Sutra* (*Myōhō Renge Kyō*), in its exposition of all beings and all things being endowed with the Buddha nature and that it is possible to open one's Buddha nature, with one's person being as it is. The technical term for this is "one's person is not separate from becoming a Buddha"; and, when reference is made to the inanimate, it is called "plants and trees becoming Buddhas".

The concept of becoming a Buddha differs according to the various schools. The Flower Garland School (*Kegonshū*) claims that one becomes a Buddha by being totally immersed in one's faith. The School of Watchful Attention (*Zenshū*) directly points to the mind of the individual and states that enlightenment is reached when the fundamental nature of things is perceived. The School of the Immaculate Terrain (*Jōdoshū*) asserts that being reborn in the Immaculate Terrain of Amida Buddha amounts to the Buddha harvest. Other schools have different notions, but none of them are the equivalent of the notion that one's person is not separate from becoming a Buddha. The significance of this concept is expounded in the *Dharma Flower Sutra* (*Myōhō Renge Kyō*). In the doctrine derived from the external events of the Buddha Shākyamuni's life and work of that sutra, it is the substantiation of the intrinsicality of the real aspect of all dharmas (things). And the teaching of the original gateway reveals that one becomes a Buddha with an ordinary body of flesh and blood, in the midst of the harsh practicalities of our respective societies. This means that, by holding faith in the Buddha teachings of the seeds planted within the text of the Utterness of the Dharma (*Myōhō, Saddharma*) of Nichiren Daishōnin, it is possible to arrive at a correct and individuated vision of society. Becoming a Buddha, which is none other than opening up our inherent Buddha nature, does not imply that we are awakened to something that goes beyond ordinary human beings, but to become fully aware of the Buddha as the final, unchanging superlative that fundamentally exists, independent of all action, and is the actual fundamental substance.

Becoming universally and correctly awakened – Japanese: *Jōtōshōgaku* [See also **Becoming a Buddha**.]

Birushana – Sanskrit: *Vairocana*
The name of this Buddha means belonging to, or coming from the sun, i.e., light. According to some Buddhist schools, he represents the real Buddha entity.

Bodhisattvas who swarm up out of the earth – Japanese: *Jiyu no bosatsu*
The innumerable bodhisattvas who appeared out of the earth, in the *Fifteenth Chapter on the Bodhisattvas who Swarm up out of the Earth* of the *Dharma Flower Sutra* (*Myōhō Renge Kyō*), are the disciples of the eternal Shākyamuni the original Buddha, who is identified with Nichiren Daishōnin. In this chapter of the *Dharma Flower Sutra* (*Myōhō Renge Kyō*), these bodhisattvas pledged to spread abroad the teachings of the Utterness of the Dharma (*Myōhō, Saddharma*) during the final phase of the Dharma of the historical Shākyamuni. These bodhisattvas alone are entrusted with this assignment. In the strictest sense, only Nichiren is the incarnation of the bodhisattvas who swarmed up out of the earth, but this term also implies the people who practise and do what they can to propagate this teaching. [See also *Treatise on the Real Aspect of All Dharmas*.]

Body and Terrain – Japanese: *Shindo*
All sentient beings possess a body that needs a terrain on which to depend for an existence. [See also **Subjectivity and its dependent environment**.]

Bonten – Sanskrit: *Mahābrahman*
According to some Hindu teachings, Bonten is the highest god and even the creator of the universe. In the Nichiren Kōmon School, he is, with Taishaku, one of the principal *deva* who protect the Dharma. [See also **deva and benevolent spirits**.]

Buddha – Japanese: *Butsu, hotoke*
From the Sanskrit *Budh*, to be aware of, to observe, or be awakened. **Buddha** – completely conscious or enlightened, has come to take on the meaning of one who enlightens – one endowed with perfect wisdom, boundless compassion, and the purpose of whose advent in the world is to set all beings on the Buddha Path. This is defined in detail in the *Second Chapter on Expedient Means* of the *Dharma Flower Sutra* (*Myōhō Renge Kyō*). There is an original Buddha, discussed in the *Sixteenth Chapter on the Lifespan of the Tathāgata* of the *Dharma Flower Sutra* (*Myōhō Renge Kyō*), who is the Buddha of the primordially infinite, original beginning and stands in contrast to the temporary Buddhas of the temporary gateways to the Dharma. He is also the oneness of the person and the Dharma of Nichiren Daishōnin and whose other attributes are defined as the actual fundamental substance of the self-received reward body that is used by the Tathāgata. There are many other Buddhas who are considered to be emanations of the Indian Shākyamuni (*c.* sixth-fifth century BCE). [See also **Shākyamuni**.]

Buddha harvest – Japanese: *Sabutsu* [See also **Becoming a Buddha**.]

Buddha's own practice, the – Japanese: *Jigyō*
The Buddha's own practice implies the Buddha's own conduct. His practice for others means his teachings for the benefit of other people.

Ceremony in Empty Space, the – Japanese: *Kokūe no gishiki*
One of the three assemblies contained in the *Dharma Flower Sutra* (*Myōhō Renge Kyō*), it extends from the end of the *Eleventh Chapter on Seeing the Vision of the Stupa made of Precious Materials* to the middle of the *Twenty-second Chapter on the Assignment of the Mission*. In the *Fifteenth Chapter on the Bodhisattvas who Swarm up out of the Earth*, the Bodhisattvas who swarm up out of the earth make their appearance. This is the moment where the original gateway begins. In the *Sixteenth Chapter on the Lifespan of the Tathāgata*, the Buddha Shākyamuni reveals his original enlightenment in the distant past of five hundred *kalpas* with all the dharmas in them ground into grains of dust. But, in the teaching that is esoterically submerged within the text, this concept of a distant past becomes the ever-present infinite in time (*kuon ganjo*).

In the *Twenty-first Chapter on the Reaches of the Mind of the Tathāgata*, the Buddha transfers the essential of the *Dharma Flower Sutra* (*Myōhō Renge Kyō*) to the Bodhisattvas who swarm up out of the earth. This can only be Nam Myōhō Renge Kyō, which means to devote our lives to and found them on (*Nam[u]*) the Utterness of the Dharma (*Myōhō*) [entirety of existence, enlightenment and unenlightenment] permeated by the underlying white lotus flower-like mechanism of the interdependence of cause, concomitancy and effect (*Renge*) in its whereabouts of the ten [psychological] realms of dharmas (*Kyō*). The Buddha transfers this to the Bodhisattvas who swarm up out of the earth led by the Bodhisattva Jōgyō, entrusting them with the assignment of broadly propagating it during the final phase of the Dharma of Shākyamuni (*mappō*). In the teaching of Nichiren, the Ceremony in Empty Space implies the whole of the original gateway.

The Ceremony in Empty Space occurred nowhere except in Shākyamuni's head. Tahō's stupa represents our objective surroundings. All of the original gateway happened in the same space as Nam Myōhō Renge Kyō. As for Nichiren Daishōnin's understanding of the theme and title, Nam Myōhō Renge Kyō – which means to devote our lives to and found them on (*Nam[u]*) the Utterness of the Dharma (*Myōhō*) [entirety of existence, enlightenment and unenlightenment] permeated by the underlying white lotus flower-like mechanism of the interdependence of cause, concomitancy and effect (*Renge*) in its whereabouts of the ten [psychological] realms of dharmas (*Kyō*) – you cannot see it, smell it, taste it, touch it, or even feel it – it is just there. It is the way existence functions. [See also **Empty Space**.]

Chain of the twelve causes and karmic circumstances that run through the whole of sentient existence – Japanese: *jūni in.nen*
 1. *mumyō*, a fundamental unenlightenment which leads to
 2. *gyō*, dispositions that are inherited from former lives;
 3. *shiki*, the first consciousness that takes place in the womb after conception;
 4. *myō, shiki*, body and mind evolving in the womb;
 5. *rokunyū*, the five organs of sense and the functioning of the mind;
 6. *shoku*, contact with the outside world;
 7. *ju*, receptivity or budding intelligence and discrimination from six to seven years onwards;
 8. *ai*, thirst, desire, or love at the age of puberty;
 9. *shu*, the urge for sensuous existence that forms the following:
 10. *yū*, the substance of future karma;
 11. *shō*, the completed karma ready to be born again;
 12. *rō, shi*, karma facing in the direction of old age and death.

Cognition of Consciousness, the – Japanese: *Ishiki* – Sanskrit: *Mano-vijnaña*

This is the consciousness of what we perceive and feel with regard to what is going on around us or inside us. The first five cognitions (*shiki – vijñāna*) have their own organs to detect whatever they are supposed to sense, such as eyes for seeing or ears for hearing, whereas the cognition of conscious mental activity (*ishiki – mano-vijñaña*) is totally dependent on the mind as the faculty of thought (*i, manas*). It is due to the cognition of conscious mental activity that makes us aware of our own existence.

Cognition of Pure Mind, the - Japanese: *Amarashiki* - Sanskrit: *Amala-vijñāna*

In Japanese, there are various definitions of this cognition – the cognition free from defilement, the immaculately pure cognition (*shōjōshiki*), the cognition of real suchness (*shinnyoshiki*). The word cognition is used to indicate a way of knowing dharmas (*or whatever may have an effect on any of our five aggregates*) whether they are inside our heads or not. The nine cognitions are as follows:

1) The cognition of the eyes – seeing;
2) The cognition of the ears – hearing;
3) The cognition of the nose – smelling;
4) The cognition of the tongue – taste;
5) The cognition of the body – touch;
6) The cognition of mental activity without precise thought, just seeing, hearing etc., as well as instinctive reactions;
7) The cognition of mind as the faculty of thought;
8) The storehouse cognition;
9) The cognition of pure mind.

Tendai (*T'ien T'ai*) refers to the ninth cognition as the sovereign of the mind and the fundamental source of all the dharmas (or whatever may have an effect on any of our five aggregates), as well as being the central axis on which they revolve. In other words, it is everything that is inscribed on the Fundamental Object of Veneration (*gohonzon*) or the very essence of life itself. In the Buddha teaching of Shākyamuni, this cognition is sometimes described as having got rid of the taints of delusion that are associated with the storehouse cognition *arayashiki, alaya-vijñāna*. Tendai (*T'ien T'ai*) also writes, in his *Recondite Significance of the Sutra on the Illumination of the Golden Light*, "The ninth is the cognition of the Buddha." However, in the Buddha teaching of Nichiren Daishōnin, it is understood that the Buddha realm (*Bukkai*) is not separate from the other nine realms of dharmas (*kyukai*). Hence, through the continual practice of the Nichiren Kōmon School and by developing a faith in the Fundamental Object of Veneration (*gohonzon*), we can open up our inherent Buddha nature with our respective persons just as they are (*soku shin jō Butsu*).

Consecrate one's life on, to [See also **Namu.**]

Corresponding body – Japanese: *ōjin* [See also **Three bodies.**]

Corresponding body independent of all karma, the – Japanese: *Musa no ōjin*

This corresponding body is the entity of materiality (*shiki shin*) of the three bodies independent of all karma. In the same way as appearance (*sō*) in the ten such qualities (*nyoze*), the term also refers to the Buddha's compassionate behaviour. In this sense, it is the self-received entity of the Tathāgata, whose freedom pervades the whole of existence and whose original source lies in the ever-present infinite in time (*kuon ganjo*). This is the physical body (*shiki shin*) and the conduct of Nichiren Daishōnin, the original Buddha (*Honbutsu*) and the Buddha for the present age, which is the final phase of the Dharma of Shākyamuni (*mappō*). In *Concerning the Practice of the Present School* by the former Patriarch Nichikan (1665-1726), he states, "When the objective realm of the Whole of Existence combines with the Buddha wisdom that is able to understand it, this understanding would certainly be endowed with an all-embracing compassion, as well as the arousal and motivation of universal loving-kindness. The result of this arousal becomes the corresponding body independent of all karma that is also the freedom from being aware of living and dying." It is the practical application of Utterness (*Myō*). The sacred title of the corresponding body independent of all karma is Nam Myōhō Renge Kyō, which is the consecration and founding of our lives on the Utterness of the Dharma (both the enlightened and unenlightened facets of the entirety of existence) permeated by the underlying white lotus flower-like mechanism of the interdependence of cause, concomitancy and effect in its whereabouts of the ten (psychological) realms of dharmas.

Daibadatta – Sanskrit: *Devadatta*

A cousin of Shākyamuni who later opposed him out of jealousy, at one point he attempted to kill the Buddha by sending a mad elephant against him. Nevertheless, it was pacified by the Buddha's all-embracing compassion. Daibadatta (*Devadatta*) committed three of the five cardinal wrongdoings – firstly, by causing a rift in the order by enticing five hundred of the disciples away from it; secondly, by trying to kill Shākyamuni by dropping a boulder on him; and thirdly, he beat a nun to death because she criticised him for his wrongdoing. On account of these actions, he fell into hell alive. In the *Twelfth Chapter on Daibadatta (Devadatta)* of the *Dharma Flower Sutra (Myōhō Renge Kyō)*, Shākyamuni revealed that in a former life he had practised under a certain hermit called Ashi, who was now Daibadatta (*Devadatta*). The Buddha (*Shākyamuni*) then predicted that Daibadatta (*Devadatta*) would become the Buddha Tennō. The importance of Daibadatta (*Devadatta*) is that the Buddha teaching reveals that a totally evil individual can become a Buddha.

Daishōnin – Japanese: *Daishōnin*
The Universal sage-like Man. The title given to Nichiren, the Buddha for the period of the final phase of the Dharma of Shākyamuni. *Dai* means all-embracing or universal; *shōnin* means sage, wise and good, upright and correct in all his character. This word, with the same feeling as "sage-like" in English, implies completeness. The *Shōnin* is the opposite of the common or unenlightened individual. *Daishōnin* carries the connotation of a Buddha and, in the case of Nichiren, that of the original Buddha.

Daitsū Buddha (also known as The Victorious Buddha of Universal Penetrating Wisdom) – Japanese: *Daitsūchisho Butsu* – Sanskrit: *Mahābhijnajnanabhibhu Buddha*
According to the *Seventh Chapter on the Parable of the Imaginary City* of the *Dharma Flower Sutra (Myōhō Renge Kyō)*, Daitsū Buddha was a king who attained to Buddhahood in the distant past of three thousand *kalpas* of grains ground into dust. At the request of his sixteen sons, he expounded the *Dharma Flower Sutra (Myōhō Renge Kyō)*. All the sons of The Victorious Buddha of Universal Penetrating Wisdom propagated the *Dharma Flower Sutra (Myōhō Renge Kyō)* as bodhisattvas. The sixteenth son was reincarnated as Shākyamuni Buddha.

Dengyō – Japanese: *Dengyō daishi*
Referred to as the Universal Teacher Dengyō (*Dengyō daishi*) and was the founder of the Japanese Tendai School. He was born

in the Shiga district in Ōmi, the present-day Shiga Prefecture, in 767 CE and died in 822 CE. He entered into holy orders at the age of twelve and studied under Gyōhyō in the Kokubunji Temple at Ōmi. He was fully ordained in 785 CE in the Todaiji temple. Some time afterwards, he returned to his native village and later built a hermitage on Mount Hiei, where he combed through in depth all the commentaries of the sutras. In 788 CE, he named his hermitage Hieiji temple, and, in 793 CE, it was renamed "The Setting the Mind at Rest in the Single Vehicle" (*Ichijō Shikan-in*). In 804 CE, he went to China where he studied the Tendai (*T'ien T'ai*) doctrine under Dōsui, Gyōman, and others. On returning to his native Japan, he founded the Japanese Tendai School, in 806 CE. Towards the end of his life, he received various honours from the Imperial Court.

Deva and benevolent spirits, all the – Japanese: *Shoten Zenjin*

In traditional Buddhist teaching, a *deva* is a heavenly being, a protective divinity. According to some accounts, the *deva* are divinities of Indian origin, and the benevolent spirits are traditional Japanese gods. Although these forces are personalised, given names and called divinities, the problem that arises is how these *deva* and benevolent spirits are understood in any "western" way of thinking. However, the *deva* and benevolent spirits could be seen to be both outside and within us. The forces on the outside, for example, are such as those that maintain the planet Earth on a proper course and the right distance from the sun. These are also the forces of nature that maintain the necessary conditions to support life and the subtle universal ecology. The forces within us are more to do with archetypes and agencies that give added strength. The *deva* and benevolent spirits are more than that for those who follow the full practice of the Nichiren Kōmon School. For, as they will testify, although life is full of problems and obstacles, there is little doubt that those who have faith in this teaching believe it will overcome their hindrances better than for those who do not. [See also **Bonten**.]

Dhāranî – Japanese: *Darani*

A syllabic invocation for bringing out the good and repressing evil in the teachings that came prior to the *Dharma Flower Sutra*

(*Myōhō Renge Kyō*). Very often *dhāranî* are regarded as the quintessence of a teaching, either tantric or sutric. It is thought that strong spiritual powers are embodied in these syllables, which rarely have any linguistic meaning, in contrast to the theme and title of the *daimoku* which is composed of words with a precise and all-embracing significance. [See also **Nam Myōhō Renge Kyō**.]

Dharma body – Japanese: *Hosshin* [See also **Three bodies**.]

Dharma body independent of all karma, the – Japanese: *Musa hosshin*
 This is one of the three bodies independent of all karma, whose origin is in the ever-present infinity in time (*kuon ganjo*). This is the real embodiment of the whole of life which in practice is the self-received body, i.e., the Fundamental Object of Veneration (*Gohonzon*) that is not separate from the lord of the teaching Nichiren Daishōnin who, for the people of the final period of the Dharma of Shākyamuni (*mappo*), is the lord of the teaching of the seeds sown in the Utterness of original cause (*Honnin Myō*). The actual reality is the consecration and founding of our lives on the Utterness of the Dharma (both the enlightened and unenlightened facets of the entirety of existence) permeated by the underlying white lotus flower-like mechanism of the interdependence of cause, concomitancy and effect in its whereabouts of the ten (psychological) realms of dharmas, i.e., Nam Myōhō Renge Kyō.

Nichikan Shonin (1666-1726) who was a former patriarch of the Nichiren Kōmon School states, in his *Treatise on the Practice of the Present School*, that the three bodies independent of all karma are the virtue and power of the self-received wisdom body of the Tathagāta, whose one entity is not separate from the three entities that comprise existence... ... our persons are the objective environment (*Kyō*) when our inherent Buddha nature is opened up. This in itself is not separate from the Dharma body independent of all karma. In the sixth fascicle of the *Universal Desistance from Troublesome Worries in order to see Clearly* (*Maka Shikan*), it says, "When we perceive the objective environment as enlightenment (*Kyō*), it then becomes the Dharma body, i.e., the whole of existence. And, when this body manifests its own wisdom, it then becomes the wisdom body independent of all karma. The effects or the actions that this wisdom brings about then become the compassion of the corresponding body."

Again, these three bodies become the three powers or virtues of the Buddha as sovereign, teacher, and parent, as well as his essential nature of being the Dharma, wisdom, and his own complete liberation. This is said to be the Dharma body independent of all karma, as the initial building block of the whole of existence – past, present, and future – as well as being the embodiment of Utterness (*Myōtai*) ... ... The sacred title of this entity is Nam Myōhō Renge Kyō, which means to devote our lives to and found them on (*Nam[u]*) the Utterness of the Dharma (*Myōhō*) [entirety of existence, enlightenment and unenlightenment] permeated by the underlying white lotus flower-like mechanism of the interdependence of cause, concomitancy and effect (*Renge*) in its whereabouts of the ten [psychological] realms of dharmas (*Kyō*). This is the fundamental part that enables all sentient beings to open up their inherent Buddha nature with their persons just as they are, as well as being the Fundamental Object of Veneration (*gohonzon*) of the three universal esoteric Dharmas (doctrines) both within us and outside us.

One of the many obstacles in the practice of the teaching of Nichiren Daishōnin is that, like so many other studies such as linguistics or mathematics, it has its own particular language. The unfamiliarity of these specialised terms is highly related to the whole problem of translating Buddhist texts.

The origins of existence are in the twists, turns, and workings of the whole of existence itself. So, if we are to talk of an original state, then it is something that potentially lives in the profoundest depths of our own minds – in other words, the existential realm of the Dharma. In the teaching of Nichiren Daishōnin, the Buddha nature inherent in all of us is understood as the three bodies independent of all karma. Apart from the fundamental Object of Veneration (*gohonzon*), the position of any concept of a pure corresponding body (*ōjin*), a pure wisdom to fully comprehend it (*hōshin*), or a combination of the two (*hosshin*) suspended in an apparent origin of time is highly hypothetical. In this present *kalpa*, it took the whole of evolution from the inception of existence right through to the arrival of living beings, through all the Buddhas from Shākyamuni, Nagarjuna, Tendai (*T'ien T'ai*), Dengyō (*Dengyō daishi*), and many others, right on up to Nichiren before we could get a grasp of how we should conceive these three bodies independent of all karma.

The contents of the Fundamental Object of Veneration (*gohonzon*) are the whole of life in their purest form. Earlier representations of the whole of life are Shākyamuni's *Dharma Flower Sutra* (*Myōhō Renge Kyō*), and the exposition of Tendai (*T'ien T'ai*), and the commentaries of Myōraku (*Miao-lo*), and others, of the *Universal Desistance of Troublesome Worries in order to see Clearly* (*Maka Shikan*). But it is only Nichiren's Fundamental Object of Veneration (*gohonzon*) that brings us face to face with the three bodies independent of all karma, all at the same time.

In the Buddhist view of the world at the time of Nichiren Daishōnin, the realms of humankind were confined to China, Japan, Korea, Central Asia, and India. So the principal languages for Buddhists were either Chinese or Sanskrit. Since the Fundamental Object of Veneration (*gohonzon*) is written out in Chinese with two germ syllables written in the Siddham alphabet of Sanskrit, I personally am in favour of the Fundamental Object of Veneration (*gohonzon*) for the twenty-first century being written out in either Latin, Greek, or Cyrillic script for the benefit of those who cannot read the Chinese ideograms. However, this is not for me to decide.

Coming back to the point, we have to be very careful not to confuse knowledge with wisdom. Although Nichiren was not aware of the worlds beyond the traditions of his time when there was no real understanding of the whys and hows of present-day science which is only knowledge, the inherent Buddha wisdom of the Daishōnin was able to penetrate the mind of each and every individual, as well as the whole of the oneness of mind. All we need to know about mind is inscribed on the Fundamental Object of Veneration (*gohonzon*), which is also the means that can make us understand why we live and die.

Dharma Flower School, the – Japanese: *Hokkeshū*
This is another name for the Tendai and Nichiren Schools, whose teaching was founded on the literal understanding of the *Sutra on the White Lotus Flower-like Mechanism of the Utterness of the Dharma* (*Myōhō Renge Kyō*). This sutra teaches that the Buddha was enlightened in a distant past of uncountable aeons ago. This sutra also points out that all sentient beings, as well as everything else that is non-sentient, has an inherent Buddha nature, which is clearly defined in the concept of the one instant of thought containing three thousand existential spaces (*ichinen sanzen*). This same teaching also emphasises that women, people of the two vehicles, and people of evil disposition, can open their inherent Buddha nature. No other sutra even suggests this. The origin is not an inconceivable distant time, but the ever-present in the infinitive in time.

Dharma or Dharma nature (The essence of the) – Sanskrit: *Dharmatā* – Japanese: *Hosshō*
If we are to understand the teaching of Nichiren Daishōnin by taking what he wrote into deep consideration, then one's existence is made up of all space, all time – past, present, and future – of all the *kalpas* and without effort. This is what is so difficult to believe and understand. In the Daishōnin's *Treatise on the Eighteen Perfect Circles*, we have, "On enquiring into the self-nature of all dharmas, we should abandon any notion of a dharma nature and replace it with the triple body independent of all karmas [i.e., phenomena (*ke*), relativity (*kū*), and the middle way of reality (*chū*) of the Dharma realm of the utterly enlightened]. If there are dharmas, then not one of them is not the triple body independent of all karma." The exception to this is the Fundamental Object of Veneration (*gohonzon*).

The essence of the Dharma is as follows:
1) The fundamental quality of all life and all dharmas;
2) The fundamental quality of life, which is explained as the enlightenment to the essence of the Dharma. This is Nam Myōhō Renge Kyō, which means to devote our lives to and found them on (*Nam*[*u*]) the Utterness of the Dharma (*Myōhō*) [entirety of existence, enlightenment and unenlightenment] permeated by the

underlying white lotus flower-like mechanism of the interdependence of cause, concomitancy and effect (*Renge*) in its whereabouts of the ten [psychological] realms of dharmas (*Kyō*). It is perceived as shining through both defiled and pure dharmas. In this case, the essence of the Dharma is enlightenment, as opposed to the unclearness of unenlightenment. Generally speaking, this essence is the eternal, unchanging, and originally endowed disposition of all dharmas. Both the real suchness (*shinnyo*) and the real aspect (*jissō*) are the same as the essence of the Dharma. This means to say that it is the real aspect and fundamental nature of all existence.

In the third Chapter on the eighteen essences in the second fascicle of the *Sutra on Controlling Existence*, it says, "When we break up the characteristics of anything at any given moment, or any particular item or items that may touch upon our senses or mental faculties either consciously or unconsciously, they are referred to as the essence of dharmas, which are explained as all existence or the essence of the Dharma or Nam Myōhō Renge Kyō. The essence of the Dharma implies that nothing has an independent nature of its own. Why is that so? It is because the essence of the Dharma has no past, no future, and no present. It is because of all the inherent karmic relations and the combination of various affinities that the essence of the Dharma can be named and explained for what it is. It is on account of ordinary people's understanding of things that the wise can conceive them – that the relativity (*kū*) of any independent nature is the essence of the Dharma, which is the essence of the whole of existence. The essence of the Dharma cannot be combined with anything, nor can it be dispersed. In the middle of the essence of the dharmas, the essence of the Dharma is without characteristics. There is neither so much, nor is there so little. This essence is expounded as an expedient means. When we put a name to the essence of the Dharma, we refer to it as its inherent quality."

It is said that the essence of the Dharma stems from the innermost origins of life itself and manifests itself in the everyday activities of our lives (*seikatsu*). The essence of the Dharma is the one instant of mind (that comprises the whole of existence).

Dharma realm, the – Japanese: *Hokkai* [See also **Realms of the dharmas.**]

Dharmas, all – Japanese: *Shohō*
The whole of existence; everything that exists either in the mind or physically. The sum total of the momentary configuration of events.

Dharmas and dharma – Japanese: *Hō*
Generally speaking, this word in most western dictionaries is defined as something that maintains a certain character always and thus becomes a standard. In order to understand this term more clearly, we should begin with dharmas in the plural. Dharmas are anything we perceive, whether it be with our minds or any other organ of perception. This implies the farthest meanderings of the mind as we drop off to sleep to the stark realities of what is in front of us. It might be said that dharmas could be equated with our word existence or life. Since our existences are subjective, we could think of dharmas as being all that comprises our lives.

Sometimes the word Dharma is used as a term for a teaching, and in this book in particular it is used for the doctrines that Shākyamuni expounded prior to the *Dharma Flower Sutra* (*Myōhō Renge Kyō*). For us common mortals, existence is a plurality of all the things that make up our lives that encumber our perception of what their real components are – which are all the single instant of mind containing three thousand existential spaces (*ichinen sanzen*) or Myōhō Renge Kyō, which means the Utterness of the Dharma (*Myōhō*) [entirety of existence, enlightenment and unenlightenment] permeated by the underlying white lotus flower-like mechanism of the interdependence of cause, concomitancy and effect (*Renge*) in its whereabouts of the ten [psychological] realms of dharmas (*Kyō*).

However, to the enlightened, the universe we inhabit becomes a unity. Just as Nichiren states in his *Treatise on the Eighteen Perfect Circles* (*Goshō Shimpen*, p.1514), "The fourth is the perfect circle of the ocean of fruition. On seeking the self-nature of all dharmas, we should put aside the notion of a self-nature and replace it with the triple body independent of all karma. There is no dharma that is not the triple body. Therefore, they are referred to as the fruition and reality of understanding the lotus flower-like mechanism that pervades all existence and all time."

Also, the word Dharma refers to the teachings that are derived from the perception of oneness. Some translators use a capital D for this concept of the Dharma. Although there is only one word in Japanese which is *hō*, in these translations I render the difference between those two concepts with a singular and a plural.

Dhyāna – Japanese: *Zenna* or *Zenjō*
Meditation or contemplation. Sometimes this word is understood as an ultramundane experience. It is also thought of as an especially profound abstract religious contemplation. Another interpretation is to be immersed unwaveringly and solely in the object of meditation. Religious ecstasy has also been suggested. Although we may come across this word in the Writings of Nichiren Daishōnin, there is no such meditational practice in the Nichiren Kōmon School.

Dragon – Japanese: *Ryū*
In China and Japan, these beings are mostly seen as benevolent divinities that live in watery places, such as the sea, rivers, lakes, ponds, and also in the clouds. In some cults, dragons are invoked to produce rain. They are also said to be the holders of the *Hoshu* [Sanskrit: *Chintamani*], the magic jewel that dispenses treasures and wisdom. They are usually represented as having long scaly bodies, with four-clawed, reptile-like feet and a lion-like head with antlers.

Dragon King's daughter, the – Japanese: *Ryūnyō*
In the *Twelfth Chapter on Daibadatta (Devadatta)*, the eight-year-old daughter of one of the great Dragon Kings sought to become a Buddha, after hearing Mañjushrī (*Monjushiri*) speak in her father's palace under the sea. At a later date, the Dragon King's daughter, on hearing Shākyamuni's exposition on Spirit Vulture Peak (*Ryojusen, Gridhrakūta*) and her body being suddenly transformed

into that of a boy, immediately attained enlightenment and became a Buddha. In the teachings prior to the *Dharma Flower Sutra* (*Myōhō Renge Kyō*), women were said not to be able to attain to enlightenment, and only men could attain it after many *kalpas* of austerities. Such notions are refuted by the example of the Dragon King's daughter becoming a Buddha. There is also the implication that our animality is endowed with the Buddha nature and that it is possible to attain to the path. [See also **Ten psychological realms of dharmas.**]

Eight classifications of Shākyamuni's teaching – Japanese: *shikyō, shi kegi*

These eight Tendai (*T'ien T'ai*) classifications of Shākyamuni's doctrine are again divided into the four kinds of teaching and the four modes of instruction. The four kinds of teaching are a progressive guidance according to the propensities of his disciples, to enable them to fully understand the gateway to the enlightenment of the *Dharma Flower Sutra* (*Myōhō Renge Kyō*) – firstly, the teaching of the three receptacles which imply all the doctrines of the individual vehicle (*shōjō, hīnayāna*); secondly, the interrelated teachings which act as an intermediate step between the individual vehicle (*shōjō, hīnayāna*) and the universal vehicle (*daijō, mahāyāna*); thirdly, the Particular Teaching that was particularly for people who were bodhisattvas; fourthly, the All-inclusive Teaching which is the perfect doctrine of the *Dharma Flower Sutra* (*Myōhō Renge Kyō*) and the real intention of Shākyamuni.

The four modes of instruction are as follows: firstly, the Direct Teaching without holding any of the truth back – the *Flower Garland Sutra* and the *Dharma Flower Sutra* (*Myōhō Renge Kyō*) fall into this category; secondly, the Graded Teachings which include most of the teachings of the three receptacles, the interrelated teachings, and the Wisdom Sutras; thirdly, the Esoteric and Secret Doctrines only understood by special members of the assembly; fourthly, the Indeterminate Teachings from which all hearers each obtain growth and wisdom according to their individual propensities.

Emma – Sanskrit: *Yama-rāja*
Often thought of as the King of Hell, he is said to try to punish all those who fall into his domain. He is the symbol of the severity of karma.

Empty Space
This is one of the most difficult concepts to be made comprehensible to ordinary people. According to the wisdom period of the teaching of Shākyamuni, each and every dharma is noumena and therefore relativity. Where did the Ceremony in Empty Space occur? I suppose it happened in the same dimension as Nam Myōhō Renge Kyō, which implies devoting our lives to and founding them on the Utterness of the Dharma (both the enlightened and unenlightened facets of the entirety of existence) permeated by the underlying white lotus flower-like mechanism of the interdependence of cause, concomitancy and effect in its whereabouts of the ten (psychological) realms of dharmas. One can only surmise that it all happened in Shākyamuni's head, so as to make such concepts available to his listeners. Nam Myōhō Renge Kyō is inaccessible to any of our means of perception. It is just there, and we can become aware of it by simply being alive.

Esoterically inaccessible – Japanese: *Himitsu*
Within the bounds of the Buddha teaching, this expression is used for something that is difficult to know or understand. An esoteric (*Hi*) gateway to the Dharma is one that is far-reaching, deep, and subtly all-embracing. As such, it cannot be fully thought out or conclusively deliberated upon. In the *Textual Explanation of the Dharma Flower Sutra* (*Hokke Mongu*), it says, "The one body being inseparable from the three is said to be esoteric, and the three bodies being inseparable from the one are said to be inaccessible. It is also referred to as that which has not been revealed since primeval times. And, only being known to the Buddha, it is said to be inaccessible."

Extent of the esoteric and almost inaccessible reaches of the mind (of the Tathāgata), the – Japanese: *Nyorai himitsu shinzu shi riki* – **(The) Reaches of the Mind** (*jinzū, abhijña*)

In the provisional Buddha teachings, this term refers to the Tathāgata's ten ubiquitous, supernatural powers, including the power to shake the earth, issue light from his pores, extend his tongue to the heavens of the Bonten effulgent with light, cause divine flowers and suchlike to rain down from the sky, be omnipresent, and other supernatural powers of the eye, ear, body, and mind. In the teachings of Nichiren, the implications are that, as there is not a single being, plant, tree, or dharma whatsoever that is not endowed with the one instant of thought containing three thousand existential spaces, the Buddha nature is everywhere, and its reaches are the totality of Utterness. [See also *Treatise on the Real Aspect of All Dharmas*, **Nam Myōhō Renge Kyō**, **One instant of thought containing three thousand existential spaces**.]

Fifty-two bodhisattva stages in the process of becoming a Buddha, the – Japanese: *Gojuni.i*

Fifty-one of these stages are those of the bodhisattvas who practised the teachings that came before the *Dharma Flower Sutra* (*Myōhō Renge Kyō*). Nichiren, in *A Collation of the Layers of the Various Teachings of all the Buddhas of the Past, Present and Future as to Which Specific Doctrines are to be Discarded or Established*, mentions these doctrines as being like the good and evil in a dream. It was also a period when the practitioners of these doctrines advanced upwards through fifty-one of these stages like the rungs of a ladder. The fifty-second stage is the ultimate and utter awakening. Also, the notion of time in all the provisional teachings is like that of a long piece of string, as opposed to the interdependence of cause and effect in the teachings of Nichiren, in which time is understood as the ever-present now in the infinity in time. These fifty-two stages are the following:

- The ten stages of developing faith (*Jusshin*).
- The ten stages of abiding in the teaching (*Juju*).
- The ten necessary activities of a bodhisattva (*Jugyo*).
- The ten stages of bestowing merit on others (*Ju.eko*).
- The ten stages of firm ground (*Juji*).
- The stage of the overall awakening (*tōgaku*).
- The stage of being utterly awakened (*myōgaku*).

Although these fifty-two stages are mentioned in various writings by Nichiren Daishōnin, they have no role in the practice of the Nichiren Kōmon Schools whatsoever.

Five aggregates, the – Japanese: *go'on*

What the five aggregates are about is how our minds and bodies react to our surroundings and the various circumstances of being alive. These five aggregates are the components of all intelligent beings – 1) *Shiki*, bodily form which involves all our organs of sense; 2) *ju*, reception, taking things in, feeling, and the workings of mind in relation to whatever is happening to us; 3) *sō*, thought in the sense of being able to make out what is happening and what things are; 4) *gyō*, choice which is the function of mind with regard to picking and choosing between like, dislike, good and bad, etc., which is influenced by the experiences of former lives, as well as the mental condition that exists between dying and being reborn; 5) *shiki*, cognition which means we have perception of what is going on, as well as what we are.

Five ideograms for *Myōhō Renge Kyō* – Japanese: *Myōhō no goji*

In Sino-Japanese the title of the *Dharma Flower Sutra* (*Myōhō Renge Kyō*) is written with five ideograms for *Myō, hō, ren, ge, kyō* and is almost invariably used for *Nam Myōhō Renge Kyō* [See also **Nam Myōhō Renge Kyō.**]

Five periods, the – Japanese: *Goji*

These five periods are a classification that the Universal Teacher Tendai (*T'ien T'ai*) utilised to indicate the gradation of the lifetime of the Buddha teachings of Shākyamuni. These doctrines were set in an order of five periods, according to their contents. What Shākyamuni taught during the first four periods were various expedient means, with which he could entice his followers to listen to and have faith in the Dharma, which was the reason for his appearance in the world. These periods are the following (for bodhisattvas only):

1. The Flower Garland Period, which was taught in three divisions of seven days each, following his enlightenment, for bodhisattvas only.

2. The twelve years of his expounding the individual teachings, in the Deer Park of Lumbini.
3. The equally broad (*hōdō, vaipulya*) period, made up of the teaching of the universal teaching, taught over a period of twelve years.
4. The wisdom (*hannya, prajña*) period, consisting of twenty years of the provisional teaching of the wisdom sutras.
5. The eight years of teaching the *Dharma Flower Sutra* (*Myōhō Renge Kyō*) and, in a day and one night, the *Nirvana Sutra*.

Flower Garland School – Japanese: *Kegonshū*
The Flower Garland School teaches that all sentient beings have the Buddha nature and that all events in the universe are interdependent. Where the teachings of this school fall short is clearly indicated in many writings of Nichiren Daishōnin.

Flower Garland Sutra – Japanese: *Kegon Kyō* – Sanskrit: *Avatāmsaka Sutra*
This is said to be the first of all the Five Periods as defined by Tendai (*T'ien T'ai*), according to whom Shākyamuni expounded this sutra immediately after he became a Buddha. But accounts vary as to whether it was on the second, third, or seventh day. The whole title of this sutra is *Sutra on Universally Spacious Flower Garland of the Buddha*. Its context is that Birushana (*Vairocana*) expounded to the bodhisattvas who had greater propensities, stating that everything that exists is bound to the rest of existence through circumstances and mutually interdependent roles. This is explained by the formula, "The boundlessness of karmic interdependencies gives rise to the realms of dharmas". He also explained that, in spite of the appearance that our individual minds are separate, existences are the oneness of mind, stating that, "All dharmas are only mind. And the three realms of form, relativity (*kū*), and desire are only knowledge". But the people who were to do the practices of this teaching had to follow the fifty-two grades of the bodhisattva in order to become a Buddha. To do this, the practitioner would have to practise these austerities over a period of twenty universal *asōgi* and hundreds of tens of thousands of *kalpas*.

Formal era of the Dharma of Shākyamuni, the – Japanese: *Zōbō* or **When the Dharma was a Superficial Ritual**

This is the second millennium after the extinction (*Paranirvana*) of Shākyamuni. The word *Zōbō* has something of the sense of "being like the Dharma". By this time, the Buddha Teaching had spread to China, Korea, and Japan. During this period, many temples, monasteries and convents were built under the patronage of each country's ruler, which gave the abbots and patriarchs enormous power. In spite of this apparently prosperous period when practices and rites became formalised, the number of believers able to derive benefit from the Buddha Teaching was few.

Four Dependencies, the

These four dependencies are the four important principles, on which the practitioner relies. They are 1) to practise according to the Dharma and not the person who expounds it, 2) to practise according to the intention of the Dharma and not just the words that are used to express it, 3) to practise according to one's inner wisdom and not according to acquired knowledge, 4) to practise according to the real aspect of the middle way, as it is expounded in the Sutra on Implications Without Bounds (*Muryōgi-kyō*), and none other.

Four Great Bodhisattvas, the – Japanese: *Shi Dai Bosatsu*

Jōgyō, Muhengyō, Jyōgyō, and Anryūgyō are the leaders of the countless bodhisattvas who swarmed up out of the earth in the *Fifteenth Chapter on the Bodhisattvas who Swarm up out of the Earth* of the *Dharma Flower Sutra* (*Myōhō Renge Kyō*). In the translation of their names, Jōgyō is Supreme Practice; Muhengyō is Boundless Practice; Jyōgyō is Pure Practice; and Anryūgyō is Peacefully Established Practice. These bodhisattvas are often referred to as the leaders of the chant Nam Myōhō Renge Kyō, which means to devote our lives to and found them on (*Nam[u]*) the Utterness of the Dharma (*Myōhō*) [entirety of existence, enlightenment and unenlightenment] permeated by the underlying white lotus flower-like mechanism of the interdependence of cause, concomitancy and effect (*Renge*) in its whereabouts of the ten [psychological] realms of dharmas (*Kyō*). Nichiren is seen as the reincarnation of these four Bodhisattvas. In the *Threefold Transmission Concerning the Fundamental Object of Veneration* Nichiren gives Jōgyō the quality of fire, Muhengyō that of earth, Jyōgyō water, Anryūgyō wind, and the Nam[u] Myōhō Renge Kyō in the centre of the Fundamental Object of Veneration (*gohonzon*), relativity. This same transmission also states that "these five archetypes are our basic composition".

Fundamental Object of Veneration, the – Japanese: *gohonzon*
The Fundamental Object of Veneration (*gohonzon*) is what we have as basis for our deepest respect and veneration. Since I do not have the wisdom to define the Fundamental Object of Veneration, there is a Transmission by Nichiren to Nikkō and written out by Nichigen, at the beginning of this book.

Fundamental Substance of the Dharma – Japanese: *Hottai*
The essential, unchanging nature that underlies all phenomena and noumena which are always subject to change. In the first fascicle of *The Oral Transmission on the Meaning of the Dharma Flower Sutra* (*Ongi Kuden*), the fundamental substance of the Dharma is Nam Myōhō Renge Kyō, which means to devote our lives to and found them on (*Nam[u]*) the Utterness of the Dharma (*Myōhō*) [entirety of existence, enlightenment and unenlightenment] permeated by the underlying white lotus flower-like mechanism of the interdependence of cause, concomitancy and effect (*Renge*) in its whereabouts of the ten [psychological] realms of dharmas (*Kyō*).

Gateway to the Dharma – Japanese: *Hōmon*
The Doctrines of Wisdom of the Buddha or Nichiren which are seen as gateways to enlightenment. [See also **Dharmas, Realms of the dharma.**]

General and Specific– Japanese: *sō, betsu*
The General and Specific view of things. These two words are a way that allows us to diagnose the teachings of the Buddha. The 'general' way of seeing things points to the whole of a teaching or a particular doctrine, whereas the word 'specific' represents a

deeper analysis, which is more detailed and accurately limited. For example, the five periods and the eight ways of teaching of Shākyamuni all show us the truth. However, from a specific point of view, only the *Dharma Flower Sutra* (*Lotus Sutra*) describes reality itself. In the same way, if we were to speak in general terms, the *Dharma Flower Sutra* represents the enlightened point of view of the Buddha Shākyamuni. However, more specifically, it is Nam Myōhō Renge Kyō that reveals the verbal formulation of his enlightenment as to how existence functions, with the added notion that existence always has, is, and will continue to exist.

Nevertheless, the terms general and specific are also used as a way of referring to the transmission of the Dharma in the *Dharma Flower Sutra* (*Lotus Sutra*). In the *Twenty-second Chapter on the Assignment of the Mission*, Shākyamuni generally communicates the *Dharma Flower Sutra* to all bodhisattvas present. But it is in the *Twenty-first Chapter on the Reaches of the Mind of the Tathāgata* that the Buddha generally transfers Nam Myōhō Renge Kyō to the *Bodhisattvas who Swarmed up Out of the Earth* and specifically to the Bodhisattva Superior Practice (*Jōgyō, Vishishtachāritra*). [See also **Ceremony in Empty Space, Five periods, General Teachings of the Individual Vehicle.**]

General Teachings of the Individual Vehicle – Japanese: *Agon Kyō* – Sanskrit: *Āgama Sutra*
With regard to the five periods of the teachings of Shākyamuni that were stipulated by Tendai (*T'ien T'ai*), this is the second. This period is referred to as the Agon Period in some Nichiren Schools. It is also called the teaching of the three receptacles. It is said that this period constitutes the first twelve years of the teaching of Shākyamuni, immediately after his six-day period, when he expounded the *Flower Garland Sutra*. [See also **Five periods, General and Specific.**]

Hell of incessant suffering – Japanese: *Abijigoku* – Sanskrit: *Avici*
The last and deepest of the eight hot hells, where those who fall into it suffer, die, and are instantly reborn to suffering without interruption.

Hossō School, the – Japanese: *Hossōshū*
One of the Ten Schools mentioned in the *Treatise on Questions and Answers Concerning the Fundamental Object of Veneration*. This school is sometimes called the Consciousness Only School. This means that the Dharma of the Buddha is a perfect oneness, as opposed to the vision of common mortals who live in a world of countless different dharmas (things) that make up the whole of existence. Therefore, in order to arrive at enlightenment, it is important to understand the real nature of all dharmas. This school also teaches that everything that is perceived, either physical or mental, stems from the cognisance of the mind's storehouse of all dharmas [Japanese: *Zōshiki*, Sanskrit: *Alāya-vijñāna*].

Humanlike non-humans or Non-humans with human intelligence – Japanese: *Ninpinin*
A classification of eight different kinds of sentient beings that were with the Buddha, bodhisattvas, and other sage-like individuals when Shākyamuni expounded the *Dharma Flower Sutra* (*Myōhō Renge Kyō*) on Spirit Vulture Peak. The eight are the *deva* who are shining god-like individuals, dragons (*ryū, nāga*) that have often been represented in far-eastern art, *yaksha* (*yasha*) that are comparable to gnomes, dwarves, etc., *kendabba* (*gandharva*) that are the musicians of the paradise of Indra, *shura* (*ashura*) that are like the titans, giants and ogres of European folklore and myth, *karura* (*garuda*) that are mythical birdlike creatures from the Brahmanic pantheon, *kinnara* (*kimnara*) that are the celestial musicians at the court of Kuvera who is a Brahmanic god of wealth, and *magoraga* (*mahorāga*) that are enormous serpents that crawl on their chests. [See also under individual headings for the humanlike non-humans.]

Implanted Seeds – Japanese: *Geshū*
This means planting the seeds for becoming a Buddha in the fields of the minds of sentient beings. It is one of the three benefits – the benefit of the planted seeds, the benefit of their maturation, and the benefit of their liberation. In the Buddha teaching of Shākyamuni, the seeds were implanted in sentient beings in a distant past by the Buddha himself. These sentient beings, after

doing various practices and cultivating themselves for a long sequence of *kalpas*, were able themselves to become enlightened. In the process of becoming Buddhas, the seeds that were sown in a distant past had to have their propensities nourished, so as to become mature and attain their liberation. The gateway to the teachings derived from the external events of the Buddha Shākyamuni's life and work of the *Dharma Flower Sutra* (*Myōhō Renge Kyō*) refers to this distant past as being three thousand *kalpas* with all the dharmas in them ground into grains of dust ago. In the original gateway it clearly defines the Buddha seeds as being implanted in a past of five hundred *kalpas* of grains of dust.

However, these two instances refer to the people who, due to their karmic relationship to Shākyamuni, were able to open their inherent Buddha nature and are referred to by the technical expression as already being in possession of good from the beginning. When these sentient beings reached the level of the *Dharma Flower Sutra* (*Myōhō Renge Kyō*), they were to become emancipated. Those sentient beings who attended the assembly of the *Dharma Flower Sutra* (*Myōhō Renge Kyō*) who allowed no deviation from the truth, as well as the people who had an affinity with the provisional universal vehicle during the thousand-year period of the correct Dharma, were able to attain to enlightenment. During the thousand year period of the formal Dharma, there were people who were able to become emancipated through the *Universal Desistance from Troublesome Worries in Order to See Clearly* (*Maka Shikan*) of Tendai (*T'ien T'ai*).

When we look at the implanted seeds of Nichiren, the sentient beings of the final phase of the Dharma of Shākyamuni had neither a relationship with him, nor were they furnished with good roots. These people are described as fundamentally not yet being in possession of goodness. But because the seeds of Nam Myōhō Renge Kyō had been implanted in the primordially infinite original beginning, as well as their acceptance of the Nam Myōhō Renge Kyō of Nichiren, they are able to directly attain to the correct view of realising that one's person is not separate from becoming a Buddha. [See also **Becoming a Buddha**.]

Individual Vehicle – Japanese: *Shōjō* – also known as the *hīnayāna* or Theravāda School

One of the two major streams of the Buddha teaching. Believers in this vehicle hold that the persons who practise this teaching work out their salvation, by holding to the way demonstrated by the Buddha Shākyamuni at the outset of his teaching. There are many adherents to this teaching in Sri Lanka, Thailand, Burma, and other parts of Southeast Asia.

Intrinsicality of the fundamental substance, the – Japanese: *Tairi*

In the *Treatise on the Whole being Contained in the One Instant of Mind*, Nichiren writes, "The intrinsicality of the substance that is the three thousand existential spaces, the three axioms of relativity (*kū, shūnyatā*), phenomena (*ke*), and the middle way (*chū*), as well as the three bodies, is inherently and infinitely existing, which has nothing to do with the makings of humankind."

Intrinsicality of the real suchness that is immutable in essence and which belongs to the temporary gateway, the – Japanese: *Shakumon fuhen shinnyō no ri*

This concept becomes apparent in the temporary gateway of the *Dharma Flower Sutra* (*Myōhō Renge Kyō*). The real suchness that is immutable in essence implies the eternal unchanging reality that is the intrinsicality of all existence. The real aspect of dharmas (things) that was expounded in the temporary gateway of the *Dharma Flower Sutra* (*Myōhō Renge Kyō*) reveals the theoretical principle of the one instant of thought containing three thousand existential spaces, which enables all sentient beings everywhere to open their inherent Buddha nature. [See also *Treatise on the Real Aspect of All Dharmas, Oral Transmission on the Meaning of the Dharma Flower Sutra* (*Ongi Kuden*).]

Jōgyō, the Bodhisattva – Japanese: *Jōgyō Bosatsu* [See also **Four Great Bodhisattvas**.]

Jōjitsu School, the – Japanese: *Jōjitsushū*

The Jōjitsu School is one of the ten mentioned in Nichiren's *Treatise on Questions and Answers Concerning the Fundamental Object of Veneration*. Jōjitsu translated literally means "attaining reality". This school taught that existence was relativity (*kū*) and took a negative standpoint with regard to everything, denying the existence of anything whatsoever. This teaching is said to be the highest point of the doctrines of the individual vehicle (*shōjō, hīnayāna*) and is thought of as the first step towards the universal vehicle (*daijō, mahāyāna*).

Kalpa – Japanese: *kō* – Sanskrit: *kalpa*

The word *kalpa* can be equated with "aeon", and it represents an astronomically long time. There are various ways that *kalpa* has been defined, and the word has even crept into English. The *Oxford Dictionary* defines *kalpa* as '(In Hindu and Buddhist tradition) an immense period of time and considered to be the length of a single cycle of the cosmos from creation to dissolution.' *Kalpas* are used in various Buddhist writings to represent immeasurably long durations of time. In the *Sixteenth Chapter on the Lifespan of the Tathāgata*, the Buddha Shākyamuni reveals his original enlightenment in the distant past of five hundred *kalpas* with all the dharmas in them ground into grains of dust. The important thing to keep in mind is that existence has always existed and will always exist.

Karma – Japanese: *Go* – Sanskrit: *Karman*

In most Chinese and Japanese dictionaries, this word has a meaning of business, trade, undertaking, conduct, and achievement. However, within the context of the Buddha teaching, all our "doings", "deeds", or workings of some kind, have an effect on our minds and bodies. For example, a bright child full of life becomes a shrewd young boy and later on turns into a bad-tempered old man. Our lives are always influenced by our past and present thoughts and deeds, which we carry beyond our intermediate existence, between dying and being born, into future lives.

Karmic Requital on Subjectivity – Japanese: *Shōhō*

Requital is a translation of the Japanese word *hō*, which is also understood as recompense, retribution, reward, or punishment. In order to take a neutral stance between reward and punishment, I prefer to use the word requital. Karmic requital on our subjectivity is how we feel in relation to any given experience at the instant it occurs. Since all sentient existence is subjective, even if we think we are being objective about it, there is no situation that is not influenced by karma. Karma should be understood as "the goings on" of the totality of existence – past, present, and future.

Karmic Requital on the Environment – Japanese: *Ehō*

Karmic requital on the environment is how our surroundings appear to us, according to our karmic relationships. A grey day can be a nasty, soggy wet morning or a romantic Bruges peeping through the mist. A hamburger can be delicious, or it is simply fast food. Whatever circumstances we may find ourselves in is a karmic requital on our environment, but it takes a long time and a lot of practice before we genuinely understand that the participation in the terror of an air raid is only mind and the Utterness of the Dharma (*Myōhō, Saddharma*). Personally, I am not capable of this.

Karura – Sanskrit: *Garuda*

These birds originally come out of the Brahmanic pantheon. They were also mortal enemies of the dragons. Only the dragons who possess a Buddhist talisman or who are converted to the Buddhist teaching can escape from them. In Japanese painting, they are represented as large, ornate birds with human heads and shown treading on serpents. In Southeast Asia, the walls of temples are often decorated with Karura, as at Angkor or in Java.

Kendabba – Sanskrit: *Gandharva*

These are the musicians of the heaven of Taishaku and the protectors of the Buddha teaching. In paintings, they are depicted as sitting in the position of royal ease. They also have a halo and are said to nourish themselves on scents.

Kinnara – Sanskrit: *Kimnara*

The Kinnara are heavenly musicians serving the court of Kuvera. They are also represented in the shape of an exotic bird with a human torso and shown holding a musical instrument. They are reputed to have marvellous voices.

Kusha School, the – Japanese: *Kushashū*
The text upon which this school is based is the discourses on the Store of Doctrinal Studies of the Dharma (Japanese: *Kusharon*). This school teaches that the self is insubstantial, whereas the dharma (things) and time really exist. Although Nichiren mentions this as one of the Ten Schools in Japan in his *Treatise on Questions and Answers Concerning the Fundamental Object of Veneration*, this school never really established itself. However, its teachings were studied by all serious schools of the Buddha Dharma.

Lesser Vehicle [See also **Individual Vehicle**.]

Life, life and destiny – Japanese: *Myō, Inochi*
This is the totality of one's existence, including karma. There are other meanings of this ideogram, which are beyond the scope of this glossary.

Magoraka – Sanskrit: *Mahorāga*
Of all the human-like non-humans, the *magoraka* are the vaguest. In some Chinese dictionaries, they are defined as "serpents that walk on their breasts". They originally belonged to the Brahmanic pantheon, and in Buddhism they have been partly assimilated by the dragons.

Mantra – Japanese: *Shingon*
This already exists in the *Oxford Dictionary*. On the whole, mantras are syllabic formulas and abbreviated Sanskrit words that are usually used as an aid to recollect the content of a teaching. This word has a relationship to the Sanskrit word *man* – to think, recollect, or suppose. With regard to the teaching of Nichiren Daishōnin, Nam[u] Myōhō Renge Kyō is not a mantra; it is the theme and title made up of seven ideograms, each of which has a profound meaning.

Memyō – Sanskrit: *Ashvaghosha*
A second century Buddhist thinker from the Kingdom of Shravasti in India. He brought many people to the Buddha teaching, due to the quality of his literary style.

Middle way, the – Japanese: *Chūdō*
There are many explanations of the middle way, but that which is relevant here is that of the Tendai School based on the *Treatise on the Median* by Nāgārjuna (*Ryūju*). This is founded in the axiom of relativity, phenomena, and the median or middle way, which inevitably are seen as fused together, and all dharmas can be understood from these three aspects. The phenomenal view of a cup, for example, would be, as it appears with its physical properties of shape, colour, texture, weight, and volume. From the view of relativity, it would be the cup in relation to its surroundings and all that one associates with the word "cup", the history of cups, or even ceramics – in other words, its spatial and noumenal qualities. However, neither noumenal nor the phenomenal aspects are the reality. Its reality is a fusion of both. Tendai's (*T'ien T'ai*) vision goes further to that which he calls the unthinkably unutterable triple axiom of existence – relativity, phenomenon, and the middle way. The unthinkably unutterable is the same as Utterness (*Myō*), which gives rise to the teaching that the three ways of seeing are contained in the oneness and instant of mind. [See also *Treatise on the Real Aspect of All Dharmas*, Such a final superlative that is equally present from the first to the last of the nine such qualities.]

Mind – Japanese: *kokoro*, Chinese: *shin, i* - Sanskrit: *citta*
Nichiren Daishōnin begins his *Treatise on the Fundamental Object of Veneration (gohonzon) for Contemplating the Mind Instigated by the Bodhisattva Superior Practice (Jōgyō, Vishishtachāritra) For the Fifth Five-hundred-year Period After the Tathāgata's Passing over to Nirvana (Kanjin no Honzon Shō)* by intimating the concept of the one instant of thought containing three thousand existential spaces through a quote from Tendai (*T'ien T'ai*), which summarily goes over it. Nichiren goes on to say, "If there is no mind, then that is the end of it. But even the minutest existence of mind is endowed with the three thousand existential spaces." Further on, there is

another quote that says, "Because it becomes what is called the unthinkably inexplicable realm of objectivity (*Fushigikyō*) [i.e., the whole of existence, irrespective as to whether it is inside or outside our heads], it is here where the meaning lies."

However, if we are to talk about existence, it is not too difficult to think of it as the whole of existence. I am here in Flanders which is part of Belgium, which again is a part of the European Union that is on the old continent of the planet Earth, which is part of the solar system that is part of the Milky Way, and so forth. Also, the inner space inside my head is just as vast. Sometimes we randomly use the word "water", which may have the nuance of water in the tap but also all the water in the sea. Life and mind are almost synonymous.

When I was in Hong Kong during the 1970s, my Chinese Teacher Hsin Kuang made me repeat at the beginning of each session, "All dharmas, i.e., anything that the mind or body can be conscious of, are only mind; and the three realms where 1) sentient beings have appetites and desires, 2) where they are incarnated in physical bodies in physical surroundings, and 3) where they are endowed with a realm of thoughts, dreams, fantasies, and concepts (*sangai*) are only three ways of perception (*shiki*)."

Myōraku (*Miao-lo*) firmly states that the whole of mind can be divided into materiality and mind. This seems to suggest that all the contents of the physical world exist and follow their own laws of 1) coming into being, 2) lasting as long as they should, 3) degenerating and falling apart, 4) then ceasing to exist altogether (*shō, ju, i, metsu*). This concept would indicate that time is a one-way direction. But if there is no mind to be aware of it, it doesn't matter.

The experience of being confronted with the experience of the physical and material worlds is the storehouse cognition *arayashiki*. The day we are born, everything is just there waiting for us to explore and resist. And it is in this way that we build up our karma.

The Buddha teaching of Nichiren helps us to understand that life, or rather living and dying, is a continual experience. But if we endeavour to open up our inherent Buddha nature with our persons just as they are, then everything we undergo becomes richer and more meaningful. The teaching of the Daishōnin is not particularly concerned with how big or how small the universe is or what it is made of. This is a problem for physicists. However, mind (*kokoro, shin, i*) is limited to all that is inscribed on the Fundamental Object of Veneration (*gohonzon*), which is held in place by the four universal *deva* kings. Needless to say, all of this is as big as life. Mind is both our conscious world, as well as having all the implications of the unconscious depths as described by the various trends in psychology. Although we may be governed by the archetypes in our respective psyches, they are nevertheless distorted by our karma. The cognition of pure mind is in no way separate from the *Gohonzon* and is the real driving force of life.

This fact is celebrated by the recitation of the title and theme (*daimoku*), Nam[u] Myōhō Renge Kyō. A rough translation would be to devote one's life to and to found it on (*Nam[u]*) the Utterness of the Dharma [entirety of existence, enlightenment and unenlightenment] (*Myōhō*) permeated by the underlying white lotus flower-like mechanism of the interdependence of cause, concomitancy and effect (*Renge*) in its whereabouts of the ten [psychological] realms of dharmas (*Kyō*). Our mind is always where it is focused on, whether we are conscious or not. But at the same time, it is the oneness of mind.

In modern Japanese, the word *kokoro* for mind has acquired many nuances, as has the same word in modern English. [Kenkyusha's *New Japanese English Dictionary*, pages 897 to 901.]

Mind, the ideogram for (Japanese: *Shin* – Sanskrit: *Hrdaya*) can also refer to the heart as the seat of thought or intelligence. In both cases, the mind or heart is conceived as an eight-petalled lotus. Both sentient beings and the non-sentient objective world possess heart and mind. Since mind is the whole of mind, it is also its own storehouse. This is the storehouse cognition (Japanese: *Zōshiki* – Sanskrit: *Alayavijnaña*) which is the source of all mental activity and the storehouse of all dharmas.

Nichiren Daishōnin, in his *Treatise on the Opposing Views of the Eight Schools* [*Goshō Shimpen*, pages 520 & 521], quotes from the fifth fascicle (scroll) of the *Universal Desistance from Troublesome Worries in Order to See Clearly* (*Maka Shikan*). It says, "The mind is a skilful artist that creates the five aggregates [which are 1) materiality, physical form, and all that is perceived through the five organs of sense; 2) sensation, feeling, and the functioning of the mind in the way we perceive the world within us and around us; 3) concepts, the power to discern, discriminate and reason; 4) volition and the ability to make informed decisions and the choice of action; 5) cognition and ways of knowing associated with the nature of mind, which is the cognition of all the mental powers]. Out of everything that is to be found in each and every realm of existence, there is nothing that is not created by mind itself – all the variations of the five aggregates that are inherent in our own realms of dharmas."

Again Nichiren quotes from this treatise towards the end: "Someone may ask, 'what does it say in the Flower Garland Sutra?' Then again you must point out that it shows what our inner and outer environment really consists of. As previously mentioned, the mind creates, but what is created is already there in the mind. Therefore, by quoting the text of the mind, creating would imply that the mind already contains what it creates. In the middle of the eighteenth fascicle (scroll) of the Sutra, the Bodhisattva Kotokurin says something like this in his metric hymn. As the mind is a skilful artist that creates the five aggregates, there is not a single dharma in all the existential and dharma realms that is not created by mind. The mind is also the Buddha, and sentient beings are just the same. The mind, the Buddha, as well as sentient beings, are not separate entities. If somebody were to aspire to know all the Buddhas of the past, present, and future, this person should see this aspiration in the following manner: It is the mind that creates all the Tathāgatas." So from the Buddhist viewpoint, mind and existence are the same. In the *Setsumon Geji*, the ideogram for mind, *shin* or *kokoro*, is defined as "The human heart is in the middle of the body."

Mind as the faculty of thought – Japanese: *I, Mano, Kokoro* – Sanskrit: *Manas, Manah*

This is the faculty that makes us think we are who we are. At first sight, this term also corresponds to mind in its widest sense, but biased towards the intellect, intelligence, understanding, with also an undertone of will and intention. It is also the individual will to go on living, due to its inherent addiction to the 'television screen of life'. It could be the catalogue of all human experience. Animals do learn words, but do not possess language to the extent of human beings. What mind as the faculty of thought cannot really understand is that the 'television screen of life' is only a reflection of mind as it is according to our karmic circumstances. Still, the impressions are funnelled in through the first six cognitions [which are 1) the cognition of sight, 2) the cognition of hearing, 3) the cognition of smell, 4) the cognition of taste, 5) the cognition of touch, and 6) the cognition of being aware of and conscious of these former five cognitions and also what goes on in the mind].

What this really amounts to is that what is perceived by these first six cognitions as well as mind as the faculty of thought is all that goes on in our lives. This faculty of thought is all that goes on in our lives. This faculty has a strong power of attaching itself to the result of its own thinking. It is constantly being aware of images, sounds, tastes, and so forth, even if they are only imagined. All of these induce the mind as the faculty of thought to presume to be the controller of the body, as well as being the part of us that makes decisions. This faculty also sees itself as independent by nature.

Mind as the faculty of thought is like one of those two-faced monsters from the realms of mythology. One face looks towards the six cognitions, and the other looks towards the cognition that is the storehouse of mind [Japanese: *Zōshiki* – Sanskrit: *Alaya*]. The faculty of thought does not know that the cognition that is the storehouse of mind is none other than mind, but we can always find some kind of faith to want to practise – a practice to dissipate our bewilderment and open our inherent Buddha nature and realise who we are.

In the *Setsumon Geji*, one of the oldest Chinese dictionaries, the ideogram *i* is defined as "The mind understands words and knows their intention."

Muhengyō, the Bodhisattva – Japanese: *Muhengyō Bosatsu* [See also **Four Great Bodhisattvas**.]

Myōraku – Japanese: *Myōraku Daishi* – Chinese: *Miao-lo Dashi*
Referred to as the Universal Teacher Myōraku (*Miao-lo*), he was born in China in 711 CE and died in 782 CE and was the ninth patriarch of the Chinese Tendai School. When he was twenty years of age, he studied the teachings of the Tendai School under Genrō, the eighth patriarch. At thirty-eight, he took holy orders and fully studied the teachings of the *Zen, Kegon, Shingon,* and *Hossō* Schools of that period. When the Tendai School was on the verge of collapse, he refuted all the arguments of each and every school and established the view that the single vehicle of the *Dharma Flower Sutra* (*Myōhō Renge Kyō*) was the truth.

Nam Myōhō Renge Kyō
The consecration and founding of one's life on the *Sutra on the White Lotus Flower-like Mechanism of the Utterness of the Dharma* (*Myōhō Renge Kyō*). Nam Myōhō Renge Kyō – which means to devote our lives to and found them on (*Nam*[*u*]) the Utterness of the Dharma (*Myōhō*) [entirety of existence, enlightenment and unenlightenment] permeated by the underlying white lotus flower-like mechanism of the interdependence of cause, concomitancy and effect (*Renge*) in its whereabouts of the ten [psychological] realms of dharmas (*Kyō*) – is the basic chant of Nichiren Shōshū and is often referred to as *daimoku* or the title and theme. It is also one of the three universal esoteric Dharmas. Nichiren says the following about Nam Myōhō Renge Kyō in *The Oral Transmission on the Meaning of the Dharma Flower Sutra* (*Ongi Kuden*): "*Nam*[*u*] is a Sanskrit word which, translated into classical Chinese, means 'to consecrate and found one's life on'. In the confines of the Fundamental Object of Veneration (*gohonzon*) to which we consecrate and found our lives on, there is both the person and the Dharma. The person is Nichiren, who is the Shākyamuni submerged within the text. The Dharma is the

Dharma Flower Sutra (*Myōhō Renge Kyō*) for the final phase of the Dharma of Shākyamuni, which is Nam Myōhō Renge Kyō and is the Fundamental Object of Veneration (*gohonzon*). This means that we consecrate and found our lives on the Universal Fundamental Object of Veneration (*gohonzon*) of the oneness of the person and the Dharma.

"Furthermore, 'to consecrate' implies that we turn our lives towards the intrinsicality of the real suchness that is immutable in essence and which belongs to the temporary gateway. 'Our lives' refers to a life founded in the wisdom of the real suchness as it is according to karmic circumstances and is a concept that belongs to the original gateway. This consecration and making it a foundation of our lives is Nam Myōhō Renge Kyō [the consecration and founding of our lives (*Nam[u]*) on the *Sutra on the White Lotus Flower-like Mechanism of the Utterness of the Dharma* (*Myōhō Renge Kyō*)]. This is explained as the intrinsicality of the real suchness that is immutable in essence and the real suchness as it changes according to the circumstances. Again, 'to consecrate' has the meaning of our physical existence, and 'our lives' implies all that goes on in our minds. The inseparability of mind and materiality is the single superlative that is the utterly imponderable, underlying principle. This is also explained as 'turning towards this single superlative because it is what is called the Buddha vehicle'.

"Moreover, '*Nam[u]*' (*Namas*) of Nam Myōhō Renge Kyō is Sanskrit; *Myōhō Renge Kyō* is classical Chinese. It is said that Nam Myōhō Renge Kyō is at the same time both Sanskrit and Chinese. In Sanskrit, it is *Saddharma Puṇḍarīka Sūtram*. *Sat* is Utterness [*Myō*], *Dharma* is the same in English and *hō* in Japanese; *Puṇḍarīka* is the lotus flower [*Renge*], and *Sūtram* [*Kyō*] means sutra. The nine syllables of *Saddharma Puṇḍarīka Sūtram* are the Buddha entity that is made up of nine World Honoured Ones which symbolise the nine dharma realms not being separate from the Buddha realm. Utterness [*Myō*] is the essence of the Dharma and dharmas [*hō*] are its unenlightenment. The single entity of unenlightenment and the Dharma essence is called the Utterness of the Dharma.

"The lotus flower [*renge*] is the two dharmas of cause and effect and is understood as cause and effect being a single interdependent entity. Sutra [*kyō*] is said to be all the speech, words, utterances, and voices of all sentient beings. This is explained as 'when the voice becomes the transmission of the Buddha Dharma, it is called a sutra'. By being constant throughout the past, present, and future, it is called a sutra. The realm of the dharmas or the Dharma realm is the Utterness of the Dharma (*Myōhō, Saddharma*). The realm of the dharmas is the lotus flower. The realm of the dharmas is the sutra. The Lotus Flower is the Buddha entity of the Nine World Honoured Ones in the eight-petalled lotus. You must ponder over this thoroughly."

Thus, Nam Myōhō Renge Kyō means to devote our lives to and found them on (*Nam[u]*) the Utterness of the Dharma [entirety of existence, enlightenment and unenlightenment] (*Myōhō*) permeated by the underlying white lotus flower-like mechanism of the interdependence of cause, concomitancy and effect (*Renge*) in its whereabouts of the ten [psychological] realms of dharmas (*Kyō*).

[See also *Oral Transmission on the Meaning of the Dharma Flower Sutra* (*Ongi Kuden*)] [This translation has been slightly simplified by the author in the interests of accessibility.]

Namu – Japanese: *Nam* – Sanskrit: *Namas*
This is a Sino-Japanese phonetic rendering of the original Sanskrit word which has a number of meanings:
1. To consecrate one's life and found it on.
2. To take refuge in and worship.
3. To venerate and worship.
4. To respect and venerate.
5. To commit oneself to the meaning.
6. Save me.
7. Carry me over to the shores of Nirvana.

To serve and hold in veneration, to faithfully follow, and to commit oneself to the meaning, refer to mental karma. To take refuge in and worship, and to bow one's head to the floor and worship, represent bodily karma. Save me and carry me to the shores of Nirvana refer to oral karma, whereas to consecrate one's life and found it on refer to the three karmas of mind, body, and mouth. However, when Nichiren Kōmon Buddhists recite this word before *Myōhō Renge Kyō* it is always pronounced *Nam*, except when reciting the drawn-out title and theme when it is pronounced *naaaamuu*. [See also **Nam Myōhō Renge Kyō**.]

Nevertheless, how the Daishōnin used and understood this word has deeper implications that go far beyond these meanings. In his *Letter Concerning a Sack of White Rice*, he writes, "*Nam* is an Indian word. In China and Japan, it means to consecrate and make something the foundation of one's life. What we consecrate and found our lives on is the commitment of our lives and destinies to the Buddha." In *The Oral Transmission on the Meaning of the Dharma Flower Sutra (Ongi Kuden)*, he extends his argument further: "*Nam* is a Sanskrit word, which translated into classical Chinese is *kimyō*, which means 'to consecrate and found one's life on'. In the confines of the Fundamental Object of Veneration (*gohonzon*) in which we consecrate and found our lives, there is both the person and the Dharma. The person is Nichiren, who is the Shākyamuni submerged within the text. The Dharma is the *Dharma Flower Sutra (Myōhō Renge Kyō)*, which is Nam Myōhō Renge Kyō and is the Fundamental Object of Veneration (*gohonzon*). This means that we consecrate and found our lives on the Universal Fundamental Object of Veneration (*gohonzon*) of the oneness of the person and the Dharma. Furthermore, 'to consecrate' implies that we turn our lives towards the intrinsicality of the real suchness that is immutable in essence and which belongs to the temporary gateway (*zuien shinnyo no chi*). 'Our lives' refer to a life founded in the wisdom of the real suchness as it is according to the changing circumstances and is a concept that belongs to the original gateway (*fuhen shinnyo no ri*). This consecration and making it a foundation of our lives is Nam Myōhō Renge Kyō."

Nichiren Daishōnin [1222-82 CE] [See also Introduction.]

Non-existence of self-nature, the – Japanese: *mujishō*
Each and every dharma (things) comes into being through cause, karmic circumstances, and affinity. There is no such thing as an inherent essence or an original nature.

One Buddha Vehicle, the – Japanese: *ichijō*
This vehicle is the only vehicle which is the Dharma that really leads people to become enlightened. In the *Second Chapter on Expedient Means*, in the *Dharma Flower Sutra* (*Myōhō Renge Kyō*), it says, "That is why the Tathāgata uses only the one Buddha vehicle to expound the Dharma for sentient beings." This term could also be paraphrased as the instructive Dharma that is the vehicle that transports people to the Buddha's own environment. In the *Second Chapter on Expedient Means*, Shākyamuni cleared away the teachings for the three vehicles (those of the bodhisattvas, the people who are partially awakened due to the search for the meaning of life, and the hearers of the voice, all of whom were at the time doing separate practices), so as to reveal to them the real truth of the Buddha enlightenment. [See also **Vehicle, Two vehicles, Three vehicles, Ten psychological realms of dharmas.**]

One instant of thought containing three thousand existential spaces, the – Japanese: *Ichinen Sanzen*
The whole of existence, the Utterness of the Dharma (*Myōhō, Saddharma*). In every instant of life or mind of all non-sentiency and sentient life, there is the whole of both subjective and objective existence. The "three thousand", which originally was a concept of Indian origin, is a term used by the Tendai (*T'ien T'ai*) and Nichiren teachings to express the totality of life. To arrive at this number, one begins with the ten realms of dharma, which refer to subjectivity, determined by karma, which consists of ten categories of ways of being or possible moods – hell, hungry demons, animals, *shura*, human beings, *deva*, hearers of the voice, those who are partially enlightened due to a profound search for the meaning of life, bodhisattvas, Buddhas.

Each one of these ten realms contains the other nine in itself, so that there are a hundred realms in total. These hundred realms are conditioned by the ten ways in which all dharmas make themselves present to any of our six sense organs – appearance, nature, substance, strength, action, cause, karmic relation, fruition, requital, and the final superlative that is equally present in the other nine such qualities which are present in every instant of life. When these hundred realms are multiplied by the ten such qualities, the total becomes one thousand.

All these various subjective mental states and their various conditions due to the ten such qualities take place in three kinds of existential space. Firstly, there is the existential space of sentient beings. According to the fifth fascicle of Tendai's (*T'ien T'ai*) *Universal Desistance from Troublesome Worries in order to See Clearly* (*Maka Shikan*), an existential space implies that there are other existential spaces which reveal the differences between beings in each of the ten realms from the Buddha realm to that of hell. Secondly, there is the existential space of the five aggregates, which are the reciprocal differences between our physical appearance, our perceptions, thoughts, volition, and ways of knowing. Thirdly, there is the existential space of abode and terrain, which may be understood as that whilst hellish beings live in hell, human beings inhabit the world of humankind. With these three kinds of existential space, the thousand subjective mental states become three thousand life conditions and their respective environments. Since existence cannot be separated from mind, this one instant of thought containing three thousand existential spaces is understood as being the Utterness of both animate and inanimate existence. It follows that nothing can exist outside it. [See also **Ten psychological realms of dharmas, Ten such qualities, Three kinds of existential space.**]

Original Gateway, the – Japanese: *Honmon*

The Dharma gateway that reveals the original terrain of the Buddha. The opposite to the expression temporary gateway. The traditional metaphor explains the temporary gateway as being the reflection of the moon in the pond, whereas the original gateway is the moon itself. Tendai (*T'ien T'ai*), in the first fascicle of his *Textual Explanation of the Dharma Flower Sutra* (*Hokke Mongu*), divided the *Dharma Flower Sutra* (*Myōhō Renge Kyō*) into the temporary gateway and the original gateway. The original gateway is the last fourteen chapters of the *Dharma Flower Sutra* (*Myōhō Renge Kyō*), beginning with the *Fifteenth Chapter on the Bodhisattvas who Swarm up out of the Earth* to the *Twenty-eighth Chapter on the Persuasiveness and Quest* [for Buddhahood] *of the Bodhisattva Universally Good* (*Fugen, Samantabhadra*). The main characteristic of the temporary gateway is its approximation to the one instant of thought containing three thousand kinds of existential space, which can only amount to the theoretical possibility of becoming a Buddha.

On the other hand, the original gateway clearly defines the original terrain of the Buddha, which is his original attainment in the primordial infinity. This implies that the Buddha realm is inherent in the ever-present infinite in time (*kuon ganjo*). Existence has always existed and will always exist. The *Sixteenth Chapter on the Lifespan of the Tathāgata* becomes the very essence of the original gateway, by destroying the notion of the gateway of the teachings derived from the external events of the Buddha Shākyamuni's life and work and other provisional teachings that the Buddha was first enlightened in Buddhagaya in his historical lifetime. The original gateway indicates the cause, fruition, and abode of his attainment to the way of Buddhahood in the primordial distance of five hundred *kalpas* with all the dharmas in them ground into dust and thus establishes the grounds for the pragmatic one instant of thought containing three thousand kinds of existential space.

In the teaching of Nichiren, this astronomical figure of the primordial distance is the primordially infinite original beginning, which in present-day language is the ever-present infinite in time (*kuon ganjo*). This concept is inherent in Nichiren's *Treatise on the Utterness of the Original Cause* as the one and only original gateway. The teachings that are called the meritorious virtues, which are based on a literal understanding of the *Dharma Flower Sutra* (*Myōhō Renge Kyō*) as well as the teachings derived from the external events of the Buddha Shākyamuni's life and work and original gateways, are taken to be the provisional gateway. But the teaching of the *Sixteenth Chapter on the Lifespan of the Tathāgata* of the doctrine of the Buddha seeds being implanted in the primordial infinity is the one and only original gateway. [See also **Real Teachings**, the.]

Primordial infinity – Japanese: *Ku.on* [See also **Primordially infinite original beginning**.]

Primordially infinite original beginning, the – Japanese: *ku.on ganjō*

The ever-present infinite in time (*kuon ganjo*). Since existence has always existed, there can be no primordially infinite, original beginning. Instead, the equation that covers the whole of existence is arrived at by reciting the theme and title, Nam Myōhō Renge Kyō, which is to devote our lives to and found them on (*Nam[u]*) the Utterness of the Dharma (*Myōhō*) [entirety of existence, enlightenment and unenlightenment] permeated by the underlying white lotus flower-like mechanism of the interdependence of cause, concomitancy and effect (*Renge*) in its whereabouts of the ten [psychological] realms of dharmas (*Kyō*). This title and theme can be applied to any existing theory of how existence works.

Provisional Teachings, the

The *Provisional Teachings* were throughout the lifetime of Shākyamuni (the *historical* Buddha) that were taught in a way so as to entice people to the Buddha teaching and away from various Brahmanical doctrines. This is clearly stated at the beginning of the *Collation of the Layers of the Various Teachings of all the Buddhas of the Past, Present and Future as to Which Specific Doctrines are to be Discarded or Established.* In these teachings prior to the *Dharma Flower Sutra* (*Myōhō Renge Kyō*), usually the intrinsic quality of all dharmas both sentient and non-sentient was relativity (*kū*). Humankind had to await the arrival of Nichiren Daishōnin to understand that the essence of all dharmas is Nam Myōhō Renge Kyō, which means to devote our lives to and found them on (*Nam[u]*) the Utterness of the Dharma (*Myōhō*) [entirety of existence, enlightenment and unenlightenment] permeated by the underlying white lotus flower-like mechanism of the interdependence of cause, concomitancy and effect (*Renge*) in its whereabouts of the ten [psychological] realms of dharmas (*Kyō*). This theme and title (*daimoku*) encompasses in the teaching all subjective existence and every possible objectiveness. On the other hand, relativity (*kū*) in the teaching of Shākyamuni is closer to a theoretical concept, whereas in the teaching of Nichiren the title and theme, Nam Myōhō Renge Kyō, entails the workings of the whole of existence.

Pure Land School, the – Japanese: *Jōdoshū*

The name of this school has also been translated as the Immaculate Terrain School. Essentially the teaching of this school is based on Nāgārjuna's (*Ryūju*) principle of the easy road to Nirvana. This school was established by Hōnen, who first taught its doctrine in 1175 CE. He underlined the need for faith and the continual repetition of the incantation, *Namu Amida Butsu*. This formula is often referred to as the *Nembutsu*. At the time of Nichiren, this school had become very popular, and its teaching still survives today in a somewhat folkloric state, for funerals only.

Real aspect, the – Japanese: *Jissō*

The actuality of something – its Dharma nature, its suchness, its essential truth or unchangeable intrinsicality. The real aspect of all dharmas (things) is revealed in the *Second Chapter on Expedient Means* of the *Dharma Flower Sutra* (*Myōhō Renge Kyō*). In the eighth fascicle of the *Recondite Significance of the Dharma Flower Sutra* (*Hokke Gengi*), it is written, "Whatever is done by thought, word, or deed is transient. All dharmas are devoid of ego and are the silent stillness of Nam Myōhō Renge Kyō." These three definitions are seen as the three tokens of proof of the universal vehicle (*daijō*, *mahāyāna*). However, in the teaching of Nichiren, everything that exists has only one fundamental "isness" which is Nam Myōhō Renge Kyō. [See also **Nam Myōhō Renge Kyō,** which means to devote our lives to and found them on (*Nam*[*u*]) the Utterness of the Dharma (*Myōhō*) [entirety of existence, enlightenment and unenlightenment] permeated by the underlying white lotus flower-like mechanism of the interdependence of cause, concomitancy and effect (*Renge*) in its whereabouts of the ten [psychological] realms of dharmas (*Kyō*).] This of course implies the mutual possession of the three thousand existential spaces that make up an instant of thought. [See also **One instant of thought containing three thousand existential spaces.**]

Realm of the dharmas, the – Japanese: *Hokkai*

The name for everything in general – noumenal or phenomenal and bridging the whole of existence. [See also **Nam Myōhō Renge Kyō.**]

Real Teachings, the – Japanese: *Honmon*
The section on the original Buddha, which is the latter half of the *Dharma Flower Sutra* (*Myōhō Renge Kyō, Saddharma Pundarîka Sūtram*). In *A Collation of the Layers of the Various Teachings of all the Buddhas of the Past, Present and Future as to Which Specific Doctrines are to be Discarded or Established* (*Sō Kan Mon Shō*), we have the following paragraph: "In the *Explanatory Notes on the Recondite Significance of the Dharma Flower*, Myōraku states, 'The provisional teachings were taught for the propensities of the people who are trapped in the first nine realms of dharmas, but it was the real teachings that revealed the Dharma realm of the Buddha, which is the ultimate truth.'"

Relativity – Japanese: *Kū* – Sanskrit: *Shūnyatā*
This concept is often translated as "the void" or "nothingness", but perhaps the definition of "relativity" which quite a number of Japanese dictionaries use is nearer to the mark. In the teaching of Nichiren, relativity is the underlying nature of the whole of existence. On the Fundamental Object of Veneration (*gohonzon*), it is represented in the centre by the Nam[u] Myōhō Renge Kyō, which means to devote our lives to and found them on (*Nam[u]*) the Utterness of the Dharma (*Myōhō*) [entirety of existence, enlightenment and unenlightenment] permeated by the underlying white lotus flower-like mechanism of the interdependence of cause, concomitancy and effect (*Renge*) in its whereabouts of the ten [psychological] realms of dharmas (*Kyō*).

Essentially, it is the implication of the one instant of mind containing three thousand existential spaces, in terms of the ten ways in which dharmas make themselves present to any of our six senses. Since we are all unenlightened, we are unable to perceive the fundamental basis of existence, which is Nam Myōhō Renge Kyō and means to devote our lives to and found them on (*Nam[u]*) the Utterness of the Dharma (*Myōhō*) [entirety of existence, enlightenment and unenlightenment] permeated by the underlying white lotus flower-like mechanism of the interdependence of cause, concomitancy and effect (*Renge*) in its whereabouts of the ten [psychological] realms of dharmas (*Kyō*). This is the empty space beyond any of our physical perceptions.

Ritsu School, the – Japanese: *Risshū*

This is one of the Ten Schools mentioned in the *Treatise on Questions and Answers Concerning the Fundamental Object of Veneration*. The doctrine of this school is based upon the rules and disciplines for monks and nuns of the universal vehicle (*daijō, mahāyāna*). The concept was that if the practitioners followed these rules they would be on the way to enlightenment. This school was founded by Dōsen (*Tao-Hsüan*) of the Tang dynasty and brought to Japan by Ganjin in 754 CE.

Samādhi – Japanese: *Sanmai*

This word is in the *Oxford Dictionary*, and its meaning is less difficult than it appears. Until now, this word has in the Nichiren Daishōnin Reader been translated as "the perfect absorption of the mind into the one object of meditation". There is no difference whatsoever between this periphrastic definition and the word *samādhi*. Some Chinese dictionaries explain this term as "When we are giving our wholehearted attention to something we are doing, it is a *samādhi*, but not necessarily a *dhyana*." [See also **Dhyāna**.]

Sanron School, the – Japanese: *Sanronshū*

Sanron literally means the three discourses, which are fundamental to this school. These teachings were brought to China by the great translator Kumārajīva. Essentially its doctrine is the middle way. While denying the reality of phenomenal and noumenal existence, it aimed at the reality of a Buddha awakening that is beyond our conception and thus barely avoided the pitfall of nihilism.

Self-nature – Japanese: *Jishō*

The unchangeable and inherent quality in all life and all dharmas (things). It is also translated as the essential or inherent property or the inner nature. However, in the first fascicle of the *Treatise on the Middle Way*, Nāgārjuna (*Ryūju*) explains, "All causes and affinities do not arise out of self-nature, but from the non-existence of self-nature." Self-nature can be explained by Nam Myōhō Renge Kyō, which means to devote our lives to and found them on (*Nam[u]*) the Utterness of the Dharma (*Myōhō*) [entirety of existence, enlightenment and unenlightenment] permeated by the underlying white lotus flower-like mechanism of the interdependence of cause, concomitancy and effect (*Renge*) in its whereabouts of the ten [psychological] realms of dharmas (*Kyō*). [See also *Treatise on the Whole being Contained in the One Instant of Mind*, **Non-existence of self-nature**.]

Shākyamuni – Japanese: *Shakason*

The historical Buddha. *Shakason* literally means the honoured one of the family of Shakyas, and Shākyamuni means the sage of the Shakyas. After five hundred or five hundred fifty previous incarnations, Shākyamuni finally attained to becoming a bodhisattva and was born in the Tusita heaven. He descended as a white elephant through the right side of his mother, Queen Maya. Simpler statements say that he was born the son of King Suddhodana. Later he was married to Yashodhara, who bore him a son, Rahula (*Ragora*). He left the royal palace at the age of nineteen to search for the truth, and, at the age of thirty or thirty-five, he realised that the way of release from the suffering of the endless cycle of birth and death lay, not in asceticism, but by purifying oneself morally and thereby erasing past karmas. He became known as the Buddha. He is said to have died in 486 BCE. The sutras mention many Buddhas and all are considered to be emanations of Shākyamuni. However, in the writings of Nichiren Daishōnin, the name Shākyamuni often refers to the original Buddha of the *Chapter on the Lifespan of the Tathāgata*. Nichiren is the manifestation of this Buddha in particular.

Shōan – Chinese: *Chang-an*

The legitimate successor to Tendai (*T'ien T'ai*), he committed Tendai's (*T'ien T'ai*) lectures and sermons to writing, which were later put together as the *Recondite Significance of the Dharma Flower Sutra* (*Hokke Gengi*), the *Textual Explanations of the Dharma Flower Sutra* (*Hokke Mongu*), and the *Universal Desistance from Troublesome Worries in order to See Clearly* (*Maka Shikan*). He also wrote commentaries on the *Nirvana Sutra*.

Six Inseparabilities – Japanese: *Rokusoku*
These are, according to the Tendai School, the following six stages of bodhisattva development:
1. The inseparability of the Buddha nature from reasoning. This is the logical concept of the one instant of thought containing three thousand existential spaces and that therefore all beings and all things can open their inherent Buddha realm.
2. The inseparability of the Buddha nature from the title and theme and their ideograms. This implies that the apprehension of Buddhist terms and those who have faith in them are on their way to becoming Buddhas.
3. The inseparability of the Buddha nature from contemplation and practice. This is an advance beyond terminology to earnest study and doing the corresponding practices.
4. The inseparability of the Buddha nature from similitude. This is the stage of semblance to purity and also that of experiencing the benefits of practice.
5. The inseparability of the Buddha nature from the discrimination of the truth. This is the ability to perceive all beings, all events, and all things in the light of the one instant of thought containing three thousand existential spaces.
6. The inseparability of the Buddha nature from the final superlative. This is the stage of having become utterly awakened.

The Daishōnin defines the six inseparabilities, in the first article of the second part of *The Oral Transmission on the Meaning of the Dharma Flower Sutra* (*Ongi Kuden*), as follows: "When it comes to setting up the allocations for the six inseparabilities, then the Tathāgata of this chapter is the common mortal of the inseparability of reasoning."

The respectful acceptance of *Nam Myōhō Renge Kyō* in our minds becomes the inseparability of the name and ideograms. This is because it is when we first begin to hear the title and theme. Hearing and reciting it is the inseparability of contemplation and practice. This inseparability of contemplation and practice is to contemplate the Fundamental Object of Veneration (*gohonzon*) of the pragmatic one instant of thought containing three thousand existential spaces. Therefore, the restraint of delusive thinking that brings about delusions is said to be the inseparability of similitude.

Setting out to convert others is seen as the inseparability of discrimination of the truth. Becoming a Buddha of the triple body independent of all action is said to be the inseparability of the final superlative. Broadly speaking, the repression of delusions is not the highest point of the *Sixteenth Chapter on the Lifespan of the Tathāgata*. But the ultimate principle of this chapter is to be able to know the fundamentally existing actual fundamental substance of the common mortal just as it is.

Spaceless Void, the – Japanese: *Kokū*

The vacuity that contains the whole of existence, space, and time and is Nam Myōhō Renge Kyō, which means to devote our lives to and found them on (*Nam*[*u*]) the Utterness of the Dharma (*Myōhō*) [entirety of existence, enlightenment and unenlightenment] permeated by the underlying white lotus flower-like mechanism of the interdependence of cause, concomitancy and effect (*Renge*) in its whereabouts of the ten [psychological] realms of dharmas (*Kyō*).

Spirit Vulture Peak, the – Japanese: *Ryōjusen* – Sanskrit: *Grdhrakūta*

The present-day Giddore, a mountain located in the northeast of Rajagriha, the capital of Maghadha in ancient India. As far as the teachings of Nichiren Daishōnin are concerned, this is where Shākyamuni expounded the *Dharma Flower Sutra* (*Myōhō Renge Kyō*). The Spirit Vulture Peak is often used as an analogy for the Buddha realm and also the Buddha enlightenment.

Stupa – Japanese: *Tō*

A *stupa* was originally a tumulus or a mound for the remains of the dead. Later, with the advent of the Buddha Teaching, a *stupa* was thought of more as a reliquary for the remains of a Buddha or relics of his mind, such as sutras, etc. Since our own bodies are supposed to be made up of 84,000 particles, King Ashoka is said to have built 84,000 *stupas* for the preservation of remains of Shākyamuni. In a later development, the *stupa* became known as a pagoda, in China, Korea, and Japan.

However, as far as the teachings of the universal vehicle (*daijō, mahāyāna*) are concerned, a *stupa* is seen as a representation of the Buddha and his Dharma realm. The proportions of this development correspond to those of the halos of the Buddha images, but put into three dimensions. In the esoteric schools, this is the concept of a *stupa* being a schematic representation of the elements of the universe, in terms of a sequence of geometric symbols. Starting at the bottom, there is a yellow square, which stands for earth. This is surmounted by a black circular disc, which symbolises water, which again has a red triangle on top of it representing fire. On top of this triangle is a white crescent moon, with its corners pointing upwards like horns, representing wind. And on top and in the centre of this moon there is a pale blue pear shape that represents relativity (*kū*).

However, in the teachings of Nichiren, a *stupa* is also conceived as being the Dharma realm, in the sense of being its Utterness (*Myō*). This is not separate from Nichiren's vision of the Fundamental Object of Veneration (*gohonzon*). [See also *A Letter to the Lay Practitioner Abutsu, Treatise on the Fundamental Object of Veneration for Contemplating the Mind Instigated by the Bodhisattva Superior Practice (Jōgyō, Vishishtachāritra) For the Fifth Five Hundred Year Period After the Tathāgata's Passing over to Nirvana.*]

Stupa made of Precious Materials – Japanese: *Hōtō*

This *stupa* is recounted in the *Eleventh Chapter on Seeing the Vision of the Stupa made of Precious Materials* of the *Dharma Flower Sutra* (*Myōhō Renge Kyō*) as being adorned with the seven treasures of gold, silver, lapis lazuli, coral, agate, pearl, and ruby. Nichiren, in *The Oral Transmission on the Meaning of the Dharma Flower Sutra* (*Ongi Kuden*), describes these precious substances as seven kinds of essential dharmic wealth needed for practising the Buddha Path. In the *Eleventh Chapter* of the *Dharma Flower Sutra* (*Myōhō Renge Kyō*), this *stupa* surged up from the earth, and its enormous size was five hundred *yojanas* high and two hundred fifty *yojanas* wide. A *yojana* is thought to be one day's march for the army. There is some suggestion that the distance covered before unyoking the oxen may have limited this. No doubt the enormity of this *stupa* has the significance of being as large as life itself.

The inside of the *stupa* contained the whole of the Buddha Tahō and his Precious and Pure Realm of Dharmas. The Buddha Tahō is understood as the objective realm of the Buddha Shākyamuni, and when these two Buddhas are seen seated side by side in the *stupa* made of precious materials, this immediately becomes the concept of the Fundamental Object of Veneration (*gohonzon*). Nichiren says, "What is precious are the five aggregates, and the *stupa* is to put them together harmoniously. When the five aggregates are put together harmoniously, they become a precious *stupa*. And the five aggregates harmoniously compiled are said to be seen as the five ideograms of the Utterness of the Dharma (*Myōhō, Saddharma*)." In his *A Letter to the Lay Practitioner Abutsu*, Nichiren writes, "Now that we have entered into the final phase of the Dharma, there is no *stupa* made of precious materials apart from the aspect of the men and women who hold to the *Dharma Flower Sutra* (*Myōhō Renge Kyō*)." [See also **Five aggregates**, *Treatise on the Real Aspect of All Dharmas, A Letter to the Lay Practitioner Abutsu*.]

Subjectivity and its dependent environment are not two – Japanese: *Eshō funi*

What we see ourselves to be is subjective. And for this subjectivity to exist, it requires a dependent environment. Buddhism teaches that oneself – or rather, what we think we are – and our environment are inseparable, since both are the *Sutra on the White Lotus Flower-like Mechanism of the Utterness of the Dharma* (*Myōhō Renge Kyō*). [See also **Nam Myōhō Renge Kyō**.]

Sutra – Japanese: *Kyō*

Scriptures which convey the Buddha teaching. Every sutra begins with the words, "I heard it in this way." The Chinese ideogram *kyō*, which is used to translate *sutra*, also has the meaning of "the warp in weaving" that runs lengthways, to pass through or by, and "canonical texts" or "classics", thus implying the concept of an eternal doctrine. [See also *Oral Transmission on the Meaning of the Dharma Flower Sutra* (*Ongi Kuden*), **Nam Myōhō Renge Kyō**.]

Tahō, the Buddha – Japanese: *Tahō Nyorai* – Sanskrit: *Prabhūtaratna*

Translated, this means "abundant treasure" or "many jewels". The ancient Buddha who, after a long period in Nirvana, appeared inside the *Stupa* made of Precious Materials at the Ceremony in Empty Space, in order to testify to the truth of the teachings of the *Dharma Flower Sutra* (*Myōhō Renge Kyō*). Due to his presence he reveals, among other things, that nirvana is not annihilation and that the teaching of the *Dharma Flower Sutra* (*Myōhō Renge Kyō*) is the highest order of understanding. In the Fundamental Object of Veneration (*gohonzon*), the Buddha Tahō represents the totally enlightened objective realm, materiality, and the function of dying of the original Buddha, whereas Shākyamuni represents the totally enlightened wisdom, mind, and being alive. [See also **Stupa made of Precious Materials**, *Treatise on the Real Aspect of All Dharmas*.]

Tathāgata – Japanese: *Nyorai*

One who has gone; one who has followed the Path and arrived at the real suchness; one of the ten titles of a Buddha. Tathāgata can be explained as a person who comes from the real suchness of existence, which is Nam Myōhō Renge Kyō – which means to devote our lives to and found them on (*Nam[u]*) the Utterness of the Dharma (*Myōhō*) [entirety of existence, enlightenment and unenlightenment] permeated by the underlying white lotus flower-like mechanism of the interdependence of cause, concomitancy and effect (*Renge*) in its whereabouts of the ten [psychological] realms of dharmas (*Kyō*) – and that person will return to it.

Tathāgata of Universal Sunlight, the – Japanese: *Dainichi Nyorai* – Sanskrit: *Mahāvairochana-Tathāgata*

The Buddha who expounded the esoteric doctrine of the Buddha teaching. According to the teachings of the Tantra or Shingon School, all other Buddhas and bodhisattvas are born of the Tathāgata of Universal Sunlight, and he is also seen as an idealisation of the truth.

Tathāgata Universally Pervading Superlative Wisdom, the – Japanese: *Daitsūchishō* – Sanskrit: *Mahābhijnājñānābhibhu*

His name is often shortened to Daitsū. He is a Buddha who, in the *Seventh Chapter on the Parable of the Imaginary City* in the *Dharma Flower Sutra*, is said to have first expounded this sutra three thousand *kalpas* of universes ground into ink ago. [See also **Daitsū Buddha**.]

Teachings derived from the external events of Shākyamuni's life and work Gateway, the – Japanese: *Shakumon*
This gateway to the Dharma is the first half of the twenty-eight chapters of the *Dharma Flower Sutra* (*Myōhō Renge Kyō*). It consists of the fourteen chapters from the *First and Introductory Chapter* to the *Fourteenth Chapter on the Practising in Peace and with Joy*. The opposite of this technical term is the original gateway. The Chinese ideogram that is used for "temporary" has a flavour of transience, as opposed to the concept of an original substance. In Buddhist teachings, there is the traditional metaphor of the moon being the fundamental substance and the actual reality and therefore belonging to the original gateway, but its reflection in the pond only being a reflected likeness, which is suspended in space and time and is similar to the teachings derived from the external events of Shākyamuni's life and work (temporary) gateway.

The Buddha who became enlightened for the first time under the bodhi tree in India is not the original Buddha, but one who is suspended in temporariness. All the teachings and sutras he expounded are defined as the temporary gateway. The first part of the *Dharma Flower Sutra* (*Myōhō Renge Kyō*) is understood as being the temporary gateway, because, in the *Second Chapter on Expedient Means*, Shākyamuni expounded the real aspect of all dharmas as the ten realms of dharmas. Each one of these ten realms contains the other nine in itself so that there are one hundred realms of dharmas in total. These in turn are qualified by the ten ways in which dharmas make themselves present to any of our six sense organs – eyes, ears, nose, tongue, body, and mind – but without any indication whatsoever as to where these oscillations of the mind occur. These thousand ways in which dharmas make themselves present are groundless, incomplete, subjective, and therefore theoretical.

It is when we come to the *Sixteenth Chapter on the Lifespan of the Tathāgata* that we have an account for the three kinds of existential space, which give a groundwork on which the thousand such qualities can happen in reality. This concept of the one instant of thought containing three thousand existential spaces also includes the idea of subjectivity and its dependent environments not being two, which is the reality of life as we live it. [See also **Ten psychological realms of dharmas**, **Ten such qualities**, *Treatise on the Real Aspect of All Dharmas*, *Treatise on the Fundamental Object of Veneration for Contemplating the Mind Instigated by the Bodhisattva Superior Practice (Jōgyō, Vishishtachāritra) For the Fifth Five Hundred Year Period After the Tathāgata's Passing over to Nirvana.*]

Temporary Buddha – Japanese: *Shakubutsu*
A Buddha who is suspended in time and space, as opposed to the original Buddha.

Temporary Teaching – [See **Provisional Teachings**, the.]

Ten psychological realms of dharmas, the – Japanese: *Jippōkai*
In the Buddha teaching prior to the *Dharma Flower Sutra (Myōhō Renge Kyō)*, the ten realms of the dharmas were thought of as the environment, determined by karma of ten kinds of sentient being who, in some cases, shared the same terrain as human beings did with animals, although each was set apart from the other. In the doctrines of the *Dharma Flower Sutra (Myōhō Renge Kyō)* and Nichiren, we ourselves are furnished with each of the ten realms as ten archetypal states of mind. The ten realms are the following:
1. Hell (*jigokukai*), which includes every possible kind of suffering and is a realm of the mind from which no sentient being is spared.
2. Hungry demons (*gakikai*) in many teachings are conceived of as ghosts who dwell in a purgatorial state, hankering after sex, food, drink, and other such things that are coveted. In traditional Buddhist iconography, these beings are depicted as having long thin necks and crawling on the ground. They are always hungry and seek a hardly attainable desire. In the teaching of the Daishōnin, these beings symbolise our own hunger, thirst, and all our other wants, such as drug addicts in need of a fix or alcoholics

in the skid rows of cities. From a positive viewpoint, the perpetual nature of such a desire enables one to defend and protect the life within us. It is acceptable to express a need for food, money, and all the other necessities for human existence. But when this realm becomes distorted, the baser elements become apparent.

3. Animality (*chikushokai*) in some Buddhist teachings means being born as an animal, with functions entirely guided by instinct. In the teachings of Nichiren, this realm is part of the human condition that is the "naked ape" – our animal qualities, defects, and tendencies.

4. The *shura* (*shurakai*), originally in Brahmanism and Hinduism, were titan-like beings continually vying with the *deva* for superiority. In the teaching of Nichiren, this dharma realm corresponds to wanting to have power over someone, or anger which might be seen as a demonstration of ferocity in order to have power over the person with whom we are at odds. From a more positive standpoint, this *Ashura* realm is the mental and physical space that we need in order to "breathe". Infringement on that space results in anger. In the *Treatise on the Fundamental Object of Veneration for Contemplating the Mind* [*Instigated by the Bodhisattva Superior Practice (Jōgyō, Vishishtachāritra) For the Fifth Five Hundred Year Period After the Tathāgata's Passing over to Nirvana*], the *Ashura* realm has the connotation of wheedling, cajoling, or using persuasive means.

5. Humanity (*ninkai*). In spite of troubles and inner torments, there is a part of us that reassures us that things are not as bad as they appear and that one is "all right". It is a human mechanism to find tranquillity or an ability to be calm in spite of all. In the teachings prior to the *Dharma Flower Sutra* (*Myōhō Renge Kyō*), the realm of humanity meant being born as a human being.

6. *Deva* (*tenkai*). In Brahmanism and Hinduism, *deva* are the gods. They are often described as living in heaven and in palaces, are said to have golden bodies, superhuman powers, and to have extremely long lives filled with joy and ecstasy. But, like all other beings, their lifespans must come to an end. From the Buddhist point of view, however, many *deva* are seen as the protectors of the Buddha teaching. Nevertheless, in the teaching of Nichiren, the *deva* is an archetype, inherent in the mind that corresponds to our ecstasy, our greatest raptures, and supreme delights. However wonderful those raptures may be, sooner or later there is a

compulsion to return to our respective realities. The *deva* realm points to the transience of our joys, as opposed to real happiness.

7. The hearers of the voice is a literal translation of the Sino-Japanese Buddhist term (*shōmonkai*) which means those who listen to, or have heard, the voice of the Buddha. It also has an undertone of those who seek meaning in their lives. Seen as a state of mind, this is the realm of learning and wanting to find out. This process starts in early childhood with continual questions, in the form of "what is...?" and "why?" This attitude can continue into old age as a lifelong search for truth.

8. Being partially awakened by a search for the meaning of life (*engakukai, pratyekabuddha*). In contrast to the desire for wisdom and knowledge, there is a part of us that knows the leaves will fall in autumn – knows that there is a body of knowledge upon which one can build. This realm encompasses those who have understood something of the essence of life but not all of its secrets. In the teachings prior to the *Dharma Flower Sutra* (*Myōhō Renge Kyō*), the people who were awakened by affinities had become partially enlightened by personal endeavour and consequently rather more for themselves than for the benefit of others.

9. Bodhisattva (*bosatsukai*). In the teachings that came before the *Dharma Flower Sutra* (*Myōhō Renge Kyō*), this realm indicated persons who seek enlightenment not only for themselves but also for the salvation of others. In the teaching of Nichiren, bodhisattvas, especially in the sense of Bodhisattvas who swarm up out of the earth, are seen as people who not only practise for themselves but seek to set others on the Path of the Buddha teaching as well. At another level, the bodhisattva realm is that part of us which wants to do something for the benefit of others. Essentially, it is our altruistic nature.

10. The Buddha realm (*bukkai*) differs from the previous nine realms, which are all within the bounds of our own experiences, in that it is more elusive, less tangible. From the Buddha teaching of Nichiren, however, if one steadfastly pursues fully the practice of the Nichiren Kōmon School, it is possible to attain a depth of perception and unshakeable happiness.

The unhappiest realm of dharmas is hell (*jigokukai*) and the suffering of its denizens. This includes all suffering, either physical or mental. Suffering begins at the stage of a thorn in your little finger, feeling the lash of pain caused by words that hurt, the pain of broken relationships, illness, injuries, and loneliness, also including the horrors of war and the almost unimaginable dimension of the perpetrators and victims of things that happened during the second World War, as well as the current bloodshed in Africa and the Middle East. Hell is also hate.

Each one of us has suffered, in some way or another. From a more conventional and stereotypical Buddhist point of view, there are, according to various teachings of the individual vehicle (*shōjō, hīnayāna*) or the universal vehicle (*daijō, mahāyāna*), eight hot hells and eight cold hells, which are situated under the world of humankind. Usually, the descriptions of these hells depict them as medieval and sadistic. In their iconographic way, these portrayals are far removed from the real pain, suffering, and mental anguish that many people experience. Among the objectives of the teachings of Nichiren, one of them is to lead people away from such torments and to bring about their happiness and inner realisation.

The second of these ten [psychological] realms of dharmas is the dimension of hungry demons. In the Buddha teaching of Shākyamuni, these hungry demons are seen more like ghosts who live in a purgatorial state which some people say is under the ground. It is their sad destiny that they are condemned to continually hanker after food, sex, drink, drugs, and other things. It is documented that there are 39 classes of these unfortunate creatures.

This dimension is the second of the three lower karmic destinations. In traditional Buddhist iconography, these beings are depicted as having long, thin necks with swollen bellies that force them to crawl on the ground. There are also a number of Japanese paintings of the Edo period, depicting hungry ghosts hanging around the more sordid and seedy establishments of the red-light districts. The present-day visualisation would be closer to heroin addicts in need of a fix, or alcoholic derelicts haunted by their thirst, or the tobacco smoker who cannot do without a cigarette. This is the part of us that craves or wants and "must have", in order to continue. From a positive view, the perpetual need for food, nourishment, money, etc., is the mechanism to defend the life within us, in order to do the things that make life worth living. Again, like all the other realms of dharmas, the mental state of the hungry demon is also endowed with all the other ten realms of dharmas.

In the teachings prior to those of Nichiren, the realm of dharmas of animality (*chikushōkai*) signified being born as an animal, even though there must be psychic entities that can only be incarnated in the animal world, such as those beings who were also animals in their former lives. One of the concepts of animality is a sentient being who is motivated by animal instincts and territorialities. Since we humans have also been described by some people as "hairless apes", then perhaps we can recognise that our animal qualities are not only limited to eating, defecation, and sex but are also partly responsible for our class systems, hierarchies, and feudalism in the office or other workplaces. However, to be born with a human body gives us the opportunity to open up our minds, so that we can understand what our existences are all about.

The *shura* (*ashura*) in the Brahmanic and Vedic mythology were originally titanesque beings, who were always vying with the *deva* (*ten* or *shoten zenjin*) for superiority. Traditionally, they were defined as "ugly", "not *deva*", and "without wings". There were four categories of these beings that depended on the manner of their birth, which means whether they were born from eggs, or from a womb, or born by transformation, or as spawn in the water. Their habitat was the ocean, which only came up to their knees; but other less powerful *shura* (*ashura*) lived in mountain caves in the west.

In popular iconography, the kings of the *shura* (*ashura*) were represented with three or four faces and had either four or six arms. They also had palaces and realms similar to the *deva* (*ten*). In the teaching of Nichiren, this realm of dharmas corresponds to the psychological mechanism of wanting to be the centre of attention, to be noticed by others, and the desire to control. Often, when these tendencies are frustrated, they easily turn into anger, rage, and jealousy. In simpler terms, it has a lot to do with our being pretentious or a show-off. In the *Thesis on the Fundamental Object of Veneration for Contemplating the Mind*, Nichiren mentions cajolery, wheedling, and "buttering up" as part of this dimension. In a more positive sense, this is the part of us that says that we need our own space, which enables us to mentally and physically carry on living, in other words, all that our egos need.

The realm of dharmas of humanity (*jinkai*) is the sense of human equanimity and rationality. In spite of all the troublesome worries (*bonnō, klesha*) that plague our lives, there is a part that reassures us that things are not as bad as they seem and that everything is all right. It is this aspect of our personalities that gets on with daily living without too many upsets, in other words, a satisfactory life. In the Buddha teaching of Shākyamuni, the realms of dharmas of humanity meant to be born as a human being.

From the viewpoint of the teaching of Shākyamuni, the realms of dharmas of the *deva* (*tenkai*) refer mainly to the merits of the divinities of Brahmanism and other Vedic teachings. The *deva* (*ten*) were said to have golden bodies, superhuman powers, and extremely long lives filled with joy and ecstasy; but like all other lifespans, at some time or another, they must come to an end. Many *deva* (*ten*) are the protectors of the Buddha teaching. According to Nichiren's writing on *Securing the Peace of the Realm through the Establishment of the Correct Dharma* (*Risshō Ankoku ron*), one concludes that the *deva* (*ten*) protect human interests and that they are also nourished by religious rites, especially by the recitation of the title and theme (*daimoku*), Nam Myōhō Renge Kyō. There are many cultures with legends and mythologies concerning this kind of sentient being that would fit into the category of *deva* (*ten*), for example, elves, guardian spirits, local gods, saints, angels, and ancestral divinities. There are a number of *deva* (*ten*) whose names are important to the Buddha teaching of Nichiren Daishōnin and are inscribed on the Fundamental Object of Veneration (*gohonzon*).

One might ask if these tutelary essences could be archaic, archetypal elements in the depths of our psyches that have an influence over our lives in one way or another. When we create so much bad karma by doing things that are wrong, these archetypes can no longer take part in what we do. Then these *deva* (*ten*) may no longer make their presences felt, thus allowing more destructive energies to take their place. For anyone who has practised the rites of the teachings of Nichiren Daishōnin, we can only be aware of forces that in some way guide our lives, often in the most unexpected way.

What I have just said about the *deva* (*ten*) is based on personal intuition. However, someone might ask the question, "What are the *deva* (*ten*)?" I thought an allusion to their existence might be food for conjecture.

Deva (*ten*) have extremely happy and ecstatic long lives that eventually must come to an end, in a protractedly distant future. The concept of the realms of dharmas of the *deva* (*ten*) in the teaching of Nichiren refers to our joys and epiphanies, like falling in love, getting the right job, a great night out, or the enjoyment of doing something useful or creative. Nonetheless, however exhilarating or joyful our experiences may be, we are always sooner or later compelled to return to the starker dimension of normal realities of daily living. The realms of dharmas of the *deva* (*ten*) refer to the impermanence of all our joys, raptures, and delights.

Next we have the realms of dharmas of the people who listen to the Buddha's voice, which is a literal translation of the Chinese ideograms. In the teaching of Nichiren, it refers to the dimension within us that wants to be informed, the desire for intellectual pursuits, or just wanting knowledge. This is the part of us that is the inquirer and the part of us where learning is still a work in progress. This concept is applicable to the intellectuals of the present day.

Historically speaking, during the time of Shākyamuni, these were the people who exerted themselves to attain the highest stage of the individual vehicle (*shōjō*, *hīnayāna*), through listening to the Buddha. [Here I use the term "individual vehicle", because these teachings were for individual enlightenment. We can say that these people were only practising for themselves, as opposed to the practices of the universal vehicle (*daijō, mahāyāna*), which was an exposition of the Dharma for the people who were prepared to practise not only for the benefit of themselves, but for others as well (*bosatsu, bodhisattvas*).]

Later, the expression *shōmon* was used to designate people who understood the four noble truths – 1) suffering is a necessary aspect of sentient existence; 2) the accumulation of suffering is brought about by our lusts and our attachments to them; 3) the extinction of such suffering is possible; and 4) the teaching of the Buddha path leads to the elimination of such lusts and attachments. These people practised with all their might to become *arhats* or *arakan*, which is an inner realisation of existence being nirvana or relativity (*kū, shūnyatā*). The object of the teaching of Nichiren, as I have said earlier, is to open up our inherent Buddha nature with our persons just as they are, which is not only within our grasp but is also a path towards a real fulfilment and realisation.

The realm of dharmas of the people who are partially enlightened due to a profound search for the meaning of existence (*engaku, hyakushibutsu, pratyekabuddha*), is a psychological dimension that is contrasted with the search for understanding and wanting to know the how and why of their circumstances. This realm of dharmas involves those people who have a deep understanding of what life entails but not all its secrets.

This kind of mental state is not only concerned with people who follow the various teachings of the Buddha, but also many scientists, writers, artists, musicians, and other people, who try and have tried to follow an enlightened existence, fall into this category.

However, from a historical Buddhist viewpoint, these partially enlightened individuals were those who fully understood the links in the chain of the twelve causes and karmic circumstances that run through the whole of sentient existence. [These are 1) a fundamental unenlightenment, which is brought about by 2) natural causes and inclinations inherited from former lives, 3) the first consciousness after conception that takes place in the womb,

4) both body and mind evolving in the womb, which leads to 5) the five organs of sense and the functioning of the mind, 6) contact with the outside world, 7) as well as the growth of receptivity or budding intelligence and discernment from the age of six to seven onwards, 8) the desire for amorous love at the age of puberty, and 9) the urge for a sensuous existence, that forms 10) the substance for future karma, and 11) the completed karma ready to be born again, that faces in the direction of 12) old age and death.]

Nevertheless, the Buddha Shākyamuni saw people of the realm of dharmas who were partially enlightened due to a profound search for the meaning of existence (*engaku, hyakushibutsu, pratyekabuddha*) as essentially seekers of enlightenment for themselves.

The realm of dharmas of the bodhisattva (*bosatsukai*) is the ninth of these ten realms of dharmas. Basically, this term bodhisattva is derived from two Sanskrit words, 1) *bodhi* which means knowledge, understanding, perfect wisdom, or enlightenment, and 2) *sattva* which has the sense of being, existence, life, consciousness, or any living sentient being. While this concept is not entirely foreign to the teachings of the individual vehicle (*shōjō, hinayāna*), it was used almost exclusively to designate Shākyamuni in his former existences. In tales concerning the former lives of the Buddha, he is often referred to as the Bodhisattva.

According to the earlier teachings of the universal vehicle (*daijō, mahāyāna*), this expression referred to any person whose resolve was to attain enlightenment, which in Chinese texts was understood as "a sentient being with a mind for the universal truth". Later, the term bodhisattva (*bosatsukai*) was used for people with an awareness that was all-embracing.

In the teachings of the universal vehicle, the people who listened to the Buddha's discourses (*shōmon, shrāvaka*) and those people who were partially enlightened due to a profound search for the meaning of existence (*engaku, hyakushibutsu, pratyekabuddha*) only made endeavours for their own enlightenment, whereas the bodhisattva aimed at the illumination and the realisation of others. Roughly speaking, this realm of dharmas designates the desire to seek one's own enlightenment, and at the same time, have the compassion to strive for the happiness of others.

The tenth of the realms of dharmas is that of the Buddha enlightenment. To describe this psychological dimension is the most difficult, since such an enlightenment is beyond any of my personal experiences. This realm of the Dharma is the oneness of existence as perceived by the Buddha. This perception of the singularity of the Dharma is understood as one of total freedom and a consciousness of the ultimate truth.

The *Dharma Flower Sutra* (*Hokke-kyō*) makes it clear that the Dharma Realm of the Buddha is inherent in the lives of all sentient beings. As an experience, this dimension is probably the clear light that is often seen by people in near-death states, which in *The Tibetan Book of the Dead* (*Bardo thos sgrol*) is described as "the point of entering the intermediary state between dying and rebirth" (*hchi khahi bar do*).

In the teaching of Nichiren, this is pointed out as "the silence and the shining light" that is in fact the fundamental nature of life itself, which also accompanies us through our respective deaths. It might be possible to define the Dharma realm of the Buddha (*bukkai*) as life and all that Myōhō Renge Kyō implies.

In the concept of the one instant of thought containing three thousand existential spaces, each one of these realms is furnished with the other nine, so that in fact there are one hundred dharma realms which in turn are modified by the ten such qualities. [See also **Buddha, One instant of thought containing three thousand existential spaces**, *Treatise on the Fundamental Object of Veneration for Contemplating the Mind Instigated by the Bodhisattva Superior Practice* (*Jōgyō, Vishishtachāritra*) *For the Fifth Five Hundred Year Period After the Tathāgata's Passing over to Nirvana*, *Treatise on the Real Aspect of All Dharmas*, **Bodhisattvas who swarm up out of the earth.**]

Ten realms, the – Japanese: *Jikkai* [See **Ten psychological realms of dharmas.**]

Ten ways ten ways in which dharmas make themselves present to any of our six senses – eyes, ears, nose, tongue, body, and mind, the **(or ten such qualities)** – Japanese: *Jū.nyōze*

The ten qualities of suchness are, according to the *Dharma Flower Sutra* (*Myōhō Renge Kyō*), the essential qualities that are present in everything that exists – a lateral and objective view of all dharmas, as well as playing a vital role in the teaching of the one instant of thought containing three thousand existential spaces.

The ten qualities of suchness are the following:
1. Such an appearance (*nyoze sō*) – sentient beings, objects, and things in the mind made manifest.
2. Such a nature (*nyoze shō*) – the inner quality of anything we can perceive including sentient beings.
3. Such a substance (*nyoze tai*) – the fundamental substance or reality.
4. Such a strength (*nyoze riki*) – intensity or potential.
5. Such an action (*nyoze sa*) – functioning, the outward manifestation of the strength or potential.
6. Such a cause (*nyoze in*) – the direct cause that brings about the fruition or result.
7. Such a karmic relationship (*nyoze en*) – the concomitance, complementary causes, and circumstances that accompany the direct cause.
8. Such a fruition (*nyoze ka*) – the result which is brought about by the direct cause.
9. Such a requital (*nyoze hō*) – the total outcome of that which is brought about by such a fruition, due to karma.
10. Such a final superlative which is equally present from the first to the last of these nine qualities of suchness (*nyōze hon makku kyō tō*) – the real aspect of the middle way.

These ten qualities of suchness are present in the hundred dharma realms, which in the doctrine of the one instant of thought containing three thousand existential spaces bring the number to one thousand. This is seen as a theory that covers most possible combinations of sentient existence. This teaching was first revealed in the *Second Chapter on Expedient Means* of the *Dharma Flower Sutra* (*Myōhō Renge Kyō*) and is referred to as "roughly clearing away the three vehicles in order to reveal the one".

In the *Second Chapter on Expedient Means* in the first fascicle of the *Dharma Flower Sutra*, it says, "The real aspect of all dharmas can only be exhaustively scrutinised between one Buddha and another. This real aspect of all dharmas is said to be (*Sho'i shohō*) in any way they make themselves present to any of our six sense organs – eyes, ears, nose, tongue, body, and mind (*Nyoze sō* [*ke*]). [For instance, a carrot is orange; it tastes sweetish and may have a smell.] Next are their various inner qualities (*Nyoze shō* [*kū*]). [These include all the words associated with a carrot, i.e., zanahoria, carotte, carota, ninjin, and all our memories of a carrot; when we see this carrot, we unconsciously see a carrot, and both what we see and the associations in our heads automatically come together.] Then there is the substance or what they really are (*Nyoze tai* [*chūdō jissō*]), which includes Nam Myōhō Renge Kyō. Next come their potential strength and energy (*Nyoze riki*), the manifestation of that energy and strength, which is their influence (*Nyoze sa*), their fundamental causes (*Nyoze in*), along with their karmic circumstances (*Nyoze en*), the effects they produce (*Nyoze ka*), and their apparent and karmic consequences (*Nyoze hō*). Also in any way dharmas make themselves perceptible to any of our six sense organs – eyes, ears, nose, tongue, body, and mind – has a coherence with their 'apparent karmic consequences', which are present in every instant of life (*Nyoze hon makku kyō tō*)." [See also – Such a final superlative that is equally present from the first to the last of the nine qualities of suchness.]

Tendai – Japanese: *Tendai Daishi* – Chinese: *Chih-i* – *Tiantai dashi* (*T'ien T'ai*)

Usually referred to as the Universal Teacher Tendai (*T'ien T'ai*), he founded the Tendai School; he is also known as Chigi. He was born in Hunan, China, in about 538 CE and died in 597 CE at sixty years of age. He became a neophyte when he was seven years old and was fully ordained when he was twenty. In 575, he went to the Tendai Mountain in Chechiang, where he established his famous school based on the *Dharma Flower Sutra* (*Myōhō Renge Kyō*) as being the summit of Shākyamuni's teaching.

Then from such an appearance to such a requital, all these nine such qualities (*nyoze*) **are from the first to the last equally the ultimate dimension of the real aspect of all dharmas** (things) – Japanese: *Honmatsu kūkyōtō*

In the *Second Chapter on Expedient Means* of the *Dharma Flower Sutra* (*Myōhō Renge Kyō*), when the Buddha Shākyamuni expounded the real aspect of all dharmas, he summed it up with a lateral and objective view of all dharmas. This is referred to as the ten ways whereby dharmas make themselves present – appearance, nature, substance, strength, action, cause, affinity, fruition, karmic requital, and a final superlative that is equally present from the first to the last of the nine such qualities. The first is such an appearance, and the last such a requital. Then, from such an appearance to such a requital, all these nine such qualities (*nyoze*) are equally the ultimate dimension of the real aspect of all the dharmas. The ultimate dimension of the real aspect of all dharmas is in no way separate from the one instant of thought containing three thousand existential spaces. In whatever way we may conceive this idea, any concept of existence must imply the whole of it. [See also **Ten ways whereby dharmas make themselves present to any of our six sense organs – eyes, ears, nose, tongue, body, and mind, One instant of thought containing three thousand existential spaces,** *Treatise on the Real Aspect of All Dharmas.*]

Three bodies, the – Japanese: *Sanjin* – Sanskrit: *Trikaya*

Three properties of a Buddha – the Dharma body (*hosshin, Dharma-kāya*), reward or wisdom body (*hōshin, sambhoga-kāya*), and the corresponding body (*ōjin, nirmāna-kāya*). The reward body or wisdom body is the reward or wisdom of being entirely enlightened to the one instant of thought containing three thousand existential spaces, which is the Utterness of the Dharma. The Dharma body of a Buddha is the fact that his existence occupies all time, all space, simultaneously and effortlessly, as does the single thought containing three thousand existential spaces. The corresponding body is the manifestation that Buddhas or Nichiren use, in order to propagate their teaching and to liberate sentient beings from the painful cycles of living and dying. In the teachings prior to the *Dharma Flower Sutra* (*Myōhō Renge Kyō*), these three bodies were expounded as being three separate

Buddhas. But in the *Dharma Flower Sutra* (*Myōhō Renge Kyō*) they are seen as three separate qualities of a single Buddha. In *The Oral Transmission on the Meaning of the Dharma Flower Sutra* (*Ongi Kuden*), Nichiren says, "The Tathāgata is Shākyamuni, which generally speaking implies all the Buddhas of the ten directions of the past, present, and future. In particular, it means the three bodies that are independent of all action and belong to the original terrain."

Three bodies independent of all karma, the – Japanese: *Musa no sanjin*
   The term independent of all karma is what there is beyond all concept of time or existence. It is the fundamental essence of all being and completely unsoiled by any activity or karma whatsoever. The three bodies refer to the Dharma (*here it implies the whole of existence*), wisdom, and corresponding bodies of the Buddha. Because the one instant of thought containing three thousand existential spaces (*ichinen sanzen*) comprises the whole of existence, both enlightened and unenlightened, and also because the ten realms of dharmas (things or whatever may have an effect on any of our five aggregates) are not separate from the nine other realms of dharmas, the three bodies independent of all karma are also the self-received entity of the Tathāgata that is used with absolute freedom, whose original source lies in the ever-present infinite in time (*kuon ganjo*) and is not separate from Nichiren or the Fundamental Object of Veneration (*gohonzon*).

Three kinds of existential space, the – Japanese: *San seken*
   From the Buddhist point of view, everything and all affairs that emerge from the past into the present and on to the future, through various causes, concomitancies and circumstances, are called existence. The intervals between these affairs and things are called space. The three kinds of existential space mean that all the different kinds of dharma, which are brought about by various causes and karmic relationships, are divided into three categories, although they do not entirely stand apart from each other.

In Nagarjuna's *Universal Discourse on the Wisdom that Carries Beings over to the Shores of Nirvana*, the three kinds of existential space are described as the existential space of the five aggregates (*go'on seken*), the existential space of sentient beings as individuals (*shujō seken*), and the existential space of abode and terrain (*kokudo seken*). The five aggregates are materiality or form, sensation, concepts, volition which is often influenced by former lives or traumas in the space between dying and being reborn, and cognition of perceiving ourselves to be what we seem that reveal the differences in sentient beings. The existential space of sentient beings means that, since all sentient beings are made up of the five aggregates, their lives are characterised by the ten realms of dharmas. The existential space of abode and terrain clarifies the differentiated dwelling places of the ten realms.

When Shākyamuni makes clear the whereabouts of his abode and terrain in the *Sixteenth Chapter on the Lifespan of the Tathāgata*, the three kinds of existential space become perfectly adjusted to the thousand such qualities, and the principle of the one instant of thought containing three thousand existential spaces is fully established. [See also **One instant of thought containing three thousand existential spaces, Ten realms, Ten qualities of suchness, Five aggregates.**]

Three kinds of Proof (through Buddhist Practice), the – Japanese: *san-shō*

These are 1) proof in the sutric texts, 2) a proof in theory, 3) a proof in actual reality. These three kinds of proof show the superiority or the shortcomings of a religious teaching.

The textual proof is to confirm the doctrine of a particular school on the basis of the sutras. The theoretical proof implies that each teaching is compatible with reason or logic. The proof in actual reality is one that is existent and underlies appearances. Nichiren Daishōnin states in his writing, *With Regard to the Three Tripitakas Praying for Rain*, "On looking into the mind that underlies the enlightened Dharma of Nichiren, it does not go beyond any logical proof. And yet, a logical proof is not surpassed by a proof in actual reality." It is here that Nichiren shows that he considers the sutric proofs and also logical proofs to be less important than the tangible proof in actual reality.

Three thousand universes ground into dust – Japanese: *sanzen jintengō* or *sanzen jindengō*

This is probably the immense amount of time since life likely appeared in the universe and when the Tathāgata Universally Pervading Superlative Wisdom (*Daitsūchishō, Mahābhijnājñānābhibhu*) is said to have first expounded the *Dharma Flower Sutra*. From the point of view of Shākyamuni, there would always be an India in existence, as it was when he was active. Three thousand universes ground into dust is often defined as the following: if a person were to grind three thousand universes from their inception to their end into dust, then were to travel towards the east with all these particles of dust and were to cross over another thousand universes and drop a single particle of dust and were to continue in this same manner until all of the original particles were used up, the term that is used for this lapse of time is referred to in Japanese as *sanzen jintengō*. Each particle of dust represents a *kalpa*. [See also **Kalpa**.]

Three Treasures, the – Japanese: *sambō* – Sanskrit *ratna traya*

In the Buddha teaching of Shākyamuni, these are the following: 1) There is the Buddha who has three aspects (*butsu, hotoke*); 2) his Dharma teaching (*Dharma, hō*); and 3) the community of monks (*sō, sangha*).

The three aspects of the Buddha are 1) his suchness or thusness, which is the true form of dharmas (*nyoze tai*) and indicates the reality which transcends the multiplicity of apparent existence. This entity of the Dharma is regarded as being identical with the embodiment of the Dharma (*hosshin, Dharma-kāya*) and cannot be expressed in words or even conceived of by the unenlightened. This concept is understood as real hard existence (*jitsu u*) and, on the other hand, as (*kū, shūnyatā* or even as *Nam Myōhō Renge Kyō*). This is the reality upon which both phenomenal and noumenal existence depends. The second aspect of the Buddha is 2) his wisdom (*hō*), which is represented by everything that is inscribed on the Fundamental Object of Veneration (*gohonzon*). The third aspect is 3) his manifestations (*ōjin, nirmāna-kāya*) to save all sentient beings such as us. [See also **Dharma body independent of all karma, Three bodies**.]

Three vehicles – Japanese: *sanjō*

These three vehicles are the two vehicles of the hearers of the Buddha's voice or the intellectuals of today, along with the people who have a partial enlightenment due to a profound search for the meaning of life, and the bodhisattva vehicle. These three vehicles were cleared away in order to reveal the one Buddha Vehicle in the *Second Chapter on Expedient Means*. [See also **One Buddha vehicle, Vehicle.**]

Title and Theme – Japanese: *daimoku*

The titles of books within the bounds of ancient Chinese literature are usually precise as to the meaning of the content. It is particularly so with the titles of the sutras. In Schools of Nichiren, the title and theme invariably refers to the *Sutra on the White Lotus Flower-like Mechanism of the Utterness of the Dharma* and to the chanting of Nam Myōhō Renge Kyō, which is one of the three universal esoteric dharmas (things). [See also **Nam Myōhō Renge Kyō, Actual fundamental substance, Dharmas and dharma, Sutra.**]

Tripitaka

Tripitaka is an expression that covers the three branches of teachings of the Individual Vehicle. These are 1) *Abhidharma*, which consist of works attributed to the Buddha's disciples, 2) the sutras, and 3) the monastic rules and regulations. The term Tripitaka is also used as a title for a person who is well-versed in the tenets of the Buddha teaching. [See also **Arhat, Becoming a Buddha, Universal Vehicle.**]

Triple body – Japanese: *Sanjin* [See also **Three bodies.**]

Troublesome worries – Japanese: *bonnō*

Temptations of passions and of ignorance, which disturb and distress the mind, are divided into six fundamental and derivative types. The fundamental types are covetousness or indulgence, anger or hatred, being misled by appearances or delusions, pride, doubt, and false views, such as that of a personal ego or that we only live one life. The derivative types of troublesome worries are (i) indulgence, (ii) anger, (iii) hatred, (iv) delusion, (v) pride, (vi) moral affliction, (vii) distress, (viii) trials, (ix) temptations, and (x) wrongdoing.

All of this may seem complicated and analytical. However, in a practical sense, troublesome worries refer to practically every kind of mental or emotional activity. Apart from those persons who can attain a perfect absorption of thought into the one object of meditation, which is the perfect *samādhi*, such mental acrobatics are of little or no importance in the teaching of Nichiren. There is very little one can do about the continual rolling of the wheels of the mind. The denizen of hell is only concerned about his release from such a place, whereas the bodhisattva is fully preoccupied with the salvation of others. What can be done is that we can change the quality of our troublesome worries by changing the quality of our lives through study and practice.

Two vehicles, the – Japanese: *Nijō*

These two vehicles are made up of 1) the hearers of the voice or the intellectual seekers of today (*shōmon, shrāvaka*) and 2) the people who have become partially realised due to a profound search for the meaning of existence (*engaku, hyakushibutsu, pratyekabuddha*). These two are usually lumped together. The two vehicles have already been defined in this Glossary in the **Ten psychological realms of dharmas**. However, during the time when Shākyamuni Buddha was teaching, many of the people who belonged to these two realms of dharmas came from the Brahman caste and, considering themselves to be superior, were unable to find enough faith to comply with what the Buddha said. Hence, in the teachings that came before the *Dharma Flower Sutra* (*Myōhō Renge Kyō*), there was an underlying feeling that the people of the two vehicles could not open their inherent Buddha nature on account of psychological problems. Nevertheless, in the *Chapter on Expedient Means*, from the *Dharma Flower Sutra* (*Myōhō Renge Kyō*), the sutric evidence of Sharihotsu (*Shariputra*) being able to reveal his own Buddha nature becomes manifestly clear. [See also **One Buddha Vehicle, Vehicle, Three vehicles**.]

Universal – Japanese: *Dai* – Sanskrit: *Mahā*

This Chinese translation of *Mahā* is based on the definition in the Chinese dictionary *Discerning the Signs and Explaining the Ideograms* (*Shuowen jiezi, Setsu bun kai ji*), compiled in about 100 CE, where it states, "Heaven is all-embracing; earth is all-embracing, and humanity is also all-embracing..." Although this ideogram is used nowadays to express size or greatness, in the Buddha teaching it has the meaning of all-pervading or omnipresent.

Universal Demon King of the Sixth Heaven, the – Japanese: *Dai Roku Ten no Ma' ō*

He is also known as the *Deva* King Independent of Those who are Converted by Another ["Another" in this case being the Daishōnin]. In the ninth fascicle of the *Discourse that Carries Beings over to Nirvana*, it says, "This *Deva* snatches away those who have been converted by another. However, since this is for his own amusement he is called 'Independent of Those who are Converted by Another'." This *deva* dwells in the highest of the six heavens of desire. He strives to prevent those who have faith in the Buddha teaching from practising, or even those who seek the truth or any form of realisation. Nichiren describes this Demon as the fundamental lack of clarity or bewilderment that is inherent in all existence.

Universal Discourse on the Wisdom that Carries Beings over to the Shores of Nirvana (*Treatise on the All-embracing Wisdom that Ferries Sentient Beings over the Seas of Mortality to the Shore of Nirvana*) – Japanese: *Daichidōron*

Attributed to Nāgārjuna (*Ryūju*) [Sanskrit: *Nāgārjuna*], it was translated into Chinese by Kumaraju [Sanskrit: *Kumārajîva*]. It is a hundred-volume commentary on the Sutra on the Universal Wisdom that enables beings to reach the other shore of enlightenment.

Universal Teacher, the – Japanese: *Daishi*

A title that is given to those such as Shākyamuni and various bodhisattvas who teach living beings the highest values. It is also an honorary title awarded to the monks of special merit by the Imperial court. The Tendai monk Saichō was given the title The

Universal Teacher Dengyō (*Dengyō daishi*) and Kūkai that of The Universal Teacher Kōbō. These are the first instances of the use of this title in Japan.

Universal Vehicle – Japanese: *Daijō* – Sanskrit: *Mahāyāna*

One of the two major tendencies of the Buddha teaching. Vehicle is a means or type of teaching that will bring enlightenment. As opposed to the Individual Vehicle (*shōjō, hīnayāna*), the teachings of the Universal Vehicle (*daijō, mahāyāna*) are not only concerned with personal salvation, but also stress the importance of setting all beings on the road to Buddhahood. The Nichiren Kōmon School is, from the viewpoint of its own teaching, the summit of the Universal Vehicle (*daijō, mahāyāna*).

Utterly awakened – Japanese: *Myōgaku*

The imponderably inexpressible supreme and correct awakening to the Buddha fruition, in which all troublesome worries are entirely cut off. In the teachings of Tendai (*T'ien T'ai*), it is the highest of the fifty-two stages in the process of becoming a Buddha. In terms of the six inseparabilities from the Buddha nature that refer to the cultivation and practice of the all-inclusive teaching, it is the superlative not being separate from the Buddha nature. [See also **Fifty-two bodhisattva stages in the process of becoming a Buddha, Six Inseparabilities.**]

Vajra – Japanese: *Kongō* – Sanskrit: *Vajra*

This word is vicariously translated as "diamond", "thunderbolt", "diamond club", etc. One Chinese definition is the "hardest of metals". Anthropologists have often thought of the vajra as being a sun symbol. The references to its hardness and diamond-like qualities are synonymous with its indestructibility and power. It seems also to have been a weapon of Indian soldiers in ancient times. However, we think of it as a diamond-like light that comes from somewhere deep inside us, such as that seen by visionaries or by people who have had near-death experiences. It is the part of us that is indestructible.

Vehicle – Japanese: *Jō* – Sanskrit: *Yāna*

A means or a type of teaching whereby the Buddha imparts his enlightenment according to the propensities of his hearers. In the Buddha teaching, this ordinary word for a cart, conveyance or vehicle, is a word for the various teachings that carry people towards enlightenment. The *Dharma Flower Sutra* (*Myōhō Renge Kyō*) refers to the one Buddha vehicle, the two vehicles, and the three vehicles. In the teaching of Nichiren, there is only one vehicle. [See also **Two vehicles, Three vehicles, One Buddha Vehicle, Universal Vehicle**.]

Wisdom body, the – Japanese: *Hōshin* [See also **Three bodies**.]

Wisdom body independent of all karma, the – Japanese: *Musa hōshin*

This entity is one of the three bodies independent of all karma, whose origin is in the ever-present infinite in time (*kuon ganjo*). Its function is the wisdom and understanding of total enlightenment. In other words, it is the wisdom and understanding of Nichiren Daishōnin the original Buddha, as well as being the Buddha for the present period, which is the final phase of the Dharma teaching of Shākyamuni (*mappō*). By holding a genuine and devout faith in the Buddha teaching of Nichiren Daishōnin as well persevering in the recitation of the title and theme (*daimoku*), those who practise will make the strength of the Buddha and the strength of the dharmas (things or whatever may have an effect on any of our five aggregates) apparent in their lives. The practitioners may even open up their inherent Buddha nature with their persons just as they are (*soku shin jō Butsu*).

Wisdom of the real suchness as it is according to circumstances that belongs to the original gateway, the – Japanese: *Honmon zui.en shinnyō no chi*

The wisdom of the real suchness according to circumstances that the Buddha expounded in the original gateway of the *Dharma Flower Sutra* (*Myōhō Renge Kyō*) is his perceptive understanding that the real principle of concrete reality is the consequence of an infinity of circumstance and karmic circumstances. The fact that the original Buddha of the original gateway revealed that his original terrain is the primordial infinity implies that every conceivable dharma must be included in his wisdom and understanding. This wisdom is essentially the fundamentally existing mutual possession of the ten realms of dharmas – the actual fundamental substance of the pragmatic one instant of thought containing three thousand existential spaces and the three universal esoteric Dharmas. [See also *Oral Transmission on the Meaning of the Dharma Flower Sutra (Ongi Kuden), Treatise on the Significance of the Actual Fundamental Substance, Treatise on the Real Aspect of All Dharmas*.]

Yasha – Japanese: *Yasha* – Sanskrit: *Yaksha*

These protectors of the Buddha teaching are often seen as the guardian spirits of nature. There seems to be no definite representation; in Java, they are portrayed as sturdy, smallish human beings, with unusually large canine teeth. Yashas are mentioned in various sutras, but most of the material concerning them is in the realm of folklore. [See also **Humanlike non-humans**.]

Yojana

A *yojana* is a distance that represents a day's march of the royal army, which I would guess might be something just under 30 kilometres. However, other dictionaries claim this distance to be 160 km, 120 km, or 50 km.

Zen School, the – Japanese: *Zenshū*

Probably this Buddhist school is the best-known in the West, due to the enormous quantity of excellent translations by Suzuki Daisetz and many other scholars. This school teaches that the true nature of one's mind can be realised through meditation and various other techniques, such as, questions and answers, riddles, and parables. Like all other schools, it does border on the truth, but lacks an all-embracing theory such as the one instant of thought containing three thousand existential spaces. This school is also harshly criticised by Nichiren in a number of his writings.

The Essential of the Teaching of Nichiren Daishōnin

The Essential of the Teaching of Nichiren Daishōnin

Printed in the USA
CPSIA information can be obtained
at www.ICGtesting.com
LVHW020952040124
768142LV00011B/293